ARMIES WITHOUT NATIONS

D1565802

ARMIES WITHOUT NATIONS

Public Violence and State Formation in Central America, 1821–1960

ROBERT H. HOLDEN

OXFORD
UNIVERSITY PRESS

2004

OXFORD

UNIVERSITY PRESS

Oxford   New York
Auckland   Bangkok   Buenos Aires   Cape Town   Chennai
Dar es Salaam   Delhi   Hong Kong   Istanbul   Karachi   Kolkata
Kuala Lumpur   Madrid   Melbourne   Mexico City   Mumbai   Nairobi
São Paulo   Shanghai   Taipei   Tokyo   Toronto

Copyright © 2004 by Oxford University Press, Inc.

Published by Oxford University Press, Inc.
198 Madison Avenue, New York, New York 10016

www.oup.com

Oxford is a registered trademark of Oxford University Press

Library of Congress Cataloging-in-Publication Data
Holden, Robert H.
Armies without nations : public violence and state formation
in Central American, 1821–1960 / by Robert H. Holden.
p. cm.
Includes bibliographical references and index.
ISBN-13 978-0-19-516120-5
ISBN 0-19-516120-3
1. Political violence—Central America—History. 2. Central America—Politics
and government. 3. State-sponsored terrorism—Central America—History.
I. Title.
HN125.2. V5H65   2003
303.6'09728—dc21   2002053090

3 5 7 9 8 6 4

Printed in the United States of America
on acid-free paper

To *Mary Louise Chubb*
and *Edgar J. Williams, Jr., 1916–1999*

ACKNOWLEDGMENTS

I drew the evidence for this book's arguments from archives and libraries in six countries, starting with the United States in 1991. In late 1992 I turned to Central America, spending more time in Nicaragua, Honduras, and Costa Rica than in El Salvador and Guatemala, in large part because archival records—especially any related to military or police matters—were considerably harder to come by in the latter two countries. Of course, public records of any kind are not easily accessible in Central America; typically they are not even catalogued, and their availability to any particular researcher is notoriously subject to the whims of the functionaries who guard them. But if there was too little in Central America, there was too much in Washington, where I was immersed in an ocean of paper records so immense that no single researcher could ever hope to read all the relevant documentation.

My debt, therefore, to information gatekeepers of all kinds—archivists, record-keepers, data analysts, and librarians—is immense. Many of them went out of their way for me countless times, cheerfully, unselfishly, and skillfully. I am especially grateful to John J. Slonaker, Richard Sommers, and David A. Keough, Historical Reference Branch, U.S. Army Military History Institute; Lou Samelson and Terry Knasiak, Defense Institute of Security Assistance Management; Jeanne Tifft, the U.S. Agency for International Development's Development Information Center; Capt. Julio Joaquín Raudales Soto and Capt. Sergio Gómez, Archivo Militar, Tegucigalpa; Luis Roberto Castellanos, Archivo y Biblioteca of the Congreso Nacional de Honduras; Miguel Angel Sánchez, Archivo General de la Nación, San Salvador; Marta Morabel and John Moran, the library of the Banco Central de Honduras; Julio Roberto Hill, director of the Archivo General de Centro America, Guatemala; Sandra Calix and Eduardo Martell, Archivo of the Secretaría de Relaciones Exteriores, Honduras; Victor Meza and his staff at the Centro de Documentación de Honduras;

Col. José Oscar Flores, director of the Colegio de Defensa Nacional, Armed Forces of Honduras, for a lengthy interview and for allowing me to consult the library of the Colegio; Ana Rosa Morales, Archivo Nacional de Nicaragua; Brenda Cortes, Biblioteca Nacional de Nicaragua; Nicole Ball and Kate Doyle, National Security Archive; Judith A. Frey, Defense Security Assistance Agency; and finally to David Pfeiffer and Cary Conn, U.S. National Archives, for tracking down references to diplomatic correspondence and for their diligent handling of numerous Freedom of Information Act requests.

It is a pleasure to thank the good people of the Perry Library of Old Dominion University, who together made the single greatest contribution to the writing of this book. They not only gave me a place to write but responded gracefully and energetically to innumerable requests for materials over the years. The patience, generosity, and good humor heaped upon me by Beverly Barco, Pamela Morgan, Giselle McAdoo, Janet Justis, and Stuart Frazer are richly appreciated.

For their singular expressions of moral, material, and intellectual support and interest in this project, I am happy to thank Richard N. Adams, Francisco Allwood, Craig Cameron, Marielos Chaverri, Jie Chen, John H. Coatsworth, Chandra DeSilva, JoEllen Dutton, Antonio Esgueva, Michael Gambone, Miguel Angel Herrera Cuarezma, Fabrice Edouard Lahoucq, John Markoff, Mary McCann, Michael McIntyre, Steve Mange, Douglas Massey, Michael Rosenfeld, Alberto Salom Echeverría, Trini Sánchez, Michael J. Schroeder, Pauline Holden Stork, Dennis and Warren Stork, Margarita Vannini, and Harold Wilson. I am grateful to Eric Zolov, Kirk Bowman, Darío Euraque, and Oxford University Press's anonymous reviewers for their comments on an earlier version of this book. I benefited enormously from the friendship, encyclopedic knowledge, and bottomless generosity of Marvin Barahona, with whom it is my good fortune to be bound in *compadrazgo* through the baptism of my son Carlos Roberto. For the warm hospitality of the Villar family of Honduras and the Rosales family of El Salvador I am especially indebted and deeply grateful. My wife Rina Villars makes up one-half of a floating seminar in Latin American history and culture that has been happily meeting, extemporaneously and ardently, in every conceivable venue for more than thirteen years. I would have been lost without both her fierce intellectual challenges and her measured encouragement. *Mil gracias, amada mía.*

In the very beginning was the John D. and Catherine T. MacArthur Foundation, whose grant for research and writing in 1991 launched this project. The J. William Fulbright Foreign Scholarship Board supplied a research and teaching grant in 2000 that supported my research in Costa Rican archives and libraries and gave me the chance to try out some ideas in a graduate seminar I taught at the University of Costa Rica. Old Dominion University provided indispensable material assistance over the years. I thank the people of all these institutions for their support. Cambridge University Press allowed me to quote from parts of my article "Constructing the Limits of State Violence in Central America: Towards a New Research Agenda," *Journal of Latin American Studies* 28, no. 2 (May 1996):438–446.

CONTENTS

A photograph section follows p. 118

ARMIES WITHOUT NATIONS

Introduction

Loose talk about globalization seems to have spawned a new historical specialty, "global history," and an interesting discussion among historians about its utility. A global historian keeps "a global vision," specializing in a problem that can be "conceived globally" but investigated locally.[1] According to historian Bruce Mazlish, there is no single global history but "many global experiences," each of which merits its own history.[2] Although not much of anything could have been globalized before about 1500, it seems clear enough that certain institutions have been globalized—that is, diffused around the globe—at different times at distinctive rates.[3]

This book seeks a better understanding of the history of two sequential but closely related global experiences. The first was the formation of modern states, one of the earliest (and lengthiest) examples of globalization.[4] The second embraced the increasing capacity of the agents of those states, as well as their collaborators and adversaries, to more efficiently monitor, threaten, kill and maim ever greater numbers of people and to destroy more and more of their property. This second trend, which I call the globalization of public violence, did not really become manifest until the twentieth century. It affected the first in a paradoxical way, enhancing the coercive power at the disposal of the state's agents, while at the same time empowering those who sought to challenge or undermine their authority. What accounted for the globalization of public violence? What kept it going? And what difference has it made?

My response to these questions begins with an account of the role of public violence in state formation. It ends by showing how that violence was globalized (and transformed) by the new opportunities for military and police collaboration with the U.S. government that arose during the Cold War. The process began with World War II, expanded tremendously during the Cold War, and has clearly outlived the end of the Cold War. Although the factors that account for the surge in the globalization of public violence during the second half of the twentieth century may be associated—only loosely in some cases, much more directly in others—with the Cold War, it would be wrong to identify the process entirely with the international rivalry between the two camps led by the United States and the Soviet Union.

This inquiry focuses mainly (but not entirely) on a region of Latin America with a distinctive political and cultural history: the five states of the isthmus of Central America, namely, Guatemala, El Salvador, Honduras, Nicaragua, and Costa Rica. The globalization of public violence was launched in this region in a decade or two with cataclysmic effects. Studying a specific region also offers unique opportunities for comparison of the process and its effects, not only among five superficially homogeneous countries that are nevertheless different in some surprising ways, but also between them as a whole and the rest of Latin America. Because certain aspects of the isthmian countries' experience can be readily observed elsewhere, those who specialize in other regions will find grounds for fruitful comparisons in this book.

I elaborate my particular use of the concept "public violence" in chapter 1 and fully define "globalization" in chapter 8. Briefly, "public violence" draws together the killing, maiming, and other acts of destruction committed by rival *caudillos*, guerrilla "liberators," death squads, and state agents such as the armed forces and police, all of whom act within what I will identify as the "field" of state power. My appropriation of the word "globalization" is meant to overcome the tendency to think only in terms of the familiar, mutually exclusive, and misleading spatial hierarchies of local, regional, national, and international. Public violence itself has been globalized, its agents and its victims linked in ways that render rigid notions of the "local" and the "national" practically meaningless; the idea of a self-contained, self-directed national "state" is, partially as a result of these very trends, anachronistic. I do not wish to make a case for indiscriminate "lumping" against some infernal clique of "splitters," but to propose a way to discriminate more precisely by crossing certain boundaries—in this case, between particular acts of violence and between particular national societies.[5] This book therefore shifts perspectives as needed—from the global, to the Latin American, to the North American, to the Central American, and finally to the level of individual countries of Central America—to illuminate connections and sharpen comparisons. Every *place* nests within an imbricated series of spatial situations, each one of which imparts meaning to the past they share. "Nicaragua" is at once inescapably "Central America" and "Latin America" and the "Western Hemisphere" and "global."

Chapter 1 defines the core problem: the relationship between public violence and the state formation process in the context of Latin American history. The pattern of public violence that unfolded in Central America after independence in 1821 did not differ substantially from that of other former American territories of the Iberian empires, where public violence has been a prominent aspect of the state formation process. Chapter 1 analyzes the expression of that violence as well as its sources. Without completely rejecting class-based sources (such as labor recruitment practices) to explain Latin American violence in general, I argue that patrimonial politics—as expressed in its Latin American form, *caudillaje*—contributed at least as much as class differences to the level and persistence of violence in the course of state formation. *Caudillaje* was governed by a rule of violence, a habitus that saturated the field of power surrounding the state.

Part I applies my formulation of public violence to Central America, elaborating it against the history of the isthmus as a whole, and then against each of the ex-states (later republics) of the defunct federation of Central America. The focus of part I is the role of public violence in the early state formation process, with special emphasis on two closely related problems: the emergence of what I call the *improvisational state,* whose defining characteristic was the continuous need to improvise its coercive authority by bargaining with *caudillo*-led armed bands of various kinds, and the concomitant problem of how those forces were gradually superceded, at different times and with different results, by a single army that was "national" but only in a narrowly juridical sense. Emerging with great clarity in the nineteenth century, these problems persisted, with awful consequences, well into the twentieth century and the Cold War period's globalization of public violence. Central America's "armies without nations" were the rival fighting forces that contended for power within each country up to the early twentieth century. Later they became the military institutions that gradually consolidated their grip on state power from about the middle of the century in Guatemala, El Salvador, Honduras, and Nicaragua. Another legacy of patrimonialism was the absence of any coherent, inclusive, and embedded sense of national purpose or identity that might have blocked the warping of the state by the tyrannical ambitions of a caudillo or the armed forces.

Part II picks up the theme of the globalization of public violence, now unmistakably manifest in the first truly world war, that of 1939–45. The opening chapter, which first summarizes the conclusions proferred in Part I, develops the idea of globalization in world-historical terms before turning to the novel systems of transnational military and police collaboration that sprang up during and after World War II. Subjected, during the Cold War, to a ceaseless process of financial, technological, and diplomatic adjustment, those systems globalized public violence for the first time. Subsequent country-specific chapters show how U.S. military and police collaboration interacted with distinctive political traditions to reshape the capacity of isthmian states to deploy violence up to 1960. That year marks the opening of a new phase of collaboration, one that responds to the abrupt appearance in Latin America of communist-oriented insurgent forces, the agents of a heavily ideologized Cold War variant of counterinstitutional public violence. An account of that phase will appear in a subsequent volume, *Armies Without Nations: The United States and the Transformation of Public Violence in Central America, 1961–1991.*

Part I

1821–1939

1

Historical Dimensions of Public Violence in Latin America

> For historians violence is a difficult subject, diffuse and hard to cope with. It is committed by isolated individuals, small groups, and by large mobs; it is directed against individuals and crowds alike; it is undertaken for a variety of purposes (and at times for no discernible rational purpose at all), and in a variety of ways ranging from assassinations and murders to lynchings, duels, brawls, feuds and riots; it stems from criminal intent and from political idealism, from antagonisms that are entirely personal and from antagonisms of large social consequence. Hence it has been hard to conceive of violence as a subject at all.
> —Richard Hofstadter

To "conceive of violence" as a subject of historical inquiry may be only slightly less challenging today than it was in 1970 when Hofstadter synthesized the range of difficulties posed by the systematic study of a subject so ubiquitous and momentous, yet disparate in form, origin, and effect.[1] Since then, a torrent of scholarship has poured forth on subjects closely allied with the expression of violence—war, rebellion, revolution, protest, terrorism, and government repression, to name a few. Although it is not hard to find the word "violence" in any bibliography of the social sciences or the humanities of the last thirty years or so, Anthony Giddens's pronouncement remains apt: "the neglect of what any casual survey of history shows to be an overwhelmingly obvious and chronic trait of human affairs—recourse to violence and war—is one of the most extraordinary blank spots in social theory in the twentieth century."[2]

To speak of violence in a general, collective way, as a social phenomenon, risks forgetting the meaning of violence at the personal level. As Hedley Bull pointed out, the personal level is the only level that counts in the end.[3] Is there a greater affront to the natural dignity and freedom of a person than an act of violence? The severity of the affront is not diminished in the least when applied by the state in its deployment of what its agents call "force," to resort to the conventional way of distinguishing legitimate from illegitimate violence. Indeed, "force" when used as a deterrent by the state against enemies internal or external is intended to be an assault on human dignity, for that is precisely what makes it a deterrent. Nor do the agents of states always distinguish between legitimate and illegitimate applications of violence.

In order to capture analytically the lived reality of a particular kind of violence experienced by individuals, this chapter stakes out the boundaries of a field of historical research that I call public violence. The concept draws together types of violence that historians usually treat independently, as when they habitually separate the violence committed by states from that of revolutionaries, by army factions from that of guerrilla groups, by *caudillos* from that of death squads, and so on. An overly meticulous concern for these distinctions can obscure their common character and purpose—and their common source. The persistence of public violence in Latin America originates in the patrimonial institutions—among them, patron-clientage—that have ruled the region since the sixteenth century.[4] By this I do not mean that the inhabitants of Latin America are more or less "violent" than anyone else, nor that the character, intensity, or scope of public violence in Latin America has remained unchanged for five hundred years. I claim that the enormous potential for violence embedded in patron-client politics is so great that it overshadows ideology or class interests, or regional, familial, or ethnic identity, as independent sources of public violence.[5]

No discussion of violence should begin without acknowledging the twentieth century as humanity's golden age of killing, in both the monumental scale and the astonishing inventiveness of the planning, organization, financing, execution, and legitimization of killing. The killing's great catalyst, advocate, and consolidator was the modern state. The production and continuous perfection of the instruments of death were typically the responsibility of firms recruited by the state and often heavily subsidized by public revenue.[6] Not merely the industrialization of war itself but the creation of what Giddens called a "world military order" emerged from the interaction of industrial capitalism and the state.[7]

The prominent role of the advanced industrial sectors of the world's richest economies, as the junior partners of their respective states, by no means implied that the killing was limited to those particular societies. On the contrary, by the second half of the twentieth century, their partnership made the killing almost entirely an export product, thus globalizing the violence. In addition to the consolidation of the joint private-public nature of the great killing and its globalization, another feature took on even greater importance during the twentieth century. As the power of states expanded, so did their ideological and coercive capacities to incite collaborative killing by groups and individuals who were not technically its direct agents—death squads, semi-private militias, secret armies, and "off-duty" officers of military and police agencies. As states concentrated violence in their own institutions and successfully held themselves out as its only legitimate source and licensing authority, violence that could merely be associated with the state—be it that of the state's own informally deputized agents or its sworn enemies—as well as violence that was directly sponsored by the state, was sanctified and ritualized as never before. Thus, although the actual "apparatus" of the state has not been the only direct source of the kinds of organized violence that made the twentieth century the golden age of killing, the state has undoubtedly constituted the main arena within which the killing took place, as the agents of states both contended and collaborated with their competitors and associates, both internal and external. As various theorists have noted, outside the confines of the state apparatus itself, political and military power are typically wielded by groups that either aspire to make their own state or to control some space within the state.[8] The spatially oriented concept of a social "field" of power surrounding the state, rather than that of a monolithic structure of state power from which springs discrete acts attributable solely to the state apparatus, is a way to acknowledge the disparate yet systemic character of twentieth-century public violence.[9]

State institutions operate within—and typically dominate—the field of state power but they seldom monopolize it. The boundaries of the field of state power, constituted not so much by structural borders but by fluid social relationships, vary over time and space. The killing, maiming, and destruction that take place in this field is "public violence," owing to its compatibility with all the conventional senses of the word "public"—in other words, its wide visibility, potential to affect great numbers of people, and connection with government.[10] Its "public" character was further enhanced by the range of acts of violence typically identified as terroristic (owing to their capacity to induce fear and submission among those who witness the violence) as well as display-oriented acts of violence aimed, in certain historical contexts, at impressing its witnesses with the protagonist's ability to rule. Public violence encompasses war in the conventional sense, within as well as among states, but also events typically associated with such disparate categories as "political violence," "collective violence," "revolutionary violence," and acts of violence committed by death squads, vigilantes, and self-declared popular armies of liberation. Under certain conditions, the violence carried out by some criminal organizations may, in its origins and effects, be practically indistinguishable from the violence of the latter groups. Examples are militias associated with business enterprises that trade in proscribed goods and services such as cocaine and prostitution, and the bandit gangs (*maras*) that began to terrorize much of Honduras and El Salvador in the early 1990s and had become, by 2003, major threats to their national security. A strong case might be made for a conceptual distinction between the legitimate, state-sponsored use of force and illegitimate violence that reflects the reality of life in, for example, Canada, the United States, or the Netherlands. But it would be much harder to make a similar case for Argentina, Mexico, or Guatemala. In a global sense, the validity of the distinction had already begun to wear thin with the massive aerial bombardment of civilian targets during World War II. It practically disappeared during the Cold War, when nuclear "strategic planning" of the most powerful states became a euphemism for the organization of mass murder, and as so-called covert action by intelligence organs of the state, proxy wars, and insurgencies sponsored by foreign states routinely targeted noncombatants.

The difference between public and private violence may be ambiguous at times, because agents of each can ally to achieve different objectives. Nevertheless, it is a decisive difference because of the vast disproportion in the potential scale of each. In the twentieth century, no person could be excluded as a potential target of public violence, and no number of victims could be considered too high. On the deployment side, no upward limit on the number of the agents who might be recruited to deploy public violence, not to mention any control over how they did it, could be imagined. The unlimited nature of public violence has remained as characteristic of civil war as it has of war between states, as characteristic of revolutionary violence as it has of postrevolutionary "pacification." Any given act of private violence, on the other hand, must be restricted to the work of just one or at most a few agents, and the scope limited to one or at most a few victims.[11] I adhere, provisionally, to Alvaro Camacho's definition of private violence as acts of destruction that operate "on the basis of the direct personal business of people in their strictly private lives," acting in "their own name" and neither challenging nor defending "any social order."[12]

Latin America

If it is true that, as one eminent specialist put it, "constructive and peaceable processes have dominated human relations" in the history of the United States,[13] it would be hard to deny that the opposite is the case in the history of the Latin American countries. Yet the overwhelming majority of Latin Americans live in nations that achieved their independence no more than four decades after the United States. These countries, therefore, cannot be grouped with the "new nations" of Africa and Asia, where violence is often attributed to a more recent colonial past. Just as the persistence of Latin America's comparative economic backwardness—despite nearly two centuries of independence—has long been the central preoccupation of economic historians, the persistence of violence after such a long period of self-government deserves investigation. Even though the disjunction between violent and nonviolent means of contesting power is one of the staple themes of the historiography of Latin America, the violence itself has not received enough attention. Instead of being treated as a variable on its own terms, public violence tends to disappear through the apertures of one conceptual or theoretical grid after another: militarization, class conflict, political instability, economic structures, democratization, revolution, authoritarianism, popular mobilization, culture, electoral freedom and integrity, identity, ethnicity, status, race, and gender. The violence is merely what happened as groups and individuals pursued certain goals—"statemaking," perhaps, or personal enrichment, identity construction, economic development, or "resistance"—goals analyzed with due reference to their "implications" for class, economic change, access to land, gender and ethnicity, but in ways that seem to blot out any consideration of the persistence and intensity of the violence itself.[14] The lacuna in question is not the absence of historical research in Latin America about violent events or violent processes like revolution, riot, *golpes de estado,* guerrilla warfare, civil war, terrorism, torture, death-squad killings, or political repression but a failure to systematically consider them as manifestations of a certain historical pattern or category of behavior. The varieties of public violence are equated with "instability," analysis of which is limited to its presentation as an "obstacle" to be overcome in the pursuit of something, such as economic growth. In the latter case, a kind of dialectical process is identified in which export-driven economic growth finally produces tax revenues allowing states to establish political stability, but at the cost of political repression and economic inequalities that merely supply the grievances for later outbursts of violence from below.[15]

Violence and the threat of violence generate fear and therefore preparation for violence. This is one of those grimly familiar cycles of human behavior that is nevertheless far from being understood, as the social theorist Norbert Elias observed.

> Up to the present, there has been relatively little understanding of how the use of violence by a particular group against another gives rise with a high degree of probability to the use of violence by the other group against the former, as soon as there is the slightest chance to do so. The violence of the second group then in many cases triggers off increased violence from the first group. If such a process, a double-bind process, is once set in motion, then it is exceedingly difficult to halt; it often gains a momentum of its own. It gains a self-perpetuating and very often escalating power over the people, the opposing groups which constitute it, and becomes a trap forcing each of the participating sides, out of fear of the violence of the other side, to fight each other with violence.[16]

The context of the quoted passage makes it clear that Elias considered his observation to have universal validity, even though he was particularly interested in the persistence of the double-bind process in the Weimar Republic, when communist and fascist groups each targeted both one another and the state itself. In that particular case, Elias blamed the escalation of violence on the weakness of the Weimar state and its limited control over the armed forces and the police.[17] This is a conclusion commonly reached by students of Latin America's history, who associate state strength with high levels of cohesiveness, clarity, and stability in the state's organizing ideology and institutions. Weak states—by definition incoherent, obscure, and unstable both ideologically and institutionally—were therefore subject to higher levels of violence.[18] A slightly different interpretation associates violence with a kind of evolutionary stage in the state's natural development from weakness toward strength, suggesting the inevitability of endemic violence in all states at certain moments as they mature.[19]

But it is not obvious why public violence should necessarily emerge under conditions of state weakness and disappear when the state is strong. "Strength" and "weakness" are such crudely conceived measures that they serve little useful purpose as explanatory variables. In Latin America, violence co-existed in a continual state of rivalry with nonviolence as techniques of both joined the repertoire of tools available to contenders acting within the field of power dominated by the state. What may be distinctive about Latin America is that this tension dominated the process of state formation for so long, well beyond any period of time that might be proposed as a standard "maturity" cycle of state growth. More pertinent than state strength was the molding of states and the dispositions of statemakers over the course of nearly two centuries by the constant tension between violence and nonviolence, by the cycle of fear and preparation for violence that "gains a self-perpetuating and very often escalating power over the people," to quote Elias. If we include the agents of extra-state violence within the field of state power, the state itself is no longer seen as a failed monopolizer or as a strong player or a weak player, constitutional or illegitimate, popular or oligarchic. Instead, the agents of the state are trapped in the same cycle of fear that also characterizes activity by others who are contending in the wider field of state power.[20]

The Agents and Sources of Public Violence

I classify the agents or perpetrators of public violence as institutional, counterinstitutional, and para-institutional.[21] Institutional violence emanates from the state itself when it deploys the armed forces, the police, judges and their accessories, instruments through which the state seeks to claim absolute sovereignty. Institutional violence also includes that associated with the formal allies of the regime in power, such as regional strongmen (*caudillos*) with their armed retainers and political parties with their respective militias. Counterinstitutional violence emanates from groups bent on seizing or reforming the state, either from within established state institutions (such as military plotters) or from without (such as a guerrilla army or a disaffected *caudillo* and his followers). Counterinstitutional agents even include the perpetrators of the more or less spontaneous, class-based violence deployed to protest, for example, food shortages or tax rises. The public character of violence may be most distinctive when it seeks either to affirm or contest the authority or legitimacy of the state.

Sharing in varying degrees the characteristics of both institutional and counterinstitutional violence, the third type of agent is para-institutional. In general, this violence is committed by groups that are loosely—and usually covertly—affiliated with organs of the state, that may depend on them for support, and that may even have been created or licensed by the state itself to collaborate in the elimination or intimidation of its enemies. Some para-institutional groups may have legal status as private, state-chartered organizations that are nevertheless led, organized, and manned by agents of the state itself. Others operate without any such charter even though they typically operate on behalf of some or all of the state's coercive agencies and under their informal (if partial) sanction. Successful bandit groups, to the extent that they depend on the political protection of local notables, may be required to pay for that protection by making war on their sponsors' political enemies. Exemplary para-institutional organizations in Latin America have been the *caudillo*-led bands that were most prominent in the nineteenth century, and the death squads and other vigilante-type groups that became informal instruments of state terror in the second half of the twentieth century.[22] Under certain conditions, official or semi-official para-institutional organizations can escape the control of their institutional sponsors.[23] An example of this sort of degeneration was the hodgepodge of armed bands known as the "contra," initially sponsored by the Argentine state and later by the United States, to undermine the Nicaraguan state in the 1980s. They frequently fought among themselves, carried out criminal operations against unarmed civilians in cross-border sanctuaries in Costa Rica and Honduras, and worked out covert but shaky arrangements with elements of the governments of the two bordering states. Like institutional and counterinstitutional violence, para-institutional violence has a theatrical dimension that encompasses selective acts of terror and other gestures intended to dramatize power.

Public violence in Latin America draws on three kinds of power—economic (emphasizing class), cultural (emphasizing status), and political (including party)[24] —in ways that account not just for the persistence of public violence but for its hardening into what has from time to time been called a "culture of violence." So, instead of deploying the concepts of class, status, politics, and culture to build models ("authoritarianism," "democracy," "militarism," "development") that filter out or subsume public violence, I will use them to try to capture it and analyze it.

Economic/Class

No explanation for public violence is more widely assumed (if not actually asserted) than economic or class differences, especially for Latin America. This is at least partially because the privileged access to resources is well known to be even more disproportionate in Latin America than in other world regions. With so much at stake, incentives among the privileged for defending the status quo are as powerful as the incentives among the lowly for challenging it. In the historiography of the five countries of the isthmus of Central America, for example, the foundational nature of an inevitable conflict between economic classes underlies nearly every explanation of social and political contention of any kind. The ultimate, subterranean source of that conflict is typically understood as an agro-export production structure that has been controlled for at least a century by groups and individuals with privileged access to land and labor. "Elite" owners and managers used the power of authoritarian states (either directly, or indirectly through military proxies) to protect their control over land and their supply of cheap labor, brutalizing the lower classes into submission and virtually forcing them to resort to revolutionary violence. The poor and weak have been oppressed, often violently, by the rich and the powerful, and responded with violence, which triggered more counter-violence. Nothing could be simpler, more obvious, nor more intuitive; societies *are* class divided, and the most violent often turn out to be the most class divided.

But class identity—how people perceive their own class situation and how they assign class boundaries to others—can shift abruptly. And even when the boundaries and identities remain stable, elements of different classes seem at least as likely to form alliances as they are to contest one another violently. Perhaps the most important question, for the claim of class-based violence to be convincing, is: Precisely what minimum proportion of any given subordinate class's total "membership" should one expect to discover among groups ostensibly fighting on its behalf? Class affiliation can be undermined rather easily, particularly by patrimonial forms of political organization, making political and military alliances notoriously fluid and almost impossible to predict on the basis of economic or class interests or identities.[25] One study of Guatemalan public violence, although sympathetic to the guerrilla movement, nevertheless speculated that the Guatemalan armed forces succeeded in liquidating the movement in part because many of the rural-based small property owners who composed a segment of the guerrilla army "deserted as soon as the repression became more intense, even joining with paramilitary groups in the service of repression, which shows that the motive for participation in the guerrilla war included a good deal of adventurism and inclination toward violence, common among the inhabitants of the eastern region of the country."[26] A study of one region of Guatemala showed how to two different ethnic-class blocs (Ixils and Ladinos) refused to kill each other in the name of either the class-oriented guerrillas or the equally class-oriented military government.[27] In Nicaragua, old kinship and regional loyalties weighed heavily among the Marxist Sandinista revolutionaries in both their insurgent (1970s) and governing (1980s) phases. In fact, it would be hard to find a better example of the weaknesses of an exclusively class-based analysis of the sources of public violence than the Nicaragua of the 1980s.[28]

Finally, it is telling that almost all of the killing carried out by armed groups of all kinds in Latin America—whether army, militia, guerrilla *frente*, or death squad—has invariably been the work of the *soldado raso*, the private who is "recruited" (often coercively) from among the poorest classes of Latin American society, whereas the intellectual authors, the ideologists, and the strategists of the killing, are usually among the most privileged. The examples of intraclass killing during situations of public violence, in which individuals target members of their own economic class, are well documented. How much more often, indeed, has violence actually hindered the expression of class interests, instead of advancing it? To the extent that violence can be used to move oneself from a lower social class to one of higher status, it can weaken class solidarity.[29] It is not that class doesn't matter, but that the concept has infiltrated the analysis of violence to such an extent that it has tended to obscure its many cross-class attributes. In the Latin American context, it is a force that must be reconciled with patrimonialism.

Culture/Status

In Latin America, culturally constructed status hierarchies have created and distributed power even more effectively than the economically constructed differentiations of class.[30] A theoretical elaboration of status hierarchies emerges in Roberto DaMatta's studies of Brazilian society, highlighting what DaMatta called the "personalistic," "relational," and "holistic" characteristics that have survived alongside or tended to overpower individualistic and egalitarian tendencies. Two separate status hierarchies (one ascriptive, traditional, and Latin America; the other achievement-oriented, modern, and North American) have cohabited, not only in Brazil but in Latin America generally: "We will not advance toward significant understanding of Brazilian and Latin American reality if we do not discover the deep relations between the impersonal commands of law (conceived as a function of 'individuals') and 'friends' (a universe governed by the implicit and personalized rules of *parentela* [i.e., extended family networks])." The "harsh impersonal hand of the law" has thus been forced to obey "the gradations and hierarchically differentiated positions that everyone occupies in a web of socially determined relations."[31]

Like economic class, personalistic status hierarchies organize power in highly asymmetrical ways, with interesting consequences for distinctive expressions of public violence. Roberto Kant de Lima has shown how those hierarchies can lead to comparatively more violent responses by state authorities in Brazil to perceived infractions of the law, as they apply "the general law of their society to a particular case."[32] The kind of particularism practiced routinely in Latin America is frequently interpreted as "corruption" in the United States, as if it were simply a matter of the police or other authorities "obeying the law" when in fact they carry contrary systems of meaning. Official or state-sponsored violence isn't so much a matter of "corruption" in the North American sense of a legal or constitutional aberration, as it is an expression of distinctive premises having to do with status. In Brazil, for example, the application of the law "is always particularized, personalized, and negotiated with respect to special social circumstances, in contrast with the system of universal application of the local laws to particular individuals and cases in the United States."[33]

Kant de Lima's reference to the prevailing pattern of rigid status hierarchies as "the core of another legal and political culture" points to one of the oldest themes in the scholarly literature on Latin America: the genealogy of an Iberian political culture, and its status as an explanatory variable for any number of purportedly distinctive traits—from underdevelopment and *machismo* to lawlessness and military rule. Richard Morse, relying heavily on DaMatta, argued that the primacy of patrimonialism over feudalism in Spain and her overseas territories led to a "relational ethic" yielding "structures of authority [as opposed to structures of legal-rational domination] and casuistical applications of principle."[34] The publication of Morse's study coincided with one of those surprising swings in academic fashion. After two decades of shunning and disparagement, political culture theory achieved a sort of comeback in the 1990s, as Gabriel A. Almond, its principal architect, was quick to declare.[35]

One of the most suggestive statements of the connection between culture and public violence appeared in a study by a special commission of the Peruvian Senate, which daringly concluded that "In a generic way one can argue that the process of socialization in Peru, through the family, school, social relations and communications media, has collaborated in the creation of a *culture of violence* [emphasis in original], which stands in the background and reinforces other manifestations of violence."[36] Observing that this kind of "structural violence" has been present in the Andes even during nominally peaceful times, Enrique Mayer bifurcated the problem into different arenas of violence, one associated with domination and the other with subordination: "First, to what extent are there long-term institutionalized patterns of violence that have been imposed by state, church, and ruling elites? Second, regarding the responses from below, is there an Andean cultural pattern of violence?"[37] In this class-oriented configuration, the state and its allies initiate the cycle of violence, generating a distinctive "popular" kind of violence in response. A more holistic approach was suggested by James B. Greenberg's study of the high level of daily violence among the Chatino people of Mexico, which he tied to the emergence of capitalist relations of production and exchange. As community violence came into contact with the patron-client structure of Mexican politics (itself, according to Greenberg, "a well-known source of rancor and violence"), local and regional political violence intensified.[38]

State/Party

"Political power," according to Mann, "derives from the usefulness of centralized, institutionalized, territorialized regulation of many aspects of social relations."[39] In the context of postcolonial Latin America, the relevant institutions have been those of the state itself and of the parties and proto-party groups organized to compete for control of the state. Politics in Latin America share what Christopher Clapham called the "neo-patrimonial" character of politics in much of the Third World. What makes it "neo" is that patrimonial relationships "pervade a political and administrative system which is formally constructed on rational-legal lines."[40] In other words, this is a political system that reflects the fusion, in DaMatta's terms, of the two ideal-type status hierarchies: one oriented toward individual achievement and organized along bureaucratic and legal-rational lines, and the other ascriptive, particularistic, and personalistic. It is not the mere survival of particularistic status hierarchies, but the way in which they combined with liberal capitalist hierarchies that may make the Latin American case distinctive. Latin America's "world time" experience with republican constitutional polities and liberal capitalist economic organization began with the infancy (or at least the adolescence) of modernity itself. The modern liberal forms did not so much displace the old status hierarchies as disguise them. That is just how Octavio Paz, writing in the late 1940s, seemed to interpret the constitutional principles that formally ruled the continent since independence:

> In Spanish America they merely served as modern trappings for the survivals of the colonial system. This liberal, democratic ideology, far from expressing our concrete historical situation, disguised it, and the political lie established itself almost constitutionally. The moral damage it has caused is incalculable; it has affected profound areas of our existence. We move about in this lie with complete naturalness. For over a hundred years we have suffered from regimes that have been at the service of feudal oligarchies but have utilized the language of freedom. The situation has continued to our own day.[41]

What those constitutions merely disguised without extirpating was *caudillismo*, the Latin American variant of patrimonial or patron-client politics, or what Paz, more dramatically but less precisely, called "feudal oligarchies." In one terrible, stunning phrase—"We move about in this lie with complete naturalness"—Paz captured, as few have, the *political* lineage of public violence. The constitutions were not mere adornments but functional disguises that enabled *caudillismo* to flourish amid electoral events and a formal but utterly irrelevant acknowledgement of the separation of powers. Hence the "naturalness" of the lie, for without the constitutional disguises that made it possible for political authorities to claim a purely legalistic but spurious legitimacy, the hard patrimonial core of politics could scarcely have survived.[42] F.-X. Guerra's analysis of nineteenth century Mexican politics brilliantly exposed that core as a "new form of *caciquismo*" whose agents enjoyed a freedom of action unknown in the colonial era; this new *caciquismo* was "an illegal power, hidden, shameful but inevitable" and the *cacique* himself was "an arbitrary authority, without juridical recourse, since legally he did not exist."[43]

By the nineteenth century, there was no longer any ideology available that was congruent with patrimonial practice, whose now lifeless ancestors were absolutism and divine right. What passed for an ideology was a hollow liberalism, shot through with a crude *pactismo*, the colonial-era relation of reciprocal rights and duties between ruler and ruled, now reconfigured "among diverse elements, which could subdivide themselves infinitely."[44] Of nineteenth-century Latin American politics, Guerra and Demélas-Bohy wrote:

> Family cliques, clientelist networks, municipal bodies, all these collective participants in the old society remained strong and healthy despite the adoption of new principles. Modern political life and its electoral dimension could not avoid being profoundly changed; electoral competition could not reflect the free opinion of individual citizens, since these were very much in the minority. Only those members of the elites . . . would confront each another in modern elections by mobilising, each in their own way, the old collective actors, . . . From this moment *caciquismo*, the structure so peculiar to the political life of the Hispanic countries, assumed the place that it was to occupy for a long time to come.[45]

The link between *pactismo* and public violence derived from two implications of *pactismo*: A broken pact could mean war or other acts of violence among the parties already pacted. Even an unbroken pact implied unbending hostility toward those not pacted.[46]

In Brazil in the 1840s, according to Uricoechea, the monarchy's vain attempt to centralize authority forced it to adopt a policy of "tacit pacts and tactical alliances with the privatized power of the local notables. Favors and privileges were suggested as moves to gain the sympathy and cooperation of local families and prominent landlords. . . . Mutual awareness that the state and the landlord each needed the other in equal measure gave rise to a tacit pact resulting in a pattern of exchanges and reciprocities, the state granting authority and status in exchange for the landlord's cooperation and service." By the middle of the century, as political parties became institutionalized, the pacts encompassed the provincial governments that were now seeking resources from the central government in exchange for electoral support: "The political system thus organized itself through a series of pacts of ever expanding radius."[47] Political banditry likewise illustrates the link between violence and patrimonialism. Agents of the state or regional power brokers, men with little coercive capacity of their own, hired gangs to kill or otherwise intimidate political enemies.[48]

Without a congruent ideology to which patrimonial political authorities could appeal in order to dissolve conflict, violence became the standard arbiter for the settlement of disputes, so much so that it came to nest "naturally" within liberal democratic constitutional shells. Elections themselves functioned as opportunities for patrons to display clientage and ultimately therefore appropriate occasions for martial engagements. Richard Graham's magisterial study of the inner workings of Brazilian imperial politics shows the system to have been an artful blend of violence and electoralism.[49] David Nugent's study of provincial Peruvian politics between 1885 and 1935 found "endemic conflict" among elite-led factions over control of the region of Chachapoyas, or as he also called it, over "their efforts to become the single privileged client of the state." In seeking power or struggling to keep it, factions persecuted each other endlessly, in whatever ways they could. Those who wished to rule had "to demonstrate their ability to dominate, shame, and impose their will on their adversaries," even as both rulers and adversaries employed the liberal rhetoric of popular sovereignty and equality.[50] Once set in motion this "double-bind process" was hard to stop.

Today, ideology still counts for much less than the particularistic ties of clientelism and corporatism.[51] One result, as Douglas Chalmers has argued in the case of modern Latin America, is the tendency for the political and electoral activities of the incumbent to merge with the administrative mechanisms of the state. To survive, the incumbent has to secure "the loyalty of factions within every accessible institution and organization" well beyond the formal authority that a constitution gives the president because "such 'personal power' is all there is, and it is necessary for survival."[52] A more concise definition of patrimonial politics in its modern guise could scarcely be constructed. The patron-client dyad is an expression of a vertically structured pact, which also has its horizontal counterpart among the more or less equal patrons and chiefs who pact among themselves. And when personal power "is all there is," violence is likely to be deployed as an enactment of personal power and to be understood by its witnesses, victims, and perpetrators alike as a demonstration of fitness to rule.

Vengeance linked patrimonialism and violence.[53] In imperial Brazil, according to Uricoechea, any bureaucratic effort to redress a private wrong was interpreted as vindictiveness. "In a context where legal penalty was likely to be interpreted as a vindictive reaction, what was meant to be extirpated was actually fostered, and institutionalized means of redress were not considered restitutive actions but further crimes."[54] The power of vengeance was also an underlying motive force of "La Violencia," the great wave of interparty strife that swept Colombia in the 1950s and 1960s: "Cruelty is inseparable from vengeance and is legitimated by vengeance," and the desire for vengeance became all the more intense as rural rebels shifted their allegiance from national political leaders to local *caudillos* (*gamonales* in the political vocabulary of Colombia).[55] In his study of *caudillismo* along the Uruguayan-Brazilian border in the late nineteenth century, John C. Chasteen argued that partisan violence was a response to moral standards of "revenge and loyalty" in which "narratives of war" were crucial in constructing the identities of the two principal (and ever-opposing) Uruguayan political parties, Blancos and Colorados.[56] Posada-Carbó interpreted nineteenth-century violence in Colombia in a strikingly similar way to that of Chasteen: "[P]artisan feelings were based on the memory of bloodshed caused by previous battles and, as elections approached, old wounds were reopened in a highly politicized society."[57] This was the politics of blood, "and not only," as John D. Kelly noted, "the kind of blood you are said to be born with, but also the kind of blood you shed." Kelly meant blood sacrificed "for nation." I refer to blood shed for the party. In either case, "It is always very difficult to argue against death stories, and the fresher the blood and higher the body count, the more difficult this becomes."[58]

The Military

In the 1960s, the Latin American armed forces suddenly emerged as a major target of social scientific research. Studies of the military mounted rapidly over the next three decades in response to the growing tendency of Latin American military institutions to seize control of the state from elected, civilian governments. Although institutional rule by the armed forces (rather than rule by an individual military tyrant) was not unknown before the 1960s, it became habitual and widespread by that decade. Moreover, unlike earlier military interventions in government, the "new militarists" typically intended to hold the reins of government indefinitely.

The surge in research on the Latin American military tended, however, to magnify the armed forces' responsibility for violence and authoritarianism, thus exaggerating the innocence of civil society and the latter's capacity for engendering a democratic transition. Taken as a whole, the research tended to suggest that military participation in government could be conceptualized as a continuum between two poles, one being direct military rule and the other civilian control. Along the continuum were points at which power was shared between civilians and the military in different proportions depending on the proximity of those points to one pole or the other. One could detect points of "accommodation" or "relative equilibrium" between the two forces, civilian and military, tending in one direction or the other. It followed that policies directed toward reducing the military's strength and augmenting civilian power would bit by bit drive society toward full civilian control of the military. Hence one could logically speak of a "transition to democracy" or "redemocratization," or of a contrary "remilitarization."

By implying that the military, along with the state of which it was a part, had somehow managed to extirpate itself from society altogether, these researchers suggested that controlling the military was a matter of strengthening civil society vis-à-vis the state, or (in the Dahlian tradition) encouraging the formation of a plurality of institutions and associations capable of counterbalancing the state. According to this view, Latin Americans have a state but no civil society, or one stunted by insufficient information, mobilization, or organization. The tendency has been to see the military as an intrusive, and even alien, presence in society even as it interacts with other social forces.[59]

Civil society, understood as that realm of public life beyond the grip of the state, is neither democracy itself nor is it necessarily capable of spawning democracy, particularly where clientelism predominates. If it is true that Latin America is now passing through a transition from authoritarianism and war to democracy and peace, it is a process whose prospects cannot properly be assessed without reaching beyond state-centered paradigms ("militarism," "authoritarianism," "democratization").[60] Everywhere today, civil society—its creation, sustenance, and survival—is celebrated as the sine qua non of democracy. But civil society is also the incubator of public violence. "While civil society can aid democracy," wrote one of the few skeptics, "it can harm and even help destroy it."[61] For example, Guillermo O'Donnell pointed out that during the dictatorship in Argentina from 1976 to 1984, the military officers could not have controlled society to the extent that they did without the collaboration of others. Thus, the inauguration of a democratic government is not enough; it is necessary to overcome the "strong authoritarian tendencies that exist in society—including in the culture—of our country."[62]

It is for this reason, perhaps, that attempts to control state-sponsored violence by copying into Latin American constitutions the U.S. constitution's fiat that the president is the military commander in chief has so often proved futile. Although military officers have often enough exercised sovereign authority over a president, even elected, civilian presidents sought to manipulate and use the military for narrow political purposes. Military admonitions against partisan meddling by a civilian president, especially when constitutions were being made, are not difficult to find, and they suggest that the armed forces' eagerness to declare itself "apolitical" should be interpreted less cynically.[63]

Latin America and the United States

The United States and the countries of Latin America have found common ground in perfecting and perpetuating public violence in response to congruent interests built on some obvious incongruities.

In Latin America, public violence is dispersed, multidimensional, and subject to constant public observation; it is, above all, highly visible, habitually crossing the porous frontier between state and civil society, and typically meant to be contained within national borders. Latin American public violence has been and continues to be lavishly diverse, spectacular, and abundant in source and form: state-sponsored terror, *caudillo* armies, party militias, death squads, guerrilla warriors, bandit gangs, peasant *jacqueries*, and the great landholder's private police.

In the United States, public violence has been practically invisible because it is almost solely a product for export, made by the state and its private-sector collaborators. Public violence has been channeled beyond the national borders of the United States in the covert operations of the Central Intelligence Agency against and for other states; in the partially overt programs of military and police "assistance" run by the Defense Department, the State Department and their private-sector collaborators; and in the occasional military invasion or bombardment of another nation.[64] As such, U.S. public violence remains embedded in the cells of minutely differentiated politico-military technocracies in which the public and private sectors overlap and combine with one another; an ideology of national security has tended to veil the less visible aspects of public violence (as an export product) from public observation and debate. Robin Luckham called these technocracies an "armament complex" that links scientists, security intellectuals, and security managers, who are in turn supported by the employees of an "armament culture"—including "interpreters," researchers, and publicists.[65] Within what is generally referred to as the "private sector," this kind of intermingling goes beyond the notorious self-dealing between defense contractors and government. The export of public violence to Southeast Asia in the 1960s and 1970s and to Central America in the 1980s relied heavily on the secret collaboration of private-sector enterprises as U.S. government "contractors." The U.S. government's secret use of private firms to carry out military missions in Colombia and Peru against drug producers and traders was exposed in 2001 after employees of an Alabama firm hired by the CIA mistakenly helped the Peruvian Air Force shoot down a plane carrying U.S. missionaries, killing two people.[66]

Thus a complementarity has emerged, between the restricted sphere of the organization and deployment of public violence in the United States, controlled by Washington and its private-sector allies, on the one hand, and the requirements of societies in which public violence constitutes an everyday form of "convivencia," to quote Ernest Samper, the president of Colombia, as he reflected on the quotidian character of violence in his own country in 1995.[67] The historical convergence of deeply embedded political, social and cultural practices in North America and in Latin America created the conditions for complementarity. Those conditions had ripened sufficiently by the late 1940s for collaboration between the United States and Latin America to intensify massively during the Cold War and to continue after it ended. Just because the relationship has been collaborative rather than being, say, a mere exchange of services or products, its proper analysis forces us to abstain from separating "external" and "internal" variables, or to impose "national" and "international" levels of analysis. Even less justified would it be to identify the relationship as one of mere "dependency" or of some species of imperialism. In the case of Central

America during the 1980s, the results of the killing were re-exported in unexpected ways back to the United States, in the form of unwanted immigration, political polarization, deformations like the Iran-contra scandal, and fears associated with the risks of an expanding and unwinnable war (the "Vietnam syndrome").

Conclusions

Instead of accepting the civil-military relations paradigm and its focus on the military and military rule, historians of public violence should draw into their research civilian bureaucrats, professional politicians, judges and their collaborators (within or outside the institutional boundaries of the state) and various contenders for state power, including self-proclaimed popular liberators, whose armies could only claim that they had better reasons than others to kill.

Latin America's enduring patrimonialism accounts for a distinctive pattern of public violence. Of course, an argument for the prominence of clientelism and other practices associated with patrimonialism in Latin America would not surprise any reader of the region's historical and social-science literature.[68] Yet when violence as an aspect of political clientelism has been considered at all, it typically has been as an expression of the coercive capacity of the patron over his clients, and not as a characteristic disposition of patrimonialism itself to which clients as well as patrons may be drawn—a disposition that became deadlier still as it was transformed through globalization in the second half of the twentieth century.

2

Binding Hatreds

Public Violence, State, and Nation in Central American History

If the level of public violence cannot convincingly be tied to some measure of state strength, then with what sort of a state can persistently high levels of public violence be associated? In the case of Central America, the relevant feature of the state seems to have been its improvisational character. With each change of government, state institutions practically had to be reassembled pro tempore from a mélange of collaborators—*hacendados*, merchants, *camarillas*, regional *caudillos* and their followers, municipal-level authorities and strongmen and, later, the armed forces themselves and more or less autonomous vigilante groups. This constant need to attract and hold collaborators made the state's incumbents much more than a mere government, for they were essentially reorganizers of the state itself.

Nowhere was that reorganizational task more evident than in the primordial requirement of every new government to attract and hold the loyalty of the fighting forces to which it owed its accession to constitutional office, and the concomitant need to buy off or otherwise co-opt anyone capable of quickly mobilizing an opposing force of fighting men. The significance of this fact goes well beyond a simple computation of relative troop strength at the disposition of the contenders. It was not the capacity or strength of the state's incumbents vis-à-vis its opponents that mattered as much as the certain knowledge among those over whom the state asserted its sovereignty that the state itself was not the ultimate source of authority. That status was held by whatever fighting forces had won the last battle.[1] In no sense were the isthmian states uniquely improvisational. Indeed, the concept would seem to apply with equal force to the rest of Latin America for much of the nineteenth century and even beyond, as well as to other regions.[2]

The Central American states' incapacity to bind to themselves or to neutralize any and all sources of organized violence in their respective territories was a manifestation of their chronically improvisational character. Under such conditions, legislative dispositions either were not applied at all, or could only be applied by an exhibition (if not an actual application) of violence on the part of the state's agents and collaborators. The state could not hope, therefore, to nonviolently induce compliance with its law because it was not perceived as the legitimate or ultimate source of any latent power to enforce compliance. Whatever power this largely hollow state might hope to deploy was instead communicated to the state by collaborating fighting entities whose interests could at any moment depart from those who held at least nominal authority over them. It was therefore frequently expedient for the nominal subjects of these nominal governments to bargain independently with the collaborating fighting entities instead of with the government itself.[3] The fighting forces in question were frequently not even from the country in question, but operated under the direction of a "foreign" *caudillo,* as in Honduras and El Salvador, for example. It remains a peculiarity of the politics of Central American historiography that, whereas much is made of U.S. military intervention in, say, Honduras, the far more egregious military interventions in that country's politics by the governments of Nicaragua and Guatemala receive much less attention.

The improvisational nature of the state was almost as evident in the 1970s as it was in the 1870s and earlier. Such a state's volatility—its capacity to adopt various combinations of democracy and authoritarianism, federalism and centralism, populism and conservatism—reveal the tentative, instrumental character of its institutions. As a result, politics remain personalistic, clientelistic, and factionalized.[4] In Central America, what changed during the twentieth century was not so much the nature of the state but that of the fighting forces, which by the 1930s and 1940s were assembled into more or less coherent organizations under unified commands. What had not changed was the improvisational character of states whose governments had to attract and keep collaborators—above all, those without which government was impossible, the *fuerzas armadas* or "armies without nations."

Until about the early to mid twentieth century in Central America, state formation remained dominated by shifts in the relative military superiority of competing party militias and *caudillo*-led bands—called *montoneras* practically everywhere in Latin America—that could operate outside the national "army" (not to mention outside the national boundaries themselves) as well as within it.[5] From about the 1930s onward, those calculations were associated mainly with what were now fairly coherent national armed forces. From the 1960s onward, insurgent guerrilla armies, grounding their appeal in a rhetoric of popular emancipation, joined the calculus, which was sometimes disrupted by violent factional struggles within both the national armies and the insurgent armies. Thus, until the 1990s, personal and factional calculations of the distribution of violence remained the keynote of state formation in Central America and a fundamental reason for the incapacity of its governments to achieve any lasting legitimacy.

Four implications flow from the improvisational character of the isthmian states. One has to do with the almost complete absence, until the present day, of nonarbitrary systems of law enforcement. As long as the law and its enforcement remain subject to the will of collaborators who could come and go at any time, there was little incentive to respect the will of governments. Without any convincing claim to monopolizing the legitimate use of violence, the states were unable to induce consent to their rules, and they found that they could only do so by appealing to their collaborators-in-violence to apply force—a tendency that soon became habitual in the thinking of the agents of the state and among its subjects. Second, the improvisational nature of the state helps explain the practical absence of a strong sense of nationhood even by the end of the twentieth century, after close to two centuries of republican self-government. In countries where ethnic identify is so blurred, it takes a state to consolidate the ideological and cultural forms of identity that constitute nationhood. Even this task cannot be successfully carried out without a state monopoly of violence, which is precisely what the Central American states lacked.[6] There were armies—typically, more than one per country—but not nations.

Third, it is not difficult to see how in this situation the United States could acquire the status of yet another foreign armed collaborator, a kind of transnational *patrón* who distributed favors and bought clients by playing on divisions within and among the governments of Central America.[7] As early as 1911, Adolfo Díaz, the U.S.-installed president of Nicaragua, offered the U.S. *chargé* in Managua a treaty that would permit Washington "to intervene in our internal affairs to order to maintain peace," in the same way, he said hopefully, that Cuba's acceptance of the Platt Amendment in 1901 authorized U.S. intervention in advance. In defense of his proposal, Díaz pointed out that politics in Nicaragua had for many years been nothing less than a "state of war" between political parties that drew inevitably on fighting forces elsewhere in the isthmus; only U.S. intervention held out any hope for lasting peace.[8] When the *jefe máximo* of Guatemala, Manuel Estrada Cabrera, began to see night fall on his twenty-two years in power in 1920, he summoned the U.S. minister to his office and, in the latter's words, "placed the entire situation and the fate of the country in our hands and would agree to abide by any decision which we make."[9]

Fourth, the improvisational nature of the state, its constant dependence on ever-fickle armed groups, or on a real army that may have been with the state but was never of it, or was really with some foreign power, prolonged the old habits of clientelism and personalism, fueling public violence. The state was seen as a mere shank around which various collaborative entities were haphazardly clamped and could drop off at any moment. Lacking the resources to command obedience nonviolently, the state had to depend on a patrimonial system of inducing collaboration through exchange relationships that were inherently subject to violence. The range of collaborators extended over time from *caudillo*-led armies and the armed forces (constantly subject to schisms that frequently erupted in violence among distinct *camarillas* within the officer corps) to political parties and their militias (organically associated with distinct social strata such as peasants, Indians, workers, the middle class, and the elite) to semi-independent death squads and the U.S. government.

And so patrimonialism, which owed its provenance to the period of Spanish colonial rule, became the core property of the improvisational state, giving rise to a habitus of a particular kind of public violence.[10] "The generations," the Honduran president (and self-styled general) Miguel R. Dávila lamented in 1910, "transmit to one another the instinct for revolt," and someday Hondurans would have to "educate themselves in another school."[11] Patrimonalism also seeded a regime type associated with that kind of state. As evident in Guatemala in the 1850s as in Honduras in the 1930s and Nicaragua in the 1970s, the regime consisted of a mythically powerful central figure at the helm of the state—Carrera, Zelaya, Carías, Somoza— who delegated a certain degree of autonomy to "his" regional military chiefs. The power of these subalterns was not absolute within their jurisdictions, and in cases of exceptional abuse they could usually be checked by the national *caudillo*, who of course remained vulnerable himself to a concerted effort by his own subalterns to check *his* power. Of course, habits can be broken, most often by shocks that result in immense destruction or absolute loss. Just as the shock of the Kingdom of Guatemala's separation from Spain eventuated in the disastrous expansion of the limits of public violence all over the isthmus, the shock of Nicaragua's seizure by the U.S. mercenary William Walker in 1855–57 led directly to the shrinkage of those limits in Nicaragua, a condition that lasted three decades before the Nicaraguans resumed their old ways.

An analysis of the intensity and scope of public violence in twentieth-century Central America should distinguish the capacity for public violence (largely a function of the technology and other material and organizational resources available to the state and its collaborators and challengers) from its limits, which emerged in the process of state formation. The limits are measured by the degree of freedom of the agents of public violence to define and control their enemies through physical sanctions or inducements; to avoid punishment for committing "illegal" acts; and to hire out or informally contract the services of other agents in the way a military high command might deputize a death squad. Variations in the elasticity of these freedoms constitute shifts in the limits of public violence. Where limits are compact or tightly drawn, violence is what Walter calls an *ultima ratio;* where the limits are most extensive we find the "terror systems" where violence is a *prima ratio potestatis.*[12]

In Central America, the state formation process embodied a permissiveness in the application of public violence that has been remarkable even by Latin American standards. The Costa Rican political scientist Rodolfo Cerdas noted that although "authoritarianism, militarism and violence" have been "transitory" features elsewhere in Latin America, they have been "quotidian, traditional and permanent" in Central America.[13] The Guatemalan writer and historian Mario Monteforte Toledo, in his two-volume history of the isthmus, wrote that violence has been "an almost permanent social state in Central America from independence until the present day."[14] In a touching confession to his fellow constitutional convention delegates in

1957, Gen. Abraham Williams Calderón, who had been vice president of Honduras from 1933 to 1948, attributed his country's backwardness to its historic tolerance of public violence, which was generous even by isthmian standards: "We've all been brawlers and the brawls haven't gotten us anywhere, except the situation we are now in, in which our country is, unfortunately, more backward than the rest of Central America. And why? Because we have not wanted to understand that politicking... and brawling, and the slaughter of brothers, are harmful to the health of Honduras."[15] In the late 1990s, the jurist and philosopher Alejandro Serrano Caldera wrote of his native Nicaragua: "We could characterize our history as a circular movement in which violence is recurrent with some spaces in which the shooting stops and temporary political arrangements arise which, inadequate in their scope and spurious in their intentions, open the way once again to violence and the 'culture of confrontation and the bullet.'... Authoritarianism, intolerance and *caudillismo* have been, among others, periodic vices that emerge on that roulette wheel that turns between confrontation and the temporary arrangements of dominant interests."[16] Of the fallen Sandinista government in Nicaragua, the distinguished historian Edelberto Torres-Rivas wrote that it was one thing for a revolutionary movement to destroy the institutions of an authoritarian regime—such as the army, courts, penal system, laws, and regulations. Substitutes could readily be fabricated, as they were in Nicaragua after 19 July 1979. Not so readily replaced, however, were "the mores, the deep-seated habits, the collective mentality that comes out in the everyday conduct between the dominant and the dominated in the variety of their relationships." Politics was war, a "sickness . . . that is contagious and endemic," and in 1992 the region was still burdened by "an authoritarian culture that infects social relations, values, and the customs of Central Americans."[17]

It is remarkable that, although the Central American provinces of the Spanish-American empire were among the few to have gained their independence without having had to fight for it, "war became a way of life" in the isthmus during the first two decades of independence.[18] On 15 September 1821, after nearly three centuries as a dominion of the Spanish monarch, the Kingdom of Guatemala (whose boundaries corresponded roughly to those of the five modern nations of Central America) proclaimed its independence from Spain. The advocates of separation were divided between republicans and monarchists, but the latter succeeded in arranging the annexation of the ex-kingdom to the newly constituted Mexican empire on 5 January 1822. The empire's collapse in March 1823 left the Central American monarchists little alternative but to accept the republican principle of government. As a result, on 1 July 1823, the provinces of the former Kingdom of Guatemala declared their independence again, this time from Mexico, as the Provincias Unidas del Centro de América.[19] On 22 November 1824 a constitutional convention established the República Federal de Centro América, transforming the provinces into five "states" of a kind similar to those of the United States of America, but with a far weaker central government. The political leaders of the new republic's five states jealously guarded what they proudly called their "sovereignty," a stance that assured the central government would never exercise more than nominal control over them. The federation's disintegration reached the point of no return in the late 1830s.[20] What had for long been the de facto autonomy of Guatemala, El Salvador, Honduras, Nicaragua, and Costa Rica was now de jure, as each state subsequently declared its absolute independence from the federal republic. It was the third time in two decades that some kind of declaration of sovereignty had been issued that was aimed at all the peoples of the isthmus.

The Properties of Public Violence in Central America

The exceptional readiness of contenders to kill one another rather than negotiate their differences stands out as one of the characteristics of public violence in the isthmus. They also demonized one another, and once in power, showed little more than cold contempt for the masses.

Evidence of the readiness to kill has been strikingly and consistently preserved in records of the language of the protagonists as they narrated events and incited their followers. Among them was Lorenzo Montúfar (1823–98), the Guatemalan politician and author of the bluntly pro-liberal *Reseña Histórica de Centro América*, first published in 1878. Sprinkled throughout its seven volumes are variations on the phrase, "there was no other solution but arms nor any other hope but the fates of war."[21] When the Honduran leader Policarpo Bonilla declared war on the government of Ponciano Leiva in 1893, the violent extremism of his words belied the fact he and Leiva represented opposing factions of the same party. "[R]ise up in mass, elderly, young, women and children, and shout with voices such that they fill the heart of the tyrants with terror: 'Abdication or war.' . . . Hondurans, to arms!"[22] Bonilla's presentation of the conflict as leading inexorably to no more than two conceivable options—abdication or war—was the premise embedded in countless acts of public violence from the 1830s to the 1980s, and repeated in a hundred variations by their protagonists.

As a rhetorical device, "no other option but war" seemed to achieve a special resonance and durability in Nicaragua. The divisions between the liberal and conservative parties in Nicaragua, wrote the legal scholar Carlos Cuadra Pasos in 1932, were so "rigid" that "They almost seem to be of different nationalities," and as a result the prospect of losing a presidential election was so disgraceful that the incumbent had little choice but to prepare for war. "Power is not acquired, it is conquered."[23] In 1977, President Antastasio Somoza Debayle, beset by the Sandinistas and feeling abandoned by the Carter administration, stirred his followers by proudly recalling that for the liberal army of Gen. José María Moncada in 1926–27, "there was no other road for liberalism than armed rebellion because honor is an inescapable law."[24] In 1983, in a belated public eulogy to the legendary Conservative *caudillo* of Nicaragua (and eternal rival of the Somozas), Gen. Emiliano Chamorro (1871–1966), delegates to a Conservative Party convention were roused by repeated references to Chamorro's readiness to throw himself into battle against the Liberal Party dictatorship of José Santos Zelaya (1893–1909). One speaker reminded his audience that in 1954, when Pres. Anastasio Somoza García violated the "Pacto de los Generales" he had made with Chamorro in 1950, Chamorro "had no other option, now elderly, than to grab the rifle of a rebel once more, when the sun of his life was setting. What a magnificent twilight for a brave man, worthy setting of the sun of a *Caudillo!*"[25]

The readiness of contenders to kill one another was no doubt related to a second pattern that emerges with equal clarity from the political writing of the isthmus: the tendency to see opponents as fiendish villains, hopelessly corrupt and so utterly beyond the reach of reason that killing them was the only rational solution to the difficulties they posed. In a personalistic political culture, demonization of the enemy (or its leaders) is the logical analogue of the adoration of one's own leader. In 1811, the Spanish colonial government of Guatemala denounced the leaders of the independence movements elsewhere in the continent as "hyenas" and "monsters."[26] Montúfar interpreted the history of the isthmus after its separation from Spain in 1821 as a period of continuous combat between two irreconcilable parties, one of which was hopelessly benighted. "From independence until today, the history of Central America has been a battle between one party that wants to return us to the Middle Ages and another that presses us forward morally."[27] In 1894, his uprising against Leiva having succeeded, President Bonilla of Honduras explained why he had no choice but to resort to violence against a government headed, not by a *servil,* but by rival liberals consumed by "selfishness, disloyalty and cruelty," "cowardice," "spite" and "perversity," under the leadership of a wicked traitor.[28] In El Salvador, the leadership of the country's first political party, the Partido Democrático Nacional, shared with the patronage networks of the nineteenth century a marked tendency in the 1920s to define the opposition as "immoral and traitorous." A small, independent political faction was denounced in 1921 by a party leader as the "sordid and perverse work of a certain diabolical spirit."[29] The tendency to demonize the opposition was such a common feature of politics that the Nicaraguan essayist Salvador Mendieta, writing in 1907, called it one of the sources of Central America's "always latent" armed conflict: "Neither those in power nor in opposition tolerate one another. Those in power do not acknowledge the justice of any kind of opposition and thus deny it all the means of serene and reasoned debate. The opponent never thinks the government is well intentioned and fights it with systematic tenacity."[30]

Demonization, as one of the signs of the relatively extensive limits of public violence in the region, survived well into the twentieth century. Even some professional historians continued to express the same distaste, if not contempt, for the conservative political faction of the early nineteenth century that had so animated Montúfar. Julio César Pinto S. consistently identified the liberal faction as "progressive" whereas their political opponents were not merely conservative but "retrógrados" or "reaccionarios."[31] The Right, by 1947, was already identifying all of its adversaries as *comunistas,* which meant that everyone else was *anticomunista.* It was a tendency that "disfigured the political and ideological development of Guatemala for more than forty years," recalled the veteran Guatemalan politician Francisco Villagrán Kramer in his memoirs.[32] Lamenting the "proverbial Manichaeism" of Nicaragua in the late 1990s, Serrano Caldera wrote: "We demonize or sacralize. We condemn or we absolve but rarely do we try to comprehend."[33]

Finally, there was the core contradiction of the liberalism of the time. Montúfar ultimately blamed not the conservatives for Central America's troubles but his beloved masses. "The ignorance of the *pueblos* is the great wellspring of that [conservative, aristocratic] system. Keep the great majority ignorant, and the power of the nobility will be sustained. The *servil* party understands all of this very well, . . . It didn't enlighten the people: it fomented their ignorance."[34] Contempt for the masses was scarcely a sentiment monopolized by liberals. In Costa Rica, the sharpest critics of liberalism after about 1900 were radical intellectuals, mainly anarchists and socialists, who nevertheless shared with the liberals a certain revulsion for urban and rural plebeians alike. In need of redemption by an intellectual vanguard, the subaltern classes were seen as passive victims of capital or the oligarchy.[35]

Montúfar's low opinion of the majority's fitness to govern itself may have incited his frequent condemnations of his own liberals for being too respectful of the rights accorded to their political enemies by the federal constitution, and for failing to energetically repress dissidents. What was needed in the 1830s, the Guatemalan historian argued, were "some days of dictatorship."[36] In 1923, the same sentiment was expressed by the thirty-three-year-old Honduran essayist and future cabinet secretary, Céleo Dávila. After a century of "crazy" politics, "we need a dictatorship, in short, to realize in any way possible the dictates of human culture and to impose reason." Elections could not be the solution to violence and disorder because they were almost inevitably the occasion for violence. Hondurans lacked the "common sense to administer the nation. With the heroism of the *montonera* and their principal virtues—fire, pillage, and murder—we have wanted to resolve national problems for more than 100 years. We don't know which are the tools of labor since we want to build with the smoking rifle and the bloody *machete*."[37]

It is not that state formation in Central America proceeded over the course of more than 180 years without any successful efforts to peacefully negotiate differences among groups with different interests.[38] But to a degree unsurpassed elsewhere in Latin America, even the nonviolent resolution of differences was almost invariably conducted in an environment in which at least one side in the conflict was disposed to force compliance should bargaining fail. Among other things, this meant that the commitment of a group or party to a nonviolent resolution of differences had to be based on a calculus of the coercive forces at the disposal of the parties. In such a setting, the use of peaceful methods was less a commitment to nonviolence per se, than an acknowledgement of the superior coercive power of one side. The readiness to kill, demonization, and contempt for the masses were common enough in the newly independent countries of Latin America.[39] What stands out in the history of the isthmus is both the frequency and the persistence over time (in comparison to the rest of Latin America) with which contenders in the field of state power resorted to violence.

In 1947, Cuadra Pasos, the sixty-eight-year-old Conservative Party leader of Nicaragua, recalled the horrors of the wars he witnessed as a combatant in the 1920s. Writing with a touching sense of urgency born of his personal fear of a resurgence of civil war in Nicaragua following yet another fraudulent election, he offered some clues to the sources of the self-perpetuating violence that had by then defined a habitus saturated by fear, hatred, and vengeance. "Hatred has been the dominant note of our politics. Hatred of one of the [political] parties intersects with the fear of the other. Generally, although it may appear paradoxical, the fear is greater in the governing party, the hatred more intense in the opposition. . . . The fear of falling is the greatest worry of the Central American Governments, because they see before them an opposition that exudes spite and demands revenge. This is the greatest obstacle to the exercise of a peaceful democracy among us."[40]

Elections as Manifestations of Public Violence

As long as the readiness to kill one's opponents, to demonize one's enemies, and to abominate the masses were such consistent features of public violence, elections were little more than opportunities to observe all three of these characteristics at once. Gen. Francisco Menéndez, a militant liberal and a coffee grower, took power in El Salvador by orchestrating a rebellion that overthrew the liberal government of Rafael Zaldívar on 22 June 1885. He promptly annulled the constitution that had been adopted only two years earlier, promised complete freedom for all political parties, and organized an election for delegates to a constitutional convention. But the general would have lost to the conservatives had he not, on three successive days, dispatched his fighting forces to the polls and ordered them to vote for the liberal candidates. At the sight "of the soldiery in uniform and file," the U.S. consul reported, "the populace became enraged and insulted the commanding officers; even the women took part for they commenced to throw stones. The general clamor was 'down with the usurpers of our rights; down with the mock liberty granted.' A serious riot seemed imminent but another body of troops made its appearance with loaded arms and obliged the people to disperse." The consul predicted that should Menéndez indulge similar tactics in the presidential election scheduled for December, "a sanguinary revolution will be set afoot."[41] In the event, Menéndez's satisfaction with the results of the election did not extend to the results of the constitutional convention, which failed to concede to the central government all the power that Menéndez desired. On 26 November he dissolved the convention and declared himself dictator.[42]

Thus elections were irrelevant as instruments of the popular will because the incumbent government would never allow a free election to take place. That left just two roads to the presidency, according to Mendieta: "the armed revolution or close friendship [compadrazgo, form of fictive kinship] with some head of state who for whatever reason feels obligated to retire from office." Between 1880 and 1907, Mendieta could think of only a single exception across the entire isthmus: the election of President José Joaquín Rodríguez in Costa Rica in 1890.[43]

The association between elections and public violence was authoritatively acknowledged in 1934 by a Honduran congressional committee in a report recommending the rejection of a bill to extend suffrage to women. Though "shameful" to admit, the environment in which voting took place involved

> vices and crimes that no mother, wife, daughter, sister, fiancé or female friend should participate in if we wish to fully preserve their decency and decorum to ensure that they are always deserving of the sweetest and highest esteem and preference. . . . [Women] would capitulate to the blows of evil, descending to the lowland of corrupting swamps, . . . The three rights—the exercise of the suffrage, having and bearing arms, and undertaking public service—are intimately related to one another by their very nature, . . . And so whoever participates in electoral propaganda resorts to supporting troops: to have and bear arms and to pledge and to guarantee public jobs.[44]

This was already a familiar argument against women's suffrage. In 1921, a Guatemalan delegate to one more organizing convention of a putative Central American Federation pointed out that "Each electoral campaign presents the most repugnant picture, where bad instincts are developed with violence. Are we going to put women into that dung heap?"[45] Even in Costa Rica, a congressman warned in 1925 that woman should avoid all contact with politics, where "hatred and revenge" reigned.[46] Even Graciela Bográn, the editor of a Honduran women's magazine, initially opposed women's suffrage in 1933: "If the women's vote is allowed now, the law establishing it would be repealed as futile. Women would refuse to use it, so as not to get themselves mixed up in political struggles that are resolved by insults, bites [*dentelladas*] and bullets."[47]

Under these conditions, electoral fraud was closely intertwined with electoral violence. The taken-for-granted link between them emerges in the following statement by Manuel Mora Valderde (1909–94), the longtime leader of the Costa Rican communist party, a deputy in the Asamblea Nacional, and the political ally of two consecutive Costa Rican governments in the 1940s. Years after the 1944 elections, in which Mora's party successfully competed in alliance with the presidential candidate of the incumbent administration, Mora recalled:

> Some say that we won through fraud. In reality it is possible that there may have been fraud by one side or the other because that's how elections were done in Costa Rica. Our classical political lords, if you will allow me to say so, had converted even our simplest peasants into true artists of fraud. Elections in our country traditionally had a meaning similar to that of football games or cock fights or a boxing match, with the object of winning the fight and making bets. . . . without understanding what there was behind their victory or their defeat.[48]

Four years later, a civil war was fought mainly over disputed presidential election results at the cost of two thousand lives. Although this was the last electoral war in

Costa Rica, voter fraud wasn't over; outgoing president José Figueres complained in 1958 that there were still *ticos* who considered electoral fraud to be a "viveza," a sign of craftiness—"there are even professionals in fraud who were trained in an earlier epoch."[49]

Parties

Widely understood to be essential elements of representative government, political parties figure prominently as nominal actors in the historiography of Central America because parties tended to be organized around leading personalities for whom ideology—like identities based on region or kinship—was merely instrumental.[50] Arturo J. Cruz, Jr. speculated that in Nicaragua, the parties emerged from the *tertulias*, social-cultural clubs centered in the homes of certain leading families of the early nineteenth century. "A combination of wealth, connections, personality and social graces were the essential attributes for leadership of a *tertulia;* given the small scale of Creole society, it is not difficult to understand how small a step it was from leadership of a tertulia, to leadership of a political faction."[51] Loyalty to an individual leader easily displaced that of loyalty to a bureaucratic organization, for it was the leader's personal ability to dominate and subdue his enemies that would dictate whatever rewards politics might have to offer; the leader's failure entailed the loss of income or status, or even exile or death. Loyalty, therefore, might logically be transferred to a stronger and more effective leader. This is what made incumbents so difficult to unseat; once in power, it was hard to pry their followers away from them and into the opposition. In 1883 and again in 1887, the Honduran liberal *caudillo* Céleo Arias found that the *comandantes de armas* or regional military authorities upon whom he had counted as his "partidarios" or political allies abandoned him the moment the name of the "official" candidate was revealed "in order to submit themselves unconditionally to the order issuing from the National Palace." Other liberals frequently deserted the party, "taking refuge in officialism, rich in honors, money and position."[52]

When Liberal Party leader Policarpo Bonilla ordered members to abandon Luis Bográn's government before the election in 1891, a *bonillista* lamented, some remained with the government "because it was more comfortable to stay in a public post acquired with a gesture of patriotism, than to run the risks of an opposition, whose triumph was more problematical."[53] An admirer of Policarpo Bonilla's archenemy, Gen. Domingo Vásquez, agreed with Bonilla's follower on this point: "the parties are personal, they are isms, so that it is not unusual to see someone, now in one group, now in another, without violence, without the need for explanations..; so that a poor *cachureco* [conservative] thinks and acts like a liberal, and a rich liberal acts and thinks like a *cachureco*. It's a question of economics, or better yet, of the stomach."[54] Under the permanent conditions of economic insecurity that characterized Central America, the opportunity costs of party loyalty were relatively high; it was more prudent to side with the strongest, and that frequently meant the incumbent.[55]

Political alignments, therefore, were not so much ordered to either a liberal or a conservative party as such but to a range of factions whose ideological orientations were vague or largely irrelevant. Writing around 1870, a prominent Nicaraguan from León who was known as a liberal noted, "It is true that the individuals who make up the parties will be either Conservatives or Liberals, because some kind of a name is needed in order to avoid confusion. But it made much more sense when they were called 'culumucos,' 'chapiollos,' 'mechudos,' 'timbucos,' 'calandracas,' 'papirones,' etc. These strange denominations were perfectly suited to our tiny, idealess clusters."[56]

Paradoxically, in spite of the often fluid character of political allegiance, a leader could also inspire immense sacrifices among the faithful, for whom it could sometimes be "something to die for."[57] The death and maiming that routinely constituted politics resulted in the accumulation of debts that could only be repaid in blood, and in commitments that bound one for life and even bound one's offspring. Hence, the contradiction of weak party organizations and blurred ideologies yet fierce loyalty to a political cause unmistakably represented by the leader. Participants did not typically speak of sacrifices to the *patria* but of sacrifices to the party or to the leader himself.

The party or the leader incurred the obligation to compensate losses or to reward a constant loyalty; claims on state resources were frankly made not as citizens but as followers.[58] Within months of Policarpo Bonilla's victory in the 1893 civil war that earned him the presidency of Honduras, a follower, Vespaciano Garín, wrote to him from a hospital:

Dear Doctor. I understand that I only have a few days of existence left, since my illness has increased so much that since yesterday I have completely lost my appetite. As a result of this crisis that I am passing through, allow me to make the following recommendation. It may happen that Francisco Martínez Garín, Manuel Carrero Garín, and Ignacio Garín Querido come to Tegucigalpa; the first two are my illegitimate sons and the last is a nephew of my own flesh. I recommend them to you so that you may serve as their father, advising you that they are liberals and that they have already fought for you. The pain that I have doesn't allow me time to say more than to wish you much happiness and prosperity.[59]

Hundreds of letters such as those of Garín were received by Policarpo Bonilla and his military chief, Gen. Manuel Bonilla, requesting jobs, money, loans, intervention in court cases, and of course the repayment of loans made to Bonilla's army during the civil war.[60] The government archives in Nicaragua bulge with letters like those of J. D. Gámez of Rivas to President Roberto Sacasa. On 10 January 1890, Gámez offered the president some political intelligence. "I hear that some mail has been sent from the hacienda of Sucuyá [?] for C. Roca. I don't know if it is political or just commercial." The following December Gámez wrote again to complain that his brother-in-law had just returned from Europe with liquor to sell, but that when he arrived in Nicaragua he found out that the tariff on imported liquor had been increased. Although other importers had been exempted from paying the extra duty, the treasury office denied his brother-in-law the same exemption, "perhaps because without knowing the firmness of our friendly relations, they assume I am your enemy because they have noticed that I have been active in the electoral opposition." Gámez asked for the same exemption that the others had received. The two letters suggest either that Gámez may have joined the opposition as a spy for the president, or that political alliances could be broken and reforged without assuming a break in personal loyalties. The second letter conveys the supreme importance of family ties; although it begins with a brother-in-law's grievance, it quickly changes into an account of a personal affront to the writer himself, who by letter's end appears to have replaced the brother in law as the aggrieved party. Indeed, in reading hundreds of letters to President Sacasa, it was remarkable how many correspondents referred to themselves as *deudo* (kin) in addition to the usual *colega* or *amigo*. The letters requested favors, reported political intelligence, and denied vicious rumors of their disloyalty.[61]

The archives of the late Somoza administration in Nicaragua reveal the extraordinary durability of the idea that relief from a perceived injustice was understood by all concerned as a condition of political or personal affiliation and not of any civil, much less human, right. When Eneyda de Aburto of San Carlos complained in 1968 that a Guardia soldier had abused her husband, she demanded that he be disciplined, and she naturally identified herself as a loyal *somocista* as if she assumed that her complaint would otherwise be pointless. However, the *comandante departamental* reported that not only was her husband drunk but that "as far as the SOMOSISMO [*sic*] goes that Señora de Aburto speaks of, I inform you that in the last [electoral] campaign, when it was desired to place on her house a portrait of the liberal Candidate Gen. A. Somoza D., she emphatically refused, which was told to me by honorable persons, such as the *Jefe Político* ["political chief," a local government executive appointed by the president], and others."[62] On 21 December 1971, six residents of Matagalpa telegraphed President Anastasio Somoza Debayle complaining that two of their number "were seized and macheted" by a member of the Guardia Nacional, Alfonso González. Demanding punishment of the guilty, they added: "We respectfully request an investigation so that this crime does not go unpunished and so that the guilty party is punished, who in this case is a member of the GN and is billeted in the Valle de San Gerónimo, taking care of private property. All of us signers are somocista liberals, who ask you for your favor and protection."[63]

From *Caudillo* Bands to National Armies

By the end of 1871, liberal-led uprisings had swept conservatives from power everywhere in Central America except for Nicaragua, whose turn would not come until 1893. Twentieth-century political contention would pit rivals of distinct species of liberalism (including some who called themselves conservatives, as in Nicaragua) and later on, Marxism, against one another. Throughout Latin America, the late nineteenth-century political shift known as the era of the liberal "revolutions" was marked by the laicization of Church-controlled institutions and property, the privatization of public land and of land held by indigenous communities, the new openness and even submission to the interests of foreign traders and investors, the commitment to cultural secularization and concomitant ideologies of progress and racial supremacy, and the enthusiastic adoption of state-led programs of export-led economic growth. In Central America, the triumph of liberalism not only failed to challenge the habitus of public violence, but led directly to the first significant enlargement in the isthmian states' capacities for violence. The readiness to demonize and then kill one's political enemies was, if anything, perfected under liberal rule.

The liberal state encouraged the creation of recognizable national institutions of rule out of the inchoate array of instrumentalities at the disposition of the region's first *caudillos*. In comparison with Guatemala's previous disorder, for example, institutional transformations in that country's political, judicial, military, communications, educational, and economic spheres seemed impressive.[64] A newspaper supporting the moderate liberal regime of Miguel García Granados, who had just seized power in the Revolution of 1871, characterized the Guatemalan "state" inherited from the conservatives as a ridiculous façade:

> Upon falling, the rotten edifice . . . turned into dust, and it has not even left ruins for rebuilding. . . . There is no regular legislation. Who knows which laws governed, among those dictated in the last half century, or where they may be found; or, among the Spanish Codes still in force, which are the regulations that have been repealed or fallen into disuse? There is no public administration, . . . [only] lazy and absurd office routine. . . . There is no plan of public instruction. . . . There is no public spirit. . . . There is no republican tradition. And without traditions of this kind, the Republic is converted into a mere farce. In a word almost all the elements that are necessary for the functioning of a free, regular and progressive government are missing.[65]

Armies were transformed, slowly and fitfully, from scattered bands under localized political control to something recognizably associated with the state. Before the liberal revolution, even Guatemala's "armies and militias," which had access to more resources than their counterparts elsewhere on the isthmus, "were no better than ad hoc, ragtag affairs based in the towns and commanded mostly by amateurs," as both the government and its political enemies recruited and then disbanded their armed forces as the need arose. Not until the liberal revolution of 1871 did a Guatemalan government begin to take seriously the creation of a national military establishment.[66] In El Salvador for most of the nineteenth century, according to Mariscal, "the officer corps was formed by political 'caudillos' with or without military experience. In reality there was no clear distinction between military and civil while the process of construction of the nation was developing incipiently."[67] In El Salvador, military commanders took orders from the leader of the political patronage network to which they had allied themselves; indeed, the commanders simultaneously held a local civilian office such as mayor. As a tendency for military commanders to take orders exclusively from the national political leader began to emerge around the late 1890s, the military men were increasingly identified with the national government. They began to clash violently with municipal authorities who objected to sharing their authority, hitherto practically exclusive, with the agents of the national state.[68]

How can this uneven but unmistakable upward displacement of violence from *caudillo* armies to *las fuerzas armadas* be accounted for?[69] *Las fuerzas armadas*, while identifying themselves with their corresponding states, remained as functionally independent of the state as the *caudillo* armies they replaced. For this reason upward displacement preserved and may even have expanded the already-extensive limits in the application of public violence in Guatemala, El Salvador, Honduras, and Nicaragua, but not in Costa Rica. In the latter, upward displacement occurred within a decade of its separation from Spain, and in a country where patrimonialism from the beginning was checked by a nationalist ideology of popular sovereignty. In the first four countries, the result was "armies without nations."

In contrast, enfolded into the process by which the European states typically monopolized warmaking was a protocol of bargaining "with ordinary people" that defined the "limits to state control, perimeters to state violence, and mechanisms for eliciting the consent of the subject population."[70] In the four northern countries of Central America, warmaking drove the displacement of violence upward from regional strongmen and local bosses to central authorities, but the authorities that emerged were the armed forces themselves, to which the other instititions of the state were more or less appended. Under the conditions that defined the improvised state, there was thus no opportunity for a bargaining process between "state" and "citizens" that might have shrunk Tilly's "perimeters to state violence." That is because there was no coherent idea of a state apart from the armed forces, no idea of a nation, and therefore no idea of citizenship.

Bargaining between the mighty and the lowly proceeded within the confines of patron-clientage, where it was subject to three kinds of contradictions: Asymmetry in power yet apparent solidarity in personal identity, a potential for coercion and exploitation under a veneer of voluntary participation, and mutual obligations with illegal or semi-legal aspects.[71] The historiography of what may be broadly classified as "caudillismo" not just in the isthmian countries but in all Latin America seems to have dwelled on the unequal and coercive features of the patron-client relationship. Yet the solidaristic and voluntary aspects, especially in combination with the historic exaltation of violence and clientelism's endless potential for coercion, decisively shaped the modern-day limits of state-sponsored violence in Central America. As the agents of the army-dominated state and the agents of the lowly bargained not over "democracy" but over special services or dispensations, the outcome favored the expansion of the limits of public violence and the privilege of impunity for the agents of that violence, notwithstanding their status as leaders or followers, patrons or clients.[72]

The process by which this kind of state consolidated its control over the means of violence included contestation and bargaining with subalterns. But the outcome should not be read as simply a failed attempt to adequately limit the state's range of violence. The terms of the bargaining had been fixed long before by the system of clientage. As a result, the intensification of public violence and the expansion of its limits were not solely the responsibility of the new centralizing states nor of the elites whose interests they basically served, but were also collaborative projects that included the lowly as well. A fundamental continuity becomes visible, then, between the age of the *caudillos* and that of the modern state. As control over the means of violence was displaced upward from the *caudillos* to the armed forces, traditions of personalism and clientage were not discarded but preserved as the army-dominated state effectively deputized subalterns to act on its behalf in return for protection and favors. In his study of this system in El Salvador, Erik Ching found that it was not the single "great pyramid" of patronage links that character-ized the Brazilian system, but rather "numerous little pyramids, distinct patronage networks which battled one another for control over the decrepit central state."[73] As army-dominated states centralized their power and markets expanded, the old patrons were replaced by brokers, spawning a clientelist state system of linked, per-sonalized power networks.[74]

The survival of personal patronage as the axis of politics in Central America was bitingly portrayed by Mendieta in 1907:

> The president is the milch cow of all the needy, real or pretend, and those who have no shame (they are not a few). From the old procuress who is pleased with five cents, to the stuck-up lady who demands an adornment worth ten-thousand, from the uncondi-tional friend, the sneak who asks for a peso for his hangover, to the eminent or uncondi-tional fellow party member who solicits twenty-thousand with a contract, all of them, every one of them turn up at the presidential audiences to cry about their troubles and receive miserable leftovers or a succulent mouthful.

Congress—which was unicameral in all five countries—was a tool of the president, who appointed its members and fired them, elections being "completely sup-pressed" and as a result, the congress was a "prolongation of the *cacique* [local polit-ical boss], forbidding the slightest opposition...."[75] The authority of the president, Mendieta continued, was represented everywhere by the local garrison command-ers. The governor of the department was "almost always" the *comandante de armas,* "and completely represents the person of the president, the only person he obeys and the only one to whom he believes he is obligated. Thus in each *departamento un caciquito* who is a faithful copy of the cacique mayor [i.e., the president], each one of whose steps he tries to follow with mathematical exactitude.... Nowhere else does one see any better the imitative character of our gorilla-like governing class."[76]

Like the problem of the upward displacement of localized bands into more or less national armies, the changing level of autonomy and personal authority enjoyed by the garrison commanders within their districts is hard to estimate. A three-stage process may be plausibly hypothesized: the upward displacement of regional power from customary authorities such as *hacendados* with their own armed followers, to relatively autonomous garrison commanders under the nominal control of a national military chief, and finally to the national command of a centralized army.[77] The sequence, if not the exact timing, of the national transitions from domination by local and regional power holders to centralized instruments of coercion and surveillance in Central America may be hypothesized as follows: The Costa Rican state was the first to achieve a significant level of unified coercive control, perhaps as early as the mid-nineteenth century. The armed forces of Guatemala and El Salvador established a practical monopoly on the use of violence at least by the second decade of the twentieth century, and those of Honduras and Nicaragua in the 1930s–40s.

From Liberal Oligarchies to Military Dictatorships

During the 1920s, movements favoring reform and even revolution broke out as governments took power that, for the first time, showed some genuine signs of seeking to broaden the social base of liberalism. Among the outcomes of this tendency was the insurrection that removed Manuel Estrada Cabrera from the presidency of Guatemala in 1920, the election in Honduras of the civilian president Miguel Paz Barahona (1925–29), in El Salvador the "laborismo" of Presidents Pío Romero Bosque (1927–31) and Arturo Araujo (1931), the further consolidation of democratic liberties and constitutional government in Costa Rica, and in Nicaragua the nationalist and reformist movements associated with Juan B. Sacasa and later Augusto C. Sandino. Although these movements "awoke a certain optimism in almost all the countries" they ended, by the late 1920s, in "chaos and destruction."[78] In the 1930s, liberal oligarchic states dissolved into openly dictatorial states. Repression intensified in reaction to labor organization and protest. Armies seized direct power everywhere but in Costa Rica, effectively eliminating the inconvenience of bargaining with nonmilitary aspirants of rule.[79] For the next fifty years, with only brief and occasional lapses, "the state" could be largely understood as "the armed forces" everywhere but Costa Rica. Regimes were known (and later, fondly recalled by some) according to the dictators at the helm: Jorge Ubico in Guatemala (1931–44), Tiburcio Carías Andino in Honduras (1932–48), Maximiliano Hernández Martínez in El Salvador (1931–44) and Anastasio Somoza García in Nicaragua (1936–56). By organizing their armies in ways that allowed them to manage their countries on patrimonial terms, they creatively joined bureaucratic methods and technological progress to the principles of *caudillo* rule. The Costa Rican governments of Ricardo Jiménez (1932–36) and León Cortes Castro (1936–40) were similar in some respects, although Costa Rica's was the only one not founded mainly on military strength. Everywhere in the isthmus the urban middle-class reform groups and communist revolutionary parties that had surged in the 1920s "were almost totally eclipsed" in the 1930s.[80] Significant openings were registered in Honduras in the 1950s, but even in Costa Rica the communist party was suppressed and unions lost much of their autonomy after the 1948 civil war. The Depression, therefore, led the isthmus back to despotism even as, in the rest of Latin America, it opened the door to populism.[81]

In the closing years of World War II, the military dictatorships of Guatemala, El Salvador, Nicaragua, and Honduras finally confronted popular challenges provoked in part by the impending defeat of fascism, which encouraged the movements for democratic reform that reemerged in the early 1940s. In El Salvador, a general strike led by middle-class professionals and young military officers forced General Hernández-Martínez to resign in 1944. The movement failed, however, to achieve any lasting reform because its leaders were shot and the army replaced Hernández with another general. Army officers subsequently carried out El Salvador's so-called "Revolution of '48," a modestly reformist project geared mainly to economic modernization. A similarly middle-class movement overthrew Guatemala's Gen. Jorge Ubico in 1944, inciting a process of radical reform that would survive an entire decade before being jointly rolled back by anticommunist army officers and the U.S. government. In Honduras and Nicaragua the forces capable of challenging the dictatorships were far weaker. Popular pressure forced Gen. Tiburcio Carías out of the presidency of Honduras in 1948, but a sixty-nine-day strike in the U.S.-owned banana plantations in 1954 had a more fundamentally reformist impact on social policy and social organization. Two years later, however, the newly institutionalized Honduran Army forcibly intervened for the first time in the political process, and remained the principal political force in the country until the 1990s. In Nicaragua, the democratic forces were so weak that National Guard director Anastasio Somoza was able to dictate the results of elections and then void their outcomes at will. Costa Rica in the late 1940s experienced a social revolution of its own, although not directed against a military dictatorship but against a kind of genteel oligarchy that had actually adopted rather generous social policies. The country emerged from the Revolution of 1948 with a social-democratic orientation that would become more or less permanent. Thus Costa Rica and Guatemala were the only two countries in which the reform movements unleashed during World War II could be said to have achieved real success, though Guatemala's only lasted ten years.[82]

Another three decades passed before such movements outside of Costa Rica could plausibly claim victory, first when the Sandinistas took power in Nicaragua in 1979, and later when the insurgency in El Salvador finally snapped six decades of military rule with the signing of the United Nations-mediated peace treaty of 1991.

Central America and the United States

The construction of the U.S.-owned Panama Canal, starting in 1903, incited in Washington a growing determination to discourage the kind of cross-border military adventures among the region's *caudillos* that could set off a regional war or instigate the intervention of some nonhemispheric power. Nonchalant disregard for national borders was by then a venerable custom among Central America's *caudillos*. The history of failed Central American Federation, and the resulting legacy of a complicated network of cross-national kinship, entrepreneurial, and political ties, supplied ideal conditions for cross-border interventions—armed and otherwise.

This tendency had an increasingly disruptive effect from the 1870s onward. Wielding national power more effectively than their conservative predecessors, the "liberal caudillos" seemed to be touched by a kind of messianism that led them into foreign adventures inspired, in part, by the desire to restore the old liberal-led federation. The United States, intent on claiming and preserving exclusive control of a cross-isthmian canal route while discouraging rival European powers from interfering in Central America, joined the fraternal strife. It alternately attempted to mediate armed conflicts and openly took sides, in both cases usually employing some combination of violent and nonviolent devices—military intervention, threats to intervene, some show of force such as a warship, or a token landing, bribes, loans, diplomatic recognition—to manipulate the government in power or its rivals.[83]

An important sign of the deepening U.S. military interest in the isthmus was the assignment in 1910 of the first military attaché to a Central American country, Guatemala. The attaché is a kind of public spy, charged with supplying politico-military intelligence from closed as well as open sources. Except for 1917–18, the United States kept the Central American military attaché's post (located in either Guatemala, Panama, or Costa Rica) filled continuously from 1910 to 1940, when for the first time two attachés were assigned. For all five countries, the attaché was expected to file detailed reports, often including photographs and drawings, on military installations, troop strength, roadways, harbors and population centers, as well as the facilities and obstacles that might be encountered by a U.S. invasion force.[84] The seriousness with which the War Department took its responsibilities in Central America even at this early stage can be discerned in a rebuke to its Panama-based Central American attaché, Maj. Fred T. Cruse. Writing from Washington in 1921, his superior, Major Churchill, complained that Major Cruse's reports on Central America were both infrequent and less complete than what he was already reading in the Boston and New York newspapers. The Division of Military Intelligence "wishes to be informed of all current events. While the armies of these countries are comparatively unimportant, the fact remains that they exist, and this office should have complete and detailed information regarding them, . . . From a geographic standpoint (Combat) these countries should be studied with reference to operation against, and in defense of, the Panama Canal."[85]

By then, the United States was deeply involved in Central American politics, a development that would not be entirely propitious for the popular mobilizations of the 1920s. Washington welcomed neither the disorder implied by this kind of social change nor the prospect of governments that expressed more than rhetorical interest in distributive justice or balanced foreign polices. Both were perceived as dangerous to U.S. lives and investments, and so the early 1920s saw a return to heavy-handed intervention by Washington, including the use of U.S. military force in Honduras and Nicaragua. By the beginning of the next decade, further demonstrations of popular discontent provoked by the economic dislocations of the Great Depression were answered by the dictatorships that seized power in the 1930s. Generally welcomed in Washington, they would prove to be different from those that had preceded it, marking the demise of the liberal oligarchic state and the onset of "authoritarian *caudillismo* and an extension of state powers."[86] The recourse to open military dictatorship that marked the 1930s in Guatemala, El Salvador, Honduras, and Nicaragua would burden the region until the 1980s and 1990s, when constitutional civilian rule and basic political liberties began to take root.

Washington's role in the chain of events that led to the political calamity of the 1930s, and therefore the extent of its shared responsibility for the half-century of authoritarian rule that followed, is difficult to assess. The U.S. preference for rulers who seemed capable of delivering stability and of complying with U.S. policies meant that Washington often used its influence to undermine political movements that looked capable of seriously challenging that preference. Everywhere in the isthmus, fear and mistrust of the United States intensified after August 1912, when U.S. armed forces, in defense of their Nicaraguan puppet government, first went into combat to defend an incumbent Caribbean government against an insurgent army.[87] Even before this turning point in the history of U.S. intervention, the U.S. minister in Nicaragua warned Washington that "the natural sentiment of an overwhelming majority of Nicaraguans is antagonistic to the United States," owing to Pres. Juan Estrada's obvious dependence on the U.S. Marines for his acquisition of the presidency in 1910 and for his tenure in office.[88] Three weeks before he wrote those words, in January 1911, the Honduran Congress angrily rejected, 32–4, a proposal for a U.S. customs receivership, denouncing it as a means to "transform Honduras from a free country into an administrative dependency of the United States."[89] Angry protests across Central America were incited by the Bryan-Chamorro treaty from the time it was proposed in 1912 until well after its ratification in 1916, when Nicaragua formally ceded to Washington the exclusive right to build a canal across the country and build naval bases on Nicaraguan territory.[90] Some Costa Ricans denounced the Wilson administration for withholding recognition of the *golpista* regime of Gen. Federico Tinoco (1917–19) and for attempting to dictate Tinoco's successor after a popular uprising forced his resignation.[91] The most spectacular popular-nationalist protest against U.S. intervention was the armed resistance to the U.S. Marine presence in Nicaragua by Augusto C. Sandino's guerrilla army from 1927 to 1933. Until the 1930s, therefore, U.S. policy in some measure fueled the nationalistic and social-reform impulses of the era, and by extension the public violence associated with their implementation and subsequent repression.

On two occasions before 1930, however, the U.S. government undertook major multilateral diplomatic initiatives aimed at encouraging the five governments of the isthmus to make and keep the peace, both among themselves and within their national borders. The failures of both initiatives were as emphatic as their objectives were utopian, and in both cases the United States contributed nearly as much to their demise as did the Central Americans themselves. The first was a conference of all five governments in Washington in 1907 that produced a treaty requiring the signatories to abstain from recognizing governments that took power illegally and from intervening in each other's political disputes. A second treaty established a five-man court charged with settling disputes among the five countries. Neither the United States nor the signatory governments respected the terms of the agreements.[92]

The second initiative, the Conference on Central American Affairs, which met in Washington from 4 December 1922 to 7 February 1923, was much more ambitious, a reflection in part of the growth in U.S. power on the isthmus since 1907. "The United States was clearly in charge this time," noted Thomas Karnes, "and the Central Americans were but secondary partners."[93] Even the agenda was spelled out in the "invitation" that Washington extended to the isthmian governments. The aim of the conference was to preserve peace among the five countries, in part by adopting what the United States considered the best solution for ending the national conflicts that so often triggered international violence, namely, the creation of "nonpolitical" constabulary forces or "national guards." Representatives of all five countries subsequently signed (and their governments later ratified) a Convention for the Limitation of Armaments obligating each one "to establish a National Guard to cooperate with the existing Armies in the preservation of order in the various districts of the country and on the frontiers, and shall immediately consider the best means for establishing it. With this end in view the Governments of the Central American States shall give consideration to the employment of suitable instructors, in order to take advantage, in this manner, of experience acquired in other countries in organizing such corps."

One of fifteen separate accords signed by the Central American countries at the conference, the Convention did not propose replacing existing armies with "national guard" constabularies but merely augmenting them with such forces. Further, the signatories were urged merely to "give consideration" to hiring foreign trainers, whose nationality was not even specified. What might appear to be a more serious commitment to international peace were the Convention's manpower ceilings on the combined forces of the signatories' armies and national guards. But even these ceilings could be ignored in the event of "civil war or impending invasion by another State" and they did not apply to officers of either the guards or the armies. With these qualifications, the following limits were placed on the combined armies and guards: Guatemala, fifty-two hundred; El Salvador, forty-two hundred; Honduras and Nicaragua, twenty-five hundred each; Costa Rica, two thousand. The accord also prohibited the signers from holding "more than ten war aircraft," as well as any "war vessels" except for "armed coast guard boats."[94] Nonetheless, the ceilings were ignored and little interest was shown outside of Nicaragua in creating a "national guard." El Salvador had already established its National Guard, with the help of Spanish military advisers, in 1912. The State Department approved Honduras's request in 1925 for assistance in creating a National Guard, but Honduras finally decided not to carry out the plan.[95] Nicaragua was the only country to invite the United States to help it create a National Guard.

Washington intended the treaties of 1923 to avert further U.S. interventions. Until then, U.S. military forces had been introduced and maintained on a significant scale only in Nicaragua. The U.S. presence in Nicaragua, far from diminishing after the treaties, would actually intensify, owing precisely to Nicaragua's compliance with the Convention's recommendation to create a National Guard. In Guatemala and El Salvador powerful national *caudillos* had by the late nineteenth century hammered together fairly cohesive national armies, maintaining a level of control adequate for averting direct U.S. military intervention. In Honduras, although U.S. troops occupied the capital and two port cities for two months in 1924, the interminable violence among the country's numerous *caudillos* did not bring the level of U.S. intervention that prevailed in Nicaragua, perhaps because Honduras lacked the strategic significance of Nicaragua's cross-isthmian waterways. Moreover, the Honduran violence was frequently incited by and therefore served the interests of the U.S. fruit companies. As long as rival *caudillos* respected U.S. property—and they almost invariably did so—U.S. military intervention was normally unnecessary. Costa Rica had by the early twentieth century achieved a level of tranquility that was the envy of the rest of the isthmus, and Costa Rican threats to the burgeoning U.S. banana interests there or to the Panama Canal were remote. Before World War II, direct U.S. military intervention outside of Nicaragua was both infrequent and statistically unrelated to the level of U.S. direct foreign investment.[96]

Thanks to the dictatorships that had taken power in the 1930s, by the end of that decade military and police institutions had become sufficiently consolidated under national military-oriented leadership to nearly monopolize the use of large-scale violence, marking a new stage in the isthmian state formation process.[97] This achievement coincided with the outbreak of war in Europe in 1939 and with the U.S. decision to make allies of the Latin American governments. As a result, throughout World War II, new and virtually unmediated channels of collaboration opened between U.S. military, police, and intelligence agencies, and Central American military authorities for the conveyance of matériel, training services, advice, and technical support. Although those channels contracted from time to time, for different reasons, in each of the five countries, the general trend over the next five decades was one of growth and diversity in tutelary military and police collaboration with the United States.

Despite the trend toward the consolidation of national armies, counterinstitutional, and para-institutional forms of public violence hardly diminished in frequency and scope. After about 1960, the counterinstitutional violence that had for so long been the instrument of dissident *caudillos*, party militias, and army factions was adopted by communistic political organizations aiming at the destruction of the state and the imposition of a revolutionary, socialist government. The agency of para-institutional violence took on new methods. Loosely coordinated mobs of street fighters preserved the party-militia tradition. In Costa Rica between 1944 and 1948, the communist Partido de Vanguardia Popular's *brigadas de choque* attacked opponents of the government; although one historian reported that the *brigadas* "reinforced" the army, in fact the army reinforced the *brigadas*, because the latter claimed six hundred members to the army's three hundred. On the heels of the U.S.-organized overthrow of the Arbenz government in 1954, *turbas* or mobs allied with the victorious insurgents plundered the homes of ex-government officials, including those "whose modest life and lack of luxury were visible even to the plunderers." Honduras's Partido Nacional unleashed its *mancha brava* in the 1960s.[98] The *turbas divinas* of the governing Frente Sandinista para la Liberación Nacional performed the same function in Nicaragua during the 1980s. In Guatemala and El Salvador, far more savage and shadowy *escuadrones de muerte* selected high-profile targets for torture and murder and publicly exhibited their work.

Conclusions

The core event in the Central American state formation process was the gradual knitting together of dispersed power centers into coherent organs of coercion. Not just violence but traditional clientelist arrangements themselves were displaced upward in this process, drawing collaborators at all levels of society into networks of state-associated violence and leaving noncollaborators little option but to resist violently. The primary purpose of the new national-level armies that emerged from this process in the second half of the twentieth century was the control of internal opponents of the state. Although the new armies' *caudillo*-led precursors had moved back and forth across national frontiers with insouciance, drawing followers and repelling enemies with practically no regard for nationality, the armies of the mid-twentieth century were almost exclusively inward looking. And they tended to stay that way, as frontiers hardened into borders to be patrolled, defended, and occasionally fortified against penetration by subversive enemies.

By then, exceptionally ample limits had already been set to the practice of public violence in the isthmus. As the states and their newly organized armies began to integrate themselves during World War II into the emerging global circuits of public violence that led back to the United States, the breadth of those limits meant that the process of globalization would have a transformative impact on public violence itself. Globalization would both intensify it and legitimize it in novel ways—as anti-communist and as anti-imperialist, as righteous struggle and just war—obstructing tendencies toward the shrinkage of its limits.

Yet the countries within which these new armies operated remained bereft of what Barry Buzan called an "idea of the state"—a popular sense of nationhood or some coherent organizing ideology. As a result, institutions took over that substituted coercion for an idea of the state.[99] Indeed, nowhere in Latin America do scholars find much evidence of a stable, unifying cross-class nationalism, which is not to be confused with abrupt surges of patriotic fervor or with the more or less steady appeals to nationalism by the intelligentsia and party ideologues. In a nation, one finds a broad consensus on "fundamental values and procedures," Samuel L. Baily argued. The absence of that consensus in most of Latin America points to the absence of nations. "There are few common interests or broadly based institutions that might bind together the diverse elements of contemporary Latin American societies."[100] Central America's armies operated within states still less likely than the Latin American norm to tap any coherent sense of nationhood. Indeed, the feebleness of national identity among the inhabitants of the Central American countries compared to other countries in Latin America—a weakness intensified by the omnipresent temptation to reconstitute the supranational isthmian federation that collapsed in the 1830s—is practically an axiom of isthmian historiography.[101]

Occasional surges of antiforeign nationalism, such as those that inspired the successful all-isthmian war of 1856 against William Walker's evanescent Nicaraguan government, were too superficial and negative to supply nation-building timber.[102] Such sentimental patriotism can in time of emergency incite, in Tocqueville's words, "great transient exertions" but not "continuity of effort." In the absence of a legal-rational ambience of respect for individual civil and political rights, a country undergoing rapid change "assumes a dim and dubious shape in the eyes of the citizens"—a fitting characterization of the four northern countries of the isthmus.[103] Only two organizing ideologies have ever gripped them. The first was liberalism, mythologized as the great gift of the "revolutions" of the 1870s. However, liberalism was never more than a thinly rooted plant, nourished with bombast and badly stunted by the authoritarian intentions of its exponents. The second was anticommunism. By the Cold War it was the only coherent organizing ideology available. Negative by definition, it relied above all on the state's capacity to generate fear, serving only the interests of the few who devised it and lived by it—above all the leadership of the armies. For them, a spiteful and destructive anticommunism had become "the official ideology."[104] Like liberalism, anticommunism was an organizing ideology that could have almost no resonance outside the institutions that sought to promote it. But what of Marxian socialism and its multiple deviations such as Nicaraguan *sandinismo*? Founded as they are on the belief that people live antagonistically in one class or another, and that one class can't help but systematically exploit another, socialism by definition could not seed the unification of a people. No less a figure than Luis Carrión, a Sandinista *comandante* and economics minister, acknowledged that the class-driven policies of the Frente Sandinista para la Liberación Nacion while it was in power in Nicaragua from 1979 to 1991 offended justice itself. Failing to distinguish innocent individuals from guilty ones, Sandinista policies led to "resentment and violence."[105]

The timing of the globalization of public violence in Central America's case was therefore crucial. It followed a secular process of state formation that gave rise to broadly extensive limits in the use of public violence. It occurred while the Central American states still lacked either deeply rooted organizing ideologies or ideas of nationhood that might have exercised some constraining influence on the local effects of public violence's globalization. Instead, anticommunism was quickly appropriated by the governing elites to justify their participation in the globalization of public violence. The effects were devastating. Nevertheless, two trends might have restrained those effects in the way that a popular sense of nationhood might have. The first was the emergence with full force, in the 1940s, of "the social question" in Central American politics, some two decades or more after it had already surfaced in Mexico, Cuba, and South America, and a half-century or more after it had first dominated the political agendas of the North Atlantic world. For the first time, the Central American states were forced to respond to popular demands for economic security and social equity.[106] The second was what might be called "the political question" of the day, expressed in demands for the reform of the systems of oligarchical or dictatorial rule that the liberal revolutions of the late nineteenth century had perfected in the 1930s. But the collision of both trends with the fear of communism effectively choked them off. Latin American states that had faced popular challenges before World War II, such as Argentina, Chile, and Brazil, could accommodate them in ways that were unavailable to those in Central America. The isthmian states met the popular challenges later than the others, and they found that their collaboration with the United States enabled them to avoid making the accommodations that had already been carried out elsewhere. In effect, they could preserve their sociopolitical structure at a low cost—until the 1980s. At the heart of that structure was a state whose legitimacy derived not from any strong sense of national identity but rather from a patrimonial ethos that made its agents readier than those elsewhere to resort to coercion. In the field of power surrounding that state, anticommunist armies without nations emerged during the Cold War as the principal agents of public violence.

3

Guatemala

Organizing for War

It looks like only force can keep him in office. His Army is large but how
true I cannot say.
—Benton McMillin, U.S. minister in Guatemala, of dictator Manuel
Estrada Cabrera, 22 March 1920, three weeks before the latter's
resignation after twenty-two years in office

In 1837, armed opposition to the policies of a transient liberal government broke out
in what was still formally the state of Guatemala of the República Federal de Centro
América. In the town of Mataquescuintla, José Rafael Carrera assembled a band of
sixty would-be insurgents. Having grown up in a poor section of the state capital,
the son of a mule driver and a domestic servant, Carrera was only twenty-three years
old but already a veteran of the Federal Army, which he had joined as a drummer at
the age of twelve. He saw combat in the first major civil war that followed the establishment of the Federation in 1824. Moving in and out of odd jobs after the war, he
ended up raising pigs in Mataquescuintla, where he settled down and married. Only
weeks before taking charge of Mataquescuintla's guerrilla unit, Carrera had led an
angry mob of two thousand residents who, while protesting the state government's
response to a cholera epidemic, killed some visiting government officials. In the first
battle he led against government troops in June 1837, Carrera turned the tide in favor
of the insurgents and immediately persuaded a regional leader of the revolt to submit himself and his men to Carrera's direction.[1]

Owing to his success on the battlefield, the former swineherd soon commanded the statewide "Army of the Constitution," which not only managed to place
a conservative government in power in 1839 but also to repeatedly humiliate the
army of the liberal-dominated federal government. The retreat of liberal-associated
montoneras all over the isthmus led to the complete collapse of the federation and
opened three decades of conservative rule in Guatemala. Carrera controlled the
country militarily until 1844, when he added the presidency of the government to

his leadership of the army. Except for a few months in 1848, the army belonged to him until he died as president-for-life in 1865. "From a nucleus of ragged guerrillas ... Carrera built the strongest military force in Central America," his biographer reported. "The army was his weapon ... and he did not hesitate to use it."[2] He turned over control of the countryside to "his" military chieftains, men he appointed to the constitutional office of *corredigor*, whose excesses were only rarely subject to their chief's rebuke.[3] It was Carrera's genius to have been able to maintain his control of this regime for the better part of three decades; no one before him anywhere in Central America had ever come close to such an achievement, which likely strengthened his army's nascent identity as the national institution it would shortly become.[4] In 1973, Carrera's role as the first organizer of the Guatemalan Army and his success in establishing "a rigorous hierarchy from soldier to field marshall" were celebrated by his successors, who like Carrera were themselves soldiers who governed the country after overthrowing a civilian government.[5]

Among Carrera's political opponents, there was never any doubt that conservative rule could only be terminated violently. Fifty years after the separation from Spain, the double-bind dynamic of attack and counterattack, kill and kill again, must have appeared to be in a state of perpetual motion, trapping all sides and forcing them to fight out of fear of the other. The public purpose of the fighting—usually to impose or resist a liberal or conservative program—must always have been subordinate to the knowledge that one had to be constantly ready to fight. Even during the relatively peaceful and stable dictatorship of General Carrera, revolts and various forms of political banditry were practically continuous and frequently crossed national borders.[6]

The first serious challenge to Carrera's control of Guatemala emerged in El Salvador, where a liberal *golpista* regime under Gerardo Barrios took power in 1858. Five years later, the Guatemalan Army invaded El Salvador under Carrera's personal command. The war widened to Nicaragua and Honduras before the general managed to defeat Barrios's army in November 1863 after a ten-month campaign that turned out to be Carrera's last. It was a costly and arduous victory that portended still more fighting. Barrios's daring act of defiance, the final defeat of Mexican conservatism four years later in the bloody War of the Reform, and Carrera's death in 1865 encouraged the liberal opposition to organize for war again. Liberal-led revolts against Carrera's handpicked presidential successor, Fd. Mar. Vicente Cerna, broke out in 1867 under the leadership of Justo Rufino Barrios (no relation to Gerardo) and Serapio Cruz, whose separate *montoneras* were launching attacks on Guatemala from the now liberal-friendly territory of Mexico. After government troops defeated Cruz in battle in 1870, the field marshall had the insurgent's head boiled in oil and displayed in the capital. Justo Barrios alone was left to command the liberal insurgents.

Building adroitly on the advantage provided by the recent victory of the Mexican liberals under the leadership of Benito Juárez, Barrios operated from Mexican soil with the personal assurances and material support of Juárez and his government. Mexico's safe haven allowed Barrios to import rifles from the United States.

Although outnumbered six thousand to two thousand by government troops, Barrios's men occupied the capital on 30 June 1871, their victory owing in large part to their superior U.S. weaponry. The government's troops, besides committing various strategic errors, "carried nothing more than ancient flint rifles while the revolutionaries were armed with different kinds of rifles (Remington, Henry, Winchester, piston rifles, flint rifles, and even hunting shotguns); but breechloading weapons predominated, which could fire three to five shots for each one that the flint rifles fired, especially when taking account of the humidity, . . ." Barrios and other military leaders authorized the liberal soldier-statesman Miguel García Granados to form a government as provisional president but Barrios, the undisputed leader of what was now the Army of Guatemala, replaced him as president in 1873.[7]

The liberals had not wielded any significant authority in the country since the 1830s, and it is arguable whether they in fact had done so even then. The most significant aspect of the liberal triumph and the permanent defeat of the conservatives in 1871 was not so much the formal supremacy of the liberal ideology but the persistence of public violence even after the permanent defeat of the liberals' great rivals. As soon as the remnants of conservative resistance had been mopped up, factions that identified themselves in one way or another as liberals resumed the fighting. Montúfar reported approvingly that President Barrios (1873–85) had managed to cast off the respect for the civil liberties of the conservative opposition that had proved to be the downfall of his liberal predecessors. History taught that allowing the conservatives the same freedoms as the liberals only made it easier for them to remove the liberals from power. That experience, according to Montúfar, "has obligated today's Chief to carry out acts of severity that are not found in the biography of don José Francisco Barrundia," a liberal leader of the federal period.[8] As Barrios liked to say, "This whip [*fusta*] is the Constitution that I govern with,"[9] and it is clear that he meant to use it against anyone who opposed him, liberal or conservative.

There was nothing new about this way of governing, except that now his "fusta"—and that of all his successors until the 1980s—was an armed force that was increasingly worthy of being called a national institution as it slowly disciplined itself and became more an army and less a collection of semi-independent *montoneras*. It is possible that this transformation was encouraged by the establishment of a military academy within eighteen months of the 1871 *golpe,* and the hiring of three Spanish Army officers to staff it.[10] The event has been widely interpreted as the beginning of the Guatemalan armed forces' "professionalization," a term that could not be applied to them without significant qualifications at any time in either the nineteenth or twentieth centuries. Apart from any conceivable effects the academy may have had on the professional formation of an officer corps, its founding could not have marked the birth of a national army, a process that was put in motion not by Barrios but by his conservative archenemy, General Carrera, and whose consummation awaited a future administration.

General Barrios acquired the presidency in 1873 by demonstrating that he commanded more destructive power than his erstwhile ally, Pres. García Granados. As Taracena drily put it, once General Barrios, then the commander of the Army of the

West, "moved to the capital with part of his army," García Granados instantly announced his resignation and made way for the election of Barrios in March.[11] The general succeeded in keeping the presidency until 1885, when he died in combat at the head of an expeditionary force organized to enforce one of the most memorable acts of official megalomania in the history of Central America. Richly representative of the discourse of demonization and the readiness to kill, the announcement by Barrios (writing in the third person) in his "Decreto de Unión Centroamericana" of 28 February 1885 said that he

> proclaims the union of Central America in a single Republic: initiates, protects, and sustains all work, operations and movements directed toward establishing it; and with this purpose assumes the character of Supreme Military Chief of Central America and the exercise of absolute command as such, until the reunification of these *secciones* in a single Nation and under a single flag. . . . Every person of either a private or official character who declares against the Union or opposes its operations and work and impedes it in any way, will be considered a traitor of the great cause of Nationality; he will remain unable to discharge any function or employment in the Republic of Central America, and will be subjected to the consequences.[12]

Despite the cautions against the use of force voiced by the governments of the United States, Mexico, and Spain, and the even more significant obstacle posed by a defensive alliance of three of the five governments (Costa Rica, Nicaragua, and El Salvador) against their unification, General Barrios organized an army of 14,500 men and invaded El Salvador on 31 March 1885. Three days later, he took a Salvadoran bullet in the heart, inspiring his army to retreat to Guatemala. The grand campaign to unify the isthmus collapsed, tragically but ludicrously, with the death of the general.[13]

The humiliation of the Guatemalan Army by tiny El Salvador crowned fourteen years of constant internal violence pitting Barrios against his enemies, and in this respect the continuity of the age of liberalism with the age of Carrera was at least as significant as the liberal political changes—"La Reforma"—that the governments of García Granados and Barrios had dictated. Barrios may have been the born leader of a rising class of rural, *mestizo*, medium-sized entrepreneurs in whose interests liberal ideology was devised.[14] But to succeed in Guatemala, Barrios would above all have to emulate Carrera, showing that he too was prepared to kill ruthlessly. In the same way that Carrera had depended on his army, Barrios made his army "uno de los pilares" of his regime.[15] Just as Carrera had to confront constant liberal conspiracies and revolts, so too Barrios had to keep his "fusta" at hand to deal with uprisings against his rule.

Chief among them was the "Remincheros" revolt of conservatives in 1872–74, which drew Guatemalan troops, in temporary alliance with El Salvador, into combat inside Honduras to defeat the rebels.[16] No sooner had the *Remincheros* been overcome than the governments of both Guatemala and El Salvador sent their troops back into Honduras in 1876 to intervene in a civil war. El Salvador's president promptly betrayed Barrios and joined a Honduran faction to overthrow Barrios himself. Now allying himself with a different Honduran faction, Barrios invaded El Salvador. As combat engulfed the whole of El Salvador and part of Honduras, El Salvador surrendered to Barrios on 25 April 1876. The Guatemalan seized the opportunity to install his own candidates as the presidents of both countries: Rafael Zaldivar in El Salvador and Marco Aurelio Soto (a cabinet member of Guatemala's liberal government since 1871) in Honduras. For the "Campaign of 1876," Barrios had organized the largest army (some twenty thousand men) and the one with the highest morale in the isthmus. Over the next nine years, until the fatal campaign of 1885, Barrios's army had to extinguish four internal rebellions that were nevertheless, in Zamora's estimation, "sin importancia."[17]

Two more liberal generals followed Barrios. Gen. Manuel Barillas, one of Barrios's *jefes políticos* seized power and ruled until 1892. Barrios's nephew, Gen. José María Reina Barrios, won the presidential election that year but in 1897 he imposed rule-by-decree in a vain attempt to ensure his own reelection. Assassinated less than a year later, he was followed in office by the first nonmilitary figure to take the presidency since before Carrera. Manuel Estrada Cabrera, a lawyer and a veteran bureaucrat who was Reina Barrios's interior minister and constitutional successor, stayed in power for twenty-two years. From the start, innovation and continuity in the state's deployment of public violence marked the administration of a master of intrigue, no less ruthless than his predecessors but exceptionally adroit in the manipulation of the men around him, and in the exploitation of political and technological opportunities to impose his will. Estrada Cabrera was the first national *caudillo* to take power and keep it without an armed following of his own. He improvised his own personal fighting force, not by the time-honored method of recruiting a new one but by remaking the national the army, gradually purging the officer corps of political enemies while playing off rivals against one another. Assassins and firing squads removed disloyal officers; the hapless Barillas was murdered three years after his electoral humiliation while he was plotting a coup in Mexico City. The military academy was razed in 1908 after a cadet conspiracy was uncovered, and then rebuilt four years later. A formidable spy network further enhanced Estrada's control, which he extended by preserving personal loyalty as the sine qua non for advancement. The bloody rivalries among *montoneras* were replaced by bureaucratic skullduggery and competition in the officer corps for the favors of the *caudillo*-cum-dictator. Estrada also reached beyond the army to the *hoi polloi*, the up-and-coming political force of the twentieth century. Relegated by his predecessors to the role of armed clients, they were organized by Estrada as electoral clients—voters. A pioneer of populism, Estrada created the first real political party in Guatemala's history. He prepared for the election of 8 December 1898, not by opening the traditional, temporary election-eve "clubs" among influential liberals but by admitting the downtrodden and the lowly to the Liberal Party, an institution whose mass membership was carefully cultivated and expanded over the next two decades. In the process, Estrada also captured the nascent labor organizations for his party. Easily winning election to a first term, he was so confident of his popularity that he declared victory in the 1904 election by a risibly fraudulent margin of 548,830 votes to 3 for General Barillas. At the same time, Estrada showed himself to be a master at exploiting and manipulating yet another new opportunity to extend his power: the desire of foreigners—above all the United Fruit Company—to invest in Guatemala.[18]

In demonstrating his ability to adapt *caudillismo* to new conditions and opportunities, Estrada nevertheless preserved and even strengthened its core attributes of personalism and violence. Perhaps the most novel aspect of his achievement was his success in converting the army he inherited from the three generals who preceded him as president into his own *montonera*, which he used to defeat one violent challenge after another to his rule for more than two decades.[19] But by March 1920, the president had become "so distrusted and condemned by [a] large majority of his people" that "only force can keep him in office," the U.S. minister in Guatemala wrote. After the legislature withdrew its recognition from the Estrada government on 8 April, the tide turned against the dictator when his army divided, with some forces joining the opposition. A four-day civil war took, by one account, an astonishing seventeen hundred lives before Estrada resigned on 13 April.[20]

His civilian successor was swept from office on 5 December 1921 in an uprising led by Gen. José María Orellana, one of Estrada's most trusted generals. Two more of his generals would follow Orellana in the presidency in the 1920s and 1930s, in effect extending the regime another two decades by relying on an army that was little more than an occupation force. "The present Government is strictly a military one, that is, one relying wholly on the army to maintain its control until it gets in good running order," the U.S. military attaché reported after Orellana's coup. The strategy for maintaining control of the country, developed by Orellana's fellow *golpista* and his defense minister, Gen. Jorge Ubico, was simple and effective: make the army visible in the main population centers. But Ubico was its only competent commander; the rest of the officers were "mere garrison commanders" whose knowledge "will probably be confined to defending a cuartel, or clearing the streets in time of trouble." The French officers who were supposed to be supervising the training of officers complained that they could accomplish little because attendance at training sessions was so spotty. As for the infantrymen, "it must be clearly understood that these soldiers are all Indians, accustomed to carrying burdens all their lives, that they are simply impressed into service when needed, sent anywhere, turned loose when their services are no longer need, no matter if it happens to be five hundred miles from their homes, and paid only twenty cents a day. To expect much of such a force seems foolish, yet General Ubico in less than a month has produced real morale and esprit de corps among them. "[21]

After a decade of relative political openness under the leadership of General Orellana and his successor, Gen. Lázaro Chacón, General Ubico won an uncontested election for president in 1931. The godson of General Barrios, Ubico had been commissioned a colonel at twenty-eight, a mere nine years after he joined the army as a second lieutenant. He served Estrada Cabrera as a *jefe político* and *comandante de armas* or regional military chief. Ubico considered Barrios a model president, and echoed his godfather's assertion that Guatemalans could be adequately governed only by the use of force.[22] On taking office, Ubico (who had served as minister of war from 1921–23) immediately implemented Estrada Cabrera's main survival strategy: the outright elimination of his political opponents, a strategy justified by what he claimed to be the imminent danger of a communist insurrection. The army's visibility and its control of the countryside were increased, as each of Guatemala's 22 departments was assigned a *comandante de armas* who was a colonel or general, and the departments were in turn divided into a total of 228 *comandancias locales*. The army's general staff boasted an almost incredible number of generals: sixteen "de división" (including Ubico himself) and thirty-four "de brigada."[23]

Seizing on the abortive uprising of January 1932 in neighboring El Salvador, which was widely attributed to that country's communist party, the government carried out a series of arrests and then claimed to have saved Guatemala from a worse disaster than that of El Salvador.[24] In September 1934 the discovery of a "plan terrorista" that "may not have been comparable to any in the world history of crime" provided an opportunity for the arrest and liquidation of still more political enemies (identified as communists) and the consolidation of dictatorship.[25] Militarization was deepened. Roderico Anzueto, director general of the Policia Nacional, asserted his preference for "military education as a means of forming virile and patriotic citizens; the barracks are the best schools of civic instruction."[26] Though he headed the national police force, Anzueto pointed out that police and the military were both "armed forces"; police service was equivalent to military service and the two bodies were subject to the same regulations.[27]

In 1940, Ubico announced what he called the "militarization" of secondary schools. All students preparing for careers as school teachers in the state-run normal schools had to undergo military training, and were assigned the army ranks according to their year in school. Students who finished the second year would be corporals; the third year, sergeants; and when they graduated with the degree of Maestro de Educación Primaria, they would automatically be named second lieutenants in the reserve infantry, and therefore subject to the army service. Similar decrees required identical training of students in the Escuelas de Artes y Oficios para Varones, the Institutos Nacionales de Varones, and the Escuela de Agricultura.[28] Guatemala's declaration of war on Germany and Japan immediately after Pearl Harbor not only triggered the conversion of these Reserve officers into regular army officers, subject to military discipline, but inspired Ubico to create a "Guardia Cívica." Made up of volunteers between the ages of fifty and sixty, the Guardia watched highways, electric power plants, and other strategic resources.[29]

Until Ubico took over, Guatemala showed little interest in the U.S. training services offered under the 1923 Washington treaty for creating a nonpolitical national constabulary. In 1927, Guatemala brushed off U.S. diplomatic efforts to convince it to buy its first warplanes from the United States and bought four combat planes and two trainers from France instead. A U.S. military mission that arrived in Guatemala in 1929 "developed into nothing more substantial than a physical training program."[30] Then, less than three months after Ubico's election, U.S. Army Maj. John A. Considine took over as director of the military academy, the Escuela Politéc-nica, on 1 May 1931, replacing a Guatemalan general. A U.S. Army officer would con-tinue to run the Politécnica until 1945, the year after Ubico's removal from office.[31] Ubico also arranged for Guatemalan pilots to receive their training in the United States and for the fledgling air force to buy their planes from the United States instead of France.[32]

More consistently than its three northern neighbors, the Guatemalan state managed to concentrate its coercive capacity in a national army that had formed itself into a coherent entity by the 1860s. To be sure, it remained vulnerable to fac-tional strife and incapable of imposing a stable monopoly of violence. But the Guatemalan Army had become the backbone of the state sooner than did the army in El Salvador, and considerably earlier than in Honduras and Nicaragua. No gov-ernment from that of Carrera on could take and keep power without placing itself on a war footing, with the army as its only important ally. Guatemala was different in another way. In no other Central American state did individual *caudillos* achieve the levels of personal power and longevity in office recorded by Carrera, Barrios, Estrada, and Ubico. In the realm of public violence, therefore, Guatemalan state for-mation was marked, paradoxically, by a personalism that depended heavily on an institutional order represented by the national army. The result was an army that became the source of endless intrigue and the matrix of a deadly and persistent fac-tionalism, which meant a state subject to constant improvisation, as aspirants to state leadership sought to neutralize any opposition from within the army by pact-ing with one or more of its factions. It was this army-centered dynamic of improvi-sation that opened the door to a promising experiment in electoral democracy in 1944, just as the army was beginning to reap the benefits of the globalization of pub-lic violence. As the capacity of the Guatemalan military increased, so did its author-ity to determine who would govern. That was an outcome as antithetical to democ-racy as it was consistent with Guatemala's past.

4

El Salvador

A Democracy of Violence

It is necessary that politics be guided along a path that little by little dispenses with the gangrene of personalism, the primordial cause of our instability.

—Pres. Jorge Meléndez, 1917

A purely impressionistic reading of Central America's past suggests that until 1932, El Salvador may have been the scene of the most frequent and intense public violence. The affiliation of this violence with the name of the Christian savior himself, *el Salvador,* is not so much ironic as grimly appropriate, as *salvadoreños* seemed driven to reenact His immolation as their own.[1] After all, what made 1932 the universally regarded turning point in El Salvador's modern history was the government's bloody suppression of a peasant uprising rather than the uprising itself; the suppression became known simply as the *matanza* or "slaughter" of eight to ten thousand partisans and innocent peasants. It came just as Salvadoran public violence was starting to order itself to the requirements of a militarized state that, uniquely in the isthmus, would preserve itself uninterruptedly for nearly six decades.

But the thirst for immolation was scarcely limited to either military men or large landowners. Ana Patricia Alvarenga reported, in her study of western El Salvador between 1880 and 1932, that peasants also resorted to violence to deter landowners and overseers from abusing their power. But concessions extracted through violence left behind nothing but fear, she observed, as "intimidation generated a growing cycle of violence. Landowners responded to the peasants' threats by arming their henchmen, who would accompany them in the countryside. . . . In short, social conflict expressed through violent confrontation was not exceptional for the different social groups that interacted in the hacienda. It was a part of the daily life in the community." When landowners feuded, each organized armed bands of their own *peones*. But even "relations between equals were frequently very conflictual" too, so that merely personal differences were often resolved violently, and among peasants, that included differences over land or grazing rights.[2]

The violence took place in a field of state power that Erik Ching characterized as a "system of numerous little pyramids" that competed among themselves for control of the state apparatus, such as it was. The amazing level of traffic through the presidency—it changed hands forty-two times between 1841 and 1861, and fifty-eight times between 1841 and 1898—becomes comprehensible when the presidents are seen as the representatives of just a few political networks. The thirty-three men who occupied the presidency from 1841 to 1898 represented thirteen rival patronage networks. In this system, municipal political leaders allied with one of the national networks and simply controlled elections in ways that favored that network's presidential candidate. Ascent from local to national posts of political leadership occurred in the national legislature, which was controlled by thirty to forty regional leaders who "arrived in San Salvador looking to form alliances with other bosses in hopes of building ever-larger pyramids, for whoever assembled the largest networks competed for the ultimate political prize, the Presidency." The power of these men was mainly a function of their ability to earn votes for candidates of allied networks, who often ran unopposed and won unanimously.[3] Successful regional leaders were rewarded with presidential appointments as governors and military commanders.[4] And successful presidential aspirants were the men of the strongest networks who had managed not only to control enough polling stations to gain an electoral majority, but also to best rival networks in the usual months-long, preelection wars among the networks' *montoneras*.[5] Of the thirteen transfers of power between rival networks from 1841 to 1898, at least nine occurred violently; many more violent attempts at such transfers failed. An opposition network, frustrated by its exclusion from the presidency, canvassed the country for local and regional leaders who might be persuaded to add their armed men to the planned revolt against the president's network, in return for appointment to higher office in the event of victory. "Officeholders did not possess a sense of belonging to an institution of government, rather they saw themselves first and foremost as members of their respective patronage network, . . . Presidents rose to power on the back of their networks and stayed in power only so long as they maintained their allies."[6]

By the 1870s incumbent national administrations were already incorporating civilians into their repressive organs as unpaid enforcers of the law at the local level. As *alcaldes, alcaldes auxiliares,* and *comisionados de cantón,* these men collaborated with the government and the oligarchy against their own peasant communities, arresting *hacienda* workers who deserted their jobs or otherwise failed to pay their debts, and evicting fellow peasants from their property. Acting as institutional agents of public violence that could metamorphose into para-institutional and even counterinstitutional agents of such violence, they "fomented clientelism and individual loyalties. The *alcalde,* the landowner, or even the administrator of the *hacienda* were the most important authorities for the civilian patrols." The civil patrols, as slightly anachronistic manifestations of the old system of *caudillo* armies, could also be impediments to the centralization of state power, and so were eventually replaced by the National Guard. Besides the "civilian assistants" (*auxilios civiles*) there were also "military assistants" (*auxilios militares*) who began working without pay for the army in 1901 to keep order and pursue the army deserters or those militia members who failed to report for their monthly training session.[7]

Both military and civilian governments depended on civilian collaborators. During a two-decade period of exclusively civilian rule (1911–32) both the "civilian assistants" and the "military assistants" were deployed. In 1918, Pres. Carlos Meléndez established the Liga Roja as the militia of his newly founded Partido Nacional Democrático (PND). Although the government did not arm the Liga, it condoned its use of violence because of its capacity to intimidate, kill, or maim the opposition without directly implicating the state, thus making the Liga an agent of para-institutional violence, a type whose perfection El Salvador would be famous for by the 1980s. The Liga members were seen by Indian-majority towns as tools to recover some autonomy from both the state and non-Indians; the Indians who organized the Ligas expected the government to reward them by appointing them to local offices. The Ligas were therefore a double-edged sword for the state. They provided a fairly disciplined source of power in the Indian towns, but they also made the Indians more dangerous, given their potential to shift from para-institutional to counterinstitutional status. When the Ligas began to challenge the power of the official repressive bodies of the state, attacking and killing soldiers in the course of punishing the opposition, they began to threaten government control and the state's long-term project of eliminating Indian village autonomy. They were disbanded by Pres. Alfonso Quiñónez Molina five years after their founding.[8]

Like some disorderly fugue, the elements of public violence overlapped, repeated and varied endlessly, with "foreign" forces merging into "national" ones, and "peasant" violence blending with "Indian" violence. Between 1841 and 1890 El Salvador fought five wars with Guatemala, four with Honduras, and one with Nicaragua, while experiencing thirteen successful coups d'état.[9] To these must be added revolts, riots, and unsuccessful coups. In these conflicts, the historian Aldo Lauria-Santiago refers repeatedly to the participation of "local militias," "peasant militias," and "Indian militias," of which some were formed by regional alliances of Indian communities that reached across the border to unite with both conservative and liberal Guatemalan governments.[10]

The precise relationship among the variety of fighting forces—national army, militias, *montoneras*, and local constitutional authorities such as *gobernadores*—remains obscure, though the overall tendency toward the upward displacement of violence into the hands of a central state became clear by the 1890s. At the same time, more informal fighting forces—often identified generically as "militias," a term that might also refer to the state's regular reserve force—were sometimes headed by men attached to some government office such as the presidency or a departmental governorship, and sometimes by men without any such formal affiliation. "Given the weakness of the central state and national identity, in which authority and legitimacy rested on a fragile balance of regional, ethnic, factional, and community alliances, political stability was an elusive goal. Order depended on shifting alliances between communities and Ladino factional leaders, most of them military men. Any leader's attempts to build a stable regime faced great challenges, given his inability to control local communities and the lack of a professional military and strong state institutions."[11]

As late as 1885, a rebel uprising against the government drew the support of an army of Indians that numbered, according to the U.S. consul in San Salvador, more than six thousand, of whom nearly seven hundred were armed with Remington rifles and the rest with machetes. The U.S. consul reported that the Salvadoran Indians captured the city of Cojutepeque from government troops "after a well contested fight," killing and mutilating the commander of the government's troops, disarming the government soldiers, and capturing seven large cannons and ammunition. "That makes the Indians formidable and an attack is feared here. The chief of the Indian rebellion is sending armed parties all over the surrounding country; there is danger that he may attempt to cut off communication between this Capital and the port of La Libertad; the Government will not be able to guarantee life or property."[12]

An era of phenomenal disorder—what Lauria-Santiago called the "popular mobilizations" of the nineteenth century—ended in 1898 when local militias carried out Gen. Tomás Regalado's successful *golpe*, the last one until 1931.[13] Regalado restored the regular operation of the military academy, the Escuela Politécnica, which produced two hundred officers between 1900 and 1919. A distinctively Prussian-oriented military tradition was endowed by a Chilean military mission from 1903 to 1907.[14] El Salvador had even established a school for noncommissioned officers, the Escuela de Cabos y Sargentos, well before the other countries of the isthmus had given any serious attention to training NCOs. Both of the schools ranked "very much above the average in Central America," in the view of the U.S. military attaché for Central America, who reported in 1919 that its graduates were both "efficient" and "snappy." He thought the morale of El Salvador's army was "probably higher than any of the other countries of Central America," owing in part to the belief among its officers that their academic training was superior to that of the other officers in Central America. That superiority in turn attracted "men of higher class" to become officers than elsewhere, though power remained an irresistible attraction: "a military *Comandante* is absolute master in the district over which he presides."[15] Perhaps owing to the Chilean-Prussian influence, El Salvador's army was, Dana Munro thought, both "better trained and equipped than that of any other Central American country" and "the chief support of the government."[16]

In 1921, the Salvadoran Army was still "by far the best of the Central American forces," according to the U.S. attaché.[17] But high morale and combat effectiveness collapsed with astonishing speed when falling coffee prices choked the flow of government revenue in 1921–22. By May 1922, soldiers had been without pay for ten months, and early that month the government quit even feeding the troops. In San

Salvador, the men of the Sixth Infantry Regiment "were therefore obliged to forage in the city for their meals and at the end of eight days they had reached the limit of their credit and were starving." As a result, on 22 May, 250 of the regiment's men revolted, beating their commanding officers and attempting to fortify a knoll a half-mile north of the Zapote garrison on the southern edge of the capital with rifles and artillery. The uprising was rapidly quelled by artillery fire from the fort, but the U.S. attaché was certain more such outbreaks would occur.[18] Despite these setbacks, a year and a half later El Salvador still had "by far the best army" in Central America in terms of personnel, training, equipment, and morale. Combat planning continued to be mainly "predicated upon political factors, such as the suppression of revolts against the government in power, Bolshevistic tendencies and labor strikes."[19]

An insurrection of cadets in 1922 led to the closing of the Politécnica. Five years later a new military school, the Escuela Militar, was founded with a more demanding curriculum and a stress on specialization.[20] Its disciplinary code was famously brutal. Until 1940, when the U.S. military mission took over direction of the school, students were "often confined for two or three days at a time to small punishment cells, no larger than a small closet, where, deprived of their clothing and given only bread and water, they were forced to remain standing because it was impossible to lie down. Also, at the whim of any officer passing through the Military School and who observed an infraction of the rules, a cadet might be sentenced on the spot to do as many as 1,500 kneebends without stopping, or other similar punishment."[21]

Meanwhile, separate rural and urban police agencies under the control of the national state were gradually depriving local governments of their policing function. The Policía Nacional usurped urban policing in the 1880s. In 1912, the Guardia Nacional was created under the leadership of Alfonso Martín Garrido, a colonel in the Guardia Civil of Spain whom the Spanish government detailed to El Salvador at its request.[22] As the country's first all-national rural force, controlled by the Ministries of War and Government, the Guardia operated as an accessory of the army, drawing its officers from the Escuela Politécnica, and its weapons and ammunition from the War Ministry. Its duties included patrolling agricultural estates, roads, ports, and rural hamlets. By 1924 there were one thousand Guardsmen and ninety-six officers, controlled by the central government and free to ignore the interests of local *alcaldes* and *gobernadores*. Guardsmen were detailed to *haciendas*, at the request of the owners, in special detachments to control the *hacienda* workforce.[23] The U.S. military attaché for Central America considered the National Guard (still directed as late as 1919 by the Spaniard, Colonel Garrido), to be "purely military" in organization, drawing its members from either the army or the Army Reserve. The Guardia was

said to be the most efficient and best trained military organization in Central America. ... The men are well uniformed and trained. ... Nearly all cart roads are patrolled at night by these Guards and horse and cattle thieves and other rural criminals are their particular object. The landowners of the country are the strongest supporters of this organization and their influence has kept Col. Garrido in his post in spite of some objection on the part of certain portions of the public against his stern discipline and the rigorous measures he takes against rural thievery.[24]

By the 1920s, therefore, the Salvadoran state seems to have succeeded in consolidating and institutionalizing the scattered sources of military power that had been dispersed among militias under the control of independent regional and local leaders, building them into a national army whose commanders also controlled the militarized National Guard and the National Police.[25] Although in doing so El Salvador had lagged perhaps two decades behind Guatemala, it managed to produce a national military establishment that exceeded Guatemala's both in morale and combat effectiveness, at least in the unanimous view of U.S. authorities.

El Salvador had also accumulated decades of experience in another realm that set it apart from Guatemala: the organization and management of civilian networks of militarized authority that collaborated directly with the state in the deployment of violence. To the organization of the civilian assistants, military assistants, and Ligas Rojas, the government of Gen. Maximiliano Hernández-Martínez added, in the 1930s, the Legión Nacional Pro-Patria and the Guardias Cívicas. The Legión was organized in February 1932 by Maj. Gen. José Tomás Calderón, who at that time was still commanding the *matanza,* the brutality of which would be felt for the rest of the century.[26] Calderón's Legion, composed originally of combat veterans of the *matanza* and assigned to identifying and capturing suspected communists, was renamed the Guardias Cívicas in 1937 and its members deputized by the state. Now under the control of the army and the National Guard, members of the Guardias Cívicas were trained by officers of the two institutions. Along with its counterpart, the Asociación Cívica, the Guardias constituted, according to the U.S. military attaché, "a network of national espionage and ready means of promptly communicating to the seat of the National Government information of any subversive activity that may be discovered."[27]

The incentives to join the Guardias Cívicas were not negligible: uniforms, power over nonmembers, freedom from arrest for misdemeanors, and the right to carry a firearm. Although the old *comisionados* hadn't been very reliable and the Ligas Rojas had degenerated into semi-autonomous gangs, Guardias Cívicas represented an unalloyed success from the point of view of the state; closely monitored and led by the upper and middle classes, they could never use their power to challenge the status quo. As the fear of communism associated with the 1932 uprising receded, so did the surveillance activities of the Guardias Cívicas, which gradually transformed themselves into social clubs and bearers of the new national ideology of anticommunism.[28]

Although a pattern of subaltern collaboration with the agents of institutional violence seems to have been characteristic of Nicaragua and Guatemala in the 1930s as well, what may set El Salvador apart from the other isthmian republics was that such collaboration seemed to have a longer tradition, to operate on a larger scale, to have enjoyed a higher level of voluntary cooperation, and to have persisted longer. A dramatic example of such continuity was the foundation of the semi-secret Organización Democrática Nacionalista (ORDEN) by Pres.—and Lt. Col.—Julio Adalberto Rivera in 1966. Its purpose was to report subversive political activities to the government; within a year it had about thirty thousand civilian and retired military members, according to a U.S. intelligence report.[29]

Yet another distinctive feature of El Salvador's past is the character of its relations with the United States. Of all the Central American countries, those relations have been the least amicable over the course of the twentieth century. El Salvador displayed a level of autonomy and national dignity in its dealings with the northern colossus that no other Central American country can match. This distinctiveness may have been related to a nationalistic pattern of economic growth that set El Salvador apart not only from its isthmian neighbors but even from much of the rest of Latin America. The country's late nineteenth-century economic takeoff was "almost entirely a local effort; economic growth took place without large-scale imports of factors of production. Local entrepreneurs using local resources built the economy, almost from scratch. They made decisions on their own, taking their clues from foreign markets and not from foreign companies or governments."[30]

As early as the first decade of the twentieth century, anti-Americanism was widespread among Salvadorans.[31] In 1916, Cuba, Panama, and Nicaragua were U.S. protectorates, the Mexican port of Veracruz had only just been evacuated by U.S. occupation forces, General Pershing's troops were scouring northern Mexico for Pancho Villa, the Panama Canal had just opened and—most troubling of all to the Salvadorans—the U.S. Senate ratified the Bryan-Chamorro Treaty between Nicaragua and the United States. That treaty not only formalized Nicaragua's status as a U.S. dependency but also turned over Nicaraguan territory on the Gulf of Fonseca, which Nicaragua shared with El Salvador and Honduras, for a U.S. naval base. The Salvadoran government's efforts to nullify the base concession failed, and fear of U.S. entrenchment in the isthmus was growing.[32]

But for some Salvadorans (as well as many others elsewhere in the isthmus) that entrenchment was an opportunity for self-aggrandizement. As the Salvadoran elections of January 1919 approached, the millionaire coffee processor Rafael Guirola emerged as a possible presidential candidate. At Guirola's request, the U.S. military attaché for Central America, U.S. Army Capt. Douglas MacDuff, agreed to meet with him on 10 December 1918, two days after an especially bloody round of municipal elections that left more than one hundred people dead. Guirola's choice of a military attaché rather than a State Department representative may indicate the extent to which Salvadorans considered U.S. policy in the region to be motivated by a strategy of conquest. Guirola informed the captain that Pres. Carlos Meléndez secretly despised the United States and was pro-German as well as a friend of the anti-U.S. Mexican Pres. Venustiano Carranza. Guirola then made a prediction, and offered the captain a deal. First, it was clear that the United States would soon fulfill its ambition of becoming the principal trading partner of Central America, and that it would also get its naval base on the Bay of Fonseca regardless of isthmian opposition. "Therefore," the captain reported,

> Señor Guirola suggested that the Government of the U.S. could no longer adhere strictly to its policy of hands off in the internal affairs in these countries but that it would be absolutely essential that the U.S. government should intervene to some extent in all the countries as far south as the Panama Canal. . . . At this point Señor Guirola reached the vital suggestion for which the interview was sought apparently. He baldly stated that he was the man the United States ought to have as President of El Salvador. . . . He stated that possibly 200,000 pesos dropped on his side would turn the balance in his favor.

Guirola added that the United States "would need a friend in the Presidency of El Salvador, that he was that friend," and that Captain MacDuff ought to ask his superior's permission to tell President Meléndez that Guirola should be the next president.[33]

No record was found of the U.S. response to Guirola's request for a bribe worth US$100,000 at the current rate of exchange, but his candidacy did not prosper. President Meléndez tapped his brother Jorge to succeed him in office, establishing the Meléndez-Quiñónez dynasty, which ruled until the fateful year of 1931, when the first fully free election in the country's history was followed by the first successful military coup since 1898 and the dictatorship of General Hernández-Martinez. The depth of anti-Americanism no doubt made Guirola think the United States would gladly buy the country's next president: "The feeling in El Salvador toward the United States may be said to be anti-American, a feeling apparently shared in by most classes and certainly by the Government [and] is reflected throughout official circles although Government officials and the educated classes are courteous enough not to show it to any extent personally. The clergy, who do not have much influence in this respect, are undoubtedly anti-American. . . . Against the United States, El Salvador would probably render the most efficacious aid possible to any possible allies of hers."[34]

During World War I, El Salvador was the only Central American country that refused to cut relations with Germany, despite U.S. pressure. Later, Pres. Pío Romero Bosque (1927–31) sent his minister of war to meet with Augusto Sandino, whose armed resistance to the U.S. Marine presence in Nicaragua was widely supported in El Salvador. Pres. Arturo Araujo himself protested the U.S. intervention in Nicaragua in 1931.[35] When Hernández-Martínez took over, there was still "widespread fear of United States intervention and economic domination," owing in part to El Salvador's rapidly increasing foreign debt and to the fact that a U.S. official was "observing" the collection of customs revenue that was being offered as security for an old debt.[36]

Perhaps no single event demonstrated the singularity, among the Central American countries, of El Salvador's stubborn pride in its dealings with Washington as the nonrecognition crisis that followed Hernández-Martínez's accession to power in December 1931. In 1923, at Washington's invitation, all five countries signed a General Treaty of Peace and Amity, Article 2 of which obligated the signatories to withhold recognition from governments that took power illegally. When the United States invoked the treaty against the *golpista* government of Gen. Manuel Orellana of Guatemala in 1930, the general stepped aside and made way for an election. El Salvador's General Hernández-Martínez ignored Washington's refusal to recognize his government under the 1923 treaty, a position consistent with El Salvador's earlier decision to sign the 1923 treaty while denouncing Article 2. As a result of the general's perseverance, Washington extended recognition in 1934. The crisis led to the abandonment of the treaty by all of its signatories.[37]

El Salvador had already become accustomed to turning to governments other than the United States for assistance in modernizing its armed forces. The army bought its first six airplanes from Belgium, not the United States, in 1926.[38] Various foreign military officers served along with Salvadorans as directors of the Escuela Militar from 1927 to 1937. Salvadoran Army officers began training in fascist Italy and Germany in 1936 and within two years the Escuela Militar had a German director, Gen. Eberhard Bohnsted. In March 1938 the government paid Italy US$200,000 for four Caproni fighter planes and spare parts, a decision that created a "shock over Salvador's inclination towards the fascist nations," according to the U.S. military attaché.[39] In October, six Caproni bombers were delivered along with three Fiat tanks and three tractors that could serve as armored cars. One of the planes crashed in December, killing the Italian Air Force pilot and completely destroying the plane. Salvadoran pilots disliked the Capronis so much—they were hard to start and their wings were thought to be defective—that the U.S. military attaché correctly predicted the country would soon be asking the United States for planes.[40]

By 1940, the state formation process in El Salvador and Guatemala seemed to have yielded identical outcomes: the creation of national armies that were the principal tools of military dictators. Yet El Salvador's experience differed in important ways. It was far less accustomed than Guatemala to long-term rule by iron-handed national *caudillos,* its two recent decades of uninterrupted civilian rule included one free election, and the country flaunted an independent spirit in its relations with the United States. These were characteristics that might have seemed propitious for a move away from public violence. On the other hand, the Salvadoran state had an integrated and comparatively well-trained force of soldiers and policemen under a single national command whose dramatic liquidation of a communist-led peasant uprising strengthened its authority and its legitimacy, and served to discourage counterinstitutional violence. As a result, the Salvadoran military found itself prepared to begin governing as an institution in the 1940s, some two decades before Guatemala. Furthermore, a robust tradition going back to the nineteenth century of village-level collaboration with the institutional, para-institutional, and counterinstitutional agents of public violence undoubtedly supplied an extra incentive for direct rule by the members of the military high command. As they began to exploit the opportunities for force-enhancement presented by the globalization of public violence during World War II, they chose to take power and try to co-opt potential collaborators by drawing them in as agents of institutional violence. The alternative was to risk a resurgence of warlord killing and destruction ignited by the inequalities of life in the countryside, fanned by communism and open to the same opportunities for enhanced capacity that the globalization of public violence was providing to the armed forces.

5

Honduras

Caudillos in Search of an Army

> The generations transmit from one to another the instinct for revolts.... [M]any years of peace are needed for the love of work to draw Hondurans away from the demented and personalistic politics that, diverting their moral sense, demand the blood of brothers constantly and on any pretext.
>
> —Pres. Gen. Miguel R. Dávila, 1910

By the second decade of the twentieth century, first Guatemala and then El Salvador were building national states capable of co-opting or eliminating the regional and local warlords, party militias and gangs that had disputed one another in the field of state power since 1821. The instruments of control were armies that looked increasingly as if they were truly national, in the sense that they were increasingly subject to a unified command structure. What distinguished Honduras and Nicaragua was the persistence, well into the new century, of the kind and degree of public violence that typified the nineteenth century. The state-directed order that Guatemala and El Salvador were managing to impose early in the century was not achieved in Nicaragua until the mid-1930s, whereas in Honduras this universal sign of a mature state did not become evident until the 1950s.

From 1824 to 1900, Honduras passed through 98 changes of government, an average of 1.3 per year. Although the rate of governmental change fell to almost one every two years between 1900 and 1933, the annual rate of lethal civil conflict rose 66 percent in the second period, compared to the nineteenth century.[1] From 1824–1950, the executive branch changed hands 116 times; only thirteen presidents held office for four or more years and most presidents gained office by the use of violence.[2] Of the eighteen heads of state between 1883 and 1948, nine identified themselves as professional soldiers (with the rank of general) who governed the country for 60 percent of the period. Of the ten administrations that governed from 1892 to 1919, only one (Gen. Terencio Sierra, 1899) was initially elected to office and only one retired

Table 5.1 Time in Office, Honduran Heads of State, 1883–1948

Military rank	Name	First date of accession	First date of exit	Second date of accession	Second date of exit	Days of first period	Days of second period	Total days	Proportion of total elapsed days
General	Tiburcio Carías	1 Feb. 1933	31 Dec. 1948			5,812		5,812	24.45%
General	Luis Bográn	30 Nov. 1883	30 Nov. 1891			2,922		2,922	12.29%
General	Francisco Bertrand	21 Mar. 1913	28 July 1915	1 Jan. 1916	9 Sept. 1919	859	1,347	2,206	9.28%
	Policarpo Bonilla	24 Dec. 1893	1 Feb. 1899			1,865		1,865	7.85%
General	Rafael López Gutierrez	1 Feb. 1920	10 Mar. 1924			1,499		1,499	6.31%
General	Manuel Bonilla	13 Apr. 1903	18 Apr. 1907			1,466		1,466	6.17%
General	Terencio Sierra	1 Feb. 1899	31 Jan. 1903			1,460		1,460	6.14%
	Miguel Paz Baraona	1 Feb. 1925	31 Jan. 1929			1,460		1,460	6.14%
	Vicente Mejía Colindres	1 Feb. 1929	31 Jan. 1933			1,460		1,460	6.14%
General	Miguel Dávila	13 Apr. 1907	23 Apr. 1907	1 June 1907	28 Mar. 1911	5	1,396	1,401	5.89%
General	Ponciano Leiva	30 Nov. 1891	9 Feb. 1893	18 Apr. 1893	7 Aug. 1893	437	111	548	2.31%
General	Vicente Tosta	30 May 1924	28 Feb. 1925			274		274	1.15%
General	Domingo Vásquez	8 Aug. 1893	22 Apr. 1894			257		257	1.08%
	Alberto Membreño	28 July 1915	1 Jan. 1916			157		157	0.50%
	Francisco Bográn	5 Oct. 1919	31 Jan. 1920			118		118	0.50%
	Angel Zúñiga H.	10 Mar. 1924	30 May 1924			81		81	0.34%
	Juan Angel Arias	1 Feb. 1903	13 Apr. 1903			71		71	0.30%
	Rosendo Aguero	9 Feb. 1893	18 Apr. 1893			68		68	0.29%
	junta	25 Mar. 1907	18 Apr. 1907	9 Sept. 1919	5 Oct. 1919	24	26	50	0.21%
All		30 Nov. 1883	31 Dec. 1948					23,773	
Gens. only								15,639	65.78%

Source: Author's calculations, from "Apéndice" in *Historia General de Centroamérica*, vol. 4, *Las repúblicas agroexportadoras (1870–1945),* ed. Victor Hugo Acuña Ortega (Madrid: Sociedad Estatal Quinto Cententario y FLACSO, 1993).

voluntarily at the end of his term (Policarpo Bonilla, 1899); the heads of all but two (Policarpo Bonilla and Francisco Bertrand) called themselves generals.[3]

The struggle to both define and create a national military force can be observed in the Honduran constitutional and statutory legislation of the nineteenth century. Having declared its absolute independence from the hapless Central American Federation on 15 November 1838, Honduras found itself for the first time in a position to govern itself without formal reference to the dictates or interests of forces beyond its borders (although Guatemala, El Salvador, and Nicaragua intervened regularly in the country's politics, from 1838 until the early twentieth century, making and unmaking presidents). Its first constitution, adopted in 1839, simply authorized the president to "Prepare [disponer] the armed force of the State" and to appoint "the military Chiefs" without even referring to the existence of an army; the word "ejército" does not appear in the document. The president was required to consult his ministers in the event he wanted to "use arms against any town."[4]

Four years later, the legislature, again without mentioning "ejército," decreed as an economic measure that the state's "permanent force" be reduced to two hundred men and officers of whom one hundred were to be posted in the national capital of Comayagua, fifty in the departament of Tegucigalpa, thirty at the Puerto de Omoa, and twenty at the Puerto de Trujillo.[5] For the first time, the constitution of 1848 used the word "ejército," but only in connection to its relationship with the president, to whom was delegated the power to "make war.... Direct and prepare the armed force ... carry out the duties of general command, and personally lead the army.... Raise the force necessary beyond that decreed by the law in order to repel invasions or contain insurrections.... Freely dismiss the Comandantes de Armas." Clearly preoccupied by the need to establish the president as the military chief, the framers of this constitution specified that the jefes políticos of the departments (appointed by the president) would have command of troops only in wartime and only with the approval of the president.[6] The provisions may seem superfluous, because whoever commanded the strongest military force was normally capable of naming himself president.[7] They are noteworthy because they indicate that any man who aspired to the presidency was assumed to possess personal experience as a military commander and to be ready to exercise it as president. The president was first of all a man of arms whose fitness for the presidency was a function of his leadership of his montonera. The "army" itself was still institutionally irrelevant and thus nonexistent in constitutional terms.

Not until 1865 did a constitution refer to an "ejército" as an agency of the state with certain functions. Its authors mandated the establishment of "la fuerza pública," to consist of both a "national militia" and "the army of land and sea." The constitution even sought to demilitarize politics by mandating an "obedient" and nondeliberative, nonpartisan army—one of the pipe dreams of twentieth-century U.S. policy toward Central America. It even prohibited military officers who were in service at the time from serving as president or legislator. The document went still further by seeking to terminate caudillismo itself, as implied by the limitation of the fuero (the privilege of being judged for crimes by a military rather than a civil court) to military men who "belong to an organized corps" but also by specifying that, from the date of adoption of the constitution, the president must "not have made war against this [republic] simply as a *caudillo* or as a military chief." It spelled out as no other constitution had the president's role as commander in chief, and for the first time prohibited a president from succeeding himself in office. The 1873 constitution was identical to that of 1865, except that it narrowed the *fuero* to exclude from its protection common crimes.[8]

But without a real army, dispositions governing its conduct and its leadership were bootless. The ephemeral nature of whatever may have qualified as a national army was evident in the remarks of Marco A. Soto, the liberal president imposed on Honduras by Guatemala's Justo Rufino Barrios, to the Honduran legislature in 1879. For Soto, who had served Barrios as his minister of foreign affairs, the construction of a national army was a high priority, perhaps because he was the third Honduran president in a row who had been seated by the combined armies of Guatemala and El Salvador. When he had acquired the presidency four years earlier, he observed, the government's arsenals were empty, and "I immediately occupied myself with procuring a modern and uniform weapon system. Today the armories have a considerable quantity of Remington rifles, Krupp cannons and machineguns, and munitions. What we have is enough to maintain the order and dignity of the country. They cost a good deal. More weapons and military equipment are about to be delivered but there are still not enough to equip the army that this Republic is capable of raising."

Although as president Soto accumulated enough weapons to keep order, the army that would carry them had yet to be established. He blamed an 1874 law that exempted everyone but the poorest Hondurans from military service, leaving Honduras without "either militias or an army," thus making it "difficult even to service the main garrisons in the Departments and the ports."[9] As a militant liberal, Soto's minister of education, Ramón Rosa (who had been undersecretary of Barrios's treasury department), understood the true source of the problem. It was the "ignorance of the people" that had permitted the flourishing of *caudillaje*, a rapacious and divisive system of rule that had brought "ruin and discredit" to Honduras, Rosa told the legislature. The Soto administration, Rosa promised, would soon establish a system of free and compulsory primary education that would end *caudillaje*.[10]

A second line of attack against *caudillaje* could be detected in the language of a new constitution that repeatedly emphasized, as none before it, the war-making supremacy of the president, who was "the Commanding General and the General-in-Chief of the land and sea forces of the Republic. He establishes all the military posts. . . . He has at his disposal the military forces, and he is responsible for their organization and distribution, according to the needs of the State." This was also the first constitution that mentioned military service, specifying that every Honduran between eighteen and thirty-five "is a soldier of the active army" and those between thirty-five and forty were members of the "reserva," while preserving the military's *fuero*.[11]

But the effort to abolish *caudillaje* by concentrating armed force in the hands of the state had as little prospect of success as Rosa's plan for universal primary education. After all, these were men who owed their jobs to the system that they sought to destroy. In addition, the most basic material conditions for the maintenance of anything other than a paper army were still lacking in 1889, when the government reported that most of the country's barracks still lacked "indispensable conditions regarding size, defense and hygiene." The barracks were nothing more than residential dwellings bought by the Government and converted for use by its troops. In Tegucigalpa and in the *plazas* or garrison towns of Santa Bárbara, Comayagua, Juticalpa, Intibucá, Gracias, and Santa Rosa, the state could quarter one and sometimes two battalions. Besides being physically substandard, Honduras's garrisons were sharply undermanned compared to those of its neighbors. All the *plazas* were manned by just twenty-seven chiefs, ninety officers and seven hundred men, many fewer than the permanent forces at the disposition of the other Central American states even including Nicaragua "whose Government is distinguished for its economy in military spending."[12] Like his liberal contemporaries elsewhere, Soto established an Academia Militar (shortly renamed the Escuela de Cadetes) in 1881 under the direction of a French engineer, and a school for noncommissioned officers two years later. Although the schools continued to enroll and graduate young men, they achieved little. "Unstable and lacking professionalism," they were reorganized in 1904, by which time Honduras still had no "professionally organized army."[13]

The constitution that Policarpo Bonilla's government (1893–99) promulgated in 1894 was the first to contain a separate article exclusively devoted to the army. Reviving the fantasy of a nonpartisan military, it sought to pacify politics by depoliticizing the country's *caudillo*-led armies, while retaining the *fuero militar.* "The public force is instituted to secure the rights of the Nation, compliance with the law and the maintenance of public order. No armed body may deliberate. Military obedience will be subject to the law and military ordinances."[14] After having gained the presidency by force, Bonilla, a lawyer and merchant, was eager to demonstrate his abhorrence of militarism. The military commanders upon which his insurrection had depended were now mere citizens, committed to respect for the law and the rights of all Hondurans. "The 'I command and you must follow' of the past disappeared with the advent of the Power of the Liberal Party," Bonilla declared shortly after taking power. He wanted to reduce the strength of the garrisons to the minimum needed to guard their arsenals, while converting the rest of the soldiers into policemen, "an effective and practical means of instilling in Hondurans love of civilian government, and of terminating militarism, the sworn enemy of the public freedoms." Yet he also promised to improve the system of military education; Honduran officers are "by and large ignorant of everything concerning their profession."[15]

Like so many of his predecessors, Bonilla had ridden to power not only behind his own militias but behind those of a neighboring government. The armies that had placed Gen. José Santos Zelaya in the presidency of Nicaragua subsequently joined forces with Bonilla's militias in his campaign for the presidency. The Nicaraguan Gen. Anastasio J. Ortiz even had overall command of the combined forces; the Honduran Gen. Manuel Bonilla was reduced to second in command.[16] Three years after taking power, Bonilla found himself obligated to return the favor when Zelaya's government was threatened by a band of Nicaraguans. At the head of the insurgents rode General Ortiz, the ex-*zelayista*, now allied with Honduran émigrés who expected in exchange that the insurgent Nicaraguans would help overthrow Bonilla's government after deposing Zelaya. The joint forces of Bonilla—who sent two thousand Honduran soldiers under the command of Gen. Manuel Bonilla, now his minister of war, to Nicaragua—and Zelaya defeated the revolt.[17]

Despite its victory, the Nicaraguan campaign revealed, Bonilla admitted, "grave deficiencies in the organization and discipline of our army," including an extraordinarily high rate of desertion. Of the 1,160 men sent to fight in Nicaragua from the department of Choluteca, only a few more than 500 returned.[18] In 1899, amid constant reports of desertions, public hostility to the army, low morale, poor discipline, low enlistment rates, and miserable living conditions in the barracks, the minister of war issued orders for "the most complete military reorganization."[19] The country's policemen seemed even less qualified than its soldiers, judging by a stream of consistently critical comments by various government from the 1890s onward. "Nothing has been gained for this institution," the interior ministry reported in 1910, "in spite of the attempts made by the Government, . . . The [police] agents are ignorant of their duties, and generally incompetent and depraved, to the extent that, when it is necessary to guarantee order in public festivities, we turn to the military force."[20]

All attempts to control public violence by concentrating it in a single military establishment under the exclusive command of the head of state had failed. A liberal uprising against Gen. Manuel Bonilla's government in 1906 was joined by forces contributed by President Zelaya of Nicaragua. Once again a combined army of Honduran liberal insurgents and Nicaraguan regulars marched into Tegucigalpa and installed a new government. The liberals agreed on Gen. Miguel R. Dávila as their new president. Yet in 1910 this *caudillo*, like Policarpo Bonilla before him, was lamenting the "demented and personalistic" *caudillo* politics of the country, as he recounted his success in frustrating both a seaborne invasion attempt by the indefatigable Gen. Manuel Bonilla in July, and a twelve-day rebellion by the commander of the Amapala garrison, Gen. José María Valladares, in October. Both events forced the government to declare separate states of siege. Speaking as a president who realized that his power remained strictly limited by that of the regional caudillos, President Dávila eloquently denounced, like those before him, the system to which he owed his bully pulpit:

> Vain indeed will all the propaganda in favor of peace be as long as the caudillos, the shapers of public opinion, remain examples that contradict the propaganda. The generations transmit from one to another the instinct for revolts, and the passage of many years of peace are needed for the love of work to draw Hondurans away from the

demented and personalistic politics that, diverting their moral sense, demands the blood of brothers constantly and on any pretext. A long period of peace is indispensable so that the generations of the future educate themselves in another school, so that they live in another intellectual environment and form a true concept of *la patria*.[21]

Vain indeed were Dávila's hopes, for in January 1911 his old adversary General Bonilla succeeded, with the financial support of the U.S.-owned banana exporter, the Cuyamel Fruit Company, in occupying various northern towns. The following month, the U.S. government brokered a settlement that saved the country from another civil war but forced Dávila to resign in March. General Bonilla was the sole candidate in the election that followed.

The general died in office in 1913. He was buried in the nave of the cathedral in Tegucigalpa, under a plaque embedded in the floor, scuffed to this day by the shoes of communicants. Seven months after General Bonilla's burial, a Honduran colonel pondered the connection between the wreckage of the Honduran state and the absence of a national army worthy of the name. Writing in the second issue of the *Boletin del Ejército,* optimistically subtitled "authorized organ of the national army," Col. P. Romero castigated the military leaders and politicians of Honduras, where there were no "true military men, since with very rare exceptions we are no more than decked-out civilians owing to the lack of training, discipline and military morale. . . . Our soldiers are revolutionaries out of custom, out of a spirit of libertinage and our Chiefs and Officers out of ambition for another promotion or a job." Men seeking a military career had no choice but to join a political party, for no victorious *caudillo* would employ any but his own commanding officers. And unless a *caudillo* gave his fighting men a job or a promotion, they turned against him and joined some other faction to seek his overthrow. The lack of discipline, morale, and instruction, Colonel Romero wrote, had made Honduras's military men "disparaged in time of peace, and viewed with horror in time of war."[22]

Colonel Romero's was not the only critical voice to be raised against the sorry state of the country's armed forces. In the first issue of the same organ, whose cover carried a photograph of the late General Bonilla, M. Bertrand Anduray observed that Honduran soldiers were "notoriously incompetent" and the army was the "most backward" institution of Honduras. "We have no army. This is the general outcry."[23] The U.S. military attaché for Central America joined the outcry in 1919. He ridiculed the pajama-like appearance of the army uniform, made in Honduras from German cloth. Soldiers typically wore "crude sandals" and carried "mostly very bad" rifles that few could shoot straight. There were not even any fortifications in the interior of the country. Young Hondurans had no ambition to serve in an army

composed usually of barefooted, ignorant, untrained Indians and half-breeds who come from the lowest social stratum. The officers with some few exceptions are of the same social standing. As a result . . . [p]ublic sentiment is one of contempt. As we interpret morale and discipline these qualifications do not exist in the Army of Honduras except to the most infinitesimal degree. The officers as a rule have had no training in discipline and except for brute force and domination of the crudest character they cannot discipline their troops. An army on the march may best be described as a horde of animals on the rampage.

Loyalty was an unknown virtue, for "it is a standing joke that when troops go out to battle in time of revolution they carry the ribbon of the revolutionists concealed on their persons, so that at the opportune moment, should expediency demand it, they may adorn themselves therewith and thereby constitute themselves a section of the effectives of their former enemies." Desertion was so common that recruiters typically bound their recruits with rope as they led them into town for military service. "With the low order of intelligence of the average Hondurean soldier and the complete and total lack of understanding (probably fortunate) of what he is fighting for and for whom he is fighting, it is useless to expect or look for the existence of morale." No foreign military mission had yet been contracted by Honduras for training purposes, the attaché continued, although the various military schools had from time to time hired Italian, U.S., French, Chilean, and Mexican instructors. Military maneuvers and target practice were never undertaken until the troops were sent to confront an enemy, and military tactics were derived from field experience.[24]

Taken together, these Honduran and foreign critiques revealed two distinct concerns: sheer military incompetence and, on the other hand, the readiness of military men to make common cause with greedy and unscrupulous politicians. The direction of change, they implied, would have to go from the military to the political system, making a professional officer corps immune to the manipulation of civilian politicians. Thus the country's salvation was the construction of a modern, professional (nonpolitical), and efficient army.

As always, elections continued to signal the most dangerous moments. Pres. Francisco Bertrand (1913–19), in imposing his brother-in-law Nazario Soriano, a resident of El Salvador, as his successor, offended the political opposition when Soriano won election in April 1919. Civil war followed, and the general who emerged victorious, Pres. Rafael López Gutiérrez (1920–24), reported the results of three armed encounters between the forces of the "gobierno" and those of the "revolución." The cycle opened at an intensive pitch of violence of 4.6 armed conflicts per week from July 1919, when General López began the war in the south until the fall of the northern city of San Pedro Sula to the insurgents under his command in September, when the United States persuaded President Bertrand to resign. General López's troops subsequently took the capital, and the general was elected president in December. As table 5.2 shows, however, he had little time to recover from the exertions of battle before being challenged by other caudillos. The intensity of the violence fell and then rose toward the end of his administration. A rebellion led by Gregorio Ferrera, Luis Isaula, and Francisco Martínez Funes was not finally defeated until September 1922. In response, President López replaced practically all local and regional civilian officials with military officers.[25]

Table 5.2   *Acciones de armas*, 1919–1922, Honduras

Beginning	Ending	Total acciones de armas	Total days	Total weeks	Acciones per week
23 July 1919	7 Sep. 1919	27	46	6.6	4.1
25 Jan. 1920	25 Nov. 1920	12	305	43.6	0.3
4 Apr. 1922	31 Aug. 1922	18	149	21.3	0.8

Source: MGH 1922–23, pp. 77–80.

The fighting inspired President López's war minister to reflect once again on the state of the Honduran Army: "We have to consider certain huge necessities for the soldier, such as his dress, food and appropriate lodging. We should care for his health and attend to his training and improvement, in all senses. [We should] accept in the ranks only individuals who are completely normal and healthy, in order not to sacrifice those who are handicapped by fate and those who are cowards by misfortune. Many of these necessities, I dare to hope, can be met in a not-distant future."[26] In a particularly radical sense, Honduras was a nation without an army, for in 1921 it was made up almost entirely of Nicaraguan and Salvadoran volunteers. "The drafting of men for service was given up about six months ago, the government being so unpopular that drafted men deserted immediately and the army practically disappeared. A great number of the higher generals and colonels are Nicaraguans," and when López had to put down a recent rebellion, "four out of five generals sent against the rebels were Nicaraguans."[27]

Although a general staff had been created in 1920, as of 1923 it had yet to begin to function. Some officers were receiving training, the war minister noted, but it was evident that any serious instruction would have to be imparted in a calmer environment; eight men went to Mexico to study at the Colegio Militar de San Jacinto and at the Escuela de Aviación while another three were in training at the Colegio Militar de San Martín in Buenos Aires.[28]

President López was nevertheless unprepared for what was probably the single bloodiest military engagement in the country's history, touched off by the presidential election of October 1923. When none of the three candidates received an absolute majority of votes, the responsibility for choosing a president moved, as the constitution required, to the national congress. Congress failed to act, President López assumed dictatorial powers, and one of the candidates, Tiburcio Carías, declared war on the López government in January 1924. The conditions under which men fought the civil war of 1924 were abominable, according to Gen. Andrés Leiva, an interim war minister of the victorious insurgents. In late 1924 he reminded congressional deputies of "scenes that chilled your soul: soldiers half naked, starving, oppressed by the weight of physical ailments, all of which made them, more than soldiers, a simple pile of cannon fodder." If such soldiers, upon taking a city, "commit abuses and outrages to get whatever way they can some relief from their bodily discomfort," General Leiva declared, they could hardly be blamed. The fault lies in having allowed the soldiers to reach such an extreme state. His solution: "Let us have an the army that is an army." Leiva's line of reasoning sounded much like that of Romero and Anduray eleven years earlier: a more professional and efficient army would guarantee peace. The country had to act at once before another war broke out. "The year 1924 has been a terrible year for the National Army. . . . Let us hope, distinguished deputies, that this will be the last war among brothers."[29]

Leiva's hopes were unavailing. Four years later, Hondurans were still "probably the poorest fighting men in Central America," in the view of U.S. Army Maj. Fred T. Cruse. Except for the Indians of Copán and Santa Barbara, who were "extremely dangerous and courageous fighters with a machete, but hardly even attempt to use their rifles," any Honduran fighting unit was "negligible in combat value." The army was nothing more than an infantry force without an organized supply system or even a supply reserve (with the exception of rifle cartridges). "Regulations provide for the organization of regiments, and brigades, but such units have not existed for years and will probably never be organized again, even on paper.[30]

Major Cruse, like the U.S. military critics who would follow him in the 1940s and 1950s, held up the garrison system as one of the prime impediments to professionalization. The army was "little more than a number of disconnected groups of various sizes garrisoning some of the cities and towns."[31] It seemed plausible that, if a centralized and disciplined chain of command could be adopted there would be less fighting simply because there would be fewer chiefs. So one solution was to eliminate the traditional autonomy of the garrison commanders and impose a single chief whose leadership the entire fighting forces of the country would obey. In theory, of course, there was a central command, but until the 1940s, commanders enjoyed a fair amount of autonomy in the disposition of the forces under their command. The president was forced to acknowledge that autonomy as long as the commanders did not challenge the regime itself.[32]

The leader of the National Party, Tiburcio Carías, took office as president on 1 February 1933 after winning the October 1932 election and the civil war that routinely followed elections. Liberal Party-led uprisings attempted to keep him from taking power, even though the liberal candidate, José Angel Zúñiga Huete, disassociated himself from the revolts. Liberal armed forces captured the San Pedro Sula garrison on 11 November but it was taken back by National forces in a few days. The La Esperanza garrison took up arms under the liberal General Umaña, who was shortly joined by liberal Gen. José María Fonseca; the liberals also held the garrisons in Tela, Santa Bárbara, Nacaome, and Danlí. Then Salvadoran President Hernández-Martínez air-shipped Carías five hundred thousand 11-mm cartridges. In exchange, Carías offered to recognize his government—a generous concession, considering Washington's strong public opposition to recognition. By the first week of December both Fonseca's and Umaña's forces had been defeated. In addition to Hernández-Martínez's timely assistance, air power was a key factor in Carías success, as well as the lack of communications among the scattered liberal forces.[33]

Adopting the same techniques as Generals Ubico and Martínez, in 1936 Carías liquidated the political opposition by jailing, killing, or exiling his enemies and clos-

ing the opposition press. After reporting in detail on his success that year in smash-
ing several uprisings by Honduran military officers and in turning back invasion
forces at the border, Carías's war minister, Juan Manuel Gálvez, concluded with the
by-now familiar refrain of isthmian dictators—there had been no alternative to violence. "It is absolutely certain," declared Gálvez, "although it may hurt to confess it,
that in Honduras as long as her bad children [*malos hijos*] make no honest effort in
favor of good sense and patriotism properly understood, peace has to be imposed
and the happiness of Honduras has to be crafted by means of strong Governments."[34] The following year, more rebellions against the government were put
down in the north, along the Nicaragua frontier, and in the interior department of
Olancho.[35] Like his Guatemalan and Salvadoran counterparts, Carías arranged new
constitutions and special laws allowing him to stay in office beyond his four-year
term. To control his enemies, he introduced the internal passport and developed a
spy network that was particularly welcomed by United Fruit as it confronted
attempts to organize its workers.[36]

Like Leiva, Romero, and Anduray before him, War Minister Gálvez argued
that by modernizing the army, Honduras could eliminate the plague of public violence: "[T]he frequent and almost always unjustified internal struggles in which
Honduras has writhed from independence to today, and which have greatly
depleted the sources of income and held back its evolutionary march toward
progress, are definitely the result of the lack of a truly front-line army" under state
control. To achieve this result, Gálvez reported in 1934, the administration had
already taken steps to "instruct" and "reorganize" the militias, to hire a European
military mission, to teach recruits the rudiments of military science as well as reading and writing, and to overcome "the prejudices, as diffused as they are erroneous,
that exist against obligatory military service among the citizens who are called by
the law to supply it."[37]

The war ministry's desire to improve both the army's potency and its public
image could not be satisfied with the meager political and financial resources at the
disposal of the Honduran state. Thus, first World War II and then the postwar U.S.
policy of communist containment became the deus ex machina of transformation
for the Honduran military. To a certain extent this was true for other Central American states as well, but the impact on Honduras was undoubtedly the most dramatic,
particularly in the creation of its air force, the one branch of military power in which
Honduras excelled from the beginning. The size and quality of the country's fledgling air force exceeded that of its neighbors from the early 1930s, owing in part to the
leadership of the U.S. government, and to the special attention that Carías lavished
on it. In the most mountainous of the five republics, the only one whose capital city
was not linked to a rail line, and the one with the most rudimentary highway system,
an air force would extend the reach of the central government more effectively than
any other single innovation. The Honduran Air Force and its school were commanded by U.S. Army colonels from 1933 until 1947, when the first Honduran, Maj.
Hernán Acosta Mejía, was appointed air force commander.[38] The United States sold
Honduras its three small training planes and five warplanes (including one heavy

bomber-troop transport, three smaller ones suitable for bombing and machine-gunning, and one for pursuit), all of which were radio-equipped.[39] When Carías's suppression of the Liberal Party in 1935 provoked a liberal rebellion in 1936, his little air force helped turn the tide against the liberals, the War Ministry reported: "In more than one clash with the rebel hordes our airplanes decided the victory in favor of the government, sowing panic and death among the former, and supplying the legitimate forces with precise information, giving them pertinent advice, encouraging and helping them with complete effectiveness." This alone justified the expense of a military aviation branch, the ministry added.[40]

In 1940, as director of the aviation school, U.S. Army Reserve Capt. Malcolm F. Stewart was "in absolute command of the Honduran Air Force," the U.S. military attaché reported, and appeared to report directly to President Carías. Captain Stewart "is well thought of by all the pilots, has the confidence of the President, and is doing an outstanding job of training, considering the equipment available." Captain Stewart personally supervised gunnery training, "in which bombs are actually dropped and guns are actually fired," and as the result of requiring similar training to that provided to U.S. airmen, the captain had produced "easily the best air force in Central America," the attaché concluded. Of the school's five other instructors, three were U.S. citizens.[41]

Except for the tiny air force, the national, unified armed forces that successive Honduran administrations had yearned for and sought vainly to build would not emerge for more than a decade; the infantry was still made up "of the very lowest type of *peones*; they are ignorant, dirty and with only occasional parts of a uniform."[42] The new armed forces would owe their existence almost exclusively to the generosity of the United States. And almost immediately, it would follow its three isthmian counterparts by establishing an unchallengable claim to supremacy over any other state institution. By 1957, the improvisational state in Honduras had been "modernized": no civilian party could rule—or even contest an election—without the consent of an institution that scarcely existed in 1947.

6

Nicaragua
A New Army Finds Its Caudillo

[W]e declare that we consider ourselves to be friends to whomever may
be his friends and enemies to whomever may be his enemies.
—Part of a secret blood pact signed by followers of Gen. Anastasio
Somoza García at midnight on 14 November 1933

The public violence that racked Nicaragua until the 1860s drew on the rivalry
between two factions associated respectively with the cities of León and Granada and
the vast hinterlands from which each of them drew their wealth and soldiery. Practically stateless during its first forty years of life, Nicaragua degenerated into little more
than a field of almost constant civil war. It was a country, a government official
lamented in 1853, "in ruin and in rags."[1] Personalism and strongly localized kinship
ties combined with the traditional loyalty owed the *patria chica*, hardening patron-
client alliances and creating a "nefarious dynamic" of destruction.[2] Although historians often analyze Nicaraguan politics as a contest for power between the Liberal
Party and the Conservative Party, expedience was the rule of political affiliation as it
was elsewhere in the isthmus. "Liberals" and "conservatives" throughout Nicaraguan
history have invariably identified themselves with particular factions aligned with
one or another party leader. Ideologically, the leadership of both parties tended to
share the same classically liberal ethos. Factional leaders associated with both parties
routinely pacted with factions of the other party and with regional strongmen. Sec-
toral economic interests were so varied and mobile that the conventional historical-
materialist breakdown of party affiliation according to, among other things, "coffee,"
"cattle," or "capital," cannot be sustained without serious qualifications.[3]

The result of interfactional strife over control of this polity was near-anarchy.
From 1824 until the 1860s, according to historian Knut Walter, Nicaragua's "central
government as such ceased to function. Nominally, government posts and offices

and constitutions and laws existed, but in practice political power reverted to landed families that dominated their respective regions." Politics were "nonnational."[4]

Just how nonnational and patrimonial Nicaraguan politics had become can be illustrated by a decision made by Francisco Castellón, the Liberal Party candidate for president in 1853, who had lost the election to Fruto Chamorro of the Conservative Party. On 28 December 1854, in an act that would reorder Nicaraguan politics for decades, Castellón signed a contract with California newspaper publisher Byron Cole that obligated Cole to produce three hundred U.S. mercenary soldiers for the Liberal Party, which was then at war with the Conservative Party. Six months later, the leaders of the Liberal Party welcomed the fifty-eight-man army of Tennessee lawyer "Colonel" William Walker to León. In short order, Walker astutely pacted with three regional *caudillos*, whose men joined his army. After Walker's combined U.S. and Nicaraguan forces captured Grenada on 13 October, he was hailed by many Nicaraguans—including the bishop of León—as the country's savior. Authorities in both Granada and León appointed him head of state. By March 1856, Walker controlled the country with a largely Nicaraguan army that included more than 1,000 Americans and 250 Cubans, whose leader joined the Tennessean in exchange for Walker's promise to lead a Cuban war of independence against Spain. Walker had himself elected president of Nicaragua in July.

Not until 12–13 September did enough Nicaraguan liberals and conservatives manage to overcome their differences and unite against Walker. Meeting in León, they signed the Pacto Providencial. By usurping power, Walker had, of course, betrayed his employer, the Liberal Party. And in response, liberals had little choice but to unite with their conservative archenemies to launch the patriotic "Guerra Nacional." The Pacto Providencial brought anti-Walker armies into the country from elsewhere in the isthmus, leading to Walker's defeat and his surrender on 1 May 1857 to a U.S. Navy captain. The three regional *caudillos* with whom the Tennessean had pacted in 1855 fought by his side until the end.[5]

The Pacto Providencial opened a singular era in Nicaraguan history. Men who identified themselves with any faction of liberalism or conservatism, or with León or Granada, overcame forty years of violent hostility and cooperated by sharing power for some three decades. The signers of the Pact agreed, in relevant part, that "There will be a general forgetting of the past and of any hostile act that the parties may have committed. There will be no criminal responsibility for official acts by the functionaries of either part up to this date."[6] That a catastrophic war might persuade former enemies to adopt a more conciliatory attitude is not surprising. What remains impressive about the Pacto Providencial is its durability, for Nicaragua was ruled according to its principles until the early 1890s. Such a record of largely peaceful, nondictatorial, and bipartisan government could be favorably compared, in the history of nineteenth-century Latin America, only to Chile and Costa Rica. What accounts for the durability of the Nicaraguan peace, above all in a country that, both before 1856 and after 1893, exemplified the much more familiar characteristics of Central American public violence?

Cruz's explanation for the long peace emphasized the horrific destruction of the National War, the absolute impoverishment of what was left of the national governing apparatus, and the shame of having practically lost the country itself to men of another race, another culture, another nationality. That was a risk that no other Central American country had yet come close to experiencing; perhaps only Mexico, whose government was removed by a French army and replaced with an Austrian monarch, had approached anything like it in all of Latin America. "The devastation and carnage had traumatized the Nicaraguans." As a result, a spirit of both conciliation and contrition seemed to animate the constitutional convention that met in 1857–58, as representatives of both Granada (now a "burned-out ruin") and León (whose politicians were now almost ostentatiously repentant) framed a constitution that protected the traditional interests of both regions and even divided the Supreme Court into a León branch and a Grenada branch. By making national elections more competitive, the constitution forced political candidates to campaign, "and not just amongst their clubmates in their own city." Each of the country's seven departments was headed by a presidentially appointed prefect with extraordinary powers—in effect a "minipresident" who acted as a liaison between the national and the local governments.[7]

The new arrangement seemed to strengthen the legitimacy of regional authorities, leaving the central government with little formal power in their jurisdictions. The prefectures weakened both the presidency and the municipality, for from their offices in the *cabeceras* (headtowns) of their departments, the prefects were the treasury agents of their respective departments, as well as the "*canton* chiefs, the *jueces de agricultura y de la mesta* (agricultural and cattlemen's judges), and the head of the police." Although the military *comandante* and the magistrates were constitutionally independent of the prefect, in practice the prefect tended to control them.[8] The autonomy of the prefect may be further gauged by considering what Cruz called the "thinness" of the Nicaraguan state, which in the late 1870s counted on a mere sixty-eight officials in its executive (including the army) and judicial branches, who supervised just eighty-eight central-government employees (not counting the army).[9]

Pleased with their newfound capacity for peaceful self-government, the Nicaraguans even allowed what passed for its national army to shrink to no more than 434 officers and men by the early 1860s. It was an "army," according to Cruz, that still "revolved entirely around the personality of the *caudillo*, as Nicaragua's many ad hoc armies and bands had done in the past. . . . From top to bottom, the army was entirely personal, not professional," and for once the weakness and fragmentation of the fighting forces was seen as a strength.[10] According to Levy, garrisons could be found that were intended mainly to keep order and watch for contraband, military commanders could be found in each *cabecera*, and a special military unit deployed in the name of the national government was dedicated exclusively to protecting the treasury. But rarely were more than a thousand men under arms at any one time across the country. In the event of war, conscription was imposed, but because of the lack of any reliable census data, recruiters simply seized "all the day laborers and poor people they meet," releasing them only if they could prove that they had been formally exempted from service. When the better-off class of men wished to serve, they did so as officers. This kind of recruitment system wreaked havoc with the economy and family life. "Many times, those who fear being drafted live entire months hidden in the woods, living miserably, to avoid having to serve. When the danger is over, most of the militiamen return to their homes." The typical soldier, "perhaps through a failure of discipline, lacks impetuous boldness; little trained in maneuvers and in the handling of his weapons, he aims poorly, hollers a lot, and breaks rank as soon as an action begins. Battles always take the form of guerrilla combat." The most common military crime was desertion and the most common disciplinary problem drunkenness.[11]

The government's fighting forces had little artillery and even fewer fortified places from which to fire it. Twenty-two cannons were divided between the fort overlooking the San Juan River and the abandoned fort at San Carlos. They were the only forts in the country, because those in Granada had fallen into ruin. During civil wars, downtown Granada was fortified by means of trenches cut across all the streets going into the plaza: "The houses above the barricades are crenellated, and the combination of houses and trenches forms a redoubt capable of resisting an assault."[12] Not until 1885, when Nicaragua was forced to mobilize its 652 officers and men against the threat of invasion by an army of Guatemalans reputed to number 30,000, did the leaders of the conservative republic begin to take seriously the construction of a national army. Although the Guatemalan threat evaporated, Nicaragua's government reacted by taking steps to establish a military academy, an artillery school, a permanent expeditionary force within the army, and an army double in size.[13]

Chastened by the realization that their failure to govern themselves for four decades had nearly led to the liquidation of their country, the political class made two moves that ushered in the long peace: They adopted both an attitude of cooperation and a set of institutions designed to encourage cooperation and bipartisan rule, as different factions of both parties (and both regions) shared power under seven consecutive Conservative presidents (most of whom were ideologically liberal) associated with Grenada and its hinterland. The immediate effect was to dampen personalist rivalries while multiplying the opportunities available to notables in different localities to accumulate "power and prestige," according to Cruz. In an ambience of toleration governed by a mutual disposition to pardon old grievances and insults, political affiliations remained remarkably fluid.[14]

Of course, the era of the "conservative republic" was not entirely free of the public violence that had tormented the country before Walker. In 1863, government forces easily put down a coup attempt by Gen. Máximo Jerez, a León liberal who fought for Walker and served briefly in his cabinet. After he was allowed to return from exile from Costa Rica and take a Senate seat in 1868, General Jerez pacted with—of all people—Gen. Tomás Martínez, the conservative hero of the war against Walker and the man who, as president in 1863, had defeated Jerez. Together, the two *caudillos* launched a war in 1869 that lasted four months and nearly succeeded in overthrowing the government. Five years later, General Jerez launched his third and final unsuccessful attempt to overthrow a conservative president. The only other significant threat to national peace occurred in 1881, when Indians aggrieved by the adoption of a series of classically liberal economic development measures seized Matagalpa and rioted. Three years later, an antigovernment conspiracy that apparently united disaffected Indians, liberals, and conservatives was broken up.[15]

None of these events, however, could account for the relapse that awaited Nicaragua in the 1890s. The long peace was fatally undermined by Roberto Sacasa, a conservative from León who succeeded to the presidency upon the death of Pres. Evaristo Carazo on 1 August 1889. Carazo's constitutional successor proceeded to violate all the most important rules that had been so carefully constructed in the late 1850s. Rejecting the principle of regional balance, Sacasa—the first man from León to govern since the Walker debacle—immediately packed his administration with cronies from the León region. A spirit of revenge against Granada for having monopolized the presidency for four decades seemed to motivate Sacasa, a francophile whose personal vanity and arrogance further divided him from the Granada wing of the party. The most telling sign of recidivism was Sacasa's decision, three months after taking office, to dispatch his own *montonera* to disarm and occupy the Granada garrison a few weeks before local elections were to take place. He wanted to humiliate and intimidate the conservative faction that Sacasa now counted as his mortal enemy. Granada's notables (including four former presidents) signed a proclamation denouncing Sacasa's move, further reviving old regional hatreds.

Then, arguing that because he had not been elected to office, he needn't follow the rule of nonsuccession, Sacasa announced his candidacy for the presidential election of 5 October 1890. He also announced an expansion of the army to five thousand men and used the opportunity to forcibly recruit his political enemies. After winning the election, Sacasa arrested the leaders of the Granadan conservatives, who reacted on 28 April 1893 by declaring an insurrection against Sacasa. The liberals of Managua, following José Santos Zelaya, joined the conservative insurgents from Granada, and together they gained the upper hand, organizing a *junta* that was nevertheless dominated by Managuan liberals. The *junta* fell apart after forces associated with León revolted and declared war on Granada and Managua. Pacting with the leaders of the León revolt, Zelaya organized a rival *junta*, and on 27 July his forces seized Managua. With the surrender of the conservatives of Granada, their republic finally collapsed.[16]

For a generation, the limits of Nicaraguan public violence had shrunk because the traditional agents of public violence had achieved something practically unheard of in the four northern republics: an all-inclusive pact of the country's main political contenders. Their successors were determined to live by it for more than three decades. As a result, the Nicaraguan state shed its improvisational character and achieved a stable legitimacy, the likes of which would not be seen again until the 1960s.

But what kept Nicaragua from staying on the Costa Rican path? The answer likely has to do with the event that triggered the long peace, the National War. By the

late 1880s, the leaders who were traumatized by it had yielded to a younger generation for whom the war, now a distant memory, could not have inspired the same
determination to avoid violent conflict. Moreover, the economic prosperity that the
long peace and government spending on public works had helped to incite produced a class of men whose desire for government employment conflicted with the
Granadan conservatives' preference for tight budgets and lean bureaucracies. In
addition, by monopolizing the presidency for so long, the Granadans needlessly
antagonized the residents of León, to say nothing of Managua.[17]

Despite Zelaya's commitment to an election of delegates to a constitutional
convention, he issued the following statement on 11 August 1893 on behalf of the
junta that he headed: "The Liberal Party of Nicaragua presents itself today, after its
splendid victory, desirous of putting into practice its principles, which are the only
ones that should govern men and which are the basis on which the prosperity of the
nations will rest."[18] If liberal principles were indeed the only ones that should govern men, elections were unnecessary and the enemies of liberalism must be the enemies of mankind. A year later, following the adoption of the new constitution, President Zelaya confided to his fellow liberal *golpista*, Pres. Policarpo Bonilla of
Honduras, his obsession with rooting out "a powerful enemy: Conservatism," not
just in Nicaragua but elsewhere in Central America. In words that echoed those used
by Montúfar when he chided the pre-1840 liberal rulers of Guatemala for their fussy
compliance with the constitutional rights of the conservatives, Zelaya asserted that
his own constitution was rather impractical for a country like Nicaragua. Not only
were the conservatives manipulating it to gain power but the constitution also gave
too much power to the municipalities, which were even raising independent armed
forces that could challenge his hold on national power. He was faced, he told Bonilla,
with two alternatives: scandalize the country by acting unconstitutionally or sus-
pend the constitution and "remain in Dictatorship." The latter "seems to me to be
the most correct step."[19]

Zelaya's preoccupation with what a later generation would call "internal security" would be disclosed more specifically in legislation that his government issued
two months after he wrote to Bonilla. The new law repealed the 1858 regulations
governing the prefect, who was replaced by a *jefe político* appointed by the president
to govern a department for a two-year term. The *jefe*'s "main effort must be directed
toward preventing disorder, uncovering and choking in its infancy every tendency
that disturbs or threatens public security." Among other security-related responsibilities, the *jefe* was authorized to request military support from the local *comandante de armas*, issue passports, keep account of any assistance provided to government troops by individuals in his department, maintain "la seguridad pública" in
the event of "uprisings, riots or tumultuous meetings" by using force if necessary,
maintain regular police patrols, move into populated areas anyone living unlawfully
in the countryside, destroy vacant huts that might be used by criminals, and report
annually to the central government the names and personal details of the owners of
all hunting weapons. The list of the *jefe político*'s functions went on for seventeen
book pages. He also enjoyed immunity from the regular system of prosecution:

"Infractions committed by the *Jefes Políticos* will be administratively corrected by the Executive Branch, with reprimands or fines of five to twenty-five pesos."[20]

Although evidently preserving the conservative republic's policy of delegating almost unlimited powers to provincial headmen accountable solely to the president, the new legislation seemed to significantly reduce the prefects' freedom of action that had so impressed Levy. Zelaya's intention was not to respect the local autonomy treasured by the conservatives but to limit it as much as possible by centralizing power in his own hands. The fact that Zelaya succeeded in staying in office far longer than any of his predecessors—or, for that matter, than any of his successors except for Anastasio Somoza García—suggests that the legislation was at least partially effective.[21] In 1905, the *jefe político* of the department of Jerez, Rafael Caldera, also served as its *comandante de armas* (military chief). His thirteen *comandantes locales* and two *subcomandantes locales* helped Caldera oversee what he called a "fuerza armada" consisting of 303 soldiers, 7 second lieutenants, 7 lieutenants, and 3 captains. All the local commandants were under orders to file daily reports of events in their jurisdictions, a measure that allowed Caldera to maintain discipline and order throughout the department.[22]

It would be wrong, however, to infer from Zelaya's apparent success in centralizing power the achievement of some new level of consensus or legitimacy. Within three years of seizing power, he was nearly driven out of office by a revolt led by fellow liberals. The León-based insurgents had played a decisive role in Zelaya's victory in 1893 and as a result they held important positions in his government, including the vice presidency and the leadership of the National Assembly. But Zelaya represented the Managua faction of liberalism, and the *leoneses* thought it was their turn to have the presidency. As the discontent of the León faction deepened, Zelaya initially chose to conciliate them. On 21 February 1896 he signed a power-sharing agreement with their representatives, who nonetheless mounted a rebellion only five days later. Identifying themselves as aggrieved "westerners," they constituted themselves as the National Assembly, removed Zelaya from office, appointed a new president, and declared a national state of siege. A proclamation signed by turncoat *jefes políticos* and *comandantes militares* accused Zelaya of violating individual freedoms, arrogating to himself judicial and legislative functions, and making himself a dictator. In mid-March, troops loyal to Zelaya, reinforced by Honduran government forces, defeated the insurgents decisively. Zelaya singled out the *comandantes de armas* of the departments of León, Chinandega, Matagalpa, Jinotega, and Estelí for special condemnation because of their disloyalty. The rebellious departments were deprived of much of the jurisdictional authority that they had enjoyed, as Zelaya seized the opportunity to further concentrate power in Managua.[23] Perhaps the most surprising aspect of the uprising was the loyalty to Zelaya's government of the Granada-based Conservative Party. In the struggle for power, men seemed to betray one another or stay loyal, to proclaim rebellions or defend incumbents, less out of ideological commitment or devotion to some communal economic interest than according to shifting calculations of firepower and troop strength at the disposition of one element or another—calculations that were heavily weighted by kinship and regional identity.

Thus the improvisational character of the state, whose agents were faced with the continuous task of maintaining and reassembling enough coercive power to protect their control of the state, often required crossing national borders. Zelaya put down internal revolts led by liberal generals in 1899 and 1903, and in 1906 he joined forces with Honduran insurgents against Pres. Manuel Bonilla of Honduras. Zelaya's attack on the Honduran government drew a counterattack by Salvadoran government forces in alliance with Bonilla, as well as attacks on Nicaraguan towns by Honduran government forces. By March 1907, Salvadoran troops were on the march in Nicaragua against Zelaya and in Honduras with Bonilla; Nicaraguans and insurgent Hondurans were closing in on Tegucigalpa, the Honduran capital; and Honduran government forces were occupying scattered Nicaraguan territory. In April, with Nicaraguan-backed Honduran insurgents in control of Tegucigalpa, Bonilla fled Honduras on a boat bound for Acapulco. The leading Honduran rebel, Gen. Miguel R. Dávila, took over the Honduran presidency. The war ended when Nicaragua and El Salvador signed a peace treaty aboard the U.S. cruiser *Chicago* on 23 April.[24]

The revolt that would finally undo Zelaya was led in 1909 by the liberal general, Juan José Estrada, whom Zelaya had appointed governor of Zelaya, the megadepartment comprising the eastern third of the country that the president had named after himself a year after seizing power. This time leading conservatives joined the insurgent liberals. The U.S. government, correctly identifying Zelaya as the region's main agent of international violence and intrigue, joined the uprising. Zelaya resigned in 1910. During the U.S. protectorate that followed, from 1911 to 1927, Washington indirectly managed Nicaragua through a series of conservative governments that were protected from liberal attempts to overthrow it by a U.S. Marine unit ostensibly sent to guard the U.S. legation in Managua.

Apart from Panama, no place in Central America has interested the United States as much as Nicaragua, whose lacustrine and riverine geography made it, like Panama, a relatively low-cost site for the construction of a transoceanic canal. However, the U.S. decision to build the canal in Panama in 1903 only transformed Yankee covetousness into something that may have been still worse for the Nicaraguans— an endless determination by Washington to prevent its favorable geography from being exploited as the site of a second, competing transoceanic canal by a rival great power. For more than a century, therefore, Nicaragua's relationship with the United States has been radically different from that of the other four republics. Its status more nearly approached that of a protectorate or semi-colony, like Panama itself, or like Haiti, the Dominican Republic, and Cuba until the 1930s. As a result, Nicaraguan military collaboration with the United States exceeds in age and intimacy that of the other Central American republics.

After Washington assisted in the removal of Zelaya from power, Nicaragua failed to achieve the level of independent stability and respect for U.S. policy prefer-

ences that the United States hoped for. The conservatives depended almost completely on the United States for their continued hold on power. Thus after 1910
Nicaraguan liberals became "anti-interventionists," because to remove the conservatives by definition meant questioning the U.S. domination of Nicaragua and
directly challenging the Marine guard. In 1921, a liberal-affiliated newspaper linked
prostitution to what it said were more than thirty-five cases of syphilis among the
Marines; twenty-two Marines retaliated by breaking into the paper's offices and
damaging some of its property.[25] But by then Washington was less anti-liberal, and
more interested in achieving bipartisan stability, than it had been in the immediate
aftermath of the Zelaya administration. The United States encouraged the ruling
conservatives to allow their opponents an opportunity to seek public office through
elections. Washington criticized the conservative government for not taking more
aggressive measures to ensure fair and competitive elections. After U.S.-proposed
electoral reforms were adopted in 1923, the United States decided to withdraw the
Marine legation guard once a new government was elected. But the incumbent
administration ignored or abrogated parts of the new electoral law and resorted to
the customary deceptions in order to ensure the victory in October 1924 of its
favorite, the newborn Conservative-Republican Party. The latter was the outcome of
a pact between José Solórzano, the leader of a Managua-based conservative faction
considered to be "progressive," and a Liberal Party faction headed by Juan Bautista
Sacasa of León, who became Solórzano's vice presidential running mate. A liberal
faction headed by Luís Corea of Managua contested the election as the Liberal-
Republican Party; the Granada-based Conservative Party nominated ex-president
Gen. Emiliano Chamorro. Despite the obvious fraud, Washington reluctantly recognized the Solórzano-Sacasa administration as the constitutional government,
and on 1 August 1925 fulfilled its promise to withdraw the legation guard. Nicaragua
was without a U.S. military presence for the first time since 1912.[26]

Proving almost immediately the efficacy of the Marines' stabilizing influence,
General Chamorro overthrew the governing coalition on 25 October. He let Solórzano, the conservative apostate, stay in office temporarily as his puppet but exiled
the liberal Sacasa. After purging the Congress, Chamorro made it appoint him president. Washington refused to recognize Chamorro's obviously unconstitutional
government. Sacasa went straight to Washington, seeking the State Department's
blessing on an armed movement to overthrow the usurper. State replied that it preferred "moral pressure" against Chamorro rather than military force, but in May
1926 Sacasa's liberals launched a war on Chamorro's government. Desperate for
material support against a superior enemy, Sacasa negotiated a pact with the president of Mexico, Plutarco Elías Calles, under which Mexico would give "direct and
active support" to Sacasa's insurgency in return for legislation that would not only
advance Mexican diplomatic and economic interests in Central America but would
also impose on Nicaragua the "social and political program" of Mexico's revolutionary government. Calles duly shipped Mexican arms and even a few Mexican soldiers
to Sacasa's forces, turning a hopeless cause into a hotly fought stalemate. U.S.
Marines returned to the eastern port city of Bluefields to protect U.S. property and

the lives of U.S. and other foreign citizens. Under pressure from the United States, Chamorro resigned on 31 October in favor of an old friend of U.S. interests, Adolfo Díaz, who as vice-president succeeded President Estrada upon his resignation in 1911 and governed the country until 1916.

Once again Washington found itself protecting a government of questionable legitimacy from the *montoneras* of a deposed government of equally questionable legitimacy. Correctly attributing Sacasa's military successes to Mexican support and citing the danger that Mexican influence posed to the region's stability and to U.S. economic and diplomatic interests (including "the Nicaraguan canal route"), Pres. Calvin Coolidge authorized the reinforcement of the U.S. military force in Nicaragua in January 1927. By March, some two thousand Marines had established "neutral zones" that excluded the contenders' armed forces. Liberal commanders—including Augusto C. Sandino—who were eager to avoid a confrontation with the United States "courteously received American officers in their camps," but despite favoring Díaz's forces, Washington was in no position to turn back the liberal tide. So in May the United States brokered a peace agreement between the liberals and the Díaz government that provided for elections in 1928 (under U.S. supervision) and the creation of a "constabulary"—a police force organized on military lines—headed by U.S. officers.[27]

The commander of the Liberal Party's armies, Gen. José María Moncada, agreed to the terms on 12 May. All his men surrendered their weapons to the United States except for Sandino, who on the same day pledged to resist "the Barbaric colossus of the North." But few Nicaraguans showed any interest in fighting the Marines, and most of Sandino's men deserted their *caudillo*. Even before the month of May was out, "Sandino's cause looked hopeless—even to him." In response to a plea from General Moncada to surrender, Sandino first demanded that the United States remove all Nicaraguan office holders, establish a U.S. military government, and supervise an honest election. The nationalist *caudillo* appears to have concluded rather quickly that, if he could not get rid of the "Barbaric colossus," he might at least use it to drive Díaz from office. But Washington declined Sandino's invitation to take over the country. "Rebuffed, Sandino felt his honor left him no other course but to resist the Marines." Issuing one anti-imperialist manifesto after another, Sandino's resistance attracted recruits and drew the admiration of leading public figures in Latin America and the United States.[28] By the time Moncada was elected president and took office on 1 January 1929, the total number of U.S. military forces in Nicaragua had climbed to five thousand. Most of them were Marines sent to defeat Sandino, who vowed to continue fighting until all the U.S. armed forces left the country. He achieved his goal on 2 January 1933 when the last Marine embarked at Corinto.[29]

But now, unlike its first withdrawal in 1925, the Marines left behind the National Guard, a robust new institution that rapidly displaced all competitors. Until it was liquidated in 1979 by an insurgency named for Sandino, the Guard effectively eliminated the need for another U.S. military intervention. The Guard was thus not only the first substantive experiment in U.S.-Central American military collaboration, but the most successful. The groundwork had been laid by the Convention for the Limitation of Armaments, which Nicaragua had signed with the other Central American countries in February 1923. That fall, the Nicaraguan government was told that the Marines would be withdrawn after the 1924 elections, and reminded that to prevent any "disorder or instability" that might follow the Marine withdrawal, the State Department might be able to help the Nicaraguan government organize a constabulary should it wish to carry out Article II of the Convention.[30] The Nicaraguan government's acceptance of this offer inspired what the U.S. military attaché called a "cry of indignation" against the project and "an almost universal disapproval" among Nicaraguans. The U.S. plan provided for a constabulary that would completely replace the existing army and police forces, and that included active-duty U.S. Marines as training officers. Public opinion appeared to favor the creation of a force that was strictly limited to police duties, but in which retired U.S. officers might be hired as nonranking instructors. On 14 May 1925 the newly seated Nicaraguan Congress rejected the U.S. plan, and instead authorized the formation of a National Guard that would coexist with the army and could hire foreign trainers. The new law did not mention any formal cooperation with the U.S. government. Washington finally agreed to arrange for U.S. civilian instructors to train the newly created Guard under contract with the Nicaraguan government.[31]

Retired U.S. Army Maj. Calvin B. Carter, formerly an officer in the Philippine constabulary, arrived on 30 June 1925 to begin work as the chief trainer. He organized a 295-man National Guard without experienced officers and without enough weapons, ammunition, or even clothing and barracks for the recruits. Pressed into service against General Moncada's liberal the army during the 1926–27 civil war, the Guard scarcely survived the war. In terms virtually identical to those that the Nicaraguan Congress had rejected in 1925, the U.S.-mediated peace agreement of 1927 committed Nicaragua to concede to the U.S. Marines the responsibility of creating a National Guard, with Marines as the Guard's initial officer corps. U.S. Marine Lt. Col. R. Y. Rhea assumed command of Carter's bedraggled little force on 21 May 1927, retaining 160 of its men and discharging the remaining 190. The reorganized Guard's character as a U.S. Marine operation was now unmistakable: "The principle that Marine Officers and N.C.O.s shall not be placed in positions subordinate to natives will be strictly adhered to," the U.S. military attaché declared.[32] Lieutenant Colonel Rhea's General Order No. 1 showed that an old chimera still haunted U.S. policy: "One of the most essential facts to make this organization a national one is, first and last, that it shall be nonpartisan in every sense of the word. If this is not true it can not possibly carry out the services and duties for which it is duly authorized and intended. Politics has its place and power but must never control the military or police organization of a country. The organization of the National Police of a country is for the maintenance of peace, law and order."[33]

Until 1929, the war against Sandino's army was fought not by Rhea's Nicaraguans but by a Marine combat brigade of more than thirty-five hundred men. As the National Guard matured, growing to 2,090 by April 1929, it began to take over the battle against Sandino. Most of the Marines went home that year, and in early

1930 the Guardia took over all remaining Marine combat duties. At the same time, Nicaraguan officers replaced U.S. Marine officers in the Guardia, a shift no doubt accelerated by the fact that Nicaraguan Guardsmen mutinied ten times against their Marine officers, killing five of them, apparently in response to Yankee insults and humiliations.[34]

Nicaragua thus became the only country on the isthmus to implement the 1923 Convention for the Limitation of Armaments provision obligating the signatories to establish National Guards and to consider employing foreign trainers for this purpose. The Convention said the National Guards should "cooperate with the existing Armies" but did not say the Guards should replace them. Nicaragua had gone a step farther, eliminating an army altogether (more precisely, eliminating references to a formal army, which did not exist) while establishing something unique in Central America—a force that combined the functional characteristics of both a military and a police unit, and would thus provide any future despot with a range of control that Zelaya would have envied.

The Guard received its first Nicaraguan "Jefe Director," as the commander was called, on 2 January 1933. Both the Marine commander and the U.S. diplomatic mission recommended the appointment of Anastasio Somoza García, a liberal general who had fought at Moncada's side and became his undersecretary of foreign affairs when Moncada became president in 1929. By now, the U.S. military attaché had learned something about Nicaraguan politics and accurately predicted the fate of Washington's constabulary. "General Somoza," Maj. A. R. Harris reported, "is energetic and clever but not too honest, and should, provided his political inclinations do not interfere with his duties as Commandant of the Guardia, make an excellent officer in charge of that organization. However, this office can not conceive ANY prominent Nicaraguan liberal keeping an organization as important as the Guardia on neutral ground. It is believed that under General Somoza's command the Guardia will develop into a highly efficient *LIBERAL* force."[35]

The assassination of Sandino in 1934, an act widely credited to Sandino's fellow liberal Anastasio Somoza, left Nicaragua, for the first time in decades, with a single armed force that would not be credibly challenged again until the late 1970s. Somoza converted the Guard into a personal instrument of power—in effect, a party militia—that he used to gain the presidency in 1937 and then to establish a dynastic succession of rule that endured until the overthrow of his son, Pres. Anastasio Somoza Debayle by self-declared successors of Augusto Sandino on 19 July 1979.[36]

While the Guard and its Marine allies were locked in combat with Sandino's guerrillas in January 1932, Conservative Party leader Carlos Cuadra Pasos gave a talk to students at the Universidad de Granada. One of Nicaragua's most distinguished intellectuals, Cuadra Pasos looked back on his country's political history and drew his audience's attention to the two most noteworthy features of its politics. First was what he called "the illness that most urgently requires medicine in our constitutional system," namely the pattern of bloody confrontation between two political parties, with one of them governing and the other outlawed by the incumbent party. Owing to the fact that, for the incumbent party, nothing could be more disgraceful than losing the presidency, politics was always a matter of civil war in which "Power is never acquired, it is conquered." The second problem, he said, was the fact that the president had been a dictator in whom all power resided. It was thus that simple people appropriately called the president "El Gobierno"— The Government. "If a common man greets the President, he says: 'I greeted the Government.' All the other collaborators of the Executive are overshadowed and nullified."[37] Perhaps Major Harris had been in the audience. In any event, the chimera of a politically neutral force capable of upholding constitutional principles disappeared from the imaginations of U.S. policy makers for good. The idea must have seemed preposterous to the Nicaraguans. Somoza's performance as *Jefe Director* of the new Guardia Nacional followed precisely the traditional logic explained by Cuadra Pasos: political conquest, proscription of the opposition, one-party rule, and an all-powerful presidency.

Before the end of his first year as Guardia director, Somoza faced calls for his dismissal. In response, a Guardia captain, Francisco B. Rueda, arranged blood pacts in which Guardia officers secretly pledged their absolute fidelity to the general. Meeting at midnight on 14 November 1933, five Guardia officers (a captain, a first lieutenant, and three second lieutenants) posted at Rivas signed, at Rueda's instigation, what they called "the following pact of honor, whose slogan is 'we for the general and the general for us.' We commit ourselves to strengthen by as many means as possible the solidarity that until now we have had with Major General Anastasio Somoza, G.N., first because of our military duty and second because of the personal affection that we profess for him; we declare that we consider ourselves to be friends to whomever may be his friends and enemies to whomever may be his enemies." Whenever Somoza may be in danger of being dismissed "we will declare that we do not accept any other Chief, reserving to ourselves the right to make the most effective protest." If transferred to other places, the signatories agreed to attempt to arrange other pacts like this one, though without disclosing the existence of the pact they were about to sign. The penalty for failing to comply with the pact did not have to be specified with great exactitude: "Whenever any of us fails to comply with what is stipulated here, the rest of us commit ourselves to punish this failure in the most severe manner. In the same way we commit ourselves to keep absolutely secret what is agreed here. When any of us withdraws from service he will be relieved of the obligations contained herein, but of course he will not reveal even a single letter of what is agreed to here." The pact would be valid until Somoza decided to withdraw voluntarily to private life. It concluded: "All the undersigned declare: 'All for one and one for all.'"[38]

Apparently not fully trustful of the Guardia, Somoza reached beyond it to create a one-hundred-man company of "Auxiliares" commanded by Mexican Gen. Juan Escamilla. "Serving in conjunction with Guardia troops, where and when needed, they have been taken from the civilian population, furnished with Government arms (but not uniformed) and were paid from Guardia funds."[39]

In 1936, though he was constitutionally ineligible to be a presidential candidate, Somoza used Guard forces loyal to him to drive President Sacasa from office before his term expired, then pressured the Congress to appoint a Somoza flunky as interim president. Somoza continued to use his power as Guard director to intimidate the opposition and win election as president later that year and still retain his position as Guard director. In his election "campaign," Somoza softened up the opposition with the Camisas Azules (Blueshirts), a gang of thugs evidently modeled on Hitler's brownshirts, who were trained by the Guardia and supplied with government money and identity cards. Another Somoza party militia was the Liga Militar Liberal Nacionalista (Nationalist Liberal Military League). After 1936 the members of the Liga became National Guard auxiliaries, some twenty-six hundred men with special identity cards.[40] The Auxiliares, the Camisas Azules, and the Liga were the Nicaraguan versions of El Salvador's Legión Nacional Pro-Patria and its Guardias Cívicas, and the counterpart of Ubico's efforts to militarize civilian institutions in Guatemala.

The political logic described by Cuadra Pasos, and the public violence that accompanied it, were practiced everywhere in Central America. What was unique to the Nicaraguans was the Guardia Nacional, upon whose continued existence as a modern, professional, and "nonpartisan" monopolizer of legitimate violence the United States rested its hopes for a politically stable future. After taking office in 1937, President Somoza made the Guardia the backbone of his government, routinely appointing its officers to nonmilitary posts, including those of director of the railroad (nationalized in 1937), the public health agency, and the mail and telegraph system. The militarization of these activities gave Somoza more control of the bureaucracy while providing an opportunity for him to reward loyal Guardia officers with promotions and opportunities for graft.[41] At the same time, the new administration threatened its enemies—foreign and domestic—by boasting of the Guardia's political intelligence capabilities. Its Departamento de Inteligencia claimed it was "the eyes of the army that constantly look and scrutinize" and could "acquire records on every person who seeks to leave the Country and if those records do not correspond to the morality of the individual who wants to travel abroad, his passport will be denied, ... The same applies to the foreigners who visit us. If they do not correspond to the purposes that every civilized country seeks they will be denied entry."[42]

Despite the violence that Somoza had used to open the path to the presidency in 1936, and the utter collapse of any pretense that the U.S.-created Guardia might be a nonpartisan instrument of law and order, President Somoza immediately "developed a good working relationship" with the Roosevelt administration. In January 1939, shortly after Somoza had announced his intention to produce a new constitution that would extend his term of office to 1 May 1947, President Roosevelt even invited Somoza to visit him in Washington.[43] "Dictator Somoza," as Time's report on the visit called him, was received on 5 May with extraordinary honors by President Roosevelt, his cabinet and the chief justice of the Supreme Court. In the lead story in Time's "National Affairs" section, headlined "Wonderful Turnout," Somoza's arrival was reported with a sly blend of contempt for Somoza and his country, and amazement at the incongruous majesty of his reception:

Brigadier General Maxwell Murray, commander of the Washington Provisional Brigade, ascended to the dome of the Capitol one day last week and trained a pair of high-powered binoculars down on Pennsylvania Avenue. Lining the street on both sides, all the way to the White House, was a solid wall of U.S. soldiers and marines. Behind the walls massed the Washington populace, patrolled by 751 policemen, 400 firemen. Overhead roared nine flying fortresses, 42 Army pursuit ships [sic]. Drawn up from the Capitol to Union Station were more soldiers, and filling the station plaza were cavalry, 30 tanks, a battery of artillery. General Murray looked at all these preparations, for which he was responsible, with anxious, critical eye.

Up to the station in cutaway & silk hat drove Franklin Roosevelt, beaming. "It's wonderful!" said he to Major Ernest Brown, Washington's police superintendent. "It's a great turnout and I am so pleased!"

Pleased too was the swart, chunky gentleman for whom this swankest military-State reception in Washington history had been staged by Franklin Roosevelt. He was only General Anastasio Somoza, President of little Nicaragua (pop. 1,133,000), but this show for him was in all details preceisely the reception planned for King George & Queen Elizabeth of mighty Great Britain next month. Fact that it was a dress rehearsal for that occasion did not diminish the fact that it came first, that it was as handsome a performance as any Latin-American heart could desire, that it was a gesture intended to honor all the Good Neighbors as well as Nicaragua.

Mrs. Roosevelt, Vice President & Mrs. Garner, the Cabinet (with only two absent), Chief Justice Hughes all followed Franklin Roosevelt in handshaking General Somoza & wife at the station. The artillery banged a 21-gun salute. With 15 tanks in front, 15 behind, the Presidential car led a parade up to the Capitol, around its plaza, down Pennsylvania Avenue to the White House. Franklin Roosevelt had assured the presence of throngs by having all Federal employes excused from work from 11 a.m. to 1 p.m. Military strictness prevailed. Officers wore their medals & decorations....[44]

The *New York Times* observed that this was the first time that President Roosevelt had ever left the White House to greet a foreign head of state, and that the parade's spectators outnumbered those who attended his first inaugural in 1933. After a state dinner at the White House that evening, President Somoza and his wife, Salvadora DeBayle, were overnight guests of the Roosevelts.[45] Three days later, on 8 May, the U.S. Senate and then the House welcomed Somoza for separate, fifteen-minute speeches, each differently worded, but both aimed at persuading Congress to build a canal across Nicaragua. His country was eager to contribute to hemispheric security by exploiting Nicaragua's favorable geography, its "most valuable source of potential prosperity" and "the most valuable natural resource of my country."[46]

Roosevelt himself had already told Somoza that an interoceanic ship canal was impractical, though he did agree to send army engineers to Nicaragua to study the possibility of "canalizing" the San Juan River sufficiently to allow for barge traffic from the Caribbean Sea to Lake Nicaragua. Of more direct military relevance was Somoza's request that Roosevelt detail a U.S. Army officer to head Nicaragua's Military Academy, which Somoza was about to reopen, as well as an aviation instructor for the National Guard's fledgling air wing, which in 1937 had consisted of one pilot and three mechanics, who had at their disposal two Boeing B-40 biplanes and two monoplanes, a Ford Trimotor, and a Taylor Cub.[47] Roosevelt complied, and an agreement was signed 22 May 1939, under which U.S. Army Maj. Charles L. Mullins, Jr. was appointed to direct the academy when it reopened on 1 February 1940, with a class of fifty cadets.[48] U.S. officers—"solely responsible to the President and Commander-in-Chief of the Republic of Nicaragua"—continued to direct the academy until 1947, when a Nicaraguan took over.[49]

From 1911 to 1927, the nominal U.S. military presence tranquilized Nicaragua but blocked action toward the upward displacement of *caudillo*-led violence into a national, state-centered military force. That process, already successful in Guatemala and El Salvador and just starting in Honduras, ended uniquely in Nicaragua. There, all but one of the country's warlords accepted the U.S. offer to rush the process by giving Washington the authority to forge a new army. Rapidly "Nicaraguanized," the National Guard almost immediately became the personal instrument of one man and his family, and stayed that way for more than four decades. In the three northern countries, the process of upward displacement led to the formation of armies that were institutionally independent. By suppressing that process in Nicaragua, Washington midwifed a modern army unique among its isthmian counterparts in the way it conserved the nineteenth-century tradition of intensely personalistic leadership. Along with the state that it protected, the National Guard would likewise suffer a fate unique among its neighbors—complete liquidation.

7

Costa Rica

Caudillos in Search of a State

> While all of Central America shook, Costa Rica was at peace.
> —Lorenzo Montúfar

Words like these, written in the 1870s by Montúfar in reference to the first serious isthmian civil war in 1826–29, have been repeated endlessly by journalists, politicians, and historians of Central America ever since the 1820s.[1] What distinguished Costa Rica was certainly not the absence of the elements of public violence that afflicted the rest of the isthmus—civil war, *golpes de estado,* election violence, *caudillo* rule, popular uprisings and military rule—but their comparative scarcity. In the history of the other four countries, the violence has flowed like a river that swells and contracts, but that hardly ever slowed to the trickle that characterized Costa Rica for much (though not all) of its history.

The last major outbreak of public violence in Costa Rica occurred in 1948, a record no other Latin American country can match. In partial response to that year's civil war, which ruptured Costa Rica's image as a nation of peacemakers, in 1949 the government took the unheard-of step of abolishing, at least in a formal sense, its tiny armed forces. In the 1950s, the other Central American countries were not only pouring more and more resources into their own armed forces, but in the face of rising popular demands for political and economic equity their states were run by men in uniform to whom constitutions were irrelevant. Costa Rica, on the other hand, immediately set out to preserve and even magnify its reputation for peaceful, constitutional rule. For the rest of the twentieth century, the esteem in which Costa Ricans were held by people everywhere seemed all the greater in comparison to the odium reserved for the rest of Latin America's governments, most of which only seemed to enhance their reputations for unpredictable violence and brutality.

At the moment of its emergence from colonial status in 1821, Costa Rica found itself embroiled in precisely the same politico-military conflict then dividing the other provinces of the former Kingdom of Guatemala. Costa Rican partisans of national independence opposed those who favored annexation to Mexico, and as each side identified itself with a particular city, the political debate flared into an eight-day civil war in 1823 between San José (the stronghold of republicanism and independence) and the former colonial capital of Cartago (whose leadership favored annexation). The independence forces defeated the annexationists on 5 April, moved the capital to San José, and declared Costa Rica's adherence to the newly formed Central American Federation on 3 August.

Nevertheless, this little war seems to have inspired—as it often did in Spain's former colonies during the 1820s—a restless and undisciplined collection of fighting men to collect more weapons and to terrorize a largely defenseless civilian population. The new government in San José reacted swiftly, sharply cutting the ranks of its own the army, closing the San José garrisons and ordering the creation of a citizen militia. To José Luis Vega Carballo, a modern historian of the early Costa Rican state, this was a defining moment in the country's early history, for it established the principle of military subordination to political authorities: "With this action a process of military ascendancy ended that, had it continued, would have ruined the emergent civil institutionality and opened the doors to an early establishment of caudillismo."[2] The government's reaction did not, however, end militarism—much less *caudillismo*—in Costa Rica. Military regimes and *patrones* with their armed followers would come and go as they did elsewhere. That the government established a principle of civilian supremacy is at least plausible. That it was an early sign of a long and uneven trend away from the habitual violence of Costa Rica's sister republics is undeniable.

Nevertheless, the rivalry between the conservative-dominated cities of Cartago and Heredia, on the one hand, and the liberal San José on the other, persisted through most of the century, as the first two continued to challenge the primacy of San José as the capital. The first, largely pacific decade of Costa Rican history was interrupted by the Guerra de la Liga of 1835. When the fighting forces of the cities of Alajuela, Heredia, and Cartago tried to impose their own president on San José, they were defeated by Pres. Braulio Carrillo's army. After expelling some of the leading dissidents and executing the Cartago garrison commander, Carrillo ran for reelection but lost to Manuel Aguilar, who represented the defeated provincial cities. Although Carrillo stepped aside and allowed Aguilar to take office, when Aguilar attempted to move the capital out of San José, Carrillo mounted a successful coup on 27 May 1838. The first in Costa Rican history, it marked the beginning of a forty-four-year period of *caudillo* rule in which military power played a vital political role for the first and last time.[3] Carrillo's coup not only settled the question of the capital's location, but also constituted a mortal blow to the conservative, clerical, and anticentralist ideology associated with the rebellion of the three dissident cities.[4]

But dictatorship was a constant invitation to violent resistance, and as Carrillo found himself obligated to quash one coup attempt after another, the country increasingly resembled its northern neighbors. More and better weapons found their way into Costa Rica. In 1842, in what was now a familiar isthmian operation, one of Carrillo's generals doubled-crossed him by joining forces with the Honduran Gen. Francisco Morazán, who had been recruited by Carrillo's enemies to help over-throw him. Driven into exile in El Salvador, Carrillo left a distinctive legacy behind him. He effectively centralized state control, rationalized the administrative appara-tus of the state, and even implemented developmentalist policies that benefited the first large-scale producers of coffee. These were unique achievements for the 1830s in Central America, and they set Costa Rica apart from its neighbors as the first state to carry out the reforms associated with liberalism.[5] Carrillo's reforms, like those that would follow forty years later in the rest of Central America, were accompanied by a rigid, military-backed authoritarianism. Unlike the others' liberal reforms, however, it was precisely that aspect of Carrillo's legacy that would wither by the end of the century.

What mattered even more in comparative terms, however, was Carrillo's cen-tralization of state power. He effectively began the process of incorporating dis-parate sources of organized violence into the state itself, making the state and not some transient collaborators the indisputable source of sovereignty. This achieve-ment allowed the Costa Rican state to substantially reduce its dependence on the kinds of patrimonial relationships that inevitably bound the states of its northern neighbors to the procession of collaborators—armed factions and, later on, the armed forces—upon which they were forced to rely as improvisational states.[6] Car-rillo's relative success in centralizing authority enabled the state to induce compli-ance with its legislation without constantly resorting to violence. In other words, a process of legitimization of the state and the enthronment of law was now under way, spurred on in part by the successful monopolization of violence.[7]

Precisely what accounted for the Costa Rican state's precociousness in gather-ing up the dispersed sources of the violence associated with state formation remains an open question. Vega Carballo repeatedly emphasized the role of a nationalist ide-ology of popular sovereignty—evident since the colonial period—in transforming private interests (i.e., those of the coffee oligarchy) into general or national interests, and in presenting the state as an entity dedicated to the common good, which in turn fomented a widespread respect for the rule of law, even when that law served the class interests of the coffee oligarchy.[8] In making this claim, Vega Carballo pro-duced strong evidence for a marked preference among Costa Ricans, even immedi-ately after the separation from Spain, for the peaceful compromise of differences, and for a representative form of government that aspired to consider the views of the majority, or at least those of the principal sectors of opinion. From the 1820s onward, both Costa Ricans and foreign visitors repeatedly observed how these pref-erences set the country apart from the rest of the isthmus. Although it is difficult to assess the role of something as intangible as ideology, it seems clear that strongly held notions of popular sovereignty, equality, national identity, and a fundamentally irenic disposition substantially facilitated state building and the control of public violence. From this perspective, the violence used to remove Carrillo from office was the result not of the kinds of particularistic interests that dominated the other states of the isthmus, but of a popular desire to preserve the integrity of the legitimate institutions of the Costa Rican state against the abuses perpetrated by a dictator. No future government would approach Carrillo's "extremos dictatoriales."[9]

Nevertheless, a twenty-four year interval of public violence that more nearly approximated those of Costa Rica's northern neighbors opened in 1846. At least seven military interventions decided who would rule until 1870, when Gen. Tomás Guardia took power at the head of a *golpe* that succeeded in restoring a Carrillo-like period of stability.[10] If those twenty-four years represent a mere hiatus in an evolutionary process of public pacification (rather than the endemic tendency that they were elsewhere in the isthmus), they nevertheless require some explanation. The violence seemed to be contained within the national army, rather than dispersed (as they tended to be elsewhere in Central America at this time) among rival *montoneras*. Another difference was that golpista officers acted not on their own initiative but in response to calls from competing civilian factions. Although they regularly rigged elections, the state's fighting forces failed to achieve the level of autonomy enjoyed by their counterparts elsewhere, and they tended to pass the government on to civilians. It was a pattern that Vega Carballo associated with a desire to maintain the constitutional character of the government, and even with a certain populist and democratic tendency within the military itself. As a result, military *golpes* were often seen afterwards as constitutionally legitimate, and were even preceded by "a climate of general support by the population . . . that gave the golpes a certain legitimacy *desde abajo*." An underlying factor was the prestige, self-confidence and war matériel that the Costa Rican military had acquired as a result of having helped to drive the U.S. filibuster William Walker and his army out of Nicaragua in 1856.[11]

Paradoxically, General Guardia's twelve-year dictatorship (1870–82) would go far toward curing Costa Rica of military rule, reducing the interoligarchic strife that had characterized the previous four decades and reestablishing the principle of the military's absolute subordination to the president.[12] The general's seizure of power marked a radical turn in the behavior of the army, which decided "no longer to be instruments or objects in service and to become the subjects of their own destiny. This time they were not going to return to the barracks, now they would decide to stay in the presidential palace, not to protect the back of the oligarchy but to exercise power in the face of the shock and anger of those who had wanted to utilize them."[13] Guardia in effect sought to finish the the task begun by Carrillo. Expanding the military power of the state beyond anything that had yet been seen in Costa Rica, he also centralized, legitimized, and modernized the institutions of the state itself. In this he enjoyed the support of many intellectuals and civilian professionals, men who were not only consciously building the institutions of a newly autonomous state but, as a modern historian put it, were even preparing Costa Rica for representative democracy.[14]

If Guardia's was a militarized state, it was markedly economical in its deployment of military men. In 1880, a full decade after the administration took power, it boasted that the number of soldiers on active duty in all the country's garrisons—those of San José, Cartago, Heredia, Alajuela, Guanacaste, Puntarenas, Esparta, Barranca San Lucas, and El Coco—totaled a mere 358, proving once again, the government added, that in Costa Rica school teachers (628 of them) outnumbered garrison soldiers. In an emergency, the government could still call on its eighteen-thousand-man Ejército de Operaciones, composed of all able-bodied men between eighteen and thirty, who were required to receive some type of military training. There were two more backup forces: The ten-thousand-man Ejército de Reserva, composed of men who had retired from the Ejército de Operaciones and were still under forty-five years of age, and the Guardia Nacional, men between forty-six and fifty-five.[15]

The military's domination of the state persisted through the two civilian administrations that followed Guardia's death in 1882, and did not begin to recede significantly until the election of Pres. José Joaquín Rodríguez in 1890.[16] The military's strong influence in government was owing in part to the fact that during this period, the threat of an externally provoked military emergency could never be dismissed, making military readiness prudent. In March 1885, when news of Guatemalan President Barrios's unilateral declaration of Central American unity arrived in Costa Rica, the country mobilized rapidly and enthusiastically against Guatemala and the latter's only ally, Honduras. Costa Rican indignation was aggravated when Pres. Próspero Fernández received this one-sentence telegram from Barrios: "I notify you that last night the [Guatemalan] National Assembly approved the decree under which, in order to carry out the Central American union, I assume the military command of Central America. Your most affectionate friend, J. Rufino Barrios." A Costa Rican army of two thousand entered Nicaragua to join the latter's forces in a joint operation against Honduras. The defeat of the Guatemalan Army by El Salvador on 2 April at Chalchuapa, and Barrios's death in that battle, abruptly terminated the Guatemalan-Honduran threat. "[N]ever," according to the war minister, "had any government ever felt so solidly supported by public opinion; never had there been such absolute uniformity." The experience, he added, also proved that Costa Rica had to be prepared to resist foreign aggression—"even the absurd emergencies of brute force."[17]

In the decade that followed the election of President Rodríguez in 1890, it became still more evident that the improvised character of the state building process that still predominated in the other countries of the isthmus had largely been overcome in Costa Rica. There, at last, was a state unencumbered by the constant need to recruit armed collaborators. Building on the achievements of General Guardia, the state had even achieved an impressive level of autonomy from the oligarchic interests that continued to dictate policy elsewhere in the isthmus, as its direct administration was gradually turned over to liberal functionaries. They used their power to further enhance the legitimacy of the state by manipulating its now substantial financial, educational and ideological resources, without having to resort much to violence, even as the electorate expanded.[18] Democratization had begun, and historians often point to the election of 1890 as a decisive turn toward competitive elections even though they remained indirect until 1913, and the secret ballot was not introduced until 1926.[19] The military, nevertheless, remained a source of intrigue and occasional violent intervention in the political process for three decades after 1890.[20]

In comparative terms, what seems to stand out over the course of state building from the 1830s to the 1890s was the success of a long line of *caudillos*, starting with Braulio Carrillo, in drawing together public institutions with real political and military resources at their exclusive disposition. This process would not have succeeded had the governments of the 1820s failed to subordinate the fighting forces and establish order on the fledgling state's own terms, which eventually would enable it to enforce its control and consolidate its legitimacy through ideological rather than coercive means. In a similar vein, Carrillo's legacy included the displacement of sociopolitical conflict from its local and estate-type horizontal grounding toward a vertical, hierarchical arena controlled by an emerging agro-export oligarchy that succeeded in identifying its own interests with those of the state and, most important, the nation.[21] A succession of *caudillos* had in effect deliberately used their power to make a state. It was a path that in every important respect made Costa Rica unique among the five countries of the isthmus.

As state building on these terms unfolded in Costa Rica, the independent authority of the army declined after 1890. The minister of war opened his report to Congress in 1900 by observing that Costa Ricans hardly thought at all about their military garrisons, and when they did so, it was with a "certain disdain." The very role and purpose of the Costa Rican Army seemed to be in doubt, a discourse unheard anywhere else in the isthmus, or in Latin America for that matter. According to the minister, the garrisons' primary purpose was to reinforce the police force when the maintenance of public order required it; beyond that, the garrisons served to store arms, munitions, and other military material, and as training centers for soldiers and officers.[22]

Two decades later, the autonomy that the army had enjoyed up to about 1890 was utterly reversed. After the fall of the *golpista* regime of Gen. Federico Tinoco (1917–19), the army almost collapsed, losing 90 percent of its men in just three years—from five thousand in 1918, to one thousand in 1920, to five hundred in 1921.[23] In 1922 the government became the first in the region (and perhaps one of the first in the world) to rename its Secretaría de Guerra (Secretary of War) the Secretaría de Seguridad Pública (Secretary of Public Security), which it has been called ever since. The decline in the army's active-duty roster not only contradicted the trend that General Guardia had set in motion, but also the militarization of politics in practically every country of Latin America. The Tinoco dictatorship's brutality, corruption, and contempt for public opinion only temporarily deprived Costa Rica of its fame as an oasis of peace. Tinoco was deeply unpopular, and he finally fell in the face of the stern disapproval of Pres. Woodrow Wilson and a series of popular uprisings that culminated in an insurrection in San José. More than a year before Tinoco was forced out, the U.S. chargé d'affaires in Costa Rica approvingly noted "the unanimity of public sentiment against the Tinocos, the odium in which they are held, the blackness of their character."[24] Thanks to Tinoco's impudence, the

Costa Rican Army never recovered from the "infamy and social disapproval" that it had earned.[25]

The downgrading of the army was not even interrupted by the threat of a border conflict with Panama in 1921. Costa Rica "had no army," according to the U.S. military attaché, and the government initially depended on four hundred infantry-equipped policemen, "the only organization which might be defined as regular troops," to protect it from Panama. U.S. mediators managed to prevent war, but the experience—which had forced Costa Rica to hurriedly assemble an army of about two thousand volunteers—only seemed to encourage subsequent governments to proceed with the dismantling of the army and its gradual replacement by a national police force. In May 1922 it had fewer than two hundred soldiers, and in 1929 the musicians in the army's bands outnumbered combat troops three to one (262 versus 85).[26]

From a geostrategic perspective, Costa Rica had little to fear despite a history of contention with Panama and Nicaragua. Sandwiched as it was between the two U.S. protectorates, it could always count on the protection of the United States, as happened in the Panamanian conflict in 1921, when the United States forced Panama to recognize Costa Rica's rightful possession of territory that Panamanian troops had seized. Pres. Ricardo Jiménez (1924–28) was evidently the first president to base the country's national defense policy on a belief in the readiness of the United States to protect Costa Rican sovereignty.[27] In 1933, the U.S. military attaché decided to find out what military plans Costa Rican officers were making to head off a rumored invasion by Nicaragua. There were "no plans of any description" to block an invasion because, the government told him, "the United States would never permit any such invasion!"[28] The strategic sense of the Costa Ricans with whom the attaché consulted proved to be unerring, for U.S. military and diplomatic collaboration would effectively shield Costa Rica from Nicaraguan aggression in the 1950s. By the same token, however, Costa Rica would be helpless against the U.S.-backed anti-Sandinista forces of Nicaraguan exiles that operated from its territory in the 1980s; no conceivable Costa Rican Army could have deterred the United States from sending its "contra" clients into Costa Rican territory.

As for internal threats to the Costa Rican state, the governments after 1919 calculated that a national police force would adequately protect it against rebellion. Although public violence was notably less frequent and intense than elsewhere in Central America, its limits were nearly as extensive. In a clientelist political system weighted heavily toward the presidency, in which personalities still counted for more than ideologies or parties, electoral fraud and violence were commonplace until 1948.[29] Until the 1940s, the tiny army regularly sought to manipulate election outcomes, contributing to the declining confidence in elections that characterized Costa Rican politics from the 1930s until at least the 1948 revolt.[30] Between 1882 and 1938, only five of eighteen presidents took office through fair elections; opposition groups launched twenty-one insurrections against the state.[31]

By the 1930s, however, electoral violence typically exhausted itself in short order. Attempts to seize the towns of Grecia, in December 1930, and San Ramón, in

June 1931, as the result of a dispute over election ballots, were easily turned aside by the authorities, but a more serious uprising led by presidential candidate Manuel Castro Quesada in 1932, with the support of the army commanders in San José, lasted four days and took fifteen lives.[32] Col. Juan María Quesada, the commander of the National Penitentiary, objected to the officer appointed to relieve him of his command of the penitentiary and revolted on 2 February 1934 with a part of his garrison. He surrendered to a force of one hundred policemen who had only to shoot several hundred rounds in the air. Pres. Ricardo Jiménez not only released Quesada, but agreed to appoint a replacement more to Quesada's liking, a result that the U.S. military attaché found as incomprehensible as Quesada's subsequent threat to sue the government for damages in order to clear his honor.[33] In comparison to the kind of response by an offended military man that was to be expected in its northern neighbors, Quesada's fatuous gesture was a welcome sign of Costa Rica's peculiarity. The idea of a defeated Honduran *caudillo* hiring a lawyer to sue the Carías government in the 1930s would have been practically inconceivable. But in Costa Rica, the idea was at least plausible.

The Quesada episode captured the contradictory, perhaps even schizophrenic, character of Costa Rican exceptionalism on the eve of its epochal civil war: lucent traces of public violence and *caudillismo* of a familiar Latin American kind persisted alongside a shrinking armed force, a solid tradition of civilian rule, contested elections, a reasonably free press, and a legal system that had earned some public respect. In 1948, that contradiction would blow up in one last civil war that ended by purging Costa Rica of the vestiges of *caudillo* violence.

Part II

1940–1960

8

Transformations

The last five chapters have attempted to show how the limits of public violence acquired the expansiveness that came to characterize the republics of Central America during the first century or so of their independence. In either seeking or exercising power, few men could act without being prepared to capture, exile, maim, or kill their opponents. By the 1920s, after a century of turmoil that exceeded anything the isthmus had experienced during the three centuries of Spanish rule, a rising number of public mea culpas by isthmian intellectuals and politicians called attention not only to the extraordinary scope of public violence, but to such associated phenomena as the improvisational character of the state and the persistence of political loyalties that were always more personalistic than institutional or ideological.

The violence was gradually militarized by drawing together, out of the rabble of caudillo-led bands, armies that could be credibly associated with the apparatus of the state. In a roughly simultaneous way, Guatemala under the presidency of Gen. José Rafael Carrera (who died in office in 1865) and Costa Rica under the presidency of Gen. Tomás Guardia (1870–82) were the first to militarize the violence. They were followed by El Salvador, perhaps as early as the 1890s, and most definitely by 1920. Only under Gen. José Santos Zelaya (1893–1909) did Nicaragua appear to come close to this achievement, but the transience of what he called his army revealed itself with his downfall. There, contending party militias were not replaced by an army until the construction of the Guardia Nacional by the United States from 1927 to 1933. Thus, armies recognizably associated with the state apparatus dominated the field of state power by the 1930s in Costa Rica, Guatemala, El Salvador, and Nicaragua, in a process that Costa Rica and Guatemala clearly led. The force on which Gen. Tiburcio Carías relied in Honduras during his presidency (1933–48) continued to retain its predominantly caudillista character even as it submitted itself to a piecemeal process of army-formation by the United States, which would not succeed in helping Honduras make an army until the 1950s. Honduras, like Nicaragua, owed the founding of its army largely to U.S. government collaboration.

Just as the agents of institutional violence in the four northern states were beginning to rely on national armies and proto-armies as they contended with their enemies in the field of state power, Costa Rica's governments were dismantling their country's army in the 1920s. As they deprived the state apparatus of all but the most nominal armed force, they opened the door to a revival of party-militia violence centered on elections that would culminate in the 1948 civil war and, two years later, a constitutional restraint on the establishment of an army. Public violence in Costa Rica had been contained, since at least General Guardia's administration, within limits that were more restrictive than those that prevailed to the north. Although militia-inspired electoral violence was common, the government's right to rule was widely acknowledged and rarely challenged. This was one place in Central America where one could find signs of an unmistakable "idea of the state," an organizing ideology that tended to unify people across the boundaries of class, party, family, and region and that served to shrink the limits of public violence. Costa Ricans alone in the isthmus had managed to devise a unifying idea of themselves as comparatively egalitarian and pacific. It was an idea that bestowed legitimacy on the state even as it propelled the construction of a nation whose army would be subordinate to civil government. The idea of a peaceful and democratic oasis in the murderous panorama of the isthmus undoubtedly fomented the gradual dissolution of the army from the early 1920s to 1949, just as the same idea had encouraged, under different conditions, the construction of a national army in the mid-nineteenth century.

Besides variations in the timing of the construction of national armies, other distinctive features of public violence can be found from one country to another. Because of the immaturity of the national historiographies, it is difficult at this point to say whether these differences are real or merely the artificial product of a highly uneven body of secondary literature and an archival record that cannot be consulted in any systematic way (where it has been preserved at all). The organization of para-institutional agents of public violence, particularly in the form of socially inferior groups acting in collaboration with institutional agents of violence, seems to have been especially noteworthy in El Salvador throughout the twentieth century. A logical counterpart of this trend were the instances of a moderate military populism—in the 1930s, the 1950s, and the 1970s—that also seems to set El Salvador apart. Both Guatemala's General Ubico and El Salvador's General Hernández-Martinez were transitional figures between the personalistic governments of the past and the highly institutionalized military rule that followed from the 1950s in El Salvador and the 1960s in Guatemala. The governments of both men adopted measures that exalted the military as an institution even as the dictators exalted themselves, an artifact of nineteenth century caudillismo that would practically disappear by mid-century everywhere in the isthmus.

In Honduras, perhaps the most nakedly anarchic of all five countries, the leadership of the country nevertheless seemed painfully and self-critically aware of the futility and waste of continuous public violence. Denouncing it, they sought vainly for ways to pacify the field of power around the state by arguing for a "real army," on the order of that of El Salvador or Guatemala. But why they thought so is hard to determine, for the record of all five countries fails to suggest any obvious linkage among the three underlying variables at play: the consolidation of the fighting forces into a single national army, the level of public violence, and the frequency of unscheduled changes in government. Figure 8.1 compares changes of government in all the countries in two roughly equal periods, 1870–1908 (thirty-eight years) and 1909–45 (thirty-six years). Honduras, whose fighting forces were the least unified, became more governmentally stable in the second period, yet it was by all accounts the country with the highest frequency of armed actions in the same period. The most intensely destructive violence of the second period occurred in Nicaragua and El Salvador. In Nicaragua, that violence was a direct result of the departure of Washington's quasi-occupation force, which led to a civil war that gave rise to the Sandino insurgency. El Salvador's well-developed army efficiently slaughtered some eight thousand or so suspected enemies of the state in a matter of weeks. The two countries were the only ones to record a significant increase in government turnover in the second period compared to the first period.

This diversity of tendencies in the expression of public violence up to about 1940 highlights the inadequacy of any attempt to sweep the four northern states of the region into a single regime type, such as authoritarian, reactionary-despotic,

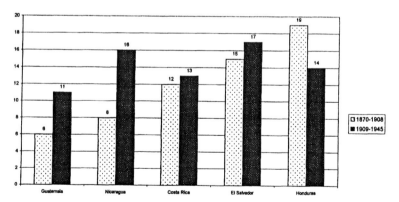

Figure 8.1   Changes of Government, 1870–1908 vs. 1909–45. *Source:* Calculated by author from data in "Apéndice," *Historia General de Centroamérica*, vol. 4, *Las repúblicas agroexportadoras (1870–1945)*, ed. Victor Hugo Acuña Ortega (Madrid: Sociedad Estatal Quinto Centenario y FLACSO, 1993), pp. 404–412.

semi protectorate, or sultanic.[1] The diversity might best be ordered as tendencies of patrimonialism. In Nicaragua, a bureaucratic tendency prevailed under both Zelaya and Somoza, men skilled at drawing power to themselves through agents who specialized in surveillance and population control, though with vastly different results that corresponded in part to the available technology and resources, not to mention the oceanic difference in the two leaders' capacities to satisfy U.S. interests. A more strictly military tendency can be associated with El Salvador and Guatemala. The most personalistic rule seemed to operate in Honduras, which was bureaucratized or militarized much later than the others, perhaps not fully until after the military coup of 1963. Even so, military rule continued to be associated closely, in a way reminiscent of the old-time caudillismo, with one man, Gen. Oswaldo López Arellano. But by that time, not even Honduras could match the personalism that imbued the Nicaraguan National Guard.

Though foreigners from time to time exploited or tried to direct public violence, its essential dynamic was largely unaffected by events or interests outside the isthmus. Neither the U.S. government's quasi-occupation of Nicaragua from 1912 to 1933, nor the participation in the violence by U.S.-owned enterprises acting as sources of ready cash for the agents of public violence, altered the basic character of the violence.[2] Although fruit-company meddling may have exacerbated that violence in the case of Honduras, the U.S. Marine presence in Nicaragua attenuated it until 1927 and then provoked the single most intense and prolonged outbreak of public violence in Nicaragua since the 1850s. The Sandino episode also represented one of the few times that the United States (or any foreign government) directly challenged or sought to change the practice of public violence as it had evolved in Central America, rather than simply adapting to it. The first two such attempts were embodied in the so-called Washington "treaties" of 1907 and 1923. The third was the U.S. government's creation of the Nicaraguan National Guard in 1927, an act that stemmed from the 1923 treaty. Not only had the treaties failed to keep the peace but the Marine-made Guard metamorphosed immediately from an exotic Yankee transplant into the familiar patrimony of a caudillo. The scope, intensity, and limits of isthmian public violence as it had emerged over the century that followed its separation from Spain remained a product of Central America until the 1930s.

Starting in the 1940s, however, that pattern would for the first time be substantially affected by practices that were genuinely global in scope. Converging in World War II and catalyzed by the Cold War, they globalized public violence everywhere in the second half of the twentieth century. Although they could not be attributed solely to the United States, it was principally the United States that carried them to Central America. Part II of this book will show how U.S. military and police collaboration, as an expression of the globalization of public violence, interacted with and changed an already well-established tradition of public violence in Central America. Before enumerating the ways in which U.S. collaboration changed public violence after 1940, let me first explain what I mean by the globalization of public violence.[3]

Today, practically everything about public violence is intensively global in ways that were almost unimaginable only fifty years ago. If public violence is an old story, its globalization is a comparatively new one. Here I am not speaking of mere diffusion but of new and expanding worldwide networks that intimately linked diplomatic, military, financial, and industrial agents of public violence across the continents, in relationships that ran the gamut from cutthroat rivalry to collaboration and solidarity, within as well as across national identities. At the nodes of these networks were not mere governments but institutional, para-institutional and counterinstitutional agents of public violence, including the private-sector entrepreneurs who operated as their contractors or stood by as bidders to supply equipment and services. It was a process that intensified notably after 1945, as practically every manifestation of public violence became an event with global implications, with linkages crisscrossing national borders. The agents of the industrialized economies fed the networks with an array of tools astonishing to behold in their ingenuity and destructive power. They also supplied knowledge of their operation, techniques for organizing and administering the violence, and technologically driven methods of surveillance and passive control over the people (the "nation") in whose name public violence was invariably administered, whether by states, their collaborators, or their guerrilla enemies. In return for the means and the knowledge to operate them, the recipients typically ceded some (often nominal) authority over the deployment of public violence, so that both the means and the power to dispose of them were globalized. The overall effect was to extend both the reach and deadliness of public violence, as twentieth-century killing became a worldwide enterprise binding perpetrators, suppliers and victims.

But how was public violence globalized? It depended not just on the growth of the nation-state but on industrial development, and the subsequent intertwining of public and entrepreneurial global networks. The trade in arms or their deployment in the service of foreign conquest did not globalize public violence.[4] The decisive step in that direction occurred when military organization and technique, under the supervision of newly centralizing nation-states with access to unheard of revenues and the loyalty of millions of citizen-soldiers, were revolutionized by scientific and technical advances in communications, power generation, transportation, and manufacturing.[5] But it was still too soon to speak of the globalization of public violence because these were strictly national networks, dependent on central authorities and organized merely to destroy an enemy force or to occupy subject territory. The great-power disarmament initiatives of the 1920s reveal just how tenuous was the commitment to building and sustaining global networks of public violence.[6] Not until after World War II would the clouding over of the boundaries between peace and war, the national and the foreign, the military and the civilian, the private and the public, make it possible to speak of the globalization of public violence.[7]

After 1945, four interrelated elements constituted the globalization of public violence.

The first and most important was the politicization or quasi nationalization of the arms trade, which transformed a private-sector activity into one controlled increasingly by the national state. Beginning in the 1930s, arms manufacturers had to request government licenses in Western Europe and North America before exporting their products, and as a result private arms makers became increasingly dependent on governments. As arms transfers became "nationalized," they became the subject of high foreign policy.[8] And as governments increased their control over the dissemination of weapons and the knowledge to use them, direct military intervention came to be replaced by intensive military and police collaboration among governments themselves and between and among governments and other agents of public violence. This collaboration was effected not by transferring troops but by transferring to local agents the tools of violence and the knowledge to use them.

Quasinationalization of the arms trade made the second element of globalization a practical option: the expansion and institutionalization of transnational military and police collaboration. To win World War II, the United States not only subsidized the armed forces of its principal fighting allies, Great Britain and the Soviet Union, but also extended those subsidies to allied but noncombatant states such as those of Central America. After the war, the massive program of military collaboration that the United States initiated with its Western European allies in 1949 (as a result of President Truman's appeal to Congress for the authority to provide "military aid to free nations to enable them to protect themselves against the threat of aggression") was extended to Asia, then to Latin America and then to Africa.

Third, a technological revolution in the production of the tools of public violence after 1945 (and a concomitant economic imperative) accelerated the second trend, as collaboration was repeatedly justified as a necessary aspect of "modernization." Military and civilian research in the "defense" sphere became practically indistinguishable while vastly inflating the military budgets of governments. The added financial burdens imposed by new technologies made it imperative to develop markets for the products of the arms industry, in order to maintain production capacity at a level sufficient to hold down unit costs. This objective was even more urgent among secondary industrial powers such as Britain, France, and West Germany: Manufacturing firms collaborated with one another in research and development while leveraging their collaboration with the state.[9] The competition among the purveyors of arms and related services for "clients" in both the commercial and political senses provided incentives to exchange weapons and related services on terms that included not only outright grants and low-interest credits but also strategic planning, organization, training, and consultation services.

Finally, the globalization of public violence during the Cold War was also constituted by the rivalry of two global political programs, communism and liberal capitalist democracy, which in turn took the form of two great politico-military alliances. The Cold War thus furnished an ideal environment for the flourishing of transnational military and police collaboration. Both of the two great alliances succeeded in linking national military establishments into giant transnational military alliances, along with scores of less formal instances of transnational collaboration among the agents of institutional, counterinstitutional, and para-institutional public violence. "Early in 1967 the United States had 700,000 soldiers stationed in 30 countries, was a member of 4 regional defense alliances and an active participant in a fifth, had mutual defense treaties with 42 nations, was a member of 53 international organizations, and was furnishing military or economic aid to nearly 100 nations across the face of the globe."[10] These commitments and their corresponding programs of military and police collaboration, not to mention their expression in innumerable "small wars," were part of the continuous war of position ("containment") that constituted the Cold War.[11] The result was an intensification of the globalization of public violence, as its agents in places like El Salvador, Argentina, Mozambique, and Taiwan, found themselves operating increasingly from within networks of public violence that led beyond their national borders. Not just states, but also a staggering variety of counterinstitutional insurgencies that called themselves organs of "national liberation" and countless covert and semicovert parainstitutional movements were no less integrated into circuits of public violence that linked Moscow, Prague, and East Berlin as well as Washington, London, and Paris. Public violence of all kinds—interstate warfare, revolutionary guerrilla movements, death-squad killings, state terrorism—became points in a network that linked governments and private businesses, military and police organizations, their collaborators and their sworn enemies.

In the United States, the authority for its worldwide program of military subsidies during World War II, and the seed of the massive programs of postwar military collaboration that would follow the defeat of the Axis, was the Lend-Lease Act of 11 March 1941. The Act endowed the U.S. president with sweeping new power in foreign economic and military relations by allowing him alone to decide which countries would be invited to collaborate, what they would get (industrial and agricultural materials as well as military material were allowed), and under what terms. The Act even empowered the President to authorize "payment or repayment in kind or property, or any other direct or indirect benefit which [he] deems satisfactory."[12]

Lend-Lease signaled the onset of two postwar trends that together radically altered the character of the U.S. state's relationship to foreign friends and foes alike. Lend-Lease not only opened the public treasury of the United States to foreign military organizations, but did so in a way that diminished the control that Congress might have been expected to exercise over the disbursal and administration of those funds and of such related resources as, for example, the disposition of the U.S. armed forces required for the oversight and training that invariably accompanied the transfer of material abroad. Although the future Cold War programs of military collaboration would include some measure of congressional oversight, those provisions were never very stringent, they were frequently underexploited by Congress itself, and in any case Congress itself endowed the president with emergency powers to supply military materials and services that were no less sweeping than those given to Franklin Delano Roosevelt in 1941. Lend-Lease, by both expanding and institutionalizing the transfer of military material and services to beleaguered friendly states, was thus the core precedent for the military and police collaboration that followed during the Cold War. In 1959, William H. Draper, Jr., chair of the President's Committee to Study the United States Military Assistance Program, observed correctly that "There is indeed no precedent in all history for what our country has done under the mutual security programs." The United States remained the largest supplier of arms in the world throughout the Cold War as well as after it; from 1950 to 1979, the United States transferred abroad more than half the world's total of arms and related military services.[13]

The legal foundations for the new system of military and police collaboration among nation-states were set by the U.S. Congress over a period of just four years, starting in 1947, when it gave President Truman the authority to help the governments of Greece and Turkey to defend themselves from communists. It was the first time that military collaboration became a paramount peacetime foreign policy tool. Two years later, Truman asked Congress to go a step further and authorize "military aid to free nations to enable them to protect themselves against the threat of aggression." The result was the Mutual Defense Assistance Act of 6 October 1949, the law upon which all subsequent military collaboration programs, including government grants of equipment and training services as well as cash sales and credit sales, were founded.[14] It authorized the conveyance, "without payment to the United States," of "military assistance in the form of equipment, materials, and services" and it defined equipment and materials as "any arms, ammunition or implements of war, or any other type of material, article, raw material, facility, tool, machine, supply, or item that would further the purposes of this Act, or any component or part thereof, used or required for use in connection therewith, or required in or for the manufacture, production, processing, storage, transportation, repair, or rehabilitation of any equipment or materials, but shall not include merchant vessels." Services included "any service, repair, training of personnel, or technical or other assistance or information necessary to effectuate the purposes of this Act."[15]

Although the act only authorized gifts of military assistance through the Military Assistance Program (MAP) to member states of NATO plus Iran, Korea, and the Philippines, it permitted the president to sell military equipment, materials, and services to any other country that may have joined the United States in a "collective defense and regional arrangement," but only so long as such a country paid the full cost of the transfers in advance. The latter was called the "408-e" program.[16] Within a year, however, as a result of both the widening conflict over Korea and the success of the communist revolution in China, Asia suddenly emerged as a military-collaboration priority, radically expanding the potential geographical scope of collaboration and calling for new legislation to replace that of 1949. The result was the Mutual Security Act of 10 October 1951, in which Congress expanded the number of countries for which assistance was authorized. This act also authorized grant collaboration with Latin America for the first time, but in doing so Congress added a restriction that would become increasingly controversial before it was finally abandoned by about 1961. Grant collaboration could be authorized "only in accordance with defense plans which are found by the President to require the recipient country to participate in missions important to the defense of the Western Hemisphere," and under the terms of bilateral agreements "designed to assure that the assistance will be used to promote the defense of the Western Hemisphere."[17] In other words, grant collaboration to protect Latin American government from internal enemies was prohibited. Grant collaboration could only be undertaken to defend Latin America against an attack from outside the hemisphere. If the fear of a Soviet attack on Latin America was a paranoid fantasy, it is well to recall that it was one that gripped the United States itself in the first years of the Cold War. In 1950, Congress created the Army Antiaircraft Command, which hastily installed gun defenses against a Soviet air attack across the United States over the next six years, when Nike missiles began replacing the guns. By 1963, 219 surface-to-air missile batteries were defending the United States against Soviet bombers.[18]

In 1955, in an effort to expand sales, Congress authorized the extension of credit to recipient governments for up to ten years, a form of collaboration that would become increasingly important after 1960.[19] Military collaboration took other, more ambiguous forms as time went by, often in order to circumvent restrictions in the sales and grants programs or to augment the executive branch's ability to act flexibly and without congressional authorization. Among the most protean was a cluster of programs known variously as "Defense Support," "Special Assistance," "Security Supporting Assistance," and "Economic Support Funds," created in the Mutual Security Act of 1954, which authorized the president to "furnish, to nations and organizations eligible to receive military assistance . . , commodities, services, and financial and other assistance designed to sustain and increase military effort."[20] Misleading and perhaps even intentionally deceptive in intent, these programs could plausibly be classified as either military or economic, depending on the political sensitivities of the moment, and have been handled by the U.S. Agency for International Development and its predecessor agencies since 1954.[21]

Other, smaller programs offered still more flexibility. Since 1950, the president has been authorized to give "excess" defense articles to other governments, allowing the recipient to pay only the costs of repairing, rehabilitating, and transporting the article. As a result, "it was possible to furnish large quantities of excess defense articles to military assistance recipient countries to augment the grant military assistance program far in excess of what the Congress had intended," a congressional committee concluded in 1976.[22] The Food for Peace program (also known as Public Law 480) let recipient governments sell U.S.-shipped food whose proceeds were used to generate additional revenues for military purposes; from 1955 to 1974, more than $2 billion in Food for Peace sales was used for military purposes in twelve countries.[23]

Under each of these categories of collaboration, the U.S. government entered the transaction as seller, donor, creditor, or loan guarantor. Of course, foreign governments and individuals could also buy direct from U.S. arms manufacturers. But even in the case of these "commercial" sales, the U.S. government intervened indirectly as a regulator with the power to block the sale. With a few wartime exceptions, commercial arms exports were unregulated by the government until 1905, when the United States began to impose limits on commercial sales to certain Latin American countries and to China in order to promote political stability. However, not until the passage of what became known as the first of the Neutrality Acts, in 1935, did Congress impose comprehensive controls over commercial arms exports.[24] In the case of Central America, however, commercial U.S. arms sales were never as important as

U.S. government transfers. From 1971 (when the government began tabulating the value of commercial sales deliveries by country and year) to 1990, commercial sales only amounted to 3.6 percent of U.S. government military transfers to Central America.[25]

It is hardly surprising to find that in the military collaboration legislation of the late 1940s and early 1950s, World War II was taken as the model threat and Lend-Lease as the model response. In the case of Latin America, these assumptions could be detected in the way that grant collaboration was restricted to hemispheric defense against an invasion attempt by a Eurasian power. But by the late 1950s, an increasing number of critics were questioning those assumptions. Grant military collaboration, they argued, should encompass defense against internal enemies in Latin America. In 1959, four months after Fidel Castro's triumphant entry into Havana, the United States's best known expert on anticommunist counterinsurgency, Col. Edward G. Lansdale, wrote to the White House: "We have concentrated on materially preparing indigenous forces against an external threat. But, what about internal weaknesses? There is much that the U.S. military can do, through working with an indigenous armed force (as a true power element of a nation), to improve the internal stability of a country we are aiding."[26]

Although a rigid distinction between police and military realms of responsibility scarcely existed in many of the countries with which the United States was now collaborating, the difference was nevertheless an important one in the minds of the policymakers in Washington. Like Colonel Lansdale, they often posed it in terms of collaboration for "internal" security (protection from subversive groups or individuals who had already penetrated national borders) versus collaboration for "external" defense against potential invaders. By the early 1950s, the United States was openly training police in Costa Rica (as well as Korea, Iran, and the Philippines), while the CIA was secretly doing so in Turkey, Thailand, and Indonesia.[27] And as police training was expanded in the 1950s, the Defense Department's "internal security" responsibilities with collaborating governments were redefined to include the training and equipping of both civil police and military units that were confronting internal enemies.

By 1957, five different U.S. government agencies—State, Defense, the International Cooperation Administration (ICA—the predecessor of the Agency for International Development), the Central Intelligence Agency, and the U.S. Information Agency—were collaborating with foreign governments in the realm of "internal security." To coordinate their efforts, the Eisenhower administration created the Overseas Internal Security Program (OISP). The Defense Department was supposed to provide training, arms, ammunition, and equipment to "police forces operating under foreign defense establishments," as well as training and equipping both paramilitary and military forces "for counter-intelligence and anti-guerrilla operations." The ICA targeted civil police agencies, supplying equipment, training, and advice under what was alternately called the Public Safety Program or the "1290(d) program" after the number assigned to one of the National Security Council's 1954 decisions. In December 1956, the only Latin American country with an

ICA-run program was Guatemala, one of ten in the world.[28] The ICA supported the "operation of country-wide communications networks, maintenance of national personal registration and identification systems, fire fighting and fire prevention, prison administration, control of customs, control of immigration, control of activities of foreigners, coast guard functions, domestic counter-intelligence and control of subversive activities, border control," and even regulatory activities.[29]

The CIA's early participation in police collaboration programs was broadened in March 1955, when it agreed to contribute to the ICA programs "a small highly trained nucleus of counter subversive specialists who would be supported by the larger conventional components" of the police program.[30] The CIA's role in covert aspects of police training expanded rapidly, as suggested by the decision of the Operations Coordinating Board (OCB)[31] in September 1956 to place the operation of the 1290-d program under the control of a "Senior Group" headed by a "Senior Official" with access "to the covert aspects of this program on a need-to-know basis consistent with the operational security considerations involved."[32] By March 1961, the CIA had thirty-three employees "integrated into ICA Public Safety programs in twelve countries and is conducting parallel activities in other countries in support of OISP objectives."[33] Robert Amory, Jr., whose tenure as deputy director of the CIA from 1957 to 1962 spanned the Eisenhower and Kennedy administrations, told an interviewer in 1966 that the CIA became the "brains" of police collaboration. From the start, the CIA was active in

helping develop internal police forces, which is a dangerous ground because you can get to Gestapo type tactics and so on and so forth, but essentially bringing to bear good police methods—good filing systems, good fingerprinting systems, good systems of riot control such as using dye so when you get the ring leaders, they can't wash the dye off their clothes, without having a riot squad that picks up a lot of innocent people who just happen to be caught on a street corner. They worked very closely with AID on this. It's a program called 1290D which could be a very good subject of a, you know, Ph.D. monograph sometime—which involved who was responsible in this police thing, and it fell back and forth between AID and CIA. Finally, under [Robert] Bob Komer's leadership on the White House Staff, a task force was set up under Alexis Johnson. I happened to sit on it, and we solved the problem in a rather rude, but practical fashion of saying, "By God, AID will be responsible for it, but the brains are in CIA, so we'll move those brains over to AID." So we just took the CIA men—I can't think of his name now [Byron Engle]—and gave them the mission of training police forces using American police forces occasionally as sort of sponsors, using Michigan State University School of Police Work, which is the best in the country, and a lot of excellent work has been done there.[34]

From its origins with Lend-Lease in 1941, the U.S. contribution to the increasing globalization of public violence changed public violence in Central America in three ways. First, coercive capacity was increasingly concentrated in the command centers of the armies and police forces of the national states and away from the garrison commanders, regional caudillos, and political party militias. This process aimed to recreate the institutional agents of public violence as legitimate participants in the world military order. The sea change in war fighting technology after World War II required technical knowledge and administrative authority, which highlighted both the indispensability and the legitimacy of centralized, state bureaucracies made up of people with access to highly specialized skills. Ideologically, the Central American states' membership in a loose, worldwide alliance of states ("the free world") to defeat an adversary (communism) whose agents could be identified as both enemy governments and individual inhabitants of the isthmian republics further enhanced the authority (and sometimes the legitimacy) of national armies and police forces. The mystification of their mission as the delivery of "national security" was the crucial ideological dimension of the transformation.

Second, the globalization of public violence endowed the isthmian republics with new means of surveillance and control, including the organization of para-institutional bodies such as secret "death squads" that operated more or less under the supervision of military intelligence officers. Such activities drew on the global networks of public violence not only for equipment and training but strategic advice and a modest tutelary responsibility for the deployment of what came to be known as state terrorism.[35]

Third, as the agents of public violence sought the advantages to be gained by drawing increasingly on global networks of public violence, a relationship of mutual dependence rather than unilateral control emerged between them and their collaborators. The preeminent example was the mutually dependent relationship between Washington and the isthmian governments. However, mutual dependence rather than outright domination and control also characterized the relationship between insurgencies and their foreign collaborators, whether Cuba, the Soviet Union, Venezuela (which supported the Sandinista insurgency), or the United States (which backed insurgencies in both Guatemala in 1953–54 and in Nicaragua in 1980–91), as well as the relationship between para-institutional agents of violence and their collaborators in the national state.[36]

After 1945, a new phase of public violence with both familiar and unfamiliar aspects opened in Central America. The limits of that violence showed no signs of having shrunk, and the patrimonial ethos that had governed political life for so long remained as strongly entrenched as ever. But the capacity for public violence—not only of the state's agents, but that of counter- and para-institutional agents as well— expanded immeasurably, with proportionately greater levels of repression and destruction. The increased capacity for violence derived not merely from advances in the technological efficiency of the means of killing, but from its concentration in the hands of state agents whose status as "nation builders" was now affirmed by their participation in global networks of violence as collaborators, principally, of the U.S. armed forces.

PHOTO 1. Costa Rican forces occupying Almirante, Panama, during a border war between Panama and Costa Rica. Here they are manning a Maxim-Nordenfelt machine gun on a seawall outside a cacao processing plant. 7 March 1921. U.S. Military Attaché, U.S. Legation, Panama. National Archives, RG165, MID 2011-3.

PHOTO 2. Six-gun battery of Bethlehem mountain guns in action in Guatemala during army maneuvers celebrating the Liberal holiday, on 30 June 1922. U.S. Military Attaché, U.S. Legation, Panama. National Archives, RG165, MID 2019-21.

PHOTO 3. Six-gun battery of Bethlehem mountain guns, packed, outside the Guatemalan military academy (Escuela Politécnica) during army maneuvers celebrating the Liberal holiday, on 30 June 1922. U.S. Military Attaché, U.S. Legation, Panama. National Archives, RG165, MID 2019-21.

PHOTO 4. Forces loyal to Augusto C. Sandino in San Rafael del Norte, Nicaragua, firing a Lewis machine gun at a U.S. warplane on 4 February 1928. Photo by Alejandro Molina, a Sandino follower; the photo was sold by Molina's brother to the U.S. Military Attaché in Honduras. National Archives, RG165, MID 2657-P-241:114.

PHOTO 5. Staff of U.S. Marine Corps Gen. Logan Feland (seated, center) in Managua, September 1928. General Feland commanded the Marine Second Brigade in Nicaragua, for which he received the Distinguished Service Medal. National Archives, rg165, mid 2657-p-241:114.

PHOTO 6. Insurgent forces at a street barricade in Guatemala City at the intersection of Tenth Street East and Sixth Avenue South, during the uprising that overthrew President Estrada Cabrera on 13 April 1920 at a cost of 1,700 lives. U.S. Army Attaché, Guatemala City, National Archives, RG165, MID 2357-106.

9

Defining Collaboration
The United States and Central America

The onset of intense collaboration between the military and police authorities of the United States and the five Central American governments, starting in World War II, not only globalized but also transformed public violence on the isthmus. The military and police agencies of all the Central American states, whose national economies were incapable of supplying their enlisted men little but the sandals on their feet and the most miserly of food rations, eagerly integrated themselves into global networks that provided material, technical, managerial, and ideological resources on a scale unmatched in their histories.[1] The global, unregulated character of the networks meant no single power could control or monopolize their operation. The United States clearly dominated the Central Americans' access to and participation in those networks. But "control," even if Washington desired it, was hopelessly beyond its capacity. Morever, the Central American governments begged for enhanced levels of military and police collaboration with the United States, while Washington often found itself in the role of suppliant, eager to draw the isthmian governments into one or another new collaborative program to advance its own interests. And because of their ever-fragile dependence on internal collaborators-in-arms, usually in the form of one or another army faction, the Central American states could only have participated in the new global networks on terms that were continuously subject to renegotiation. Thus, the globalization of public violence made the isthmian states neither clients nor allies of the United States but collaborators.

In the South American countries, World War II had also opened the door to a fundamentally new military relationship with the United States, abruptly replacing a hodgepodge of well-established European training and supply linkages with a single, U.S.-coordinated channel that led back to Washington. The relative familiarity of the U.S. military presence in Panama and the Central American countries made the war's impact on external military relations there less dramatic. Still, apart from the organization and training of Nicaragua's National Guard from 1927 to 1933, and the intimate collaboration during that time between the Guard and the U.S. Marine Corps in the attempted destruction of the guerrilla forces led by Augusto Sandino, no substantial military collaboration between Washington and the isthmian countries occurred until the enactment of the Lend-Lease Act of 11 March 1941.

That year Nicaragua and Guatemala agreed to allow the construction of bases for use by U.S. military personnel in the air defense of the hemisphere. At the outset, a certain prewar continuity was established in the way U.S. Lend-Lease was justified in the isthmus, as opposed to the rest of the continent. In anticipation of Lend-Lease and the base construction agreements, President Roosevelt had already approved the War Department's rationale for military collaboration with the Central American states, namely, "to insure internal stability" rather than to enable them to assist in the defense of the hemisphere, which was the rationale for the rest of Latin America.[2] Washington considered the isthmian forces so inferior as to be practically useless as wartime allies. According to Col. Joseph B. Pate, the U.S. military attaché for Central America, Germany could "arrange for the overthrow" of every government in Central America "at a moment's notice," enabling it to launch a surprise air raid on the Panama Canal. In the case of Guatemala, for example, the most that Washington could reasonably expect to achieve would be to train and equip the nucleus of an army sufficient to defend the country until U.S. forces arrived.[3] But the *New York Times*'s military correspondent, Hanson W. Baldwin, warned against underestimating the men who had just fought the U.S. Marines to a draw in Nicaragua.[4]

In October 1941 Nicaragua became the first isthmian country to sign a Lend-Lease agreement. Costa Rica, El Salvador, and Honduras signed theirs in January and February but negotiations with Guatemala dragged on until November 1942, when it signed the largest Lend-Lease agreement of the five Central American states, for $5 million, more than three times that of the next largest agreement (El Salvador's). In every case, the value of transfers proposed in the agreements vastly exceeded the amounts actually delivered. Only 55 percent of the $9.75 million in proposed Lend-Lease military assistance ever reached Central America, and 57 percent of that went to Guatemala.

The $5.4 million in Lend-Lease transfers shipped to the five Central American countries appears insignificant when compared to total worldwide Lend-Lease shipments of $48.9 billion, or even the $493 million shipped to all nineteen Latin American countries combined. But from the point of view of Central America's political and military history, the only relevant comparison is with the isthmian countries' own military spending patterns. Guatemala's entire defense budget for fiscal year 1941 was the equivalent of $1.9 million; El Salvador's was $1.5 million,

Table 9.1   Lend-Lease Transfers

Country	Date	Anticipated value of transfers ($ millions)	Actual value of transfers ($ millions)	Repayment terms
Guatemala	16 Nov. 42	$5	$3.10	0% up to $3 m.; 60% over $3 m.*
El Salvador	2Feb. 42	$1.60	$0.88	55%
Nicaragua	16 Oct. 41	$1.30	$0.89	69%
Honduras	28 Feb. 42	$1.30	$0.37	9.20%
Costa Rica	16 Jan. 42	$0.55	$0.16	55%
TOTALS		$9.75	$5.40	

*The value of the first $3 million was considered paid for by various Guatemalan concessions.

Source: For anticipated values, *FRUS* 1941 v. 7, 411 (Nicaragua); *FRUS* 1942 v. 6, 431 (El Salvador); 443–44 (Guatemala); 480 (Honduras), *FRUS* 1942 v. 236–37 (Costa Rica); for actual values, U.S. Congress, "Thirty-Ninth Report to Congress on Lend-Lease Operations: Message from the President of the United States . . . for the year ending December 31, 1957," 85th Cong., 2d Sess., House Document No. 449 (Washington, D.C.: Government Printing Office, 1958), Appendix I (b).

Honduras's $1.2 million, Nicaragua's about $970,000, and Costa Rica's only $563,209. Of these totals, pay and personnel allowances, pensions, and operational expenses consumed well over half. Average annual procurement expenses for ordnance and equipment almost certainly never exceeded 20 percent before 1941 and were probably much less.[5] In all cases—except for Guatemala—Lend Lease transfers were shipped from about mid-1942 to about mid-1945. During those three years, the shipments accounted for 97 percent of El Salvador's estimated annual procurement budget, 46 percent of Costa Rica's, 52 percent of Honduras's, and 153 percent of Nicaragua's. Only Guatemala received Lend-Lease shipments after 1945; as of September 1946, the United States still owed Guatemala about $2 million in Lend-Lease shipments.[6] Even assuming that all Lend Lease equipment was not shipped until 1950, Lend-Lease would still have accounted for about 102 percent of Guatemala's estimated annual procurement budget over the eight-year period.

The impact of Lend-Lease was even greater than these numbers suggest because most of it was concentrated on building the air forces of countries that were extremely mountainous, with primitive highway networks and weak motorized ground transport support systems, and with a politico-military tradition of semi-autonomous regional garrison commands. The Lend-Lease air-power transfers meant that the coercive power at the disposal of these states-in-formation must have risen by at least half and probably much more in the span of just three to four years. Just over half of all Lend-Lease shipments to the isthmus consisted of "aircraft and aeronautical material," with Honduras's air force benefiting the most.[7]

Thus, World War II was a deus ex machina for the new isthmian dictators at this decisive moment in Central American state formation. The Lend-Lease program delivered aircraft, weapons, tanks, and other vehicles in quantities and on repayment terms that would have been unobtainable without the war. The U.S. military

Table 9.2 Comparison of Lend-Lease Shipments with Estimated Annual Procurement Budgets

Country	Defense Budget	Estimated Annual Procurement Budget (EAPB)*	Annualized Lend-Lease Shipments as % of EAPB
Guatemala	$1.9 million (FY 1941)	$380,000	102%
El Salvador	$1.5 million (1941)	$303,120	97%
Nicaragua	$970,000 (FY 1940)**	$194,030	153%
Honduras	$1.2 million (1941)	$236,800	52%
Costa Rica	$563,209 (1939)	$112,642	46%

Notes: *Upper-bound (see text). **Defense budget not published; estimated at 19% of total budget of $5.1 million, as reported in Migone et al., 389. Migone et al. reported defense spending at 17–21% for the three northernmost countries, and 8% for Costa Rica.

Source: For Lend-Lease totals, Table 10.1; for defense budgets, Raul C. Migone et al., eds., *Inter-American Statistical Yearbook 1942*, New York: Macmillan, n.d., pp. 379ff.

trainers and the U.S. military missions that typically accompanied Lend-Lease shipments not only supplied instruction in the use of the new matériel, but also created officer training programs and reorganized the armed forces with a view to centralizing command structures and making them more responsive and efficient. Between 1931 and 1941, all four northern countries hired U.S. military officers to direct their officer training academies. Beginning in 1941 with Costa Rica and ending with Nicaragua in 1952, all five countries requested and received U.S. military missions whose purpose was invariably identified in diplomatic agreements as "enhancing the efficiency" of the collaborator government's army, air force, or military forces in general. U.S. mission members thereby became temporary employees of that government, which paid their salaries and expenses. The duties of the mission personnel were decided on by the collaborator government and the chief of the mission but the mission members were responsible exclusively to that government, usually its minister of war or the commander of the armed forces. U.S. mission members were even entitled to "all benefits and privileges" that the collaborator government extended to its own military personnel of the same rank. Repeatedly renewed, usually at four-year intervals, the mission agreements extended the life of the missions into the twenty-first century.[8] (See figures A-10, A-11, and A-12 in the Appendix for trends in U.S. direction of the military academies and in the founding and growth of the U.S. missions.)

Even though the isthmian countries had almost nothing to do with the course of World War II, as combatants or even as significant suppliers of raw materials, the war's impact on their states' capacity for public violence was decisive. Besides the exponential growth rate in their tiny armed forces and the sudden expansion of war supplies of all kinds, Lend-Lease also provided the platform for more than five decades of U.S. collaboration in the organization, training, and equipping of military and police forces. The main elements of that collaboration would be conserved

Table 9.3   Distribution of Lend-Lease Transfers by Type

Country	Ordnance	Aircraft & aeronautical matériel	Tanks & vehicles	Other	Total	% Total
Costa Rica	$34,422	$0	$51,541	$70,367	$156,330	3%
El Salvador	$146,114	$423,369	$259,495	$49,296	$878,274	16%
Guatemala	$731,993	$1,754,759	$372,895	$226,382	$3,086,029	57%
Honduras	$46,785	$257,371	$24,626	$39,581	$368,363	7%
Nicaragua	$90,622	$469,529	$133,039	$194,009	$887,199	17%
All Central America	$1,049,936	$2,905,028	$841,596	$579,635	$5,376,195	100%

Source: U.S. Congress, House, Committee on Foreign Affairs, "Thirty-Second Report to Congress on Lend-Lease Operations, Message from the President of the United States," 3 October 1951.

and elaborated in the Cold War programs to come: bilateral military negotiation over the scope of changes in the local military force structure, followed by the transfer of services and materials from the United States on terms that ranged from long-term credits to outright grants.

Although it had a major impact on capacity, U.S. military and police collaboration would not significantly enhance the limits of state-sponsored violence in Central America. By the 1940s, the expansive character of those limits had already been defined by the inhabitants of the isthmus. Washington's collaboration with regional military and police bodies served mainly to increase both their effectiveness and their legitimacy as bulwarks against fascism and later communism, and by extension any individual or group that might plausibly be associated with fascism and communism. On the other hand, the U.S. program of modernizing and expanding the capacity for violence unquestionably inhibited tendencies that may have favored the reduction of the limits of state-sponsored violence. Still, the modernization of capacity must not be confused with the creation of conflict or with the augmentation of the limits of public violence.

The isthmian states' participation in World War II as members of the grand democratic alliance carried a certain ideological burden for the governments at their helm, because most of them could easily be confused, at times, with the fascism of the enemy. Although the burden would prove to be evanescent in the sense that democracy was quickly subordinated to the containment of communism after World War II, its timing was unfortunate for Guatemala's General Ubico and El Salvador's General Hernández-Martínez, both of whom were driven from power in 1944 by popular movements inspired partly by the democratic discourse of two of the main Allied forces, the United States and Britain, and to a lesser extent that of the third ally, the Soviet Union. These popular movements clearly weakened Honduras's General Carías in 1948, and nearly forced Nicaragua's General Somoza out of the presidency in 1944.[9] The U.S. State Department, in a note to its representatives in all five isthmian countries in 1944, acknowledged "an increase in the scope and intensity of political activities in Central America in recent months" characterized by "bitter open or covert opposition to virtually all of the administrations in power." The movements seemed so strong that it was "almost inevitable" that they would take power in some countries.[10] In no case, however, did such movements succeed in reversing the trend toward an institutionalized and "modernized" species of military-led authoritarianism that, with the collaboration of the United States, took hold in the late 1940s in El Salvador, Nicaragua, and Honduras, and in 1954 in Guatemala, and would characterize the isthmus (outside of Costa Rica) until at least the end of the Cold War.[11]

The immediate postwar agitation was quickly identified with communism by the "administrations in power," and even inspired the negotiation of an anticommunist pact in 1947 among the generals who headed the governments of El Salvador, Honduras, and Nicaragua; they signed it between 25 and 27 April, and Costa Rica's Pres. Teodoro Picado added his signature on 15 May. The pact began by acknowledging "a state of anti-social agitation" in Honduras, El Salvador, and Nicaragua orchestrated "by interests opposed to the traditional meaning of their democratic institutions." In response, the signers promised "the immediate planning of a campaign of economic improvement, either agricultural or industrial, that raises the living conditions of the masses," while promulgating labor laws premised on "harmony between labor and capital." The presidents—evidently as concerned to preserve the "history" and "traditions" of their countries as they were to address what they called the "social problem"—agreed to "organize a cultural campaign to confirm the basic feelings of nationality, such as family, *patria*, democracy, in accord with the special conditions of each Nation; in matters concerning land and population density, edicts will be issued and institutions created to organize production, always within the historical meaning of our economy; . . ." The three generals (but not Picado) also established a joint "secret information service" among their police agencies to "control the movement of communist agents" from one country to another. They further agreed to begin working immediately to produce within one month "a treaty of immediate assistance, which will include economic and military obligations, in case a movement of a communistic nature tries to disrupt order in any of the States." (This provision would be superceded four months later by the signing of the Inter-American Treaty of Reciprocal Assistance or the "Rio Treaty.") The pact was to remain open for signing by any Central American governments that "demonstrate their anticommunist tendencies and formalize a corresponding policy." To President Picado's signature was added a note that excluded Costa Rica from the obligation to negotiate the mutual assistance treaty, owing to "the idiosyncrasy and tradition of the Costa Rican people who in general are opposed to contracting obligations that may imply commitments of a military character."[12]

The pact presaged two of the ways public violence would soon be transformed through U.S. collaboration. First, it was a move toward regional military collaboration on a scale not contemplated since the National War of 1856–57, when the combined forces of Guatemala, El Salvador, Honduras, and Costa Rica (along with nationalist Nicaraguans) defeated Walker's army in Nicaragua. The inadequacy of the hermetic authoritarianism of the 1930s must have been clear to presidents Carías, Somoza, and Castaneda. What they could not have foreseen was that the potential for regional collaboration in the deployment of institutional public violence (as well as collaboration in the deployment of para-institutional and counterinstitutional public violence) would shortly be overtaken by unilateral collaboration with the United States. Second, the pact correctly identified the signers' only serious enemies as their fellow Central Americans, thus anticipating by at least a decade the official shift from "hemispheric security" to "internal security" that would justify U.S.-Central American military and police collaboration from the 1960s through the end of the Cold War. Instead of Walker's gang of light-skinned, English-speaking invaders, the common enemy were their own countrymen, subversives against whom the most important preventive weapons, the dictators realized, were intelligence and a disposition to share it among themselves. Like other forms of military and police collaboration— the transfer of equipment and weapons, training services, and strategic and organizational guidance—collaboration in the collection and dissemination of intelligence would also be subject to globalization in the years to come through unilateral collaboration with Washington.

The pact's acknowledgement of the pressing nature of the region's "social problem" and the need to raise living standards foreshadowed the adoption of public policies that led to diversification of exports, economic growth, industrialization, freer trade, unionization and minimum-wage legislation, and rudimentary social security institutions.[13] The post-1945 dictatorships in fact displayed a surprising political suppleness, a capacity to assimilate, deflect, and co-opt challenges to an extent that suggests a significant if intermittent level of either popular support or at least popular indifference. The newfound resilience of the regimes may also have been owing to the adoption of a more flexible assortment of managerial techniques by the agents of the state. If, in the 1930s, the military tended to replace the landlords as direct rulers, in the 1940s "the army was joined by lawyers, administrators, technicians and professional politicians in directing the state apparatus."[14] And so the late 1940s marked the beginning of a period of state formation in Central America characterized by a major amplification of the state's reach and of its repertoire of practical techniques of persuasion, co-optation, surveillance, control, and coercion. These were themes that the framers of the 1947 pact outlined with admirable foresight, while linking them to the preoccupations with communism and national security that would define Cold War collaboration with the United States.

The pact's stress on regional cooperation in the sharing of intelligence also pointed to an effort to replace the exhausted and highly divisive model of Central American unification, which had engendered so much violence over the previous twelve decades, with a more feasible alternative. On 14 October 1951 came the "Carta de San Salvador," a joint declaration by all five governments to establish the Organization of Central American States (ODECA), whose members would seek to "strengthen the ties that unite them; consult mutually to guarantee and maintain fraternal coexistence in this region of the Continent; prevent and unite against all disagreements and assure the peaceful solution of any conflict that may break out among them; assist one another; seek joint solutions to common problems; promote their economic, social and cultural development through cooperative and solidaristic action."[15]

All five governments ratified the Carta immediately, but the first meeting of ODECA, set for 2 May 1953, was postponed when the Arbenz government of Guatemala abruptly withdrew its ratification, alleging a plot by the other governments to overthrow it. Arbenz was right, on at least two counts. First, the Nicaraguan government had already joined an aborted CIA plot to invade Guatemala ("Operation Fortune") the previous year. Second, White House adviser Adolph Berle, after a trip to Central America in March, had just recommended that the United States organize the other isthmian countries for "the clearing out of the communists in Guatemala." Berle's plan would be rejected, but the CIA's Operation Fortune would be reborn as Operation Success in the coming summer. Guatemala's participation in ODECA had to await the *golpista* regime of Castillo Armas, whose accession to power in 1954 opened the way for ODECA's first meeting in Antigua, Guatemala, from 17 to 24 August 1955.[16] Considering the leading role that the armed forces were playing in the governments of Guatemala, El Salvador, Honduras, and Nicaragua, it is not surprising that military collaboration immediately assumed an honored place on ODECA's agenda. In January 1956 the defense ministers met in Antigua and proposed the formation of the Central American Defense Council (CONDECA) as an organ of the ODECA, "for the purpose of studying military problems," including the joint defense of the isthmus.[17]

CONDECA did not hold its first meeting until 1964, undoubtedly because the U.S. government's role as the tutelary collaborator in military and police affairs of each of the five isthmian governments made it superfluous. Washington was the region's military and police coordinator, unilaterally and secretly deciding what the appropriate "force levels" were for each country, albeit with little control over the actual achievement of those levels. U.S. influence was exerted by offering or withholding the means to achieve a certain "force level," as well as through its power to dispense advice, transfer intelligence data, provide training, approve commercial transactions between private U.S. arms dealers and the isthmian governments, sell U.S. government-owned equipment and services (with or without a discount, with or without credit), or give them away via the grant-based Military Assistance Program (MAP). Anxious to avoid upsetting what it conceived to be a rough military equilibrium among the five countries, Washington was both eager to "modernize" the isthmian military and police forces and to discourage them from collaborating with the governments of nonhemispheric countries. As a result, after the Guatemalan *putsch* of 1954, the United States in effect adopted a policy of encouraging military modernization but at a pace gradual enough to avoid disturbing the military balance or provoking complaints that it was "militarizing" the isthmus.[18]

Until the Cuban Revolution of 1959, nothing contributed more to the intensification of U.S.-Central American military collaboration than the policies adopted by the administration of Guatemalan President Arbenz. More than a year before the U.S.-sponsored invasion of Guatemala in 1954, the State Department was advocating programs of grant collaboration through the MAP with Honduras, Nicaragua, and El Salvador for "political and psychological" reasons related to Guatemala, rather than military ones. The purpose would be to isolate Guatemala politically by establishing "a political climate in Guatemala of benefit to anti-communist Guatemalan elements, including elements in the Guatemalan armed forces disposed to combat communist domination of the present Guatemalan Government," according to Secretary of State John Foster Dulles. But Dulles had to contend with the Mutual Security Act's prohibition of grant collaboration with Latin American governments for purposes other than "hemispheric defense." So Dulles asked the Defense Department to give "high and urgent priority" to creating some plausible hemispheric defense mission for Honduras, Nicaragua, and El Salvador—the same states whose dictators had signed the anticommunist pact of 1947—even if the missions were "only relatively minor."[19]

The Joint Chiefs of Staff refused to cooperate in Dulles's manipulation of the law. Although grant collaboration with Nicaragua might be justified to defend the Panama Canal against air attacks or guerrilla infiltration, grant collaboration with El Salvador and Honduras was militarily indefensible "since the specific tasks which El Salvador and Honduras could effectively perform with limited United States grant assistance would be of negligible military value."[20] But leaving out El Salvador and Honduras would diminish the "psychological impact" on Guatemala, the State Department replied, and on 17 November 1953, Defense finally agreed to "develop hemispheric defense missions" for El Salvador and Honduras. Three weeks later, President Eisenhower made the legally required declaration that "defense plans require the participation of Nicaragua, El Salvador and Honduras in missions important to the defense of the Western Hemisphere," thus authorizing the opening of negotiations with their governments on the level and type of grant collaboration.[21]

By authorizing negotiations with the three governments for bilateral grant collaboration agreements, Eisenhower opened the door to the single biggest expansion of U.S. military collaboration with the Central American military establishments—and of course, their own expansion—in their short histories. Though a momentous decision for Central America, for Washington it was no more than a low-cost tactical move to increase the pressure on the Arbenz government while bolstering isthmian support for the U.S. policy of isolating and destabilizing his administration. But grant military collaboration, a move the Pentagon had resisted, would shortly be seen as a handy device for ensuring the loyalty of the military forces to U.S. policies. After all, Guatemala's traditional, "banana-republic" army of barefoot Indian conscripts and corrupt backwoods colonels actually appeared to be sustaining a communist-oriented government in power.

In February 1954, the U.S. military officers assigned to create the "hemispheric defense" plans that would justify grant collaboration with Nicaragua, Honduras, and El Salvador worked from a one-size-fits-all draft devised by the Joint Chiefs of Staff. The draft asserted that the security of both the intended collaborator and the United States, "together with that of the other countries of the Western Hemisphere, is threatened by the imperialistic designs of the USSR," thus calling for joint action to defend the hemisphere. The United States, which "because of extra-hemispheric requirements" had to reduce her forces in the hemisphere, would, according to the draft plan, provide "such additional equipment, materials and services" as may be necessary.[22]

While negotiations with El Salvador bogged down, delaying a grant collaboration arrangement there until the 1960s, Nicaragua and Honduras readily agreed to the conditions imposed by Washington and signed Bilateral Military Assistance Agreements on 23 April and 20 May 1954, respectively. The "mutual" nature of the collaboration was stressed in the agreements, which opened by requiring the United States and its collaborator to "make or continue to make available to the other," and possibly to third governments, "equipment, materials, services, or other military assistance . . . so designed as to promote the defense of the Western Hemisphere and be in accordance with defense plans under which both Governments will participate in missions important to the defense of the Western Hemisphere." Because it was unlikely that either Honduras or Nicaragua could do much for the United States, the agreements required both of them "to facilitate the production and transfer to the Government of the United States of America for such period of time, in such quantities and upon such terms and conditions as may be agreed upon, of raw and semi-processed materials required by the United States of America as a result of deficiencies or potential deficiencies in its own resources."[23] The military plan agreed to by both countries required them to furnish one infantry battalion—outfitted and trained by the United States at practically no cost to them—for "hemisphere defense." Guatemala became a grant collaborator on 18 June 1955, the first anniversary of the U.S.-sponsored invasion that led to the collapse of the Arbenz government even though the sole, initial objective of isthmian grant collaboration—the overthrow of Arbenz—had already been achieved.

Although grant collaboration was publicly justified as a way to help Central America protect itself from a Soviet attack, the CIA claimed that not one country had a fighting force that was "worthy of consideration as an army." The forces of Guatemala, Nicaragua, and El Salvador were capable of maintaining their own internal security, whereas those of Honduras and Costa Rica could only be counted on to suppress "minor civil disturbances."[24] As a result, the United States found itself in a paradoxical position. Under what all parties agreed was nothing more than a pretense, Washington was vastly increasing the scope of military collaboration with three governments (and considering doing so with El Salvador) for which the only conceivable application of their new U.S.-derived military power would be within their own borders rather than against some external, common enemy of the whole hemisphere. By 1961, as soon as the "hemispheric defense" justification for grant collaboration was legally replaced by one of internal defense against a subversive enemy, the paradox was neatly resolved and the collaboration of the 1950s appeared to be an example of good planning.

Legal niceties aside, grant collaboration began to be informally reshaped as an instrument of internal security almost as soon as Washington's isthmian partners had signed their agreements. On 22 May 1956, Dulles asked all the U.S. diplomatic posts in Mexico, the Caribbean, and Central America to ascertain what steps the governments there were taking "to reduce the effectiveness of the communist conspiracy with particular emphasis on the detention of dangerous communists in the event of an emergency." He wanted the information in order to "assess the danger to the internal security of the US that hard core communists and possible sympathizers could render by assisting the Soviet Union in both peacetime and wartime clandestine operations." By U.S. reckoning, Guatemala still presented the greatest internal threat; its total communist party membership was thought to be more than six times that of Costa Rica's, which had the second-biggest party in the isthmus.[25]

Military guidance from the Pentagon began to reflect the rising concern with internal subversion. By 1957 it was ordering its military mission chiefs to encourage all five Central American governments to build up their air forces by developing fighter-bomber and transportation squadrons.[26] In 1958, Pentagon planners began urging each of the four northern countries to establish, in addition to their grant-supported infantry battalions, infantry battalion "combat teams."[27] A combat team is an infantry unit whose commander has operational and administrative control over elements—such as artillery, tanks, and engineering units—that an ordinary battalion commander would not have. By creating a new military unit with more mobility and independence than the traditional battalion, the governments of Central America would be preparing themselves to confront guerrilla-like enemies that might spring up within their own territory. An example of such an enemy was even then being paraded before their eyes—that of Fidel Castro's 26th of July Movement, which in 1958 was rapidly gaining control over the countryside of Cuba. And this in the only Caribbean-area nation whose army the CIA judged to be "worthy of con-

Table 9.4   U.S. Government Estimates of Communist Party Membership in the Greater Caribbean Region, 1956

	"Hard Core Communist Party members"	Additional Communist Party members	"Total Communist Party members"	"Communist Party sympathizers" or "possible sympathizers"
Cuba	13,000		25,000	
Canada	5,000	5,000	10,000	
Mexico	2,000		4,000 to 4,500	75,000–100,000
Martinique			2,600 to 3,000	30,000–40,000
Guatemala			2,000	2,000
Costa Rica			300	4,000
El Salvador			200	400
British Honduras			100	400
Panama			100	250
Nicaragua			80	120

Source: NA. FOIA. RG59. 720.5/5-2256. Dulles to various diplomatic posts in the Americas, 22 May 1956.

sideration as an army."[28] In all the capitals of Central America, the question must have been asked repeatedly: if the Cuban Army—the only "real" army in the Caribbean region—couldn't stop Castro's men, what would happen here if a few score *montoneros* alighted from a boat (as had the Cuban insurgents in December 1956) and headed for the hills?

Castro's movement undoubtedly encouraged the expansion of collaboration in surveillance and intelligence collection, a dimension of internal security that would become the most controversial aspect of Cold War military and police collaboration. The U.S. government had already been acting unilaterally to collect information on Central American citizens of all political affiliations, as well as those suspected of having communist connections. Detailed reports were being filed by informants and State Department investigators, who also gathered data collected by the Federal Bureau of Investigation (FBI) and CIA on the movements and activities of what must have been many hundreds if not thousands of Central Americans. For example, the State Department's labor attaché in Mexico City, Ben S. Stephansky, reported 23 August 1954 on "three or four Hondurans possibly attending" the Universidad Obrera of the Mexican communist party. Many of the reports were dotted with references to rumors and hearsay about drinking, adultery, and vague interests in communism. A Honduran who was *thought* to have been a communist, and who *appeared* to have some (unknown) position in the government, "divorced his wife, a schoolteacher and member of a respectable family of Tegucigalpa, by whom he has one son, and in 1950 remarried a woman of questionable reputation." Another report, produced in 1955 on the activities of a U.S. citizen residing in Guatemala, stated that he was heard to have "openly derided U.S. Congress and U.S. foreign policy in Central America while at a party in Frederiksted, St. Croix." Antonio Salazar, identified as a Salvadoran cartoonist and caricaturist who was also the Salvadoran chargé d'affaires in Montevideo in 1954, also attracted the State Department's interest for reportedly having

> entertained the former Chilean communist Senator and poet Pablo Neruda, who transited Uruguay to and from visits to various Commie [*sic*] congresses in Europe. . . . Salazar obviously belongs to the unfortunately rather large group of Latin American intellectuals who seem for one reason or another to have been taken in by Communism at one stage or another of their careers. How active a communist he may be, or just what undesirable activities if any he may be indulging in, we do not know. I did observe at one of the monthly meetings of Counselors and Chargés that he was greeted effusively by the Russian Chargé d'Áffaires and that they sat together and conversed animatedly throughout the meal.

Salazar "was presumably Secretary General of the Salvadoran communist party and was given the appointment in Uruguay [in 1952] to get him out of the country."[29]

It did not escape the notice of either the U.S. government or the governments in the region that collective access to such information would be useful to the regimes in power as they sought to limit or otherwise control political opposition.

For example, the U.S. government claimed to know the names of all "active commu-nists" in Costa Rica in 1956, and was equally confident that the Costa Rican public security ministry could not name "a large number" of them. As a result, should it ever be necessary to detail all the communists in Costa Rica, the U.S. government would be in a position to help the Costa Rican government do so, according to an official in the U.S. Embassy in San José.[30] In 1957, Guatemalan Col. Enrique Peralta Azurdia (who in 1963 would take power in a military coup against an elected presi-dent and rule until 1966) told a U.S. diplomat that "the way to combat communism was to bring about an intimate exchange of intelligence information and plans between the military establishments of Guatemala, El Salvador, and Honduras, and to support the steps which have been taken in this direction by the ODECA minis-ters of defense."[31] When the U.S. president's brother, Milton Eisenhower, visited Guatemala the following year, President Ydígoras told him that "he would like to establish a system of cooperation with the governments of the other republics of Central America in keeping track of and controlling the movements of communists. He was setting up an agency in Guatemala for this purpose."[32]

Colonel Peralta's idea, seconded by Ydígoras and perhaps advanced by Milton Eisenhower, must have been well received, for by 1960, the U.S. Army Caribbean Command had established a "highly successful" pilot program of exchanging infor-mation with the chiefs of intelligence of several Latin American countries. They traded data on "communist personalities, techniques, plans, objectives and opera-tions," as well as on activities of local communist parties and "the communist Inter-national movement." The Defense Department proposed expanding the program, beginning with unclassified information and moving up to classified information later, with the support of the FBI, which would collect nonmilitary data. As part of the expansion, U.S. military attachés and other U.S. intelligence agencies would be asked to make collection of intelligence on communists a higher priority. In addi-tion, the Defense Department proposed, reserve officers employed by "major U.S. corporations" in Latin America could be asked to report to U.S. military attachés any pertinent information "received through normal business, social or personal contacts only."[33] By August 1961, the governments of Guatemala, Honduras, and El Salvador had already agreed on a "system for exchanging information," according to the U.S. ambassador in San Salvador.[34]

Just as these collaborative programs to collect and share intelligence were get-ting off the ground, President Eisenhower authorized the CIA to organize an inva-sion of Cuba by exiles to overthrow the government of Fidel Castro. The decision of President Ydígoras to let the CIA use Guatemalan territory to train the Cuban inva-sion force contributed to an attempted *golpe* against Ydígoras on 13 November 1960 by a secret organization of military officers.[35] On the same day, the chief of the Costa Rican Guardia Civil, Col. Alfonso Monge, was killed in a shootout between Guardia troops and anti-Somoza guerrillas who were evidently inspired by the Cas-tro movement operating in northern Costa Rica. Like Guatemala, Nicaragua was also lending its territory to the CIA for the training of the Cuban invasion force.[36] The Guatemalan coup attempt and Monge's death occurred less than a month after a reformist military *junta* in El Salvador overthrew the strongly anticommunist government of Pres. (and Lt. Col.) José María Lemus.

These events happened so close together that it seemed plausible, both to Secretary of State Christian Herter and CIA Director Allen W. Dulles, that some kind of pro-Castro conspiracy was behind them. On 16 November, Herter told President Eisenhower that he and Dulles believed that the governments of Guatemala, Costa Rica, and Nicaragua "have insufficient capabilities to deal effectively with the sustained threat posed by pro-Castro and pro-communist elements, particularly the threats of force or subversion from abroad. I request that you authorize me to inform them that the United States is prepared to consider promptly and favorably any official written requests from the affected Central American governments . . . [for] our air and sea forces to seek out and prevent any reinforcement or supply from abroad of rebel movements within their countries."[37] The next day, 17 November, the White House announced that, in response to the requests of Nicaragua and Guatemala for protection from the government of Cuba, the aircraft carrier *Shangri-La* and four destroyers were sailing off the southern coast of Cuba to prevent a communist invasion of Guatemala or Nicaragua.[38] A new phase in the cruel history of public violence was about to open in the isthmus.

Conclusions

In Central America, the World War II military collaboration that had seeded the region's single greatest expansion in its capacity for public violence accelerated further in response to the growing conviction, between 1952 and 1954, that the Guatemalan government of Jacobo Arbenz had become a security threat to the United States. Intensified collaboration with Honduras, El Salvador, and Nicaragua was not a military move but a diplomatic maneuver to isolate Guatemala. Yet even as it celebrated its secret victory over Arbenz, the CIA acknowledged that the region's social and political environment threatened U.S. interests more formidably than a left-leaning government. The republics of Central America and the Caribbean, the agency reported, were marked by "social immobility, economic underdevelopment, and political immaturity," and they were inhabited overwhelmingly by "illiterate, poverty-stricken, and socially and politically inert" people. At the same time, the "traditional ruling elements have been faced by steadily increasing demands for social, economic, and political change, voiced by small but growing urban middle class elements with increasing popular support." The late Guatemalan revolution was an expression of that movement, and while it was ripening in El Salvador and Honduras it was being "effectively contained by strongly entrenched authoritarian regimes" in Nicaragua and the Dominican Republic. "The pressure for change will continue to grow. . . . Whether eventual change is orderly will depend in large measure on whether the existing regimes can bring themselves to promote social, economic, and political progress, or whether, through static repression, they make virtually certain an eventual violent explosion. In any case, no substantial improvement in basic conditions is likely to occur for many years." In Central America and Latin America generally, the CIA warned, the "issue of 'democracy' versus 'dictatorship'—that is, of social and political change versus traditional authoritarianism—is a matter of far greater importance than the question of Communism or anti-Communism."[39]

Three years later, another CIA report repeated that demands for reform would intensify in Central America and the Caribbean republics. "The present military leadership [in these countries] can provide no more than a braking action against pressures for change. The growing size and importance of the educated professional and middle classes will increasingly threaten the position of the traditional ruling groups." The "probable" outcome was "more broadly-based, reformist, nationalist regimes, similar to that in Costa Rica."[40]

The CIA analysis revealed the central contradiction of U.S. military and police collaboration in Central America during the Cold War. Washington's partners were the very "military leadership" that was providing the "braking action against pressures for change" favored by the United States. How Washington found itself intensifying its collaboration with the side that it assumed would be defeated is examined in the next five chapters.

10

Guatemala

"Showcase of Latin America"

> It is to be doubted that the Guatemalan Army could ever rise, put on
> shoes and rush to the defense of the hemisphere or anything else with-
> out substantial U.S. support.
> —L. D. Mallory, U.S. Ambassador to Guatemala, 11 August 1958

As the United States was drawn into World War II, the prospect of a closer military
relationship with Washington impassioned President Ubico. In June 1940, he
assured the United States of his absolute loyalty to the Allied cause. To prove it, he
revealed that he would soon issue a decree, already drawn up and awaiting his signature, "stating that anybody whose activities disturbed the independence or security of the State would be immediately shot," the U.S. ambassador reported.[1] In
return for that loyalty, Ubico wanted weapons for what he said was a badly underequipped army. Washington was prepared to cooperate but it had reservations. On
the one hand, U.S. political as well as military authorities recognized the strategic
necessity of supplying enough arms and training to Guatemala to enable it to
defend the country "against the first brunt of sudden internal or external aggression." On the other hand, Ubico's munitions wish-list was "inflated," and the quantity of arms sent should not be so great as to represent a risk in the event the government falls to "an openly pro-German dictator." The proposed solution was to
offer Ubico a large U.S. military mission to train Guatemalan soldiers, but whose
real function was to control and protect the transferred arms. But the dictator succeeded in defeating that plan, evidently concerned over both the cost of such a mission (whose members would have to be paid by Guatemala) and the implied
affront to nationalist sensibilities. Not until 1945, the year after Ubico's overthrow,
would Guatemala consent to a U.S. military mission, composed of separate army
and aviation units.[2]

As it turned out, the U.S. combat presence in Guatemala expanded so quickly that anyone considering a pro-German *golpe* would have had to give up any hope of victory. Since the Marines left Nicaragua in 1933, no isthmian country north of Panama has welcomed so many U.S. troops, with the possible exception of Honduras during the contra war of the 1980s. In 1941, the War Department chose Guatemala as the site of two of the twenty-five Latin American airfields that would have to be built from scratch or substantially improved for use by the U.S. Army and Navy in the air defense of the hemisphere. Construction work by Pan American Airports Corporation, under contract to the War Department, took place at La Aurora airfield in Guatemala City and at the San José airfield on the Pacific coast throughout 1941. Within three weeks of the attack on Pearl Harbor on 7 December, six B-18 bombers were flying out of La Aurora on long-range patrols over the Pacific Ocean. A bomber squadron was set up at the San José base, where six more B-18s arrived in January.[3] By mid-1942, there were at least 1,793 U.S. military personnel stationed in Guatemala. In November of that year Ubico formally agreed to an extraordinary series of concessions that included authorizations for the United States to take over, for military purposes, not only La Aurora and the San José field, but also the airfield in Puerto Barrios on the Caribbean coast; to use all the country's "ports and anchorages" for military defense purposes; and to "use all means of communications in transporting troops across or within the Republic of Guatemala." In return for the military concessions, the United States agreed to grant Guatemala $3 million in military equipment under Lend-Lease.[4]

By then, the U.S. government had already begun training Guatemalan officers outside the country. Five air force officers took courses in U.S. nonmilitary schools in 1941, on scholarships provided by Washington. The next year, more scholarships supported Guatemalan officers in the Command and General Staff School, Ft. Leavenworth, Kansas; the Infantry School, Ft. Benning, Georgia; Canal Zone installations; the Artillery School, Ft. Sill, Oklahoma; and various private institutions, including Massachusetts General Hospital, Northwestern University, and Harvard University.[5] In 1943, Washington built three more military airports and agreed to turn over the U.S. military base in Puerto Barrios to Ubico's government. As a result of these and other measures, the Ubico government boasted, rarely in its history had the Guatemalan armed forces been as powerful as they were now. All of the country's air force officers were being trained in the U.S. air base at Guatemala City as well as in the Canal Zone and the continental United States.[6]

The Guatemalan government was eager to publicize Ubico's skill at negotiating tangible benefits for his armed forces in exchange for Guatemalan cooperation "en la defensa americana."[7] But by 1943 the dictator's popularity was waning fast, and his ability to add more firepower to his army scarcely impressed his government's opponents. His involuntary departure from the presidency on 1 July 1944 after two weeks of public demonstrations against the dictatorship was followed in October by a one-way flight to New Orleans, where he died in 1946.[8] Within three days of Ubico's resignation, Gen. Federico Ponce Vaides seized the presidency, but his obvious determination to restore the dictatorship led to further public unrest. A group of young army officers organized a revolt, forced Ponce from office, and paved the way for the constitutional government and the free elections held on 19 December 1944 that the population of the capital had been demanding since June.

"Once famous for its dictators, guns and torture, Guatemala is now an example for all people who struggle for their freedom," announced President-Elect Juan José Arévalo on 10 February 1945. Demonizing Ubico and associating him with the worst of the liberal dictators, the former professor echoed the battle cries of the political wars of the nineteenth century, repeatedly denouncing the "servilismo" and the "moral and political wretchedness" of the previous administration.[9] Indeed, Ubico's downfall turned out to be a momentous event in the history of Guatemala, opening a period of government under two elected presidents—Arévalo (1945–51) and Jacobo Arbenz (1951–54)—that was more democratic and responsive to popular interests than any in the country's history.

At the outset of what became known immediately as the Guatemalan Revolution of 1944, the Arévalo administration welcomed the new opportunities for military collaboration that promised to emerge after the termination of Lend-Lease. On the morning of 9 May 1945, the day the war in Europe officially ended, representatives of the general staffs of the United States and Guatemala gathered in the office of the U.S. military attaché in Guatemala for a thirty-minute organizational session. Lt. Gen. George H. Brett headed the nineteen-member U.S. military delegation. Among the thirteen Guatemalan officers was the future president, then-Captain Arbenz, who was Arévalo's defense minister and had already established himself as the leader of the army's reform faction. Arbenz and his followers were opposed by the army faction led by Maj. Francisco J. Arana, the chief of the country's armed forces. No doubt aware of the fragility of the factional standoff within the army, the U.S. ambassador, Edwin J. Kyle, urged the delegates to maintain "an atmosphere of frank cordiality, in the security that all of us are seeking the same end in all matters related to the security of the Americas in the postwar era." Lt. Gen. Brett promised "a minimum supply of arms" enabling Guatemala to contribute to hemispheric security and urged the delegates to maintain whatever information they received on each other's forces in "the greatest secrecy" and to work "sincerely and openly." The U.S. side immediately declared the minimal precondition for any further discussions on military collaboration, one that it imposed everywhere in the isthmus: the reconstitution of the army according to U.S. tables of organization. The Guatemalans quickly assented, and in response Col. Lloyd R. Besse, who headed the U.S. Army delegation, proposed that the United States equip the newly reorganized Guatemalan Army. Offering to supply cost estimates, Colonel Besse handed the Guatemalans a list of questions that revealed Washington's preoccupation with defending the hemisphere against the type of threat represented by Germany, which had just surrendered.[10]

The answers indicated the Guatemalan Army officers' eagerness to acquire more U.S. arms and training services, to reorganize their forces along U.S. lines, and above all to expand the army. The Guatemalans asked Washington to replace 94 percent of the army's inventory of 46,094 rifles, 85 percent of its 157 artillery pieces, and 40 percent of its 270 machine guns. Most strikingly, they wanted to quadruple the army, from about 2,400 effectives to about 10,300—only a year after the overthrow of a military dictator and just two months after the inauguration of President Arévalo. A plan of expansion of this magnitude under Ubico would not have been surprising. That the army could propose it at the moment when hope for democratic change had never been greater highlights the premature character of those hopes. It is hard to believe that Arévalo was convinced of the need to organize and equip an army of 10,300 men when his authority over a chronically improvisational state remained subject to the will of the army leadership.[11]

At the conclusion of the staff conversations on 21 May, a four-year mission agreement was signed stipulating the purpose of the U.S. military mission as that of both "enhancing the efficiency of the Guatemalan Army" and advising its general staff and the heads of the military academies. Under the agreement, Guatemala consented to pay the mission members their salary and accepted a clause forbidding it from hiring the military services of any other foreign governments without U.S. permission.[12]

Even before the May staff meetings began, and undoubtedly in anticipation of them, the Arévalo administration had already issued orders to do away with the army's hallowed *cuartel* (garrison) system, considered by U.S. officers to be ridiculously old fashioned and ineffective, and to replace it with a single light division, thus matching the U.S. Army's system of organization. The *cuartel* system reflected the *caudillismo* of the past, when each garrison was commanded militarily and politically by the regional strongman who ruled the whole district. Now, command and control of military power was to be formally separated from political authority; concentrated, not dispersed; and bureaucratized, not personalized. This is what the U.S. military advisers meant when they insisted repeatedly on reorganization "along U.S. lines." On 14 March 1945, the *comandancias de armas* (one for each of the country's twenty-two departments, each headed by a colonel or general), the *mayorías de plaza* (the latter's subaltern, one for each department), and *comandancias locales* (228 subdepartmental commands that could be headed by anyone from sergeant to colonel) were abolished and replaced with seven *zonas militares*, each with its assigned units. The traditional dispersal of forces in small garrisons, the government explained, "was not only uneconomical but impeded the tactical and strategic cohesion necessary for a modern armed forces." The general staff was reorganized to match the U.S. system, with separate staffs for personnel, intelligence, organization and training, supply, and evacuation.[13]

Reorganization along U.S. lines led to an expansion in U.S.-supervised training programs. Twenty-nine men were admitted for advanced study to the U.S. Command and General Staff School at Ft. Leavenworth in 1945.[14] In Guatemala, an Escuela Militar de Instructores was established that all Guatemalan officers would eventually be required to attend. Under the direction of U.S. Army Lt. Col. Charles W. Wiegand, the training of the first class of seventy-two men began in December 1945; just twenty-six survived after the rest failed their first examination. The school's library was donated by the U.S. military mission, which also began offering ninety-day English courses to officers in 1945.[15]

On paper, the collaboration agreement was between two civilian governments. But in fact, the first genuine civilian government in Guatemalan history was scarcely relevant to either the negotiation of the agreement or its implementation. The central figure at the U.S.-Guatemalan staff conference was Major Arana, who owed his position as chief of the armed forces to his success both in organizing the coup of October 1944 and in subsequently blocking the unconditional transfer of power from military men to civilian authorities. Arévalo's easy victory in the December 1944 presidential election was the first to be won by someone who did not command some kind of fighting force, which made it that much easier for Arana to successfully threaten Arévalo with blocking his inauguration unless Arévalo promised to appoint him to the newly created post of armed forces chief. From that lofty perch, Arana could control not only the armed forces, but (he undoubtedly reasoned) Arévalo's government as well.[16]

In his position as armed forces chief, it fell to Major Arana, at the closing session of the conference, to assure the United States of the Guatemalan Army's disposition to collaborate effectively with the U.S. Army,

> to whom we owe so much, not only for assistance that it has given us, but also for the conquest of freedom with the victory of its divisions in Europe. Likewise, we wish to make it known also that you may rest assured that the Army of the new Guatemala, which is to say the Army of the Revolution, will know how to collaborate effectively with its older sister in the event that a foreign power tries to attack a sister [state] of the American continent.[17]

It is worth emphasizing Arana's reference, not to the reliability of the *Government* of Guatemala, but to the *Army* of Guatemala. Indeed, the Arévalo administration's reliability as an ally of the United States would start to be questioned in Washington less than two years later as a result of its tolerance of communism. The problem was delicately addressed by the Guatemalan military attaché in Washington, Col. Oscar Morales López, in a letter to his good friend Major Arbenz, the defense minister, on 12 March 1947:

> [I] had heard rumors here about communism in Guatemala, not in our army but in the Civil Government and its political party, rumors that I try to discredit as far as I can, declaring that what was believed to be communism was perhaps a slightly disordered democracy, the logical consequence of the recent revolution against totalitarian regimes. Unfortunately it was believed, and based on what I have been able to observe it still seems to be believed, that communism does exist in Guatemala, and, the most delicate thing, I think, about this, is the fact (which naturally reinforces these rumors) that a certain individual here and who is believed to be one of the principal advisers of the Dr. [President Arévalo] and of his political party, is being fingered insistently in different circles as a communist.

Morales wrote that he tried to defend the Guatemalan Army in Washington by arguing that, although it was "apolitical," it opposed any "totalitarian system and especially a communist one" and that Guatemala's highest ranking officers "cannot and will not tolerate any communism at all." Thanks to his efforts, Morales reported, Washington's confidence in the army's reliability remained high despite its doubts about the Arévalo government. "The result, I believe, you will have noted and appreciated, since militarily they have treated us, in spite of everything, as they have very, very few countries in this continent." Morales urged Arbenz to keep his warning secret, "since any indiscretion could close the door to us for future opportunities. . . . [T]he world situation has become so delicate, and in this situation ideology has been defined in such a way that I have thought it not only necessary but indispensable to inform you about the matter. I think it would be very good for you to talk to Paco about this letter. I am with you. The Army must stay united and clean at all costs." "Paco"—the traditional nickname for "Francisco"—must have been Arana.[18]

Morales's letter illustrates both the pull of institutional and personal loyalties over loyalty to a mere civilian government (even one that enjoyed democratic legitimacy), and the importance of pleasing the U.S. government in order to maintain the flow of equipment and training services. Of course, the disunity so feared by Morales already divided Arbenz and "Paco" Arana. Politically conservative and distrustful of civilian rule, Arana was not only a sworn enemy of Arbenz but by late 1948, Arana—"the elite's only hope to seize power," according to Gleijeses—was plotting a coup to take over the presidency. On 20 July 1949, two days after Arana was killed during an attempt to arrest him for the plot, his followers launched the twentieth military rebellion since 1945. They were defeated by forces loyal to Arbenz, then in the midst of organizing his presidential election campaign.[19] His principal antagonist eliminated and his military enemies exposed, Arbenz won election in a landslide on 10 November 1950 at the age of thirty-seven. It was the first peaceful, on-schedule transfer of executive power in the country's history. However, as both grim reminder and as augury, only five days before the election Arbenz was forced to snuff out yet another coup attempt, this one led by Lt. Col. Carlos Castillo Armas, director of the Escuela Politécnica, and the man whom the CIA would choose to lead the successful overthrow of Arbenz in 1954.[20]

Arbenz's election was not welcomed in Washington. The country's request to buy eighteen F-51 fighter jets was turned down on Election Day. Not only were they needed elsewhere to fight "Soviet communist imperialism," the State Department informed Guatemalan officials, but Washington found it difficult to allow the sale to a government that "has demonstrated a sympathy and friendship for the agents of Russian imperialism."[21] Significant material support was now regularly denied the Guatemalan military forces, whereas training and advisory activities were maintained and even intensified, so as not to disrupt the all-important personal relationships with key military figures that Washington continued to count on. The development of those relationships depended less on the delivery of commodities like rifles, tanks, or airplanes than on the U.S. mission's readiness to provide advice and to help resolve practical problems while building a sense of solidarity within the Guatemalan officer corps and between the latter and the U.S. officers. This kind of "soft" collaboration could be seen, for instance, in a 1946 U.S. Army Ground Mission proposal to reorganize the recently created general staff in order to clarify command responsibilities by "placing the various functions in a more logical and efficient relationship to each other."[22] Col. Clyde E. Steele, the mission chief, even sent Defense Minister Arbenz a sample of an onion, garlic, and chile-flavored bean-and-meat field ration that the mission had cooked up at the request of the Guatemalan general staff; in the works was a coffee-and-sugar packet to accompany it.[23] In 1947, Colonel Steele's plans for the reorganization of the Escuela Politécnica were implemented, while the chief of the U.S. Air Mission, Lt. Col. Stephen D. McElroy, took practical measures to resolve what he considered to be one of the biggest problems of the fledgling Guatemalan Air Force—the lack of one-hundred-pound practice bombs. The colonel designed one that could be manufactured locally.[24] U.S. Army personnel instructed Guatemalan Army officers in nonmilitary subjects like polo and English, activities no doubt undertaken to strengthen personal ties among the Guatemalans as well as between the latter and the U.S. officers. In 1948, a U.S. Army colonel and two Guatemalan officers even flew to the United States and bought fifteen horses for Guatemala's 1950 Olympics equestrian team, which was made up of officers and civilians trained by the U.S. mission. When the first Guatemalan officer to replace the U.S. Army director of Guatemala's Escuela de Aplicación de Armas y Servicios was appointed in 1948, he had received two years of training in U.S. Army schools.[25] A U.S. Army colonel acted as the technical adviser to the head of the Escuela Politécnica, none other than the future CIA-collaborator, Castillo Armas, who was also a guest of the U.S. Army during a six-day visit to West Point in 1947.[26] By that year, the army mission was joined by a U.S. Air Mission with four permanent members as well as numerous temporary personnel who presided over the creation of the Guatemalan Air Force.[27] In 1949, the U.S. Air Force turned over to its Guatemalan counterpart the airbase it had built in 1942 at San José.[28]

The strategic value of these kinds of activities for demonstrating U.S. friendship with Guatemalan officers and influencing their views no doubt increased to just the extent that political relations between the two governments deteriorated after 1949. The Guatemalan armed forces were now emerging as the key instrument through which the United States would seek to dislodge the increasingly leftist government of Arbenz. When it became clear that the army was unwilling to throw Arbenz out of office before his constitutional term of office expired, efforts to ensure its indirect cooperation were undertaken in 1952. As distance and hostility increasingly characterized diplomatic relations, U.S. military mission personnel intensified communications with Guatemalan officers, staying "in constant touch" with them and urging them to betray Arbenz while denying them any significant requests for equipment or material.[29] Four days before the U.S.-organized invasion by Castillo Armas's men from Honduras on 17 June 1954, U.S. military officers were still training army and air force personnel while continuing to deny their requests for weapons and equipment.[30]

By that time, nothing that Arbenz could promise his army would be enough to persuade it to challenge a U.S.-sponsored invasion. The democratic-reform faction of the officer corps, which managed to maintain control of the army since 1944, loyally turned back more than thirty coup attempts in a decade. But Arbenz's refusal to back away from his reformist social policies convinced the army that the price of loyalty would be retaliation by the U.S. government. The army was right. Perhaps its leaders knew then that among the CIA's plans was the assassination of at least fifty-eight Guatemalan leaders, which did not become public knowledge until 1997. Although the killings were never carried out, the prospective killers were duly trained. By not defending Arbenz's government, more out of an instinct for self-preservation than a commitment to anticommunism, the army left the president no choice but to resign and earned the gratitude of the United States.[31]

The ability of the United States to pit the Guatemalan Army against the Guatemalan government is evidence of the success of the program of military collaboration that had begun during the Ubico dictatorship. U.S. policy in this respect was consistent with its military policy elsewhere in Latin America from World War II onward, thus making the Guatemalan case an early example of how military collaboration in Latin America was intended to work from the beginning of collaboration in the 1940s. The latent authority that collaboration gave the United States, either to manipulate the armed forces into removing an undesirable government, or to merely shape the policy of governments that depended for their survival on men in uniform, represented the only real value that military collaboration with the Central American governments had for Washington until the 1960s.

Just before midnight on 27 June, Arbenz surrendered the presidency. Five provisional governments succeeded one another between 27 June and 7 July, when the last *junta* elected Castillo Armas its president before moving to dissolve itself on 1 September and making Castillo president of Guatemala, thus fulfilling Washington's main political objective.[32] The United States now undertook what it began to refer to as the "modernization" of the Guatemalan armed forces. In response to U.S. ambassador John Peurifoy's urgent request, Washington delivered three P-51 aircraft and twelve thousand rounds of .50-caliber ammunition on 1 August, a week after Castillo dropped off a check for $105,000 at the U.S. Embassy. According to Peurifoy, the planes were needed to convince the public that the country's armed forces were united behind the military *junta* that succeeded Arbenz.[33] In addition, Peurifoy had just mediated a political arrangement intended to ensure Castillo's undisputed control. On 22 September the *junta* announced a snap vote (with just nineteen days' notice) for delegates to a constituent assembly and for a "yes" or "no" response to the question whether Castillo should remain the president for a term to be fixed by the future assembly. Having banned all political parties and required that voters proclaim their votes publicly at the polls, the *junta* announced the expected results of the 10 October "elections": the *junta*'s delegate slate had won unopposed, and the vote for Castillo to stay in office was 485,699 "yes" and 400 "no." The assembly's first act was to decree that Castillo's term would continue until 15 March 1960.[34]

Following the *junta*'s advancement of Guatemala's long-stalled ratification of the Rio Treaty, the counselor of the U.S. Embassy in Guatemala, Thomas C. Mann, urged the State Department on 13 October to respond to this sign of Guatemalan loyalty to the United States by promptly delivering "appropriate military aid." After years of blocking Guatemalan efforts to obtain military equipment in the United States and elsewhere, Washington should now "collaborate fully with Guatemalan armed forces in effort create new and friendly atmosphere." Intensified collaboration, Mann argued, would help inoculate Castillo against a coup (by increasing Castillo's stature among his officers) and ensure a friendly government in the event of a coup, because "it is armed forces which in last analysis in best position to determine successor and orientation government. A friendly anti-communist military establishment would be a good ace in the hole."[35] Three days later, Guatemala submitted a huge request—undoubtedly encouraged by the U.S. military mission—to buy 26 aircraft, 499 trucks, 260 handheld radio sets, and ponchos, helmets and mess kits for eight thousand men.[36]

Secretary of State Dulles, evidently swayed by Mann's argument, asked the Defense Department on 27 October to construct a hemispheric defense role for Guatemala so that grant collaboration via the MAP could begin. Although the economic aid the United States was providing to Guatemala would help generate more popular support for Castillo, it wasn't, according to Dulles, "winning and maintaining the support of the Guatemalan military establishment, which probably will assert the determining influence in any political crisis in Guatemala." Grant military collaboration, Dulles continued, would ensure Guatemalan military support of Castillo Armas while preserving "friendship and cooperation of the Guatemalan army because it is, in the final analysis, in the best position to determine the successor government and its orientation."[37] The Joint Chiefs of Staff were soon instructed that unspecified "political considerations" dictated grant collaboration with Guatemala. By then a U.S. military survey team had returned from the country and recommended sufficient grant assistance for an infantry battalion. While they were there, they "encouraged and assisted in purchasing" four fighter aircraft and disposing of non-U.S. military equipment considered to be "excess." The Joint Chiefs felt compelled to observe for the record that the tasks that Guatemala might perform in defense of the hemisphere "would be comparable to those assigned to Nicaragua and Honduras and, hence, of negligible value."[38]

But by now, the State Department was working almost desperately to ensure the army's loyalty to Castillo. What the army wanted in return for its loyalty, a series of Embassy cables stressed, was a downpour of military equipment. Defense Minister Col. Enrique Close de León and a Castillo Armas aide, Maj. Enrique Oliva, spelled out what it would take at an eighty-minute meeting on the morning of 5 November 1954 in Colonel Close's office, with Mann and Col. Aloysius E. McCormick, the U.S. Army attaché. For starters, they wanted nine hundred beds; food rations; housing; thirteen hundred officers' uniforms; three hundred live rockets, and three hundred practice rockets. The latter were intended for an F-51 fighter plane to fire on Air Force Day, 1 December, a demonstration that Colonel Close and Major Oliva predicted "would have a terrific psychological impact on the Guatemalan populace" and deter a rebellion.[39]

Before the year was over, the United States had approved Guatemala's request to buy, on credit, three F-51D Mustang fighters, three hundred rockets, ten armored cars, twelve trucks, and twenty jeeps—all in time for a parade on 22 December, "for the purpose of indicating to communist elements in the Central American area the capability and determination of Guatemala to resist communist conspiracy by armed forces, if necessary," according to the State Department. Apparently, the rockets couldn't be delivered in time for the 1 December demonstration and instead were to be fired from the F-51s during the 22 December parade. An affirmative response to a variety of other purchase requests, including the new officers' uniforms, "would help keep armed forces loyal and contented," U.S. diplomats concluded. Implying that Guatemala's military need for the equipment was practically nil, a U.S. official who approved the transfers observed that "the political advantages of granting the desired credit in this case are sufficient to be controlling." The Embassy agreed with Castillo that "it was highly desirable that a demonstration of military strength be held to deter anti-government conspiring." The equipment was evidently delivered on time.[40]

According to the Embassy, "next to the projected equipment of an infantry battalion, the building of military housing would be the most effective means of working towards strengthening of the loyalty of the Guatemalan military to President Castillo Armas' regime." Quarters for soldiers and officers alike "especially in the provinces are often in subhuman condition." The Embassy urged Washington to pick up the $5.8 million in construction costs, but to disguise its assistance by making an "economic aid" transfer of cash straight to the Guatemalan treasury so that Castillo Armas and not Washington would appear to be the source. And why not throw in the "modern military hospital" that Castillo also promised the army? None of this spending was exactly "hemispheric defense," a worried Bureau of the Budget official pointed out, but because it was intended to improve the living standards of military officers, it would qualify as "economic assistance."[41] This was the kind of military collaboration whose costs fail to appear in the official tables of military assistance but rather as "defense support," "special assistance" or "technical cooperation," the standard names for disguised military collaboration. Two-thirds of U.S. transfers between 1953 and 1960, according to the official tabulation, consisted of "special assistance" or "technical cooperation" as opposed to "military assistance," as table 10.1 records.

On 4 March 1955, the State Department finally recommended to President Eisenhower that he find Guatemala eligible for grant collaboration via the MAP because the economic aid that the United States was supplying "makes no direct contribution to winning and maintaining the support of Guatemalan Armed Forces, which probably will assert the determining influence in any political crisis," and because grant military collaboration would help assure the armed forces' support for Castillo Armas.[42] Just as Mann had recommended, Washington was playing the hand that would win it the game whether the armed forces cooperated with Castillo Armas or threw him out of office. The state was no less improvisational than

Table 10.1 U.S. Outlays for Guatemalan Economic and Military Collaboration, 1953–1960

	1953	1954	1955	1956	1957	1958	1959	1960	TOTALS
Special assistance			$8,039,000	$12,681,000	$15,423,000	$10,250,000	$423,000	$70,000	$46,886,000
Technical cooperation			$1,814,000	$1,833,000	$2,189,000	$2,266,000	$2,708,000	$2,400,000	$13,210,000
Inter-American Highway construction			$70,000	$2,902,000	$8,845,000	$9,440,000	$2,375,000	$3,500,000	$27,132,000
U.S. Army mission	$67,000	$68,000	$68,000	$81,000	$84,000	$77,000	$92,000		$537,000
Grant funds to equip and train one infantry battalion				$607,000	$153,000	$93,000	$147,000	$218,000	$1,218,000
U.S. Air Force missions	$60,000	$64,000	$58,000	$71,000	$77,000	$78,000	$92,000		$500,000
TOTALS	$127,000	$132,000	$10,049,000	$18,175,000	$26,771,000	$22,204,000	$5,837,000	$6,188,000	$89,483,000

Note: Fifty-two percent of the total was accounted for by the huge "special assistance" appropriations (also called "defense support") of 1955–58, which were often, if not always, military in nature.

Source: NA. RG59. L. D. Mallory, U.S. ambassador to Guatemala, to Department of State, 21 September, 1959, 714.5-MSP/o-2159.

it had been a century before; ultimately, it wasn't so much the man in charge who mattered, but the collaboration of his *montonera*. In order of priority, the Embassy advised, grant collaboration should first be used to equip the infantry battalion, followed by the construction of officers' quarters and barracks, and the equipping of a combat engineer battalion.[43]

But if he was going to legally justify the use of MAP funds for purposes other than the creation of the infantry battalion (which was the "hemispheric defense" measure), President Eisenhower would have to invoke a loophole in the Mutual Security Act allowing him to declare that MAP aid was "important to the security of the United States." The State Department urged him to do so on the grounds that Guatemala was the "exceptional" Latin American country whose grant military assistance should be provided "on a broader scale" than mere hemispheric defense.[44] The Pentagon remained "strongly opposed" to any MAP aid for Guatemala beyond that required for its infantry battalion.[45] On 2 May, President Eisenhower sided with the State Department, authorizing negotiations with Guatemala for grant collaboration and three days later issued his finding that "the increased ability of Guatemala to defend itself is important to the security of the United States," thus opening the way for the broader grounds for collaboration that would supposedly ensure the loyalty of the Guatemalan Army to the Castillo Armas government.[46]

The next day, the Latin America desk at State proposed a near tripling of "special assistance" and related grants from the $5 million set aside for 1955 to $14 million in 1956, because the "position of the Castillo Armas regime is more precarious than had been previously thought" and its survival depended on increased military spending. "The prestige of the United States is so involved with the stability of the anti-communist regime in Guatemala that we cannot afford to take risks." All but $2 million should be spent on highway construction, which would enhance the mobility of an army that, without a decent road system, could scarcely be expected to "reorganize itself on U.S. lines," and overcome its traditional garrison mentality. That left $1.5 million to resettle five thousand families occupying land that had been seized by the Arbenz government for redistribution under the agrarian reform law, and whom Castillo's political allies wanted to evict. Another $500,000 was needed for construction of the Roosevelt Hospital.[47]

The persistence of the clamor in the State Department for a larger collaboration budget in order to buy the army's loyalty implied that the threat in Guatemala was no longer communism but the army, an assessment that U.S. Ambassador Norman Armour made explicit on 9 May 1955. Now that the "overt communist apparatus" had collapsed as a result of the coup, the main threat to Castillo Armas had become "dissident or ambitious groups to left and right" that might find allies in an officer corps still divided between the insurgents, who favored "tough authoritarian rule with widespread purges," and those who stood pat in 1954. Castillo was struggling to satisfy both groups. If he failed, the opportunities for communist subversion would increase, although the danger of a "successful communist insurrection" remained remote.[48]

The MAP agreement was finally signed on 18 June, the first anniversary of the U.S.-organized invasion by Castillo Armas and his men from Honduras.[49] But grant collaboration alone, the CIA acknowledged in a report in July, would not be enough to save Castillo, whose survival in office also depended on his personal popularity and the support of the Guatemalan armed forces. Nevertheless, the support of the U.S. government was decisive, for if Castillo's enemies thought Washington no longer backed him, he would be overthrown.[50] One of the best ways, therefore, to shore up support within the armed forces and to discourage his enemies was to flaunt the new U.S. military equipment that had been flowing in since Arbenz's resignation. For an Independence Day parade on 15 September, State approved Castillo's urgent request for $70,000 worth of helmets and cartridge belts, promising on-time delivery and a two-year credit arrangement. "It is highly desirable that we strengthen and support Castillo Armas and his pro-United States policies by giving the fullest cooperation reasonably possible," the State Department reported. "This is said to be part of the President's [Castillo's] plan to favor military elements thereby helping to ensure army support for the regime."[51] By the end of September, the United States had delivered 10 armored cars, 32 trucks, 450,000 cartridges, 10 radio sets and 6 F-51 airplanes. Mess kits, haversacks, first aid kits, ponchos, and other field equipment were on the way.[52]

Meanwhile, Ambassador Armour's worries about the stability of the Castillo government had bubbled up to the U.S. Operations Coordinating Board, the summit of U.S. national security decision making at the time. The overthrow of Castillo Armas "might well open the door for the return of the pro-communist exiles and permit a resumption of their activities. Such a development would be a disastrous blow to United States prestige," the board concluded.[53] This made Guatemala a demonstration case for noncommunist development, and no effort could be spared to ensure success. "Guatemala's reconstruction efforts," according to the Eisenhower administration, "are being attentively watched by her neighbors and people throughout the world as an acid test of competing methods of achieving economic and social progress." A U.S. congressional delegation, fresh from a visit to the country in 1955, reported: "Guatemala is the showcase of Latin America and has become a political, social and economic laboratory. She is engaged in the great experiment of proving that a country under the Communist heel can throw off the Communist yoke, and can achieve the well-being of its people not through force, not through artificial means, but through democratic processes."[54]

By late 1956, the exiled opposition, especially in Mexico, Costa Rica, and El Salvador, seemed to be threatening the "great experiment." The Embassy had heard "many reports that these exiles will attempt to assassinate the President and then overthrow the Government with support which they claim to have from both military and civilian elements within the country." The State Department even thought Castillo was becoming too tolerant of the left opposition, and criticized his decision to let some exiles return in November.[55] Anxiety about communist infiltration only increased after Castillo's assassination on 26 July 1957 by a soldier who immediately committed suicide.[56] Secretary of State Dulles instructed the Embassy in November to persuade the provisional president, Guillermo Flores Avendaño, to bar the return of exiles, communist and noncommunist alike. "We consider allowing return of undesirables on list identified by Embassy to be most dangerous, and hope Flores appreciates this also," Dulles said.[57]

Of the two main presidential candidates competing to succeed Castillo Armas, the man least favored by the United States, Gen. Miguel Ydígoras Fuentes, received a plurality of the votes on 19 January 1958, in "fair, clean and democratic" elections that were even open to the anticommunist left.[58] In the absence of a simple majority for either candidate, Ydígoras pacted with the runner-up, a general associated with the single-minded anticommunism of Castillo Armas's administration. Ydígoras's inauguration on 2 March marked a veritable redemocratization led by a general, of all people, who left no doubt that he was far more inclined than the Castillo and Flores administrations to respect civil rights and political pluralism.[59] This was just what troubled Dulles, who before the election reported that he was "surprised and concerned about extent to which Ydígoras Fuentes has apparently played with leftists and communists in effort achieve his own personal ambition."[60] The secretary's doubts about Ydígoras must have seemed prophetic to some; after he had been in office for fifteen months, the State Department's Central American desk reported: "Ydígoras' approach to the communists has been a source of grave concern to us. . . . The great defect in Ydígoras' handling of the communist problem has been his unwillingness to clamp down on clearly identified agitators and organizers."[61]

Not only had the Guatemalans elected a president who tolerated communists, but the Guatemalan Army was in a shambles five years after the resumption of U.S.-Guatemalan military collaboration, the Pentagon reported. The logistical system was so weak that "during combat, units would have to 'live on the country,'" and maintenance was "on a breakdown basis." The army was issuing four different kinds of rifles and there were no spare parts for any of them.

> The equipment on hand is so varied that there are no two like units in the Army that are equipped with the same type, age or serviceability of either major items or individual items. Present plans for reorganization of the Army anticipate complete reequipping of four battalion combat teams with U.S. equipment. Under present conditions, no new units can be activated. Training in schools and units is supported by borrowing equipment from the Mission of the MAP battalion [sic]. Combat effectiveness is very low, and there is practically no repair of disabled vehicles.

The army would be unable to defeat a well-planned national "uprising" and it was probably no better prepared to defeat a "determined invader" than it had been in June 1954. Although the air force was reasonably effective, the army could handle police duties and civil disturbances only as long as the army commanders supported the government. But the army probably could not last more than three days in the field without a logistical system or a way of replacing casualties. Among the obstacles to military modernization, according to the Pentagon, were "normal Latin lethargy" and the fear that real change would make Guatemala's neighbors think that the country was being dominated by the United States. Officer promotion was a function of age, so the result was an "inverted grade structure" of 300 full colonels and 140 lieutenants; army training "is predominantly the parade ground type," with a strong preference for "garrison life" instead of field training. "Practical field work is engaged in for show purposes rather than for field training." The U.S. military missions "have brought all of these deficiencies and problems to the attention of the Ministers of Defense, the Chiefs of Staff, the General Staff, and other authorities on every possible occasion throughout the past year—sometimes more bluntly than normal diplomacy would condone."[62]

U.S. diplomatic and military officials tended to attribute the lack of progress to different causes. The Embassy said the high command of the Guatemalan Army was a source of "deep-seated opposition to the status and prerogatives of the United States Military Missions members"; some Guatemalan officers were "envious of the advantageous position enjoyed by United States Military Mission members in matters of pay, housing, free entry privileges, medical benefits and annual leave privileges, among others." Their hostility was the main reason for the failure of the two countries to quickly negotiate new military mission agreements to replace those that expired in 1953.[63] However, U.S. military officers in Guatemala tended to interpret the source of Guatemala's numerous military shortcomings as the absence of a legitimate military function. "The national military policy of Guatemala" made the armed forces "the main props of government authority (hence supports of the faction in power), to suppress dissident factions tending to get out of control, and to furnish the majority of government officials," reported the U.S. military officers in charge of grant collaboration in 1959. This was even true of the pride of the Guatemalan Army—the newly established MAP battalion, which boasted the army's "newest and best equipment" and whose combat capability far exceeded that of any other army unit.[64] Evidently aware of its army's shortcomings at the command level, Guatemala asked the United States at the end of 1959 to help it establish both a command and general staff school and an advanced war school for senior officers, and to start sending U.S. Army mission members who had "perfect" command of Spanish, because the limited Spanish of most members had reduced their utility to the government.[65]

The immediate threat to both the Ydígoras government and to U.S. security interests in 1959 was understood to be the pending return to Guatemala of ex-president Arévalo, whose popularity had both governments worried. Washington told Ydígoras to keep him from entering the country.[66] In a meeting with the president on 11 November, U.S. Ambassador Mallory even seemed to encourage the president to manipulate the country's justice system in order to keep Arévalo out. "I dilated extensively on Arévalo, pointing out his arrival physically or to political power in Guatemala would be nothing short of disastrous," an estimate that Ydígoras did not dispute. If Arévalo were allowed back, Ydígoras asserted, he would take over the entire left and even "a considerable portion President's own Party Redención, who would go out of fear," Mallory reported. Ydígoras assured the ambassador that he was "taking every possible step prevent Arévalo getting favorable position. He had caused to be instituted seven processes [court actions against Arévalo] ranging from the murder of Arana, the violation of two girls, through robbery and other things. I remarked I understood a court action per se would not prevent Arévalo from returning, that such needed [sic] court judgement against him. President confirmed this saying he was pushing for action."[67]

The threat represented by the father of the 1944 revolution was beginning to merge with a much newer threat, Castroism. In March 1960, President Eisenhower secretly authorized the CIA to organize an invasion of Cuba to overthrow the Castro government, and Guatemala was the primary training site for the invasion force of Cuban exiles. In April, Guatemala broke relations with Cuba and the U.S. government agreed to sell Guatemala eight B-52s; a "special assistance" loan of $3.5 million was also in the works. By October, the Guatemalan government was falsely denying public reports that it was allowing the United States to use a ranch owned by a government official, Roberto Alejos, as a training base for the Bay of Pigs invasion. Some 420 Cuban exiles were training there by mid-November, a number that would eventually rise to about 1,400 in a "covert" training operation that was already an open secret throughout Latin America, including Cuba.[68]

As Ydígoras's denials of complicity with the U.S. invasion plan diminished in credibility, his already isolated government became ever more dependent on the United States. Already the target of communist subversion, Ydígoras was regarded "with hate and derision" by the right, in part for his failed economic and fiscal policies, the U.S. ambassador reported. Washington, convinced that Ydígoras was the best alternative because he was both credibly democratic and anticommunist, responded by intensifying military and economic collaboration, including road construction and a $10 million "budget support" grant, in the vain hope that it would have the effect of unifying the right and other anticommunist elements.[69] On 13 November the long-feared military revolt against Ydígoras broke out. With the Guatemalan armed forces severely divided and unable, initially, to put down the coup attempt, Ydígoras received permission from Washington for the Cuban exile air-force-in-training at Retalhuleu to assault Puerto Barrios on 15 November, where rebel troops were holed up. That operation was cancelled after it was reported, mistakenly, that the rebels had abandoned the port. The CIA still had to lend Ydígoras two of its training-camp transport planes to airlift Guatemalan troops to Puerto Barrios. The revolt was declared defeated five days after it erupted.[70]

Two grievances within the military inspired the revolt: the government's political interference in military affairs, and the president's servility to U.S. interests at the expense of Guatemalan interests.[71] By year's end, disgust with Ydígoras had increased so much that the three opposition parties representing the right, the center, and the left signed a secret pact establishing a "national front" against the government.[72] An anti-U.S. species of nationalism within the armed forces was more notable and would persist longer in El Salvador. In Guatemala, however, it was a tendency that metamorphosed into a leftist guerrilla insurgency under the leadership of two army lieutenants who had helped lead the 13 November revolt, Marco Antonio Yon Sosa and Luis Augusto Turcios Lima. Their guerrilla movement would provoke a stupendous increase in what was already the isthmus' most ambitious program of U.S. military and police collaboration, encouraging the Guatemalan military to remake itself into one of the most ruthless counterinsurgency forces in the world.[73]

Thomas Mann's 1954 trope—"A friendly anti-communist military establishment would be a good ace in the hole"—hadn't quite got it right. Guatemala's military establishment may have been anticommunist. It was almost always friendly. But it was never a card that Washington could simply choose to play, not in 1954, nor in 1960, nor in 1978. The freedom of the armed forces to act within the broadly defined limits of Guatemalan public violence was never subject to any practical, U.S.-imposed sanction. Even Washington's ability to enhance the coercive capacity of the armed forces was undermined by the fundamental incoherence of its rationale for intensified collaboration. On the one hand (at least publicly) the United States aimed to modernize the military to improve its ability to defend Guatemala against both internal and external communist threats. On the other hand, in their nonpublic discourse, U.S. officials repeatedly justified collaboration above all not as a military measure but as political maneuver to buy off potential coup plotters in the officer corps. Although these aims were not necessarily contradictory, the failure to clarify them helps to explain why Washington was unable to exert more control over the military collaboration process, and why it was ultimately disappointed by the outcome.

In response, perhaps, to the muddle that military collaboration had become, an alternative form of collaboration began to emerge in the 1950s that seemed to promise quicker and more tangible results in both securing the country against communism and stabilizing its governments.

Collaboration for Internal Control: Policing and the Hunt for Subversives

Since the 1940s, military collaboration had been preparing the isthmian countries' ability to resist threats emanating from enemy states. However, as the preoccupation with "internal defense" intensified in the mid-1950s, so too did the desire to improve the ability of collaborator states to watch their own citizens and gather intelligence on them. Attention turned naturally to police agencies, which were increasingly seen as the first line of defense against internal subversion. In Guatemala, collaboration in this realm surged far ahead of that in the rest of Latin America during the 1950s, and because of both its scope and its novelty, merits separate treatment. The novelty lay primarily in its inward-looking focus on subversion stemming from nonmilitary threats such as political parties, foreign travelers, and individuals associated with ideas or movements that challenged the status quo. Because of the breadth and inexact nature of the threat, "internal control" collaboration engaged police and military agencies alike, in part because the police agencies in Latin America were typically controlled by the armed forces. Some aspects of this collaboration—such as traffic control and criminal investigations—were more strictly police-oriented. But whether the threat was communist subversion, petty theft, or reckless drivers, the effect in Central America was to deepen the U.S. government's contribution to the state formation process, as Washington became involved in an array of both open and secretive operations that inevitably identified it with governments associated more with repression, torture, and assassination than with traffic flows and crime solving.

The scope of collaboration in Guatemala broadened considerably in March 1955 when the U.S. Army agreed to send an intelligence adviser there—its first ever in Latin America. His job: to offer training in "internal security and counter-intelligence." This was a spy-plan within a spy-plan, for it would not only help the Guatemalan government secretly keep track of its opponents but make it easier for the State Department to secretly stay abreast of changes inside the armed forces.[74] By May, Washington was transferring its own data on Guatemalan communists to the Guatemalan government's Committee for National Defense Against Communism (CNDAC), despite the fact that it "has often proved incompetent, overzealous, and arbitrary and has aroused public disapproval and even ridicule," according to the CIA. Ambassador Armour even urged Washington to transfer to the Guatemalans not only the information it had collected on Guatemalan communists in exile, but also on "others potentially linked with communist underground here. They [the Guatemalan government] cannot do this for themselves." Writing in the elliptical style of the diplomatic cable, Armour pointed out that the Castillo government was unable to "apprehend single top communist most of whom appear to have escaped country. Since then less than half dozen second echelon communists rooted out within country." Although about five thousand people had been arrested, "some several times, on suspicion communist activities, most in first weeks after revolution," the ambassador was dismayed that practically all of them had been released after "administrative hearings."[75] In June, the Embassy assigned its second secretary, Jacob D. Esterline, to handle the exchange of intelligence on communist activities with Carlos Lemus, the Guatemalan subdirector of national security in the Interior Ministry.[76]

The U.S. Army's special counterintelligence adviser arrived in June 1956 and immediately began to help the Guatemalan Army reorganize its intelligence section.[77] Lemus's agency had taken over the CNDAC and renamed it the Section for Defense Against Communism, which according to the U.S. Embassy had achieved such success in compiling a "register of communists and communist sympathizers" that "it seems likely the government could round up, within a short time, most of the dangerous communists now in the country" although by that time, there were probably no more than 150–300 communists in Guatemala.[78] But progress on the intelligence front was slow. In November, the U.S. National Security Council received alarming news about the state of Guatemalan agencies charged with "suppression of subversion." The Policía Nacional (PN) were "seriously deficient in organization, training, staffing, and equipment"; the CNDAC "has not proven highly effective in uprooting the clandestine communist organization"; and the

army's nascent military intelligence section only had "slight capabilities for controlling activities of communists."[79]

Counterintelligence operations were thus seen as a police responsibility as well
as a military one, and the deficiencies of the Guatemalan police forces (split into five
agencies with separate jurisdictions, as reported in Appendix table A-13) led Washington into a program of police collaboration that remained, until the early 1960s,
the largest and most ambitious in Latin America, quickly overshadowing the
$45,000 that Washington spent in 1955 to train seventeen Guatemalan police offi-
cials in the United States and Puerto Rico.[80] In 1956, just as the National Security
Council was considering the news about the inadequacy of the PN and other "internal security" agencies, the Castillo government formally asked for a U.S. instructor
to train Guatemala's police "in anti-communism and counter-intelligence."[81]

A critical U.S. government evaluation of the Guatemalan police in early 1956
pointed out that, although the three-thousand-man PN was the country's principal
police agency, it was little more than a branch of the army. Its director, Army Col.
Carlos De León, had no police experience and "looks upon his current assignment
with disfavor and disciplinary in nature [sic]," according to Fred G. Fimbres of the
U.S. International Cooperation Administration (ICA). Army officers not only
staffed the top three positions of the PN, but all key units and stations, and even
wore their army uniforms on the job. Command rested almost totally on Colonel
De León, to whom some fifty-one persons were responsible, "a staggering and
administratively unsound span of control" that seemed to result in "an almost fear-
ful reluctance and resistance on the part of unit commanders to make decisions,"
overwhelming the colonel with operational and administrative details. Because
authority was so centralized in a single man, who gave orders to others without even
informing their superiors, the result was "animosity, distrust and general poor
morale among unit heads," according to Fimbres. Among other deficiencies, he
found a lack of professional training, "unwieldy spans of control," poor management, "very low morale, " improper deployment of line personnel, a poor records
system, and poor vehicle maintenance.

Much of the PN's equipment was unusable owing to poor maintenance practices. More than 40 percent of its vehicle fleet of seventy-one motorcycles, twenty-
eight automobiles, twenty-three jeeps, six trucks, four boats, two buses, and two
ambulances was inoperable. The force appeared to be well armed, however. Its men
had 1,788 .38-caliber revolvers, of which 1,314 were in "good" condition, and 500 new
ones were on the way from the United States. In addition, they could count on
eighty 9-mm semi-automatic revolvers, and sixteen hundred 7-mm Spanish Mauser
rifles; a "confidential" number of submachine guns were on loan from the army. In
any case, the traditional police functions of the PN were only secondary, because its
main job was stopping "subversive activity and communist attack." Because the
Castillo government itself took power on the basis of a "revolt" by "some 200
'minute men'" it was acutely aware of how easily it could be overthrown, and so "the
ever present driving thought is the 'alert' to communist activity and attack. . . . In
fact, the preparedness and functional operations are more and more directed

toward this constancy of alertness to near obsessive-compulsive acts closely border-ing on the neurotic. . . . Its fulfillment of its police function is at best to be rated as fair." That the PN enjoyed little public support was implied (but not stated directly, probably because the report was to be shared with the Guatemalan government) in Fimbres's recommendation for an increase in technical and material collaboration. One hope, Fimbres said, was that "a higher and new found degree of rapport between the police and the citizenry will further strengthen the public acceptance, confidence and support of the government by the people."[82]

As a result of the Fimbres study, a team of three U.S. police consultants—a number that would rise to seven by 1970—were assembled in the summer of 1956. At a cost estimated at $75,000 for the team's first year of operation, Guatemala became one of just ten countries in the world with an ICA police program, and the first in Latin America.[83] The funds for police collaboration were drawn from three distinct sources, perhaps in order to obscure the full cost of police collaboration: the MAP, the ever-flexible "defense support," and the ICA.[84] After a quick survey, the U.S. police advisors concluded in November that the PN was "basically a pedestrian force of 3,000 men and not a mechanized unit of proficient mobility and communica-tions. The Guatemalan Government considers this to be hazardous to internal secu-rity. We agree." In a meeting with President Castillo, Colonel De León, and Col. Alfredo Castaneda, the head of the Guardia de Hacienda (which controlled the bor-ders and the customs posts), the consultants persuaded the Guatemalans to trim their request for police equipment and training services back from $306,500 to $217,000, as reported in table 10.2.

Some further notion of the backwardness of Guatemalan police operations may be inferred from the U.S. police consultants' list of its objectives in 1957: Estab-lish a records system, traffic and criminal patrols, "reduce accidents and promote orderly traffic," develop police training and safety education programs.[85] A more

Table 10.2 OISP Recommendations for Grant Collaboration with Guatemalan Police Agencies, November 1956

	National Police	Guarda de Hacienda
Military Assistance Program	24 motorcycles ($24,000), 18 jeeps ($36,000), 1 radio transmitter ($2,000); 2 personnel carriers ($12,000), 500 .38 cal pistols and ammo, $30,000	16 jeeps ($32,000), 12 motorcycles ($12,000), 200 .38 cal pistols ($12,000)
International Cooperation Administration	1 tow-truck, ($6,500), 2 ambulances ($7,500), 1 crime lab ($7,500)	
TOTALS	$161,000	$56,000

Source: NA. WNRC. RG286. OPS/Oper/LA Guat 1955–61 Box 60, 1955–58. ICA/Guat to ICA/W, 14 November 1956.

specific "work plan" was devised in April that called on the United States to integrate four police agencies (the PN, the Guardia de Hacienda, the Departamento de Policía Judicial, and the Section for Defense Against Communism) under a single, more efficient command. Administrative efficiency was clearly uppermost in the minds of the U.S. planners, who emphasized the need to instruct the high command in administrative procedures and functional organization, and to train unit leaders in equipment maintenance. In the view of U.S. planners, Guatemala's police suffered less from material shortages than from certain attitudes and values. The "hysteria over communistic threat" had to be replaced with "a rational approach to the problem of locating and eradicating actual subversive elements and activities," and the police had to be convinced that the pursuit of criminals was no less important than the pursuit of subversives.[86]

The extraordinary scope of these reorganization plans, and above all the expectation that they could be implemented quickly and show results immediately, were signs of a startling lack of prudence on the part of the U.S. police advisers. In May 1957, barely five months after the program had begun, Dave Laughlin, the head of the police consultant team, told his boss in Washington, Byron Engle, that his greatest disappointment so far was the lack of cooperation by the Guatemalan police in carrying out his recommendations for reorganization. Laughlin, who did not speak Spanish, was nevertheless pleased to report that "All of our correspondence with local officials, as well as all training materials, are sent to them in Spanish. We believe that this is not only a gesture of cooperation but, what is more important, it means that the material is more apt to be used."[87] The earnest innocence of a chief police adviser who considered the use of Spanish in Guatemala to be a mere "gesture of cooperation" no doubt accounts in part for both his own outlandish expectations and the lack of interest among the Guatemalans in attaining them.

The State Department's top Latin Americanist, Roy R. Rubottom, Jr., on the other hand, held a considerably narrower view of the police collaboration program. Demanding more practical, strictly anticommunist measures, he wrote: "First, we do not undertake programs to increase the efficiency of Latin American police forces per se. Where we do render them technical and material assistance, it is for the stated objective of increasing their capability to combat communist subversion." Concerns over traffic control, accident investigation forms, filing cabinets, and like matters didn't trigger U.S. interest in police collaboration, he pointed out. The threat of communist subversion did. Some Latin American police forces seem to have "too many arms which they are too quick to use" and in any case usually can afford to buy their own.[88]

Rubottom's comment on filing cabinets probably stemmed from the recent observation by U.S. consultants that "The National Police has no records system and cannot actually define its problems and needs. . . . Drafts of record forms have been made by our technicians, a Guatemalan police lieutenant has been trained by our technicians to supervise a records system but nothing more can be done on this project until filing cabinets are available."[89] For Rubottom, the Guatemalan police were nothing more than another anticommunist tool. But the U.S. police advisers, no doubt trained in "criminology" and accustomed to working with the latest technology, saw themselves as missionaries of modernization. To them, "efficiency" was all that mattered. They continued to insist—and their view prevailed over Rubottom's—that the scope of their responsibilities extended well beyond the mere control of subversion. In 1958 they summarized their ever-ambitious objectives this way: Improvements in pay and working conditions in order to attract better recruits, reduction of turnover, more public support for the police (who "are not held in high regard"), consolidation of the Guardia Judicial and the PN, better coordination between the capital and outlying police units, creation of a central records bureau and training schools for the PN (already underway) and the Guardia de Hacienda, improvement of traffic conditions, further "specialized training" for a just-created "security police" trained to protect public officials and "combat subversives," improvement of the Guardia de Hacienda's ability to stop "contrabands and subversives" from crossing the borders, and increasing the mobility of Guatemalan police by doubling its vehicle fleet.[90]

Later that year, with the number of U.S police advisers rising from three to four, the advisers boasted of having established a training academy for PN recruits and a separate one for PN supervisory officers. Two years ago, police in the capital had exactly four "worn-out patrol cars" and those outside the capital had a few motorcycles. Since then, the U.S. government had provided eighteen radio patrol cars, thirty-two motorcycles, thirty-four jeeps, two ambulances, and a tow truck, and the Guatemalans bought an additional sixteen patrol cars. The U.S. supplied a radio transmitter and a patrol car in Quetzaltenango, as well as a "modern crime lab" for the PN. Although no report forms of any kind had existed in 1956, the U.S. advisers had managed to print a variety of "forms and reports" for use by the police. Although they did not say that the forms were actually being used, they did point out that filing cabinets to store them in had been delivered and a record bureau had even been set up. Traffic and parking control had improved, and so did the PN's ability to "maintain internal security and protect lives and property" and the Guardia de Hacienda's control of the borders.[91] The U.S. advisers were also pleased that the Guatemalans were now better armed; "the majority of the police throughout the country carry side arms." In 1956 only the capital police carried sidearms and those in the countryside were typically armed only with nightsticks. Since then, the ICA had delivered five hundred .38-caliber Smith & Wesson revolvers to the PN and two hundred to the Guardia de Hacienda, leading to the purchase by the government of two thousand more revolvers for the PN and another one hundred for the Guardia.[92]

Among the most pressing reorganizational tasks was strengthening the reach of the PN across the whole country while combining it with the Policía Judicial in order to further centralize control of what appeared to the U.S. advisers as a hopelessly fragmented and personalistic, and therefore inefficient, police operation. The PN's officers, based in the capital, had little contact with PN forces outside the city. "The Director of the National Police paid the PSD [Public Safety Division of the ICA] technicians a dubious compliment when he stated that they knew far more about police activity and operation in the Departments than did the responsible police officials in the Capital."[93] A related problem was the high turnover of top police officials. In the passage of eighteen months, from June 1957 to November 1958, the PN alone had gone through five directors and six subdirectors. In the same period, the Policía Judicial had six directors, a record that would be superceded between January 1960 and July 1961, when it had eight directors, one of whom served for just twelve days. At the cabinet level, there had been four ministers, and experienced officers were often discharged without cause by top officials and replaced with political appointees.[94] In the new crime lab created by the United States for the PN, only the lab director can operate most of the equipment. "Although extremely competent, the Director does not want to pass along his knowledge to others as it tends to assure his continued employment."[95]

Tightening control of the country's borders and improving security for the chief of state were among the highest priorities of the U.S. police program. E. DeWitt Marshall, deputy chief of the U.S. Border Patrol, spent six months in Guatemala in 1957 and 1958 to help the Guardia de Hacienda stop both "communist subversives and smugglers of arms and other contraband" from entering the country at will.[96] Probably as a result of the assassination of President Castillo on 26 July 1957, Howard R. Keough, a U.S. police adviser, took over the training of a fourteen-man team of Guatemalan Army bodyguards assigned to protect the president, teaching them the use of firearms, judo, and protection techniques. During Independence Day celebrations in September, Keough reported, "it was necessary for me to go everywhere with the President in order to show the members of the unit how to go about accomplishing each segment of the protective scheme. At the end of each day's work I held critiques on each phase of the operation. The results of these critiques have had the desired effect on the unit members." Nevertheless, he assessed their performance as extremely poor, and developed a reorganization and training plan for submission to the Guatemalan government. By February 1958 Keough had succeeded in convincing the president to issue a decree creating the Servicio Secreto, which was placed in charge of presidential protection.[97]

The lack of public support for the police to which Fimbres had alluded was, the United States discovered, a serious impediment to reform.

> One of the greatest problems facing PSD [Public Safety Division] in Guatemala is the general relationship between the police and the public. Generally poor and low-standard working conditions have resulted in a general apathy and disinterest from all sides. This has been brought about mainly by a rapid turnover of personnel in public security forces. . . . The people of Guatemala have little respect for the Police and little desire to cooperate with them. . . . The police are so underpaid that they are not concerned about losing their jobs and this naturally has a bearing on the way they handle themselves.

Accepting bribes was standard procedure.[98] The inauguration of the Ydígoras Fuentes government in 1957 further hindered progress in police-public relations. The president "has concentrated his patronage efforts on the police with Jacksonian vigor," leading to more turnover in the PN in two years than in the last thirty. "Police are being taught that their primary function is to serve the people, not suppress them. . . . It is important that these positive aspects be constantly emphasized lest the U.S. be accused of aiding a repressive arm of the Government."[99] Beyond that, a lack of training, a high attrition rate, placement of "unqualified political appointees" in key posts, inadequate records, lack of equipment and "excessive military influence in administration, discipline, and training" persisted into 1958.[100]

In 1960, after three years of work in Guatemala, the U.S. police advisory operation claimed some modest successes. Thanks to its intervention, the Guatemalan police "have been able to make advances in their administration, organization and operations which might have otherwise taken from twenty to thirty years to accomplish." More than one thousand policemen from various agencies had received both general and specialized training. The Guardia de Hacienda, acting on U.S. recommendations, opened four new stations. Before the U.S. program began, police operations outside the capital were almost completely unsupervised; now there were periodic inspections and tighter control. Police training academies had been established for the National Police (which graduated seven hundred from its three-month course), and the Guardia de Hacienda (more than one hundred graduates). The U.S. program could take credit for improved police work schedules, life insurance policies and intensive training, as well as for "better methods of escorting prisoners, establishment of property control records, eliminating of unnecessary duties and assignments that have released over 300 policemen for regular police duties."

Traffic and crime control had improved. U.S. trainers had given police "materials on patrol methods, interrogation of suspects, and criminal investigation methods," as well as crime lab equipment, and had trained six technicians in taking fingerprints. A test was now needed in order to receive a driver's license, thousands of traffic signs had been posted, traffic police had been trained in proper hand signals, and a new system of issuing drivers' licenses had been implemented. Thirty police were trained in accident investigation, and a traffic light survey had been conducted by a U.S. firm.

Police records were better. In 1956, police used narrative style daily logs instead of report forms; now they had a records bureau, report forms, a filing system and ten employees trained in records processing.

Washington also took credit for extending police communication and mobility across the whole country. Before 1956, there were no motorized police vehicles outside the capital. Now, every department had a jeep and the capital had thirty radio patrol cars, half provided by the ICA and half by the Guatemalan government. There were now thirteen radio transmitters in nine departments, covering "all important areas of the country."[101]

Collaboration in "improving special investigative services" intensified, at Ydígoras's request, as internal political opposition to his government mounted in the summer of 1960. A draft plan by U.S. police adviser Rex D. Morris recommended the creation of a Special Investigations Bureau (SIB) for the Policía Nacional, the training of its personnel, and the establishment of a Central Records Bureau "as a source of reliable intelligence information." The SIB would "have the authority to arrest and prosecute individuals charged with crimes threatening constitutional government" as well as the following responsibilities: "to investigate and be informed concerning a) political interests of social, business and labor organizations as these effect [sic] the Government, b) political activities and interests of foreign nations (e.g., communists and other agents with interests adverse to the State's), c) Guatemalan citizens with outside political interests and/or allegiances, and d) Guatemala citizens who otherwise have political interests contrary to the interests of the Country."[102] By the following May, the SIB had a staff of fifty.[103]

In the decade to come, U.S. military and police collaboration with Guatemala would grow in response to the rise of the guerrilla insurgency that emerged from the November 1960 army revolt. The insurgents naturally targeted the United States, the principal collaborator of the Guatemalan state. In 1968, the U.S. ambassador and the top two U.S. military advisers were machine-gunned to death. The war ground up the country for thirty-six years before it ended in 1996 with the signing of a peace treaty between the government and an alliance of insurgent factions. By then, even though most Guatemalans had lived their whole lives under the shadow of the longest and most destructive civil war in the history of Central America—a war in which more than two hundred thousand people were said to have been killed or disappeared—few could probably say what had started it.[104] But everyone knew which side the United States had been on. "For the United States," U.S. President Bill Clinton said in a visit to the country in 1999, "it is important that I state clearly that support for military forces or intelligence units which engage in violent and widespread repression . . . was wrong, and the United States must not repeat that mistake."[105] It was not an apology. But it was a remarkable acknowledgement of a systematically mistaken policy that endured more than three decades in "the showcase of Latin America." Whether the death toll would have been lower had the United States declined to collaborate with the police and military agencies of the Guatemalan state will never be known. What is certain is that, even as the United States began in the 1940s and 1950s to strengthen the overall capacity of the military and the police, the source of Guatemalan public violence was a political culture made in Guatemala, by Guatemalans.

11

El Salvador
Distrustful Collaborator

[It is] the Salvadoran military which, as the Department knows, is the
basis on which we must build our hopes for political stability and for
effective resistance to the growing communist problem in this country.
—Thomas C. Mann, ambassador to El Salvador, 16 May 1957

Just as it did for the rest of Latin America, World War II forced an abrupt about-face
in El Salvador's military training and supply lines, with the United States replacing
Europe. Gen. Maximiliano Hernández-Martínez, whose government declared war
on Germany and Italy immediately after the United States did so, had already consolidated his dictatorship. Rolling back the modest social welfare legislation of the
1920s, he outlawed labor unions and all political parties but his own and imposed
censorship while strengthening the power of the central government at the expense
of the municipalities. Like his fellow dictator General Ubico in Guatemala, Hernández-Martínez, an alumnus of Guatemala's Escuela Politécnica Militar, was a pioneer
in the technique of "disappearing" recalcitrant dissidents that South American military dictatorships would perfect in the 1970s.[1]

But these were scarcely reasons for Washington to question the wisdom of
wartime collaboration, and El Salvador was quick to take advantage of the opportunity presented by the war. Three Salvadoran Army captains enrolled in a six-month
infantry course at Ft. Benning in 1941, and received additional training at other loca-
tions in the United States afterward. Three more officers studied at U.S. Army
schools in 1942, and another five were sent to both continental United States and
Canal Zone training sites in 1944.[2] El Salvador signed a Lend-Lease agreement on 2
February 1942 for $1.6 million worth of military material, of which it was obligated
to pay back just 55 percent—terms similar to those accepted by Guatemala and
Nicaragua, though not as generous as those provided to Honduras.[3] The U.S. Army
was invited to take over the direction of the Escuela Militar and its associated Acad-

emia Militar, which trained general staff officers. In 1941, Col. Robert L. Christian became the first of a series of U.S. Army directors of the School and the Academy, which did not have Salvadoran directors until 1953.[4]

But the tensions characteristic of U.S.-Salvadoran diplomatic relations for decades reproduced themselves in the nascent military relationship. Hernández-Martínez denied a U.S. request for permission to station troops in El Salvador during the war, apparently the only Central American leader to do so.[5] In August 1943, the State Department turned down a Salvadoran request to buy one thousand Reising submachine guns, plus ammunition and parts, in part over concern that Hernández-Martínez might use the guns "for the repression of civil disorders" should he amend the constitution in order to secure a fourth term as president.[6]

By then the regime was beginning to totter, and although Washington clearly would have preferred to maintain the status quo, neither was it eager to associate itself too closely with a man whose brutality and deceit were turning much of the country against him. Economic growth after 1940, induced in part by rising coffee prices, and the sudden surge in pro-democracy propaganda that perforce accompanied El Salvador's declaration of war on the Axis, probably contributed to more intense demands for reforms such as social security and a minimum wage. A "modest renaissance of labor activity" included the revival of unions, organizing drives, and demands for wage increases, causes that the dictator—reviving the populist discourse that had served him in the 1930s—sought to co-opt.[7]

But the attempt at co-optation frightened the rich, some of whom even accused the dictator of communist tendencies. A broader section of the population opposed legislation to let the government regulate various private-sector groups, such as the cattle and coffee-growers associations and working-class mutual aid societies. Then, when Hernández-Martínez signaled his intention to change the constitution again so that he could stay in office after his third term as president expired on 28 February 1944, popular outrage began building. Congress obediently passed the enabling legislation for the constitutional amendment on 24 February. A military revolt on 2 April was bloodily repressed. In response, a strike initiated by university students was joined by employees of factories, shops, banks, clinics, and even some government workers. The strikers refused to return to work until Hernández-Martínez resigned. He quit on 8 May 1944, some seven weeks before General Ubico was forced to follow suit. Elections were scheduled for January 1945.[8]

Large public demonstrations for immediate social and political reforms, and the evident popularity of a strong, multiparty coalition that was preparing to sweep the January elections, generated a strong reaction among the "landholding, export-oriented oligarchy; the old upper bureaucracy; the former high command of the traditional Army; and the whole Catholic Church." They fought the reform process, undertaking their own "reactionary counteroffensive" founded on the supposed threat of a communist takeover. On 20 October, a big public demonstration in San Salvador celebrated that day's successful coup by the Guatemalan Army against the triumvirate of generals that was vainly trying to preserve the dictatorship following Ubico's forced resignation in June. Distressed by the signs of a radical turn away from dictatorship, the Salvadoran Army seized power the next day, deposing the complacent general who had been Hernández-Martínez's vice president.[9] Just as the Guatemalan Army had intervened on 20 October to open the door, however gingerly, to democracy, the Salvadoran Army rushed in to preempt democracy.[10] El Salvador thus became the first Latin American country where a personal dictatorship was replaced by institutional military rule, which would not become a hallmark of Latin American politics until the 1960s.[11] In March 1945, the army handed over the presidency to one of its own, Gen. Salvador Castaneda Castro (who had been Hernández-Martínez's interior minister), after suppressing the civilian political parties and proclaiming him the winner of the January 1945 elections.

As planning proceeded in 1945 for a meeting between U.S. and Salvadoran military authorities on postwar collaboration, the U.S. ambassador to El Salvador, John F. Simmons, began to doubt the wisdom of encouraging the governing *junta* "in the belief that we wish to build up their military establishment to a point beyond what many people here may consider to be the normal minimum requirements." Any U.S. military transfers may be used "for political purposes and as a means of maintaining a given government in power" instead of strengthening hemispheric defense, Simmons added. The State Department brushed off his concern, emphasizing that the meeting, like those being conducted elsewhere in Latin America, "are purely preliminary and exploratory in character," are "confined to technical military and naval subjects" and excluded any commitments to supply arms or other equipment.[12]

A military buildup nevertheless commenced in 1947 with the signing of a four-year U.S.-Salvadoran military aviation mission agreement, hailed by the government as the opening of a "new era" in Salvadoran military aviation history with the arrival of the four sergeants, two captains, and the lieutenant colonel of the U.S. Army Air Force mission on 16 December.[13] In 1949, Salvadoran Air Force officers flew to the United States and returned with a Douglas C-47 transport plane and ten training aircraft, plus motors and spare parts, as the air force adopted the organization plan recommended by the U.S. air mission, which continued advising and providing flight training for the Salvadoran airmen.[14] By 1950, the Salvadoran Air Force was described by the U.S. ambassador as consisting of "four or five more-or-less qualified officers, 14 students, and 10 or 12 mechanics."[15] U.S. influence on the military was considered strong outside the aviation unit as well, in large part because the colonel in charge of the U.S. Army ground mission was also the director of the Salvadoran military academy.[16]

The Salvadoran military moved swiftly to institutionalize its rule after the collapse of the country's last personal dictatorship, decisively consolidating its power when a *camarilla* of majors overthrew General Castaneda on 14 December 1948 and proclaimed a "revolution." Annulling the constitution of 1886, and with it the liberalism of the age of oligarchy, the coup leaders signaled a remaking of the state, one that would intervene more in social and economic matters, occasionally in favor of working-class interests but most consistently for commercial and industrial development, within a framework of isthmian economic integration. The majors ended personalism at the top by enforcing a ban on reelection and welcomed civilians to the highest circles of government. They also quickly identified themselves with that streak of anti-U.S. nationalism that was by now a distinguishing feature of Salvadoran political culture. When railroad workers struck the United Fruit Company's International Railways of Central America to demand the firing of its manager, J. H. Wilson, the *junta* settled the dispute by agreeing to expel Wilson and decreeing that no less than 90 percent of the employees of foreign-owned enterprises had to be Salvadorans, who also had to receive at least 85 percent of the payroll.[17]

The Partido Revolucionario de Unificación Democrática (PRUD) became the majors' official party in 1949, which outmaneuvered the opposition to win the 1950 elections for the leader of the 1948 *golpe*, Maj. Oscar Osorio, and the majority of deputies to a constituent assembly. Osorio's pre-coup exile in Mexico had impressed him with the efficiency of rule in a one-party system. The PRUD became the party of the state and drew on state resources to sustain its organization and support its candidates in election campaigns. Of course, General Hernández-Martínez could be credited with having established such a precedent with his Partido Nacional Pro-Patria, which operated as part of the state apparatus. But it was Osorio's strategy of seeking to monopolize power through co-optation, force, and fraud while appearing to encourage political competition that made it so congruent with the Mexican model. A 1949 decree sought to legally narrow that competition by prohibiting the communist party, any political parties that took foreign assistance, any organized on the basis of sex or class, and any with a religious affiliation.[18]

As the majors' promise to establish competitive democracy became less and less credible, and as electoral fraud and repression became routine, popular enthusiasm for the 1948 "revolution" dissipated.[19] On 9 March 1951, the *junta* imposed a state of siege, claiming to have evidence of simultaneous communist and reactionary conspiracies. The emergency allowed the government to jail opposition labor leaders and politicians, silencing the legal opposition. Another state of siege, for exactly the same reasons, was declared on 26 September 1952, followed by the arrest of more students, union leaders, and politicians, signaling the end of hope for democracy under the majors' "revolution."[20] On 4 December, President Osorio signed into law the Legislative Assembly's "Ley de Defensa del Orden Democrático y Constitucional," which not only outlawed communism, nazism, fascism, and anarchism, but also set jail terms of up to seven years for anyone attacking "constitutional order" in any one of twenty specified ways, including a work slowdown, the dissemination of disruptive "tendentious information," and insulting the integrity of public officials.[21] Though they campaigned, no opposition party won a single legislative seat from 1952 to 1964.[22]

As the army sought to perfect its political control of the country, it was increasingly frustrated by its inability to acquire all the military equipment that it imagined would materialize as a result of its collaboration agreement with the United States. The supply bottleneck not only threatened Washington's near-monopoly on military collaboration, but according to a 1949 U.S. Army intelligence report was delaying much-needed improvements in the capacity of the Salvadoran military. Salvador's army "does not comprise an efficient field force," and although it could maintain "internal security," and even prevent "widespread communist disorders in the event of emergencies," the army "could not prevent sporadic or isolated instances of subversion, particularly in the initial stages of a war, and it would be very difficult to prevent clandestine use by the enemy of isolated regions of the country."[23] This assessment was not to be tested for another three decades, when the Salvadoran armed forces—despite a huge leap in capacity during the intervening years—was able to fend off certain extinction only through the massive emergency intervention of the Pentagon.

In 1950, Ambassador George P. Shaw urged an acceleration in the flow of military equipment to El Salvador in order to pacify the high command, which was becoming increasingly irritated by Washington's failure to deliver on its promised support for arms standardization and for reorganization and training along U.S. lines. Most Salvadoran weapons were still of European origin. One European arms dealer—Dada, Dada y Cia., representing Madsen of Belgium—was already in San Salvador, had already sold some equipment to the army, and was "standing ready to supply the country with such arms as it may not be able to obtain from the United States," Shaw warned. Awash in cash after a nearly fivefold rise in coffee prices between 1945 and 1954, the Salvadoran government was eager to spend some of its surplus on rearmament, and it was one of the few countries in the hemisphere that could pay cash for its arms, Shaw argued. Although the government wanted to buy several million dollars' worth of equipment, it would be content to place an order for just $400,000 in arms and ammunition, and Washington should act now to guarantee the order.[24]

The State Department approved a request by El Salvador to buy $657,801 in weapons and equipment, but its decision to raise the prices of some equipment and deny the sale of other items so irritated the Salvadorans that they cancelled the order in October 1950.[25] By then, U.S.-Salvadoran military relations had clearly taken a more contentious turn. As Shaw explained the following May, "There is a long chain of incidents . . . which have caused increasing irritation with the United States military forces on the part of the Salvadoran officials and a consequent loss of prestige and influence by the United States Government." Besides what the Salvadorans considered a lack of cooperation in building up its military force, the first air mission chief, Col. George H. Hollingsworth, so offended the Salvadoran military with his tactlessness that the defense minister requested his immediate removal. His replacement, Col. James A. Smyrl, "received a cold welcome" and had numerous personal conflicts with the rest of the air mission. There were shipping delays and price increases for arms and ammunition. In addition, El Salvador had requested training in the United States for its air force pilots; the government thought the training would be free, and then was informed it would cost $10,000 per pilot.[26]

Yet another grievance was Washington's failure to respond to the Salvadoran request in 1949 for two U.S. military officers to establish the equivalent of a command and general staff school ("Escuela de Aplicación"). All of these factors probably contributed, Shaw speculated, to El Salvador's decision to contract a Chilean military mission on 28 September 1950. The Salvadoran government let it be known that the pay of the Chileans would be much higher than that of the U.S. mission members. The five officers of the Chilean mission, who arrived on 1 December 1950, were hired on a three-year contract to establish the command and general staff school, to act as its head professors, and to advise the Salvadoran general staff.[27] El Salvador was the only Central American country to welcome a non-U.S. military mission after World War II.

The arrival of the Chileans provoked a highly critical assessment of the nine-year-old program of U.S. military collaboration by Ambassador Shaw. "There are really very few concrete results to show for this long and extended effort. El Salvador has never really accepted the American system and it has not adopted United States arms or practices. The country has a Chilean military tradition and it is returning to Chilean practices." Instead of agreeing to renew the U.S. air mission agreement for the standard four years when it expired in May 1951, the Salvadorans grudgingly extended it a year at a time.[28] The government signed its first army mission agreement with the United States in 1953—but without the usual clause requiring Washington's approval before hiring other foreign military advisers, an omission that suggested that Washington was willing to compromise in order to strengthen its ties with the Salvadoran military.[29]

An opportunity for the United States to recover the confidence of the Salvadoran military presented itself on 9 December 1953, when President Eisenhower found El Salvador, along with Honduras and Nicaragua, eligible for grant military collaboration via the MAP. No doubt sensing the opportunity that Arbenz was handing him for a major military buildup at Washington's expense, President Osorio had already sent a delegation headed by his armed forces chief of staff, Col. Marco Antonio Molina, to Washington in February 1953 with the outlandish request that the United States secretly pay the entire cost of equipping twenty-six battalions of about 650 men each, a measure that would result in a nearly six-fold increase in combat-ready soldiers, from 3,000 to 17,000. The extra troops were needed to train reserves and secrecy was needed, according to El Salvador, because "communists" would oppose the deal on the grounds that the money was not being spent on schools and hospitals. Another reason for secrecy was that the transfers might provoke an attack by Guatemala. Although the Salvadorans were told that the Mutual Security Act of 1951 required public notice of any aid, they nevertheless "argued at great length their need for secrecy and asked over and over again if there was a way around this problem," according to a State Department report of the meeting.

With final presidential authorization for MAP negotiations still months away, the State Department told the Salvadorans they would have to pay for it all themselves, at a cost of about $5.3 million. "It is quite probable that Salvador does not expect even half of what it is asking for but the list from any viewpoint is so large as to be almost ridiculous," a State Department functionary commented. In April, Osorio pared the list to $2.9 million, enough to arm ten thousand men over a period of four years, and offered to pay for the equipment in four installments beginning in September 1953, but the Pentagon's counteroffer was rejected by El Salvador because of the high prices of some items and the unavailability of others.[30] By October 1953, the Salvadoran government was "extremely annoyed, if not angry" and Colonel Molina was "exceedingly disappointed" by the U.S. response, according to the U.S. Embassy.[31]

In early 1954, with the opening of formal talks on a MAP deal, President Osorio continued to insist not only on the total secrecy of any resulting agreement, but that El Salvador not be asked to contribute troops for military actions outside Central America and the Caribbean.[32] During a negotiating session on 31 May 1954, Osorio observed that the MAP agreement with Honduras "placed Honduras in a position of subservience" using language that, if applied to El Salvador, could be used by communists and the Guatemalan government against both the United States and El Salvador. For psychological reasons, MAP agreements "should be drafted to show an equality in the partnership even though no one could claim that actually Honduras or El Salvador was equal in military or economic power with the United States."[33] Unlike Honduras and Nicaragua, El Salvador clearly wanted to keep its distance from the United States even while signing a grant collaboration agreement. Secrecy and the appearance of reciprocity were essential, though it is not clear why Osorio should have cared about the appearance of reciprocity in a secret agreement. In order to accommodate these concerns, the State Department accepted wording that referred to reciprocity, but Osorio and the U.S. ambassador agreed in private conversation that El Salvador "was naturally not thinking of sending any mutual assistance mission to the United States or supplying any arms, et cetera."

That conversation took place on 24 June 1954, one week after the U.S.-organized invasion of Guatemala under the leadership of Col. Carlos Castillo Armas had begun and three days before the invasion would secure Arbenz's downfall. In the course of the conversation, Osorio also told the U.S. ambassador that his government "has officially adopted a policy of 'neutrality,' believing it the best policy at the moment for El Salvador and for Central America," citing pressure from the Left. Osorio thought Castillo Armas had insufficient ground forces to defeat the Guatemalan Army, despite his air superiority. Should Castillo be defeated, Osorio feared that Guatemala would declare war on Honduras (the platform for Castillo Armas's invasion) and that El Salvador would then "incline" toward Honduras. "It was evident that there is a prior understanding on this matter between Salvador, Honduras and Nicaragua and that Salvador will come to the support of Honduras if necessary," the U.S. ambassador reported.[34]

As of January 1955, El Salvador had still not accepted the terms of the U.S. proposal for a grant military collaboration agreement like the ones that had been speedily negotiated in 1954 with Honduras, Nicaragua, and the newly installed Castillo Armas government of Guatemala. But El Salvador's obstinacy and its constant demands for additional concessions had led the Defense Department to channel the grant military aid reserved for El Salvador to other purposes. With Arbenz gone, Washington now viewed the matter with indifference, and the U.S. Embassy was instructed to avoid encouraging the Salvadorans to renew MAP talks.[35]

As they dickered with Washington over the scope of collaboration, Salvadoran military leaders began to fashion a theory of national security congruent with the

Cold War. At hand were the newly fashioned discourses of "continental defense," anticommunism, and Pan-Americanism. New institutions—the United Nations, the Rio Treaty, and the Organization of American States—"have made El Salvador an American entity of defense," the defense ministry declared in late 1953 or early 1954. "At 700 miles from the Panama Canal, we are within the radius of common bombing operations and it is fitting to ask, 'What would be the consequences of a lack of foresight if we consider defense only within the limits of our borders?' Are we prepared for defense? Is it possible that El Salvador is threatened? The questions are enigmatic and strike one as fantastic unrealities but, be that as it may, in the high-speed atomic age, all precautions, over time, turn out to be inadequate."[36] Answers were being offered by the members of the Chilean military mission who were teaching in the Command and General Staff College. Chilean Col. Juan Forch Petit taught an early version of what would become known, in the 1960s, as national security doctrine. National security, he wrote,

> starts by organizing the whole nation. National Defense is not an exclusive attribute of the Armed Forces. . . . Modern strategy—like the police security of a town—is a permanent operation and starts and has its main activities in peacetime. . . . To prepare the resources of the country does not mean just to have a certain number of weapons, to be ready to use them and to face the enemy. More than that, much more than that, it means to restructure the economic, military, political and spiritual resources of a nation. . . . Each people must be ready to organize itself to facilitate its defense in the main areas of national activity. Therefore, total planning is necessary.

What Forch Petit called "internal security" required that the authorities reject any differences between civilians and military men, and prepare the whole nation for a new kind of war. Missiles could now travel two thousand miles. "Basically, there will be no battlefields in the war of the future and forces will be needed both in the areas of operation and in the interior zones."[37] Strikingly absent from Forch Petit's account of national security strategy was any reference to the enemy—who it was, what it looked liked, and above all, what made it an enemy. Because everyone ought to be a soldier, the enemy might be anyone who declined the role, an implication that became operative in the next three decades as techniques of internal counterinsurgency warfare, surveillance, and intelligence replaced older strategies of continental defense.

Clearly, this was a line of military thinking that could offer common ground with Washington. Despite its indifference to a MAP agreement, the United States remained eager to demonstrate its friendliness. The Salvadoran government's request in April 1955 to buy eight 105-mm howitzers, four thousand shells, related artillery equipment, tents, twenty-four trucks, spare parts, and telephone equipment, for $555,599, was approved by the State Department the day it was submitted. Both the Embassy and the army mission, State advised Defense, "attach particular importance to this request because it is a major request by El Salvador," and it represents "a victory for those in the Salvadoran Government who believe that Salvador's military equipment should be standardized along United States lines."[38]

The political value of military collaboration with El Salvador was emphasized in a dispatch written at the end of the 1955 by the new U.S. ambassador, Thomas C. Mann, who no doubt drew on his experience as the counselor of the U.S. Embassy in Guatemala immediately after the success of the CIA coup against President Arbenz. Like the Guatemalan officer corps, that of El Salvador was divided between men who were sympathetic to the United States and those who distrusted it, and Mann undoubtedly perceived the Salvadoran Army just as he had Guatemala's—as Washington's "ace in the hole." Even though the Salvadoran officer corps, unlike that of Guatemala, was impeccably anticommunist, the challenge in El Salvador was incomparably greater, owing in part to the presence of the Chileans and the Salvadorans' prideful petulance:

> Since my arrival here have been impressed with importance of army mission to our overall political interests in this country. It is our principal link with Salvadoran army officer corps which in turn largely determines who is to govern Salvador and what Salvadoran policies will be. Currently a large number of Salvadoran officers are distrustful of United States and inclined look elsewhere for help and guidance. Courses taught by Chilean mission in Escuela de Guerra can only result in further orientation away from United States of officers who soon will occupy key positions. We do not (repeat not) believe Salvadorans will continue indefinitely maintain two separate army missions here. We are competing with Chileans who have several advantages already reported to Department including especially a common culture.

Because the Chileans "still have inside track," U.S. military mission members should be of the highest quality. "The most important task of the new chief of army mission will be to gain confidence and esteem Salvadoran officers including those not (repeat not) now disposed to be friendly. This will not (repeat not) be an easy task. Request instructions."[39]

As if to prove Mann's point, the armed forces took no chances with the 1956 presidential election. Five of the six candidates were military officers; the sixth was a civilian who had been Osorio's foreign relations minister. After the ruling PRUD chose Lt. Col. José María Lemus, the government used its resources to promote Lemus while disqualifying all the opposition candidates but two. Declaring Lemus the winner with 94 percent of the votes, the *junta* demonstrated beyond all doubt the futility of the democratic hopes it had incited in 1948.[40]

Lemus's government then sounded out the Embassy about the possibility of renewing talks for a grant collaboration agreement. The Embassy speculated that the sudden interest in the subject might have been owing to three possible sources: "increased communist activity in the labor movement," a desire to "make the military forces more attractive to its members" or the "probable military growth" of its neighbors.[41] Another explanation was the budgetary impact of a sharp drop in international coffee prices in 1957, which reduced both government revenues and economic activity to such an extent that it forced an overall reorientation of government policy. Coffee accounted for 80 percent of the value of all exports, and 60 percent of government revenue depended on taxes associated with coffee production. The coffee collapse forced the Lemus government to seek support abroad for international price controls and for Central American economic integration. These goals naturally inspired Lemus to seek U.S. cooperation in resolving the economic crisis, which he adroitly linked with the communist threat.[42]

But in response to the renewed expression of interest in a MAP agreement, the State Department told the Embassy: "The United States has no further interest in concluding a military assistance agreement with Salvador and any initiative on this subject should be left entirely to the Salvadorans."[43] Six weeks later, in May 1957, Mann urged the State Department to take a more cooperative attitude to requests for military transfers by El Salvador, recommending a speed-up in the delivery of military equipment that the government had already ordered and paid for, as well as the same low prices and credit terms enjoyed by other Central American countries. He also noted that El Salvador had not received any of the economic development funds set aside for the other countries. Moreover, the military government worried about its military weakness compared to its neighbors.[44]

Nevertheless, the ambassador continued to discourage the Salvadorans from pressing for a MAP grant by "pointing out that the reason for our original demarche, the enabling of Guatemala's neighbors to resist pressures of the Arbenz regime, no longer exists and furthermore, that United States funds for this purpose are no longer available." But in his correspondence with the State Department, Mann continued to argue for a change. Although relations with the Salvadoran military had improved, they would remain good only so long as the United States tried "to satisfy their wants which are small indeed in comparison with the assistance which we render virtually every other part of the world." Only the Salvadoran military could serve as "the basis on which we must build our hopes for political stability and for effective resistance to the growing communist problem in this country."[45]

Besides the need to ensure political stability by means of the Salvadoran military and to resist communism, there was another argument for finding ways to enhance U.S military cooperation with El Salvador. El Salvador's habit of buying weapons from non-U.S. suppliers not only deprived U.S. manufacturers of orders but made a mockery of the U.S. goal of standardization of equipment along U.S. lines. From 1953 to 1955 alone, El Salvador had purchased sixty Danish mortars, eighteen French mortars, five hundred Danish submachine guns, one thousand Belgian pistols, and two thousand Belgian fragmentation grenades. In December 1954 a West German-registered ship had offloaded two hundred cases of light machine guns and one hundred cases of small arms ammunition; four months later a French-registered vessel delivered fifty-four tons of .30-caliber ammunition shipped from a London dealer. Japanese walkie-talkies and German cots, motorcycles, and cars were also purchased.[46]

The main justification for collaboration, however, remained the need to fend off a possible communist takeover, as Washington believed it had just succeeded in doing in Guatemala. The Salvadoran communist party was thought to have no more than 400 members, of whom just 150 were "militants"; it could likely count on a maximum of 600 "symphatizers."[47] In 1957 the Embassy initiated "frank discussions" with the government on methods of "combating" communist activity, "which reportedly has increased under the more liberal Administration of President Lemus." In response to the Embassy's report of these conversations, Secretary of State John Foster Dulles told the Embassy on 10 June 1957 to encourage the Salvadoran government to undertake the "legal suppression" of the communists, and to advise President Lemus "on anti-communist measures and programs to the extent he requests it and it appears to be welcomed." The Salvadoran Congress should be encouraged to enact "adequate communist control legislation. The suggested harassing tactics could be carried out effectively" within the framework of the new legislation "and should prove effective in keeping the communist leaders off balance as suggested. The Department would hope that Salvadoran authorities find it within their power to carry out these activities without compromising their professed dedication to democratic and constitutional procedures." The use of the definite article before the phrase "harassing tactics" suggests that the phrase referred to an earlier Embassy dispatch; its meaning was not spelled out in Dulles's telegram. The government, Dulles added, should also be encouraged to organize private citizens into anticommunist groups (a technique that Salvadoran governments had already mastered and would use again in the 1960s and 1970s), and to "influence" the labor movement.[48]

Meanwhile, U.S. representatives in El Salvador continued to pressure the State Department to intensify military collaboration to overcome what the U.S. military mission believed was a Chilean-instigated "anti-United States military ideology." Apparently, the duties of what was now a two-man Chilean mission were limited to teaching in the Escuela de Guerra, but because future Salvadoran leaders, including presidents, pass through the school, "It is important that officers not receive this [anti-U.S.] orientation." Furthermore, France had just sent a naval captain to direct the small naval school, which was still part of the army. In order to bridge the distance between the U.S. and Salvadoran militaries, the ambassador urged Washington to invite the Salvadoran defense minister (who had recently been decorated on a trip to Chile) and other officers to visit Washington.[49]

Nevertheless, Washington continued to brush off Salvadoran requests for a MAP agreement. As late as April 1959, three months after Fidel Castro's guerrillas toppled the Batista regime in Cuba, Roy R. Rubottom, Jr., assistant secretary of state, told the Salvadoran government that he "could not be optimistic" about its desire for a grant collaboration agreement because "the present trend of public and Congressional opinion in the U.S. was away from defense expenditures and in the direction of economic assistance." Not only was there "the new probability of any future war being an atomic conflict," but the Organization of American States was now available as an effective instrument to avoid inter-American wars. The Embassy continued to oppose a MAP agreement because "any money contemplated for the enlargement of the military capacities of El Salvador could far better be employed in productive enterprises necessary for its economic development." The State Department position was fully supported by the Pentagon, except for one dissenter, the U.S. Army's Caribbean Command, soon to become the U.S. Southern Command. It argued that the United States should sign a MAP agreement with El Salvador as well as with other Latin American countries that lacked one.[50]

But the Salvadoran government did not give up. By November 1959, President Lemus was begging for grant collaboration because of the "growing instability of the area, especially communist agitation and possibilities of attacks by El Salvador's neighbors." The country's aircraft were insufficient and in poor condition; Lemus contrasted El Salvador's situation with the jets "now contemplated for purchase by Cuba." The Salvadoran government had fifty pilots "but no planes to fly" and no money to buy them. Lemus, according to the U.S. ambassador, was looking for grant collaboration or credits as well as help in reorganizing the armed forces. Six months later, the ambassador's request for instructions was answered in the usual terms: Discourage El Salvador from thinking that Washington would sign a MAP treaty. The State Department cited Congress's disposition to annually reduce collaboration-related spending, and the Salvadorans should be told that U.S. policy was focused on economic development. Although military aircraft, armored cars, or similar military equipment were out of the question, a request for police collaboration aimed at strengthening the control of coasts and borders and maintaining public order would be welcomed.[51]

Police collaboration between the two countries had already commenced, somewhat precariously, in 1957. The Policía Nacional, according to a U.S. assessment at that time

> were not well-organized and were commanded at top level by Army officers. There was no police academy or in-service training. Recurit training consisted of military drill. Most of the mobile and communications equipment was inoperable. Much of the other equipment was ill-suited to civil police needs. Relationship of the police with the public was poor. Administrative and operational procedures of the police were so poorly conceived as to make the police ineffective. Salary and working conditions were inferior and result in an excessive turnover of personnel. Moreover these same conditions attracted poor quality recruits.

After two years of collaboration, the U.S. police advisers reported that they had managed to establish a police academy, had broadened training, and supplied some new equipment.[52]

By July 1960, the Embassy was convinced that the gravest threat to Salvadoran security was really a police matter, namely, border infiltration of "subversive agents, introduction of subversive literature, smuggling of arms, traffic in contraband items, etc." But even after three years of police collaboration, equipment and vehicles were still so scarce that deportees, for example, had to be walked to the border by the National Guard. "Castroism working in concert with international communism has made serious inroads, and, because of the combination of conditions existing here, El Salvador appears to have been selected as a prime target." A big increase in police collaboration was necessary. "Reports of clandestine movements of agents and arms are reaching the Embassy in increasing volume. And overt threats to public order and safety have shown a decided increase in both number and boldness over the past several months."[53] In August, the U.S. police advisers convinced the State Department to make an emergency $2,000 purchase of four hundred tear gas grenades for the Salvadoran police in response to a demonstration on 16 August by about three hundred people "believed communist-inspired"—in front of the U.S. Embassy and later in front of a newspaper office—and in preparation for another scheduled for 24 August.[54]

Meanwhile, the U.S. Army mission chief, Col. Robert A. Matter, along with the U.S. Caribbean Command, continued to press for grant military collaboration. Although it was not justified for military reasons, there were strong political reasons to do so. President Lemus had made a MAP treaty a "major policy objective" and "No amount of explaining can, for example, make President Lemus accept the fact that the United States provides military grant aid to El Salvador's neighbors, Guatemala, Honduras, and Nicaragua, and yet refuses to assist this country which has repeatedly demonstrated its friendship for, and has given its support to the principles and policies of the United States." One advantage of a MAP for El Salvador would be that it would "greatly enhance the now limited influence of the United States Military Missions on the Salvadoran Armed Forces policy, doctrine, training and operations along desired United States lines." There was no record, Matter lamented, of any U.S. Army mission members being briefed by the Salvadoran armed forces on any plans or programs or being asked to assist in developing any plans or programs despite U.S. offers to do so. Grant collaboration would automatically provide more information to the United States about the Salvadoran military. Another reason for a grant agreement was that social unrest might break out across Central America generally. As an "oasis of political stability," El Salvador would be an ideal place for a U.S. military staging area and the location of a "bastion of U.S.-oriented political-economic-military strength. . . . Having a basic bilateral agreement in force would permit the almost instantaneous buildup of strength in this area, which might well prove to be decisive in time of emergency."

Colonel Matter proposed U.S. grant support for creating a mobile maintenance support unit ($109,540 in equipment); an antisubmarine warfare squadron ($840,000 in equipment); a signal support company ($509,000 in equipment); and a heavy weapons battalion ($511,253 in equipment). Although a MAP treaty could help El Salvador overcome "major deficiencies" in its armed forces—including recruitment, the lack of standardization in weapons and equipment, ammunition supply in combat, combat logistics, and training—it was "primarily for political reasons" that the United States should seek grant military collaboration because El Salvador was too small and weak economically to contribute to hemispheric defense. The MAP agreement "would be so worded as to increase U.S. influence in the organization, operation and training of the Salvadoran Armed Forces."[55]

But the Embassy continued to recommend against grant collaboration and in favor of urgent police-type assistance to protect Salvadoran borders against the rising danger of "subversive agents, introduction of subversive literature, smuggling of arms, traffic in contraband items, etc."[56]

The recommendations of neither Colonel Matter nor of the Embassy were acted on immediately, even though El Salvador's isolation from the general trend of U.S. military collaboration in Central America was obvious. Its share of total U.S. transfers to the region from 1950 to 1959 was just 15 percent, identical to that of Costa Rica, which did not even claim to have an army. And like Costa Rica, those transfers consisted of government sales instead of the grant aid provided to the other three countries. (See Appendix, figures A-1, A-2, and A-5.)

On 17 October 1960, nine days before his overthrow, President Lemus seemed even more desperate than he had a year earlier for any sign of U.S. support for his government. Now, instead of lamenting the backwardness of the armed forces, Lemus played the anticommunist card, telling U.S. Ambassador Thorsten V. Kalijarvi that El Salvador was about to be overrun with communists from Honduras, a country that was "rapidly gravitating towards Cuba." Deserting the tradition of national dignity that had set El Salvador apart from its neighbors for so many decades, Lemus argued that the best solution was for the United States to "deal with El Salvador exactly as she would with one of her own states, Texas or Louisiana, that might be in danger from communism," Kalijarvi reported. Lemus wanted Washington to provide him "with a group of experts skilled in combating communism, who can participate in building up the country. Smilingly he said: 'I do not want a police force.'" Kalijarvi clearly relished the opportunity to keep Lemus's attention trained on the country's few communists. The National University's medical school, for example, had "a number of communists" on its faculty, of whom Kalijarvi discussed two in particular, though their names were not reported in Kalijarvi's dispatch. Lemus agreed, the ambassador reported, that "it was time to clean house, and he was holding up funds from the School until improvement could be made."[57]

Lemus had little time left to clean house. On 26 October 1960 a left-leaning military-civilian *junta* associated with ex-president Osorio removed Lemus from office. It imposed new taxes on coffee exporters, hinted that it would depoliticize the military, and promised absolutely free elections, a decision that "was in itself tantamount to a political revolution."[58] The CIA, the U.S. Embassy, and the Defense Department initially considered the coup a "Castro-communist plot," thus delaying U.S. recognition of the *junta*. Although the Defense Department continued to insist on isolating the government, which it predicted "will come under communist domination," both the State Department and the CIA urged President Eisenhower to recognize it. After conducting an "impartial survey of the problem," they were satisfied that the *junta* was "attempting to maintain its independence of Castroist or communist policies and personnel." Eisenhower ordered the restoration of diplomatic relations on 1 December.[59]

A countercoup on 25 January 1961 seemed to open a new era of U.S.-Salvadoran military collaboration. The Embassy reported that the warmth and enthusiasm with which the new military regime welcomed Lt. Gen. Andrew P. O'Meara, commander in chief of the Caribbean Command, for a visit on 4–5 April "clearly demonstrated the desire of the Salvadoran Government for closer military cooperation with the U.S."[60] Nine months later, Pres. John F. Kennedy at last authorized grant military aid to El Salvador (as well as to Costa Rica and Panama, the only other Central American countries that had not previously signed MAP agreements).[61] Because El Salvador's participation in the MAP was specially authorized by the President Kennedy, no bilateral agreement was necessary, nor apparently was such an agreement ever negotiated, a factor that no doubt pleased the *junta*, considering El Salvador's aversion to the standard terms of these agreements.

If the Salvadoran military were indeed the first of the Latin American armed forces to govern "as an institution," its highest ranking officers may also have been among the first to have learned, via the Chilean adviser, Col. Juan Forch Petit, the ideology that would justify the shift to institutional military rule practically everywhere in the region beginning in the 1960s. Both of these marks of El Salvador's military precocity were consistent with two other features of the country's twentieth-century history: its uniquely nondeferential attitude toward the United States and its military superiority to the other governments of the isthmus. One might also add its reputation for merciless ferocity against its own people (especially when they were unarmed), as had occurred in the *matanza* of 1932 and would be repeated in the 1980s.

It was therefore not surprising that twice during the Cold War, the Salvadoran military, acting out of a sense of wounded vanity, should have slammed the door on military collaboration with the United States—in 1954 and in 1977, when the ruling *junta* publicly renounced collaboration owing to U.S. government criticism of its human rights record. Yet in both instances, the military quickly found itself knocking on that door again. When its greatest test came in the 1980s, it was nearly wiped out by the very internal enemy—now armed and organized—that its own national security doctrine had been denouncing for years, and found itself utterly dependent for its survival on the United States.

From 1948 until 1960, Washington showed little inclination to deepen military and police collaboration with the *junta*. It was a logical position to take with a military government thought to be the best in the isthmus, anticommunist, and capable of acting with impunity. Closer collaboration might have risked public criticism of the United States for sustaining the most nakedly militaristic regime in Central America. The State Department opted instead for jawboning the military into deploying its unfettered power against Salvadorans suspected of disloyalty.

12

Honduras

Remaking an "Armed Rabble"

We've all been brawlers and the brawls haven't gotten us anywhere.
—Gen. Abraham Williams Calderón, vice president of
Honduras, 1933–48, speaking as a delegate to the
constitutional convention of 22 October 1957

Following the German invasion of France in the summer of 1940, the United States appealed to the Honduran government for information: How many German, Italian, and Japanese nationals were living in Honduras? How many of them were born in Honduras? Where were they living?[1] Washington also needed the permission of Honduras for U.S. armed forces planes to regularly fly over its territory and to land if necessary, to become "better acquainted with military men, particularly air men," as well as to expose U.S. pilots to Central American weather and flying conditions.[2] Honduras complied, placing "at the disposition of the U.S. government the ports, coasts, islands and territorial waters of the Republic in the Caribbean sea and in the Gulf of Fonseca, and the airports and landing fields, private as well as public, for the use of its warships and its military aircraft during the armed conflict." The Carías government also conceded free access to U.S. troops, either in transit or for longer-term posting, while promising to take steps to prevent "fifth-column activities."[3]

A week after the Japanese attack on Pearl Harbor, and immediately after Honduras's declaration of war on the Axis powers, Honduras extended the scope of its earlier permission for U.S. overflights and landings, allowing U.S. military craft to fly over Honduran territory "without limitation as to number or type of plane or personnel and arms carried," to use Honduran airports and all their facilities without any advance notification, and to photograph "all territory of Honduras as may be necessary from a tactical and strategic point of view or as may be desirable for the compilation of air and navy charts," with copies of the photographs to be supplied to Honduras. Two U.S. navy lieutenants were soon sent as "naval observers" to the

Gulf of Fonseca, with the freedom to move in and out of Honduras, El Salvador, and Nicaragua, all of which border the gulf. The U.S. Navy considered building an air base on the gulf's Tigre Island, a Honduran possession.

In return, Honduras would receive weapons, and both its military and nonmilitary pilots, as well as aircraft mechanics and aeronautical engineers, would receive training in the United States. A request for U.S. Army officers to "inspect and render technical assistance on the present condition of the Honduran infantry" had been readily granted in December 1940. But the country's principal reward for cooperating with the U.S. war effort was negotiated within three months of Pearl Harbor: a Lend-Lease agreement signed on 28 February 1942 under which Washington pledged to transfer to Honduras "armaments and munitions of war" worth about $1.3 million, of which Honduras would only have to repay 9.23 percent of the cost over a period of six years—the lowest repayment rate negotiated by any Central American Lend-Lease recipient. In exchange, Honduras agreed to provide the United States whatever "defense articles and defense information" it needed, "to the extent possible without harm to its economy."[4]

Modest U.S. requests for cooperation continued to arrive at the Honduran Foreign Ministry. The U.S. legation asked the government to "remove" from the port city of La Ceiba three Germans and one Italian who were recently discharged by the Standard Fruit and Steamship Company. Although Washington had no evidence that they were working against the Allies, there was nevertheless a risk that, now being unemployed, they might "conspire in favor of the pro-Axis interests or to propagate their political beliefs," perhaps interfering with the power plant, radio station, or telegraph system of La Ceiba in the event of a submarine attack on ships docked in the harbor.[5] A shortage of shipping in 1942 and a desire by Washington to improve land communication between the United States and the Panama Canal Zone led the United States to seek the cooperation of Honduras (as well as the other isthmian countries) in expediting completion of the Inter-American Highway from the Mexican border to the Canal, "to facilitate passage of officers and men of the United States Army with their arms, provisions and other military matériel and equipment." Most of the survey and grading costs of the gravel road segments would be paid by the United States, thus saving Honduras money and allowing for completion of the road, it was hoped, by mid-1943.[6]

As the war drew to a close in March 1945, Washington turned its attention to what it called "the problem of the postwar military security of the Hemisphere," and proposed to Honduras the same negotiations on military collaboration that were being arranged throughout Latin America that year.[7] By then the Carías dictatorship was beginning to crumble, weakened not only by mounting public demonstrations in favor of democratic change like those that had already driven neighboring presidents Ubico and Hernández-Martínez into exile, but by an evident distancing of Washington from Carías's government now that its military and political cooperation was no longer necessary.[8]

General Carías had not only succeeded in holding office longer than his fellow dictators (surpassing Ubico's record by four years and Hernández-Martínez's by three) but also managed to stanch, with considerable bloodshed, precisely the kinds of popular demonstrations against his regime that had so abruptly terminated the other two regimes. Carías also made that rarest of choices for a dictator—the voluntary cession of power. After arranging for the election of his war minister, Juan Gálvez, as president, Carías retired to his farm in 1948. Avoiding both a violent death and the ignominy of exile, he continued to direct—at least nominally—the Partido Nacional until dying peacefully in 1969 at the age of ninety-three.[9]

Mario Argüeta attributed Carías's occupation of the presidency for sixteen years to his skill in purchasing the support of a range of influential groups: conservative landlords and *hacendados*, peasants, and the United Fruit Company. The company provided Carías loans to meet the government's payroll and to buy weapons and other necessities, in exchange for the president's willingness to prohibit strikes, wipe out unions, persecute labor leaders, and grant other concessions. Upper-level state bureaucrats defended Carías's regime as long as he respected their right to steal public goods. Moreover, the dictator adroitly manipulated such resources as government jobs, scholarships to the national university and other state educational institutions, and state lands to build and maintain political alliances and a wide network of support. Perhaps most important, Carías superbly managed the local *comandantes de armas* and *mayores de plaza*, respecting the local strongmen's traditional right to pursue the usual opportunities for personal enrichment and to enjoy a certain level of autonomy from the central government, even while leaving no doubt about the limits of their freedom.[10] Finally, Carías deliberately withheld resources and training from the army, except for elite units under his direct command. After all, he had every reason to distrust an army "with a self-sufficient organizational structure, with the necessary level of power in its hands to establish itself as the arbiter of Honduran political life." Carías wanted an army that was just strong enough to keep him in power, yet weak enough to keep it from acting on its own.[11]

This was exactly the mentality that divided Carías, Ubico, and Martínez-Hernández from the men who followed them in power in the 1950s. The men of the 1950s recognized that the age of the tyrant was over, and that tyranny could only survive were it exercised collectively by the armed forces, in the name of democracy and the nation, and as collaborators of the world's preeminent military power. But to an extent unrivaled by El Salvador and Guatemala, where centralized control over a national military force had already been achieved by the 1920s, the Honduran armed forces owed its establishment in the 1950s as a distinct institution to the United States. Washington's principal collaborator in this endeavor was President Gálvez, an ex-United Fruit lawyer. After winning the uncontested 1948 presidential election he relaxed controls over the opposition Liberal Party while expanding the reach and power of the state, enabling it to more actively direct the country's economy.[12] As Carías's war minister from 1933 to 1948, Gálvez had often expressed his desire to transform the Honduran Army into a respected, fighting force. Just before ascending to the presidency Gálvez noted that, although the lack of economic resources was still the main obstacle to making a modern army, the government also had to "combat the indifference, hostility and ignorance" with which the general public regarded its duty to take up arms in the service of the Patria.[13] Gálvez's knew that his hopes for creating a "truly front-line army" rested almost entirely on the United States, and his astute exploitation of the opportunities for U.S. collaboration earned him the permanent gratitude of the Honduran armed forces.[14]

More so than for any other Central American country, World War II was the turning point in the Honduran Army's modernization. Right after the postwar collaboration planning talks in 1945, Honduras welcomed a combined, eight-man U.S. Army and Aviation mission, the largest in the isthmus, which arrived shortly after Honduras had bought eighteen military aircraft, including seven bombers, from the United States.[15] The U.S. Mission immediately organized the Escuela Básica de Armas for enlisted men and noncommissioned officers in downtown Tegucigalpa's Francisco Morazán garrison. The school opened on 20 July 1946 under the direction of U.S. Army Lt. Col. Walter C. Mayer, who modeled the curriculum on that of U.S. Army schools. At first, the school delivered basic infantry training but soon added courses in engineering, mechanics, and electricity.[16] In addition, the mission was in charge of both the training and the administration of the Honduran Air Force, which was under the command of U.S. Army Col. M. F. Stewart. The mission oversaw the construction of Toncontín airfield in Tegucigalpa, still the capital's main civilian airport, while acquiring equipment for the army and the air force.[17] The U.S. mission also organized an army general staff along U.S. lines, with separate sections for personnel (G-1), military intelligence (G-2), operations and training (G-3), logistics (G-4), and civil affairs (G-5). On 14 February 1946, the U.S. government delivered its naval base in Puerto Castilla to the Honduran govenrment.[18] By 1949, the U.S. mission had expanded to an extraordinary fourteen men, of whom eight were air force specialists. On 2 May, the ground specialists opened an officer-training academy with a class of thirteen officers. The aviation section took over the construction of the Toncontín airport, acquiring equipment, training and supervising construction workers, and laying out the runways.[19]

A U.S. Army intelligence report that year still found nothing to praise in the Honduran armed forces, and the State Department acknowledged that it was "impossible" for Honduras to defend itself "with any conceivable level of expenditures on a military establishment." As a result, the United States sought to discourage the country from buying too much military equipment and to rely instead on collective security arrangements. The U.S. military mission should not, therefore, try to do the impossible (namely, to make Honduras self-sufficient militarily), but rather to help it "in the development of an efficient air force, an engineer battalion, and a presidential guard as aids in assisting it to perform its appropriate role in hemispheric defense."[20] As a result, Washington rejected the Honduran request to buy five thousand M1 rifles and a million rounds of ammunition in 1950 but agreed to a sale of fifteen hundred M1s and 1.2 million rounds of ammunition for $221,650.[21]

In 1949, the U.S. ground mission shifted from basic infantry training, by now the responsibility of Honduran officers who had been trained in the United States, to the systematic training of Honduran officers and NCOs in an Escuela de Aplicación de la Misión Militar. The breadth of the 1,360-hour curriculum, nearly a third of which was devoted to weapons and tactics, is indicated in Appendix table A-14. In 1952 the school was "nationalized" with the appointment of its first Honduran director, Capt. José López Aguilar, a Honduran graduate of the basic infantry course at Ft. Benning, Georgia, and renamed the Escuela de Aplicación del Ejército de Honduras. Separate U.S. Army and air force missions were established in 1950 as they continued to supervise the construction of runways and taxiways at Toncontín airport.[22] The U.S. Air Force Mission set up a supply system for the Honduran Air Force in 1951 and organized a survey of all Honduran airfields to determine their adequacy for receiving transport aircraft, gathering data on runway lengths, soil, and gradients. The air mission bought $1,200 worth of "uniforms, clothing and personal hygiene supplies" for Honduran airmen from various stores in the United States and Panama, provided flight instruction to cadets in training, and trained pilots and copilots in instrument and night flying. Fourteen more Honduran airmen were trained in the United States or Panama that year.[23]

By 1952 the U.S. Army Mission had expanded to eleven and the Air Force Mission to six,[24] easily the largest combined U.S. military mission in the isthmus, and probably the largest in Latin America. One of the missions' chief successes was considered to be the Honduran government's refusal to even consider buying any non-U.S. military equipment, a U.S. official observed in June 1953.[25] In 1952–53, Washington sold Honduras, under the 408(e) program, $489,256 worth of weapons and equipment—enough to equip a light infantry battalion, as detailed in Appendix table A-15. A hodgepodge of German, Belgian, Czech, and Mexican equipment had made weapons training practically impossible.[26]

While that equipment was being delivered, Honduras and the United States signed the grant collaboration agreement on 20 May 1954 that committed Washington to organizing, equipping, and training the MAP infantry battalion that President Eisenhower authorized the previous December. Although Eisenhower authorized grant collaboration agreements with Honduras, Guatemala, and El Salvador as a political move to increase pressure on the Arbenz government of Guatemala, some plausible military justification in the Honduran case could be found in four distinct but closely related developments stretching back to 1952. They accelerated the negotiation of the MAP agreement with Honduras and the shipment of the equipment it called for.

The first was the U.S. government's choice of Guatemalan Col. Carlos Castillo Armas on 9 September 1952 to lead an invasion of Guatemala from Honduras to overthrow the Arbenz government. President Gálvez's collaboration was quickly secured.[27] But should the invasion fail, the Guatemalan Army could be expected to give chase, overrunning Honduran territory. Thus both Gálvez and President Osorio of El Salvador (where the risk of a counterinvasion was considerably less) "wanted US security guarantees, military aid, and promises to restrain [Nicaraguan President] Somoza," who was also collaborating with the U.S. government's anti-Arbenz operation.[28] Castillo Armas, who had been living in Honduras since escaping a Guatemalan prison in 1952, began to publicize his leadership of a CIA-created Guatemalan "liberation" movement from his Honduran quarters, announcing his "Tegucigalpa Plan" on 23 December 1953, two weeks after Eisenhower's authorization of grant collaboration. Any doubt that Honduras was cooperating with the invasion was erased when one of Castillo Armas's co-conspirators betrayed the CIA plot to President Arbenz, and Guatemalan newspapers published planning documents on 29 January 1954 that were signed by Castillo Armas and others.[29]

The second development was the general strike from late April until June 1954, centered on the north coast and sustained largely by at least twenty-five thousand employees of the U.S.-owned United Fruit Company, at the same time that the company was conspiring with the U.S. government in the overthrow of Arbenz.[30] The United States quickly sought to associate the strike with Arbenz, interpreting it as evidence of a Guatemalan-communist conspiracy against Honduras.[31] In a memorandum to President Eisenhower on the same day, Secretary of State Dulles assured the president that the Defense Department was already preparing to take action if Honduras were attacked by Guatemala or some other country.[32] The U.S. Caribbean Command in the Canal Zone was ready to drop 3,580 army airborne troops and to disembark a Marine Corps Rescue Coordination Team at La Ceiba, Tela, and Puerto Cortes to evacuate U.S. nationals and "maintain order."[33]

The strike's potential for justifying further military collaboration was multiplied by the third development: the State Department's announcement on 17 May of the arrival in Guatemala of the Swedish freighter *Alfhem*, loaded with thousands of tons of Czech weapons for the Arbenz government. Both the Honduran and the U.S. governments immediately linked the arms shipment with the strike, and Gálvez asked the United States to land Marines if necessary.[34] On 20 May the Hondurans signed the grant-collaboration agreement with the United States, and the first deliveries of equipment for the planned First Infantry Battalion started to arrive just five days later, with the all-important publicity arranged by the Embassy.[35]

The fourth event was a presidential election campaign that, because of its eerie similarity to that of 1923–24, raised the familiar specter of civil war in an already-turbulent year, as well as the remote possibility of a victory by the Liberal Party, out of power since 1932. The party, Washington believed, had not only been penetrated by communists but had even accepted funds from the Arbenz government.[36] The campaign opened on 15 May, the day that the *Alfhem* dropped anchor in Puerto Barrios and as the general strike was spreading across the country. Two rival *caudillos* associated with the National Party—the seventy-nine-year-old General Carías and his sixty-year-old ex-vice president, Abraham Williams, leader of a newly constituted National faction, the Movimiento Nacional Reformista (MNR)—and Ramón Villeda Morales, who was forty-six, the leader of the Liberal Party, announced their candidacies for the 10 October presidential elections. The Honduran constitution required a clear majority for a candidate to take office, but the improbability of such an outcome meant that the election of the president would probably be forced into the Honduran Congress, at which point the crisis was likely—given the historic intransigence of Honduran presidential candidates—to be resolved violently.

Expecting the worst, U.S. Ambassador Whiting Willauer urged on 8 June that, notwithstanding the U.S. legal prohibition on grant collaboration for internal (as opposed to hemispheric) defense, the MAP-supported unit be prepared for action before the 10 October election. He attributed the likely election disorder to "communist infiltration of the Honduran labor movement," which in turn "may require extraordinary internal security measures at any time between now and the forthcoming elections."[37] Willauer had taken up his job in February (the same month that the CIA had begun training the invasion force inside Honduras) as a member of what he later called the "team" of U.S. diplomats and CIA operatives who were organizing the overthrow of Arbenz. One of his main responsibilities, he testified years later, was "to keep the Honduran government—which was scared to death about the possibilities of themselves being overthrown—keep them [sic] in line so they would allow this revolutionary activity [the CIA's training of the Castillo Armas forces] to continue, based in Honduras."[38]

Notably absent from any of the sources—primary or secondary, Honduran or U.S.—consulted on the events of 1954 was any substantive reference to the Honduran armed forces as a significant political factor. The omission is telling. Unlike the armed forces of El Salvador, Guatemala, or Nicaragua, those of Honduras still lacked the leadership, cohesion, and even the institutional identity necessary to have acted politically. There was not even a coherent chain of command through which orders might have been issued for any kind of general mobilization; in this sense, it would be accurate to say that Honduras had no army.

This is the conclusion that the reports of U.S. authorities in Honduras at the time pointed to. The *comandante* system, they suggested, should not be confused with an army. Writing to his commander in the Canal Zone in June, U.S. Army Col. M. C. Shattuck, the head of the MAP advisory group, described the "small, separated and almost autonomous military units permanently located in what are called 'cuarteles' in almost every village and in every city," varying in size from ten to two hundred men depending on the size of the town: "There is no organization in the sense of organization into squads, platoons or companies. The arms are a heterogeneous collection of obsolete arms with an extremely small number of modern US arms. There are no transportation facilities, nor communication facilities belonging to the army. . . . The commanders of the 'cuarteles' are political appointees and in the approach of a national election their loyalties are a matter of conjecture."[39] That system, Willauer noted, "has long tradition behind it and is a potent source of political patronage, as well as political strength, and its early elimination does not seem probable."[40] No one, Colonel Shattuck wrote, even seemed to know how many troops were on duty; their total might be somewhere between four thousand and seven thousand. Without centralized record-keeping and owing to near-autonomy of local commanders, it was hard to guess how many men might be fielded in the event of an invasion by Guatemala or some other serious threat. "Without transportation, communication, messing facilities and with poor arms, the total field force would approximate 2,500 men. It would not be unjustly deprecatory to call whatever force that might be fielded an armed rabble."

In contrast, the Honduran Air Force was "organized, disciplined, integrated and well-commanded" and its officers "have a professional officer's viewpoint concerning loyalty to country rather than to political party or leader." The Gálvez government tended to trust the air force over the army, having put it in charge of storing $400,000 worth of just-bought army equipment as well as all grant-collaboration shipments "until a reliable army force is organized."[41] Urging the extension of grant collaboration to the air force (for twelve training aircraft, four B-25 light bombers, and twelve F4U-4 fighter bombers), Colonel Shattuck argued in June that the general strike, a possible Guatemalan counterattack should Castillo Armas's forces be pushed back into Honduras, and the 10 October presidential election "placed the ability of the Government to maintain internal order in a precarious balance." The Liberals might win in October, and they were not friendly to the United States. "The chances for a revolution before the October elections are possible and quite likely probable."[42] Shattuck's last point seemed to indicate a willingness to deploy the planned MAP battalion in support of continued National Party rule.

By the end of June, President Gálvez was persuaded "by current events" to let the United States transform the country's "military philosophy," according to Shattuck. "The objective is to create and to organize a reliable, strong, military force with a professional attitude of loyalty to the country," and Gálvez was letting the U.S. Army mission decide on "the size, composition and organization of the force." Shattuck and Willauer thought the United States should use the MAP grant to build a "hard striking infantry-air force team," an objective dictated by Honduras's topography and its primitive road system. The army would have to have an infantry battalion (including a company of parachutists), an infantry heavy mortar company, and an engineer company. The mountainous nature of Honduras meant a small hostile force could easily "cut the road system by demolitions," thus requiring a relatively high percentage of engineers. The infantry-airforce team should be ready by 1 October 1954—nine days before the presidential election.[43]

In the meantime, the Pentagon continued to take steps to defend Honduras against a possible Guatemalan counterattack. On 12 July the Joint Chiefs of Staff cabled the Caribbean Command in Panama to prepare "for employment of US mil [military] forces in Honduras, Nicaragua, El Salvador, Costa Rica and Guatemala as may be nec [necessary] to repel Guatemalan invasion and to enable Honduran Govt to exercise con[trol] over its territory."[44] The readiness to deploy U.S. forces in all five countries, in response to a possible conflict between just two of them, showed how strongly the Guatemalan crisis was interpreted as a regional one that could ignite the whole isthmus. The order may also have reflected the Pentagon's concern over the anarchic situation in Guatemala City, where five successive provisional governments had ruled between 27 June and 7 July.

Colonel Shattuck's proposal to have an infantry-airforce team ready just in time for the election exposed the chicanery of the "hemisphere defense" justification for grant military collaboration with Honduras. The Pentagon's resistance to inventing a hemisphere defense mission for Honduras, because of the country's transparent incapacity to implement one, was finally overcome by the State Department's insistence that grant collaboration "would be desirable for political and psychological reasons, taking into account our objectives in Guatemala." Nevertheless, Holland's reply on 16 July to the Honduran team's plea for an unbudgeted $1.5 million increase in grant transfers was not encouraging: Neither the money nor the extra planes were available, the Guatemalan invasion threat had practically disappeared, and the internal-defense character of the transfers would make an even greater mockery of the hemispheric-defense justification for grant collaboration.[45]

The State Department tried anyway to get the Pentagon to approve at least the transfer of two more C-47s because communist activity in Honduras "has recently been manifested in labor strikes and riots" and "It is of overriding political importance to the interest of the United States that such disturbances be prevented at this time." The Defense Department rejected the suggestion out of hand. It was too expensive, it might encourage Nicaragua to expand its air force and besides, the Defense Department had only reluctantly approved grant collaboration in the first place as a political maneuver to show the Arbenz government that "non-communist governments could receive grant aid" and to show Guatemalan anticommunists that Washington was behind them. Now, Arbenz was gone. Moreover, the combat readiness of the Honduran Army battalion that grant collaboration was supposed to generate was still "too low to estimate" and "practically all of the equipment (which was airlifted) is still in storage."[46]

As it turned out, the Embassy team's hope that the MAP battalion would be ready to fight nine days before the election was wildly unrealistic. On the last day of the year, the Joint Chiefs estimated that it would take another year for the battalion to be combat ready.[47] But even if the battalion had been ready for action by Election Day, there is no evidence of just what the Embassy thought the battalion might achieve should violence erupt. Because the troops would be commanded by President Gálvez, they might have been used by him to ensure his own continuity in office.

Whether Willauer wanted the battalion to be used for that purpose is open to question. However, it is certain that he wanted Gálvez remain in office, unconstitutionally if necessary. Ramón E. Cruz, a *caríísta* and the chief judge of the Supreme Court, reported in his memoirs that on 14 September Willauer tried to persuade General Carías to withdraw from the race. He told the general, according to Cruz, that a constitutional convention should then be convoked, an act that would justify Gálvez's continuance in office, thus blocking the liberals from taking power. The United States, Willauer said, did not want an Arbenz-type government to take power in Honduras. The old general rejected the idea, Cruz said, because it would amount to a *golpe de estado*. As a result of Carías's objections, Willauer withdrew his proposal and instead urged all three factions to agree on a single presidential candidate, or at least arrange for the two National Party factions to back one National candidate.[48]

Ten days after Willauer's first meeting with Carías, the ambassador told the State Department he was trying to arrange a coalition between the Liberal Party and Williams's faction, but his efforts were bootless and "Almost all Honduran and diplomatic sources continue prophecies of serious trouble" as long as the race was contested by three candidates. Confirming Cruz's account of the ambassador's sympathy for a Gálvez coup, Willauer wrote "Gálvez is still privately considering a 'golpe de estado' before or after the elections but he is personally profoundly averse to this course and will act only in the most extreme circumstances. I believe, however, that his continuance would receive great popular acceptance. Gálvez, the man, as President would be more desirable than any of the other three candidates."[49]

As expected, none of the three candidates won a majority of votes, though Villeda Morales came closest with 48 percent. After bargaining among the three groups failed to produce the coalition government favored by Washington, Willauer asked the State Department for permission to signal to Gálvez that Washington would not be displeased should he decide to stay in office, unconstitutionally, for another year or two. The State Department told Willauer to let the Hondurans work it out themselves.[50] The crisis was resolved in a way nearly identical to Willauer's preference. Gálvez left Honduras abruptly on 16 November, claiming he needed medical attention. Vice Pres. Julio Lozano Díaz took power as acting president. The deputies who were elected on the two National Party tickets boycotted the opening session of the new Congress on 5 December, thereby depriving it of a quorum and preventing it from selecting a president from among the three candidates. As a result, Lozano declared himself "Supreme Chief of State" the next day, unconstitutionally blocking the Supreme Court from choosing a president, who almost surely would have been General Carías—a solution that Willauer opposed almost as strongly as he opposed a Villeda Morales government. The United States formally extended its recognition to Lozano on 16 December. The crisis was over, to the satisfaction of Willauer and both National Party factions, for it effectively checked a takeover by the liberals, the most popular (but least predictable) political party in the country, avoiding civil war. Villeda Morales accepted the outcome cheerfully in return for Lozano's promise that he would let some liberals join his government.[51] Precisely why Gálvez resigned remains a mystery; perhaps he simply didn't have the stomach to carry out the *auto golpe* that he sensed Washington preferred, and offered to let his vice president do it.

The remarkable chain of events in 1954—a genuine threat of Guatemalan aggression (induced by the U.S. government's covert operation against Arbenz), a stunningly successful, nationwide general strike; and a potentially violent political campaign that ended in a U.S.-approved coup—must have seemed shockingly incongruent in a country without a real national army. The incongruity of the situation undoubtedly made collaboration, in U.S. eyes, a more urgent matter in Honduras than in any other Central American country. Because there was so little for Colonel Shattuck's U.S. Army Mission to work with, it had to create the MAP battalion from the ground up, building housing and sanitation facilities and importing uniforms for recruits before training could even begin. "In general," Shattuck wrote, "this country manufactures nothing and every item necessary to equip the unit . . . must be imported." The plan: to create an infantry battalion, an infantry heavy mortar company and an engineer company that, after eight weeks of training, would have "fairly good discipline, and would know enough about shooting, etc., to give a good account of themselves against any local opposition."[52]

Over the next ten months, the mortar and engineer companies were dropped from the plan.[53] The grand contradiction that had haunted grant collaboration with Honduras (as well as, to a lesser extent, Nicaragua and El Salvador) ever since it was authorized in December 1953 was beginning to overwhelm the members of the U.S. military mission: The United States was supposed to be creating an army unit capable of contributing to hemispheric defense under the Rio Treaty but the Honduran state wasn't even able to control its own territory because what passed for an army was practically useless even for that purpose. Why train a Honduran battalion to defend the hemisphere from outside attack, when there wasn't so much as a credible police force? In an extraordinary letter (written with the approval of the ambassador, the U.S. Army attaché and the head of the Air Force Mission) to the U.S. Secretary of Defense, Maj. Gordon A. Schraeder, the acting head of the U.S. Army mission, insisted that an exclusively hemispheric defense mission for the Honduran MAP battalion was "completely unrealistic" for a country that lacked the forces needed to "contravene or control a determined communist-inspired mass action to install a government unfriendly to the United States." The State Department's insistence that the MAP battalion be forbidden to act against internal threats to Honduran security and yet trained to defend the Panama Canal contradicted U.S. interests, the major argued. The politically fragile Lozano government was facing threats that emanated not from outside Honduras but from "the use of arms by irregular groups within Honduras. . . . There is evidence that a potentially strong communist underground is being formed in Honduras. . . . The strike in 1954 was at least partially communist-inspired and led. The military weakness of the previous Nationalist government [was] glaringly exposed when mass labor groups took over de facto civil power of five communities for a period of seven to nine weeks." But militarily, the government was "extremely weak" and resented Washington's rule against using the battalion for internal defense. "Military command structure is nonexistent, and the forces in being are small, not tactically organized, poorly equipped, and even more poorly trained. These weaknesses, political, economic and military, make it problematical whether the government can continue in power." Major Schraeder thought the government could obtain "an efficient internal security force" with three battalion-sized units and one fighter-bomber squadron with twenty-five aircraft. The air force was crippled by obsolete equipment and the lack of spare parts. He recommended that the primary mission of the MAP unit be changed to internal security, and that it become the "nucleus for reorganization of Honduran security forces."[54]

The record of the final disposition—if there was one—of Major Schraeder's plea for an internal-security orientation of U.S. grant collaboration could not be found, but it is probable that the assistant secretary of the army's curt response was definitive: "MDAP aid is for mutual hemispheric security. Honduras should provide their own internal security forces."[55]

U.S. reluctance to change its rules on the purpose of grant collaboration prob-ably fomented more purchases through the 408(e) program. On 16 June 1955, the day after the assistant secretary of the army issued his dictum, the U.S. Embassy strongly recommended a sweeping restructuring of the Honduran Air Force via purchases. Its only planes were those it bought in the United States in 1946–48, and the scarcity of spare parts made it "virtually impossible" to keep them in the air. The Pentagon should sell Honduras twenty training aircraft over the next two years, plus ten tactical aircraft, the Embassy recommended. Besides the straightforward mili-tary reasons for the sale, there was a political one. It would raise the morale of the air force and thus discourage it from intervening in politics. Thus, "the most liberal possible terms" of sale should be offered, because of the poverty of the Honduran government, and the sale should be made quickly, before the election season, when the air force might be tempted to become active politically.[56] By December, State had approved the sale of thirty "excess" but "rehabilitated" planes (twenty tactical aircraft and just ten trainers) plus related equipment and spare parts for $1.3 mil-lion. The sale would more than double the fighting capacity of the Honduran Air Force, which claimed just nine, scarcely operable fighters. On 2 December, Willauer urged haste. "It is felt that the Air Force continues to be apolitical and a great source of stability in the country. If the Air Force appears to be well equipped the chances for peace in the forthcoming elections now likely to be held in April will be notably increased." Thus, the political motivation for the sale had changed since June. No longer was the sale intended to deter the air force from intervening in politics—the air force was now touted as essentially apolitical—*but to empower it sufficiently to deter civil war.*[57] Equipment problems aside, the "overall effectiveness of the Air Force is excellent at the present time," a year-end evaluator reported. "It is well-qual-ified for close support of the ground forces, interdiction work, and attacks of a strategic nature."[58]

In contrast, the army remained almost hopelessly backward in the eyes of U.S. authorities. Still organized in urban garrisons of 40 men or less (except for the San Francisco *cuartel* in Tegucigalpa of 150 men and the San Pedro Sula *cuartel* of 250), the country's 1,180 soldiers "generally are not trained on a unit basis, but are used and have value only as a municipal police force," without a staff or even much of an organization. Without a command structure, training would be pointless.[59]

The great collaborative success of 1955 was the long-awaited organization of the grant-funded "hemispheric-defense" battalion. On the last day of the year it was about one-third under strength (400 troops instead of the 596 for whom weapons were furnished) but basic training was "virtually complete," whereas full training awaited the completion of training facilities under construction. The unit was still quartered in "tents and improvised shelters under virtual field conditions." About nine-tenths of the battalion's efforts were spent building the housing and training facilities, which were expected to be finished by July 1956. Morale was much higher than in the rest of the Honduran Army. "Men are proud of being a member of this unit because of its training and equipment, and to a lesser degree, its pay. A some-what higher pay schedule has been adopted for this unit. The number of aspirants for the unit far exceeds housekeeping space and money available." Even at two-thirds its authorized strength, the MAP battalion was 1.6 times bigger than the regular army's largest unit, the San Pedro Sula garrison.[60]

By the end of 1955, therefore, Honduran-U.S. military collaboration had, in less than a decade, yielded a sizeable transformation in the Honduran state's capacity to deploy public violence. The air force was now well trained and capable, if lacking in dependable equipment. The MAP battalion—organized, advised, trained, and equipped at U.S. government expense—exceeded the strength of any other armed force in the country. Pleased with the results, the Embassy claimed that the grant collaboration effort encouraged the Honduran military to look toward the United States and promoted "professional pride" among the military, which might in turn discourage it from meddling in politics. The MAP battalion, as "an elite professional unit, could become an important stabilizing factor in Honduras's internal security" and might eventually encourage the government to abolish the "wasteful *comman-dante* [i.e., *cuartel*] system."[61]

The Embassy's desire for a rapid improvement in Honduras's military capacity was no doubt inspired by a surge of popular opposition to Lozano's unelected and increasingly dictatorial government. Both the Liberal and the National parties were calling for his resignation. On 9 July, the government arrested and exiled three eminent liberals, including Villeda Morales. Discontent peaked on 1 August, when groups associated with the Liberal Party and striking university students, along with some military officers, seized the San Francisco garrison in Tegucigalpa, hoping to spark a national revolt. The uprising was put down by the MAP battalion, in violation of its exclusively "hemispheric defense" mission, in what was evidently its first taste of blood. The death toll was about twenty-six.[62] The Lozano government reacted by placing a large order for weapons and other equipment, insisting on delivery before the 7 October election of a constitutional convention. U.S. Army Col. Corston A. Greene, the head of the Army Mission, strongly recommended approval of the purchase order, insisting that the Honduran Army and Air Force were utterly apolitical. The State Department approved the purchase on the Embassy's recommendation and promised to expedite it, though it had some misgivings about "possible misuse" of the arms, which included 1,000 M1 rifles, 150 pistols (.45-cal.), 225 M1 carbines, 45 mortars, 40 rifle grenade launchers, 15 machine guns, 5 armored cars, and 2.5 million rounds of ammunition.[63]

Convinced that the Lozano government would fix the elections, both the National Party and the Liberal Party withdrew their candidates during the first week of October. Lozano's Partido Unidad Nacional won with 89 percent of the vote, sweeping all fifty-six delegate seats in the constitutional convention. At least eleven people died in armed confrontations on election day.[64] The hour had arrived for the Honduran armed forces to act, for the first time ever, as an independent agent of the state, against a Honduran government, twelve years after the armed forces of Guatemala and El Salvador had undertaken similar rebellions in 1944. On 21 October, the two key U.S.-supported units, the First Infantry (MAP) Battalion and the air force, led the country's first real military coup.[65] Its leaders removed the widely detested Lozano and replaced him with three military men: Gen. Roque J. Rodríguez, the director of the Escuela Militar; Maj. Roberto Gálvez Barnes, son of the former president; and the air force commander, Col. Héctor Caracciolo Moncada. Not a shot was fired, and the military's popularity soared in gratitude for its intervention against an unconstitutional government. The *junta* freed all of Lozano's political prisoners and abolished the death penalty, earning warm praise from Villeda Morales when he returned from exile on 10 November.[66]

The coup of 21 October was remarkable not only because it signified the birth of an autonomous military force while removing an unpopular and unelected government, but also because it delivered the country's first peaceful and honest national elections. The *junta* announced that a constitutional convention would be elected on 22 September 1957, and in July 1957 made what the Embassy recognized as the government's customary preelection request for a major arms purchase. In August, State approved the $540,720 deal for thirty-two hundred M1 rifles with bayonets, eight hundred M1 carbines with bayonets, two hundred .30-cal. Browning automatic rifles, plus ammunition, parts, and radios—all to be delivered before the new government was scheduled to take office in December.[67] The day before the elections the military high command issued a manifesto proclaiming its new-found destiny as the guardian of Honduran institutions, as defined by the high command itself:

> The Armed Forces cannot go on being a passing phenomenon in the institutional life of the country. In developing their activity, they show themselves to be something inherent to the freedom, order, decorum and happiness of the Patria. In that sense, to suppose that the country could do without their tutelary vigilance, would be like thinking that the State could continue to subsist without the presence of the people.... Now and forever, they [the armed forces] assume the irrevocable, historic and well-deserved function of permanent guardian of the fatherland's institutions.[68]

The Liberal Party crushed the two factions of the National Party, gaining 62 percent of the votes and the freedom to write a new constitution. It was the first clear victory for the Liberals since 1932. The nascent armed forces' decision to stay neutral and let the Liberals win a fair election—despite the fact that most officers were National Party sympathizers—may have been the armed forces' first and last act of civic virtue. Little of that virtue was evident in the Liberal-dominated Assembly, which met from 21 October to 19 December. On 15 November, the Assembly voted 37–21 to make Villeda Morales the new president for a six-year term, effective 21 December, in what could only be called a nonviolent coup, justified by the Liberals on the grounds that Villeda had already proven his popularity in the presidential election of 1954, and in the constitutional convention election in September. Twelve days later, on 27 November, the convention passed an extraordinary constitutional provision that delivered to the armed forces a measure of autonomy from the government that is probably unique in the history of Latin America.

These two decisions have been interpreted ever since as a simple exchange between the Liberal Party and the *junta*, in which the latter agreed not to stand in the way of the convention's acclamation of Villeda Morales as president, in return for the military's permanent and categorical freedom to act independently of Villeda Morales or any of his constitutional successors. A secret U.S. Embassy dispatch two years later indicated as much: "In order to ensure the transfer of the Government to itself in December 1957 the Liberal Party leadership conceded unusual Constitutional powers to the Armed Forces."[69] Although no written evidence of a deal—known as the "Pacto de Agua Azul"—has emerged, it seems unlikely that the convention would have liberated the armed forces from presidential control without an incentive to do so.[70] In a letter to Pres. Villeda Morales on 8 December 1958, the armed forces high command referred in passing to the fact that on 14 November 1957 it accepted the convention's decision to elect him president, "signing to that effect" along with the leadership of the convention, the Liberal Party, and Villeda himself.[71] Gautama Fonseca, the independent-minded liberal and lawyer, reported years later that a pact was signed by at least five military officers and several Liberal Party leaders in the home of Col. Oswaldo López Arellano, the *junta*'s defense minister.[72]

What is not open to dispute is the convention's responsibility for having created a system of state power in which the armed forces existed, not as an autonomous force parallel to the government but superior to it. The constitution of 1957 defined the armed forces as "essentially professional, apolitical, obedient and non-deliberative"; created the new rank of armed forces "jefe," whose holder was effectively independent of the president; gave control over the Defense Department budget to the armed forces rather than to the president; bestowed on the *jefe* the right to challenge, and by implication to disobey, the orders of the president; and even prohibited the president from appointing the *jefe* by giving Congress the power to choose among three candidates proposed by the armed forces itself. From the point of view of anyone hoping for stable, civilian government, the Liberal Party produced what may have been one of the world's worst constitutions. Its guarantee of military autonomy continued for forty-two years as it was reproduced without substantial alterations in the constitutions of 1965 and 1982 until it was abolished by the Honduran legislature on 25 January 1999.[73]

The United States did not necessarily welcome the emergence of a military force capable of controlling the country's politics. The coup of 21 October 1956, Ambassador Willauer acknowledged, was a "fine action." But it "has built up the ego of the armed forces and the problem from here out will be whether a monster has been created or whether the armed forces can proceed in an orderly fashion as an integrated part of the government, without trying to play too big a role." The Embassy's proposal for discouraging the army from becoming too important politically was, characteristically, to expand its responsibilities even more. The United States, Willauer proposed, should collaborate in the formation of engineering construction battalions [ECBs] that would keep the military busy with nonpolitical activities. "The Embassy fears greatly that in the present climate, if the military remains simply an infantry outfit devoted to training itself, undesirable consequences may arise." At the same time, the new government should be encouraged to act quickly to strengthen internal security. Villeda Morales was already "thoroughly persuaded as to the necessity of a frontal attack on the problem of Communism in their labor movement and elsewhere," and the best way for Washington to ensure action on that front would be to help finance it. Washington, in short, should do all in its power to welcome the passage toward "constitutional democratic government" by intensifying both economic and military collaboration.[74] Having gained the approval of State and Defense for the creation of the engineering battalion, Willauer proposed it on inauguration day to Villeda Morales, who quickly accepted the offer and announced it publicly.[75]

Evidently, the United States sought to link military and economic collaboration in a way that would simultaneously boost internal security and stimulate economic growth. The centerpiece of this strategy was the "Guayape River Valley Area Development Project" in the department of Olancho, an ambitious plan devised ten days after Lozano's overthrow by the Tegucigalpa office of the U.S. Operations Mission without consulting a single Honduran. The project would expand the livestock industry in the eighteen hundred square-mile valley, which also happened to be, according to the proposal, "lawless, open and full of cattle rustlers, *contrabanderes* [*sic*] and simple gunmen." The plan therefore provided for "the establishment of a strong military base with forces capable of patrolling the area [which] would alleviate the question of security of investment and of productive effort." The base would be the headquarters of a U.S.-funded ECB that would build roads and bridges while patrolling the area. Valley development would begin with livestock and continue with the construction of a meat packing plant, and eventually lead to timber and pulp processing for export. Hydroelectric energy could be produced by damming the Patuca River and exploiting the country's known coal deposits. The proposal estimated the cost to the United States of equipping and training the ECB at $3 million.[76] On 31 May 1957 the *junta* signed a loan agreement with the United States for $1.75 million for highway construction in the Guayape Valley, and another $1.25 million for municipal sewer and water construction in thirty-two communities around the country.[77] By August 1958, what a U.S. Embassy official called the "opening up" of the Guayape Valley was underway; construction equipment for the engineering battalion was being bought in November.[78]

By drawing the armed forces into economic development, the plan promised to "build up the ego" even more of military officers already intoxicated with the authority that constitutional autonomy had bestowed. Next came the centralization of the command structure that the United States had been advocating for so long. The new constitution mandated the division of the country into six military zones, each one commanded by a superior officer appointed by the armed forces chief, eliminating the garrison system along with the *comandantes de armas* and *mayores de plaza*. The measure was implemented in May 1958.[79]

As military and economic collaboration projects proceeded under the new Liberal administration, however, there was no evidence of the march toward stable, civilian government that collaboration was supposed to encourage. In a letter delivered to President Villeda on 8 December 1958, the armed forces' high command, the

Consejo Superior de la Defensa, criticized his government for fomenting public contempt for the armed forces, with the aim of destroying them. The letter accused the Liberal Party of arming its own "shock troops," inflaming tensions between the military and the party to such a degree that war between the two was widely considered imminent. The Consejo demanded that Villeda include National Party figures in his government, stop the anti-armed forces campaign, and join the military in an "active and systematic campaign tending toward the eradication of communism in our country."[80]

The letter coincided with a sharp decline in the political authority of the Villeda government, which a State Department official blamed on fiscal mismanagement and the ability of the armed forces to spend revenue with little or no accountability to the government. Worse yet, "there have been many indications of insurrectionary plotting. Our Embassy has been approached several times on behalf of some fairly influential citizens of Honduras in an effort to enlist U.S. support for a military coup. The Embassy has of course discouraged all activities of this sort. Still the plotting continues unabated. Some of the military seem to be involved." There were rumors that Colonel López Arellano, the armed forces chief, would sound out the U.S. attitude toward a coup when he met with State Department officials on 2 December. The Embassy strongly recommended that State tell the colonel that any forceful action against Villeda's government would be regarded as "most unfortunate for Honduras."[81]

Had López Arellano indeed been planning a coup, there is little doubt that the disposition of the MAP battalion and the air force would be decisive. The battalion's strength was now up to 650 "fairly well trained, equipped and housed" men, and still the "only effective unit of the Honduran Army," according to the U.S. Defense Department. By February 1959, the United States had supplied the battalion with $465,000 worth of weapons and other equipment and had spent $96,000 on training. For the coming fiscal year (1960), Washington planned to spend, on the MAP battalion alone, $200,000 for additional training and $115,000 on twenty-one vehicles, as well as machine guns, rifles, and ammunition.[82] Beyond the First Infantry Battalion, "Almost all the officers and men in important positions in the Honduran Army have attended U.S. Army schools" in the United States or the Canal Zone. "To have graduated from a U.S. Army service school is a mark of prestige among the Hondurans, and most graduates wear the school crest on their uniforms to indicate their attendance."[83] In September, the engineering battalion (whose status had been downgraded to a mere "unit") was building its first road in Olancho, outfitted with $309,400 worth of U.S. gift equipment.[84] An air force request for the guns, gun sights, ammunition chutes, and other weapons needed to fully equip ten of its newly purchased fighter planes for combat had received State Department approval.[85]

But outside the air force and the First Infantry Battalion, the Honduran armed forces by the summer of 1959 could scarcely be said to have advanced much beyond the "armed rabble" that Colonel Shattuck had found in 1954. Most of its three thousand men could be found "in small detachments of from ten to fifty men, located in the various villages throughout the country. These troops are usually untrained and spend the majority of their time sitting in the waiting room outside the 'coman-dantes' office. These people are not soldiers, and would be relatively ineffective in combat as they now exist." With no logistical support system, "each unit operates on its own." On the other hand, the MAP battalion commander, "as the commander of the largest and best equipped army unit in Honduras, answers directly to the Chief of the Armed Forces; he has no other command lines to hinder him. . . . The only army unit in Honduras which is adequately equipped, has proper living and train-ing facilities, and even makes a pretense at training is the MAP battalion."[86]

As relations between the armed forces and the Villeda government deterio-rated, the country seemed to be collapsing, again, into civil war. The two trends were undoubtedly linked. In February 1959, some army officers and civilian *montoneras* collaborated in a revolt that briefly captured the garrison in Santa Bárbara. Attacks on military outposts by armed civilians and "bandits" continued to be reported in northwestern Honduras through May. The series of uprisings were attributed to Lt. Col. Armando Velásquez, who was said to be operating from Nicaragua and later Guatemala. President Villeda thought the rebels were members of the two National Party factions, or else just "misguided adventurers."[87] The old, banana-republic pol-itics of *caudillo*-led revolts and party militias seemed to have returned to Honduras, and the "new" armed forces were emerging as one more contender. Zone command-ers who had replaced the old *comandantes de armas* were accused of using their authority to harass and intimidate Liberal Party members. Francisco Milla Bermúdez, the liberal president of the Supreme Court, infuriated the armed forces and embarrassed Villeda Morales when he supposedly told the *Miami Herald* that Honduras's problems could be solved by abolishing the armed forces.[88]

On the night of 11 July, Lieutenant Colonel Velásquez nearly succeeded in over-throwing the government. With the cooperation of some army officers and civilian groups, as well as the leadership of the Policía Nacional, he and his men took over the city of Comayagua, and in Tegucigalpa, the Policía headquarters and other strategic sites. The armed forces leadership succeeded in dislodging the rebels and restoring government control, but took four days to do so, and its initial hesitation only widened the gap between the government and the military.[89] Armed civilian groups were evidently joining the fighting on both sides. A Liberal Party militia was reported to have assisted the army in putting down the rebellion.[90]

The government responded to the treachery of the Policía Nacional by replac-ing it, eight days after the aborted uprising, with a new police agency, the Guardia Civil, controlled not by the armed forces but by the Interior ministry. Its recruits were widely understood to be drawn from the Liberal Party. The armed forces vehe-mently opposed the Guardia, both for its liberal affiliation and its freedom from military control.[91] To National Party opponents of the government, the Guardia was nothing more than an attempt to institutionalize the Liberal Party militia, known among its enemies as the Ejército Negro, the name subsequently applied to the Guardia.[92]

Relations between the armed forces and the Villeda Morales government wors-ened in October. The commander of the First Battalion ordered the execution of two civilians accused of killing a battalion lieutenant in a bar brawl, and a battle between elements of the Guardia and the Second Battalion left one dead and several wounded. The Embassy blamed the Liberals for handing over too much power to the armed forces but also for scaring the National Party with a partisan Guardia. And, of course, the communists were exploiting the situation.[93]

Because of the tension between the armed forces and the government, Washington was reluctant to accede to Villeda's requests for weapons, including two thousand carbines, and trainers for the Guardia. As a police force, the Guardia should carry pistols, not carbines, U.S. Ambassador Robert Newbegin told the president and his interior minister in a meeting on 10 February 1960. The Hondurans replied that carbines were a more potent "symbol of authority" than pistols. Newbegin told them that he, like the armed forces, was worried that an untrained heavily armed Guardia might "combine" with armed civilian groups. Pressing the point, Newbegin pointed out that some in the Liberal Party even favored abolishing the army. The conversation ended when the president agreed to Newbegin's suggestion that the ICA's police expert, Harold Hardin, be asked for recommendations on police training.[94]

In less than two weeks, Hardin submitted his evaluation. The Guardia Civil; the Seguridad Pública, a plainclothes investigative agency that was also under the interior ministry; and the Guarnición del Presidio or prison guards were "badly in need of technical advice, training and selected items of civil police equipment." The Guardia had about 1,200 members, with about 425 in Tegucigalpa and 100 in San Pedro Sula. Although the Tegucigalpa detachment has revolvers, "those outside the Capital are armed with a nondescript assortment of army rifles dating from Civil War [i.e., U.S.] to 1917. These are extremely dangerous and their only value is for junk." The Guardia planned to expand to 2,032 men. But its desire to buy 2,183 carbines and 75 machine guns revealed a law enforcement strategy that was

> over-simplified with excessive emphasis being placed on the importance of firearms. I see the greatest need for the Guardia Civil to be the adoption of sound organizational patterns and administrative procedures, an intensive civil police training program, and acquisition of selected items of civil police equipment.... Under no circumstances do I recommend the acquisition by the [Honduran government] of fully automatic firearms, and I believe that the number of carbines requested is far in excess of actual need. As I have pointed out in discussions, fully automatic weapons are far too powerful and dangerous. The desire of the police to possess them probably results from a lack of proficiency in marksmanship.

Hardin went on to explain why shoulder weapons were inappropriate for police work. They were cumbersome, tied up the hands, increased the risk of having the weapon snatched, the range was excessive for urban police use, and the risks of ricochet were higher. Although carbines were fine for rural areas, in urban settings the .38 revolver was the best choice. Recommending a three-man ICA training team for a period of two years, Hardin proposed that the Guardia be supplied with five hundred .30-cal. carbines; one thousand .38-cal. revolvers with five-inch barrels; seventy-five .38s with three-inch barrels; one thousand tear gas grenades; and nonlethal equipment such as riot sticks and radios.[95]

A second evaluation in March by David L. Laughlin, the head of the U.S. police mission in Guatemala, was more critical of the Guardia. Its nonlethal equipment consisted of one inoperable radio base transmitter; three patrol cars with inoperable radios and twenty jeeps it had received from the United States immediately after it was formed. Guardia officers did not use report forms but entered all activity narrative style, chronologically, on daily logs, making it impossible to analyze criminal activity or find information on specific cases. "A number of things indicate the 'backward' condition of the Guardia. Loaded revolvers, unattended, were observed laying [sic] on tables and on beds. On one occasion, nine prisoners were seen in the Headquarters contained in an area about ten by ten by a single strand of rope around four stakes. Headquarters and cantones [precinct stations] are full of policemen loafing and lying around, since they are on duty, active duty or standby duty in the stations, all the time except for an annual vacation period."

Seguridad Pública, the report continued, had seventy-five employees, of whom fifty were doing police work. They were trained for two to three hours a day by two Guatemalans in a "classroom" barren of furniture or equipment, so that students had to sit on the floor or stand. Its equipment consisted of one inoperable base transmitter and four vehicles, of which two were inoperable and of which none had radios. There was no laboratory. "At one time, nineteen prisoners, girls whose ages ranged from twelve to eighteen, were observed on the roof of the building of the Seguridad Pública as there was no other place to detain them."

There was one bright spot: An Identification Department where fingerprint files "are modern" and maintained "in good metal cabinets." But there was no equipment for lifting latent prints from crime scenes. Laughlin agreed with Hardin that revolvers were better than carbines. But Honduran officials "are completely convinced that firearms (the larger the better) are the answer."[96]

The Honduran government had submitted a formal request on 26 February to the Embassy for the three-man police mission and approval to buy the equipment, but insisted it only needed two hundred revolvers, and wanted to wait for the recommendation of the police mission on whether carbines or revolvers were best.[97] Both the State Department and the Defense Department approved the program.[98] The only firearms delivered to the Guardia and Seguridad Pública before the armed forces overthrew the Villeda government (and abolished the Guardia) on 3 October 1963 were 986 revolvers.[99]

Even as it was trying to restrain the Villeda government's desire for police carbines, the Embassy and the Defense Department's Caribbean Command were recommending a $900,000 increase in grant collaboration with the Honduran military. Both the army and the air force were low on ammunition and weapons, the national defense budget had been cut, and as a result, the army's morale was low, thus threatening the stability of the Honduran government. The Embassy and the Caribbean Command recommended 175,000 rounds of ammunition for the air force ($32,000). The army should get three thousand M1 rifles and one thousand carbines ($213,000), four hundred thousand rounds of ammunition ($29,000), six M-41 tanks ($359,000), and four 105-mm howitzers ($269,000).[100] The State Department bluntly rejected the idea. Not only would it illegally augment the army's internal-security capacity as opposed to hemispheric defense (a decision that would require a special presidential determination), but the 650-man First Infantry Battalion "obviously could not absorb 3,000 rifles and 1,000 carbines."[101]

Evidently, in the continuing rivalry between the Honduran Army and the Guardia, U.S. officials inside Honduras leaned toward the army, no doubt out of concern about the open partisanship of the Guard. Moreover, the international situation had become distinctly unfavorable for a Liberal Party administration that was so dependent on U.S. government support. Liberals were suspected of joining and collaborating with Honduran-based, anti-Somoza guerrilla groups associated with the leftist governments of Fidel Castro in Cuba and Rómulo Betancourt in Venezuela.[102] Villeda in turn accused the Nicaraguan government of Luis Anastasio Somoza, and the dictator of the Dominican Republic, Gen. Rafael Leonidas Trujillo, of fostering the adventures of Velásquez and his National Party collaborators.[103] Villeda's charges were confirmed seven years later.[104]

The U.S. priority was to prevent Cuban-supported insurgencies, and in Honduras the only reliable instrument available was the armed forces. After President Somoza reported to the U.S. Embassy in Managua that a forty-five-man "invasion" force had entered Nicaragua from Honduras on 2 January 1960, Newbegin was told to remind President Villeda of his duty to prevent further invasions. Villeda replied that he had sent fifty troops to the Nicaraguan border area. "I expressed some surprise," Newbegin reported, "at the small size of the group but President Villeda said he was certain that this was sufficient." Villeda, eager to please the ambassador (whose report exuded skepticism about the president's reliability) told him that "in line with his policy of getting rid of undesirable characters, he had given orders for the apprehension and deportation of Alejandro Bermúdez, a Nicaraguan communist, husband of a well-known Chilean communist." Newbegin seized the opportunity to report that Nestor Alvarado Puerto, the Honduran head of immigration, was the president of a group called Amigos de Cuba, but Villeda assured him that Alvarado had quit the organization.[105] The Cuban menace continued to supply the Nicaraguan government with opportunities to bedevil Villeda while drawing closer to the United States. In October, the Nicaraguan ambassador to Honduras informed the U.S. Embassy that not only had forty-eight more Cuban guerrillas just entered Honduras, but that in the last two weeks, "more than 100 Chinese with Cuban identification cards have landed on the north coast of Honduras, mostly from small craft and have moved inland."[106] Apparently, no story about a Cuban threat was considered too preposterous for Uncle Sam's ears.

The pact of 1957 was the latest manifestation of the ever-intimate relationship between violence and elections. In 1957, just as it had ever since the 1930s, the Liberal Party could not count on winning a national election because it was still outgunned.[107] To take power, therefore, it had to buy off its traditional enemy, the

National Party, whose leadership—Carías, Gálvez, Lozano—had just managed to convert what was, in effect, its party militia into the armed forces of Honduras. The armed forces' strong identity with the National Party would persist through the 1980s. In just three years, from 1954 to 1957, the Honduran armed forces had been transformed from a rabble that barely qualified as a party militia to the only political institution that counted, thanks to the U.S. government's lavish support of the air force and the First Infantry Battalion.[108]

A historic opportunity had been missed. Honduras, perhaps with the right kind of encouragement from the United States, might have seized upon the miserable condition of its armed forces after World War II as an opportunity to bypass— much as Costa Rica had done—the militarism to which Guatelama, El Salvador, and Nicaragua were succumbing. Instead, by deciding that Honduras should catch up to the military capacity of its neighbors, the Honduran and U.S. governments moved decisively toward the entrenchment of military rule. Once Honduras had begun to replace its "armed rabble" of garrisoned *montoneras* with a real army and air force, the political trajectory of its chronically improvisational state was fixed. The most telling event in this process was the Liberal Party leadership's eager embrace, in October–December 1957, of permanent military autonomy, in return for nothing more substantial than the *junta's* temporary permission for Villeda Morales to become president. Like the scores of governments that had gone before them, the Liberal Party took its turn at reorganizing the improvisational state by making the necessary pact with the fighting forces whose consent they needed in order to stabilize their rule. When the armed forces tried to control the government, Villeda Morales's acted the old fashioned way, by attempting to balance the army and the air force with a party militia disguised as a police force. A move like that would have been practically inconceivable in Guatemala, El Salvador, or Nicaragua, where the military would never have tolerated the existence of a fighting force that it did not control.

Failing to attract the collaboration of the United States in the development of the Guardia, the government of Villeda Morales would be unable to match the power of the armed forces, now the only fighting force that counted. Among the armies without nations, that of Honduras occupies a place of honor. The Salvadoran military regime's vanity, tinged perhaps with a stroke or two of the nationalism that had characterized its attitude toward the United States since at least the 1920s, kept it from wishing to collaborate too intimately with the United States until the late 1950s. Nicaragua's National Guard had already been organized by the U.S. Marine Corps in 1927. In both countries, U.S. military collaboration in the 1950s merely strengthened the armed forces. In Honduras, collaboration helped make them.[109]

13

Nicaragua

"Ready to Receive Orders from Uncle Sam"

We are here, I personally and the army of Nicaragua, ready to receive orders from Uncle Sam. We are together now and will be forever.
—Pres. Anastasio Somoza García, in a speech at a U.S.-Nicaraguan military staff meeting, Managua, 28 May 1945

Ever on the lookout to strengthen his Guardia, President Somoza responded with his usual ebullience to Washington's proposal, in May 1940, to all the Latin American governments for secret military collaboration negotiations to coordinate the defense of the hemisphere. He offered to recruit an army of forty thousand Nicaraguans, who would of course require far more weapons than his government actually possessed. "He suggested," the U.S. minister in Nicaragua reported without comment, "that it might be advisable to construct a small arsenal on the Gulf of Fonseca to store enough arms for his proposed army. He was quick to add that naturally such an arsenal would be under the protection of American troops," and that it could also be used to store arms for the other Central American governments.[1] Nicaragua became the first isthmian country to sign a Lend-Lease agreement on 16 October 1941, under which the United States obligated itself to transfer "armaments and munitions of war" worth about $1.3 million.[2] Managua had the only Central American airfield outside of Guatemala that was substantially improved at U.S. government expense and made available to U.S. military forces for defense of the hemisphere.[3]

Nicaragua was the only isthmian country in which U.S. wartime collaboration extended significantly beyond military matters. During Somoza's visit to Washington in 1939, President Roosevelt had agreed to send U.S. Army engineers to Nicaragua to study the possibility of "canalizing" the San Juan River sufficiently to allow barge traffic between the Caribbean Sea and Lake Nicaragua. When the engi-

neering team concluded that the project was "economically impracticable" the following year, Roosevelt decided to shelve the idea. Still feeling obligated to help
Somoza improve the country's communications with its isolated Atlantic coast,
Washington agreed to construct, at U.S. expense, a paved, 150-mile road from San
Benito, about twenty-two miles north of Managua, to the Escondido River port
town of Rama, which could receive barge traffic from the Atlantic port of El Bluff—
in effect opening the capital to the Atlantic coast. Like the U.S. government plan to
develop Honduras's Guayape Valley in the 1950s, the Rama Road project illustrates
the porosity of the boundary between military collaboration and economic collaboration. To the U.S. War Department, the construction of the Rama Road was a
desirable military objective, increasing stability and providing a tactical advantage
to the United States, "should it become necessary for United States troops to intervene, either because of attempted uprising by the enemy nationals [sic] along the
western coast, or because of an attempted hostile raid." This view must have been
wholly agreeable to President Somoza, whose control of Nicaragua depended significantly on his ability to mobilize the Guard against potential internal enemies. The
construction of a paved highway through a frontier region in which Augusto
Sandino's men had operated—the "enemy nationals" that the War Department
probably had in mind—must have been exceptionally welcome. The moment
Nicaragua declared war on the Axis on 11 December 1941, Somoza imposed martial
law and repressed the political opposition and a year later both countries signed an
agreement under which the United States would build the road.[4]

As the war in Europe was ending in 1945, Nicaragua also became the first of the
isthmian countries selected for bilateral talks about the future of military collaboration. U.S. military authorities made their objectives clear in conversations with U.S.
diplomatic personnel in Managua: "to determine what Nicaragua had in the way of
armaments, what it wanted, and then, taking into consideration the country's
budget, what it should have." Beyond that, the War Department sought "to modernize the Nicaraguan Guard with respect to training and weapons so that it might be
easily integrated into the American Army in case of need," while trying "at all costs"
to keep Nicaragua from signing military mission agreements with nonhemispheric
countries.[5]

The tension already evident in Washington between the State and the War
departments over the propriety of arming dictators—with State seeking to restrain
the U.S. armed forces' desire to strengthen the Latin American forces—came out
clearly in Managua. Reporting in February on his discussions with the U.S. military
officers who would be conducting the bilateral staff conversations with Somoza,
Harold D. Finley, the U.S. chargé d'affaires in Managua, said his plea that the U.S.
military not "burden the country with armaments" seemed not to have been taken
seriously. The U.S. officers "gave me no indication that they were really concerned
with any other consideration than that of developing a modern army in Nicaragua
and the extent to which the Nicaraguan budget would stand such an organization."[6]

In preparation for the meetings, U.S. Army Col. LeRoy Bartlett, Jr.—who as
General Bartlett of the Guardia Nacional was also the director of the Academia Mil-

itar de Nicaragua—recommended the expansion and reorganization of the Guardia
in a report to President Somoza. After making the standard argument in favor of
adopting the U.S. Army's system of organization, equipment, tactics, and training in
preparation for combined operations in defense of the hemisphere, Bartlett proposed a reorientation of the Guardia's mission toward internal surveillance and
control. He made no mention of Somoza's use of the Guard to silence his political
enemies, a "mission" protected by the declaration of martial law (which remained in
force until November 1945) and by a 1941 statute, "Ley de defensa de la democracia,"
aimed at controlling subversives. In line with the blended character of the Guard as
both a military and police force, Bartlett suggested the creation of two principal
forces within the Guard, a mobile "Battalion Combat Team" of 55 officers and 1,299
men that would be poised for immediate action; and a reduced-force infantry regiment of 103 officers and 1,858 men stationed throughout the country in units called
Tropas Departamentales. A separate presidential guard of 73 officers and 809 men
would also be established. Bartlett recommended a 14 percent increase in overall
Guardia troop strength (from 3,677 to 4,197) but failed to offer a rationale either for
the overall increase, or for his proposed redistribution, which would have added 34
percent to the troop strength in and around Managua and 47 percent to the Granada
area, while decreasing Estelí by 25 percent. The plan would entail "a great increase"
in military spending, while putting all training under the control of the U.S. Military
Mission.[7]

Three days after Bartlett submitted his report, Somoza addressed the bilateral
military staff meeting in Managua, assuring the United States not only of his personal loyalty but that of the Guard and, by implication, all Nicaraguans:

> I want to repeat once more what I have stated many times, that we have to, we need to,
> and we must be friendly to the United States; that we must be heart and soul with the
> United States. . . . Nicaragua will never be a problem to the United States, but will always
> be ready to do its best to show its good will and sincerity. We are here, I personally and
> the Army of Nicaragua, ready to receive orders from Uncle Sam. We are together now
> and will be forever.[8]

Eager to demonstrate his devotion, Somoza further noted that Lake Nicaragua was
the fourth largest in the world and declared that Nicaragua would be glad to offer it
to the U.S. Navy for fresh-water repair and reconditioning facilities. The country's
air base as well as any additional land that might be needed were put at the disposal
of the U.S. military.[9]

Somoza's servility, which was expressed not during a military emergency but
after whatever Axis threat to Nicaraguan security had vanished, may well have been
inspired by his desire to gain Washington's approval for his candidacy in the presidential election of 1947. When confronted in mid-1944 by demonstrations against
his government much like those that had toppled the dictatorships of Guatemala
and El Salvador, Somoza defused the crisis by announcing that he would not be a
candidate in the 1947 elections. By the time the military collaborations talks opened,

however, he was showing every sign of going back on his word, and searching for Washington's blessing. Somoza knew that the United States could undercut his legitimacy—far more seriously than a broken promise to his own people—by denying recognition to his government should he win the election.

The dictator would be disappointed, however, in the U.S. response both to his military and political ambitions. Bartlett's plan to expand the Guard, and his separate recommendation for a seven-man U.S. military mission to supervise the reorganization, found little support either in the State Department or even the War Department, which by July was considering a plan to reduce rather than to expand the Guard.[10]

Somoza's servility turned to petulance over the summer of 1945 as he and his son Luis, a Guard captain and Nicaragua's military attaché in Washington, jointly accused the State Department of standing in the way of Nicaragua's military modernization. A request for ten thousand rifles and cartridges, on Lend-Lease terms, had been stalled for two years, and the State Department was asking Nicaragua to pay more than the country could afford in salary for the members of a new U.S. military mission. Indeed, the State Department was going to extraordinary lengths throughout 1945 to prevent Nicaragua from receiving weapons either from U.S. arsenals or—when in frustration Somoza turned elsewhere—those of Canada and Great Britain. The reason was State's opposition to his reelection plans: "Any arms which we might ship him at this time could only be taken by him, by the Nicaraguan public, and by the other Republics of Central America and of the hemisphere as a demonstration of our complete support of his plans. This impression would not only be erroneous but extremely embarrassing," State told its Managua Embassy in August.[11] The State Department then tried to convey its opinion, in meetings with Somoza and others from August to December 1945, that his participation in the 1947 presidential elections would be unwelcome. Somoza didn't seem to be listening. On 29 November, the U.S. ambassador said it plainly in a conversation with Somoza at his *finca*: "Your government is considered to be that of a dictator." Somoza withdrew his candidacy.[12]

But he chose as successor a man he thought he could control: seventy-year-old Leonardo Argüello, who won a Guardia-supervised election on 2 February 1947 that was denounced as fraudulent by the losing Conservative Party candidate. The day after taking office, Argüello turned on the dictator, replacing *somocistas* on the Guardia's General Staff with his own men. Then he appointed a cabinet that included opponents of Somoza. Argüello's reappointment of Somoza as *jefe-director* scarcely calmed the furious general, who made it clear he would resist these and other affronts to his authority. In response, on 25 May, Argüello demanded Somoza's immediate resignation as Guard chief. Late that night Somoza unleashed his troops, taking control of the government and forcing the president out of office.[13]

The hapless Argüello had survived just twenty-five days as president. He was the last non-Somoza president to challenge the family's authority until the dynasty collapsed in 1979. The Somoza-controlled legislature, meeting within a day of the coup, dutifully impeached Argüello, removed him from office, and appointed its own president, Benjamín Lacayo Sacasa, as provisional president of Nicaragua. Forced to seek a way out of a constitutionally untenable situation—both Argüello's removal and Lacayo's appointment were clearly unlawful—Lacayo resorted to custom by tearing up the Constitution, dissolving Congress, and announcing elections on 3 August for a convention that would write a new constitution.[14]

Washington deplored Somoza's coup, reminding him that he had broken promises not only to refrain from using force against Argüello but to withdraw from politics altogether, and refused to recognize the Lacayo government.[15] U.S. Army Col. John F. Greco, the head of Nicaragua's military academy, was told to return to the United States "pending the establishment of an internationally recognized Nicaraguan Government."[16] His departure marked the beginning of a five-year hiatus in U.S. military collaboration with Nicaragua—the longest period of noncollaboration in Central America during the Cold War, except for the era of Sandinista rule in the same country, from 1980 to 1991. Stung by Washington's hostility, Somoza hastened to assure the U.S. chargé d'affaires in Managua that the new constitution would be harshly anticommunist, and would allow the use of Nicaraguan territory for foreign (i.e., U.S.) military bases during a "continental emergency." A week before the opening of the Rio Conference on hemispheric security (in which Nicaraguan participation was barred, owing to the coup), Somoza "promised unconditional support for United States policies at all times, including the Rio Conference."[17]

Lacayo had already arrested the leaders of the communist Partido Socialista de Nicaragua, perhaps partly to appease the United States, but the State Department hinted that it was the departure of Somoza—along with the installation of a government that included some members of the opposition Conservative Party—that was most likely to achieve a restoration of diplomatic relations.[18] The Conservatives refused even to participate in the 3 August election for delegates to the constitutional convention, which quickly voted to make Somoza's seventy-five-year-old uncle, Victor Manuel Román, the "constitutional" president of Nicaragua. As the U.S. chargé d'affaires commented, "it is difficult to understand how a constitutional president can be selected before there is a constitution."[19] A rebellion by a Conservative *montonera* on 7 September was easily suppressed by the Guardia, but apparently inspired Somoza to reactivate his own liberal militia in the guise of a new Guardia "reserve" force.[20]

General Somoza continued to balance his defiance of U.S. pressure for constitutional government with extravagant offers of collaboration in other realms. When U.S. negotiations with Panama over military base lease renewals broke down in December, General Somoza hastened to tell a United Press reporter: "We offer the United States any requisite territory in Nicaragua for construction of the long-discussed canal. We offer any requisite territory anywhere else in our country for military bases to protect the canal."[21] In case Washington hadn't been listening, his son-in-law Guillermo Sevilla Sacasa, Nicaragua's ambassador to the United Nations, repeated the offer two days later, and the constitutional convention even held a special session on 28 December in which it agreed to offer the United States unconditional rights for naval bases to protect any future U.S. canal.[22] Three weeks later,

Somoza reminded Washington of his anticommunist credentials by arresting forty "communist leaders" and seizing party documents.[23] Sensing the opportunity for further ingratiation offered by the leftist government of Guatemala, Somoza publicly—and correctly, as it turned out—accused Pres. Juan José Arévalo of fomenting revolution in Nicaragua.[24]

As Somoza promised, the constitution enacted on 22 January 1948 outlawed communist political parties (as well as fascist ones and those with international connections), and authorized the installation of bases for foreign troops in case of a hemispheric security crisis. Although the constitution extended Román's term of office to 1 May 1952, Somoza nevertheless yielded to U.S. insistence on a government that included the opposition Conservative Party, thus removing what appeared to be the main impediment to a restoration of friendly relations with Washington. On 26 February, Román and Somoza signed a pact with the leader of the "civilista" faction of the Conservative Party, Carlos Cuadra Pasos, promising free elections before 1 May 1950 (thus shortening Román's term of office), a free press, a nonpartisan Guardia, amnesty for political prisoners, and the appointment of conservatives to government posts, all contingent on U.S. recognition of the Román government.[25] The pact's immediate repudiation by Gen. Emiliano Chamorro, the seventy-nine-year-old Conservative chief, in exile in Guatemala, was ignored by its signers, because Somoza's incentive for signing the pact was undoubtedly limited to its potential for winning U.S. recognition of the Román government.[26] In apparent reward for Somoza's willingness to conciliate the opposition, the United States did not object to seating the Nicaraguan delegation at the Ninth International Conference of American States in Bogotá (30 March–2 May), and on 5 May the State Department finally recognized the Román government.[27]

General Chamorro's exclusion from the Cuadra-Somoza pact became such an obstacle to its implementation, however, that Somoza was forced, on 3 April 1950, to conclude a new pact with Chamorro himself, setting 21 May as the date for elections for yet another constitutional convention and for president. The "Pacto de los Generales" limited participation in the election to the Liberal and Conservative parties, stipulating that the party that won the most votes would win the presidency and get forty-three of the sixty seats in the convention. Upon the adoption of the new constitution, the convention would become the national legislature, with the terms of its members expiring in six years, the same period as that of the newly elected president. The pact also guaranteed stronger representation in the courts and at the municipal and regional levels for the losing party, as well as electoral freedom, a nonpartisan army, freedom of expression, and a ban on presidential reelection.[28] It was understood, of course, that the losers would be the Conservatives. Like most *pactos*, it was strictly limited to the dominant political force and its most serious rival, and thus sought to impose a bipartisan system on a political field that actually included a wide range of other, but weaker, opposition movements and parties. With the political crisis resolved, Somoza and Chamorro jointly organized a dairy farm that was destined to become, not surprisingly, the country's largest, with Chamorro as board president and Somoza as vice president.[29]

The election campaign pitted General Somoza, the Liberal candidate, against the Conservative businessman, Emilio Chamorro Benard, but the death of President Román on 6 May—just fifteen days before the election—led the Congress to appoint Somoza interim president the next day. The election was a disaster for the Conservatives, who took just one out of every four votes—not so much because of fraud, according to Walter, but because of their lack of popularity.[30] "At last," Cuadra Pasos lamented, we "made it to elections [but] suffered a grand failure. At a glance one could see that the people, who pay for all mistakes, had lost many false hopes, and with them, faith in their leaders." Cuadra Pasos blamed the party itself (implicitly, General Chamorro) for the loss, owing to the dictatorial character of the leadership, its mishandling of the Pacto de los Generales, and the brief period allowed for campaigning.[31] Although the Guardia soldiers with fixed bayonets at each polling station did not appear to intimidate the voters, a U.S. journalist pointed out that such a crude form of pressure was simply unnecessary, because ballots were marked "in the presence of two members of President Somoza's Liberal Party, one on each side of the ballot box." Those who voted for Somoza "received a card, called 'la magnífica,' bearing a handsome photo in color of General Somoza attesting the fact that the bearer voted for him. Possession of this card is required for employment in any department or dependency of the Nicaraguan Government and is said to be a 'safe conduct' in minor violations of the law. This card is also sometimes required by liberal employers, thus projecting politics into business."[32]

The restoration of formal relations between Nicaragua and the United States in 1948, after the one-year interregnum, did not automatically restore military collaboration. Nearly nine months after the resumption of diplomatic relations, General Somoza publicly and bitterly attacked the U.S. government for its nearly two-year-old ban on arms shipments, even boasting to a reporter that he was illegally importing U.S. arms in order to circumvent the embargo.[33] It was widely assumed that most of the weapons were probably acquired to bolster Nicaraguan military operations against the Arévalo government in Guatemala and to support the Picado government in Costa Rica. Even before the restoration of relations, Somoza had already confided to U.S. diplomats that Nicaraguan troops had entered Costa Rica, and military tension between the two countries only increased with the victory of José Figueres's rebel forces over Picado.[34] In 1949, Washington learned that Somoza was supporting Guatemalan exile military operations against Arévalo.[35]

Washington continued to withhold military collaboration in part, no doubt, because of Somoza's unpredictability, and his potential for complicating two delicate politico-military situations at the geographical extremes of the isthmus. In addition, Somoza's well-established image as a power-hungry dictator must have discouraged U.S. military authorities as well as the State Department from seeking an early renewal of military collaboration. Not only was the Guardia the "foundation" of Somoza's power, a U.S. Army intelligence analyst reported in 1949, "to the masses of the people the Guardia represents absolute authority and is an object of hatred."[36] By May 1951, Somoza's requests for military collaboration had been turned down so routinely that he had quit asking, according to a State Department official, who saw no good reason to continue denying the Guardia access to U.S. training facilities and recommended bringing Nicaragua back "under all phases of the military program."[37] A week later, the U.S. Army told the State Department it was time to send an army mission back to Nicaragua, which was one of only three countries in Latin America (the others being Mexico and the Dominican Republic) without a U.S. military mission.[38] Over the next few months, a new cordiality crept back into the U.S-Nicaraguan relationship. It was almost as if Somoza had managed to reacquire the prestige that had got him invited to the White House eleven years earlier. Indeed, President Truman was even persuaded to have him over to the White House for lunch on 2 May 1952. In the presence of Secretary of State Dean Acheson, Somoza genially offered to get rid of the Arbenz government in Guatemala in return for U.S. arms. The offer was taken as a jolly jest by all present, who were no doubt amused by what one may surmise to be the excitable Somoza's imitation of a Hollywood Mafia hit man. By August, the laughter had stopped. Arbenz's government was now carrying out Decree 900, the land reform legislation that had been passed in June and was threatening the United Fruit Company's immense holdings. Arbenz's communistic tendencies were now irrefutable, and U.S.-Guatemalan relations became considerably more hostile. Truman, reminded of Somoza's offer by one of his military aides, authorized the CIA to send a shipload of arms to Somoza, who would supposedly use them, with the help of the United Fruit Company, to overthrow Arbenz. A horrified State Department official learned of the scheme, code named "Operation Fortune," after the ship had sailed. Acheson hurriedly convinced Truman to redirect the ship to Panama, where the arms were stored in the Canal Zone. Perhaps Acheson pointed out to the president that Nicaragua and Guatemala were separated by Honduras, or that Somoza was as likely to use the arms to invade Costa Rica.[39]

Truman's cancellation of Operation Fortune, evidently around the first of October, did not interrupt the recovery of full-scale military collaboration. The United States signed agreements for a four-year air force mission (on 19 November 1952) and an army mission one year later (on 19 November 1953) of indefinite duration.[40] Nicaraguan pressure for a resumption of arms sales—or, better yet, participation in grant collaboration under the Military Assistance Program—intensified during the one-year period between the signing of the two agreements. U.S. Ambassador Thomas E. Whelan backed Somoza, arguing that not only was Somoza "not a dictator in the true sense of the word," but that during World War II the general "virtually offered to turn this country over to us. He says (and we believe him), he would do so again. . . . He has repeatedly said that he would do exactly as we say, and we know of nothing in his record that shows any inclination to fail us in international matters."[41]

Besides the scent of a communist conspiracy, Somoza knew that nothing got Washington's attention faster than evidence that a Latin American government might be seeking a collaborative relationship with the military forces of a nonhemispheric government. "I have just learned from a reliable but confidential source," a U.S. Embassy official reported on 9 March 1953, "that Nicaragua is negotiating with

France for military equipment. At the present stage, the discussions have revolved around $50,000 worth of material—mostly mortars."[42] Two days after the Embassy swallowed the bait, the dictator's son, Col. Anastasio Somoza Debayle, chief of staff of the National Guard, informed the Embassy that he had "received offers from several European suppliers—that a Czech armaments manufacturer had made a particularly attractive offer. None of the offers, however, exactly fitted his needs. . . . In the event of a world wide conflict, he thought it might be helpful to the United States, in a small way, if his Guard used standard American military equipment."[43] The general's son-in-law, Sevilla Sacasa, Nicaragua's ambassador in Washington, received an encouraging reply to his fervent appeal in May for grant collaboration under the MAP. Having cited communist threats from Guatemala and Costa Rica, he was told that the State Department was considering grant collaboration.[44]

As if to emphasize its determination to rearm, later that month the Nicaraguan government paid $154,500 to a private dealer, Western Arms of Los Angeles, for five hundred Danish-made Madsen submachine guns and one thousand Belgian automatic pistols, as well as a sample order of one hundred U.S.-made Johnson automatic rifles, plus two million rounds of ammunition.[45] France sold the government twenty mortars.[46]

By now, the dictator was freely letting his impatience show over U.S. reluctance to fully resume military collaboration. "President Somoza," the Embassy reported in June, "has frequently expressed puzzlement, if not displeasure, at what he regards as our reluctance to help him re-equip the National Guard, especially since he has, on all occasions, demonstrated that he is a staunch supporter of United States policies." The dispatch described the mélange of Czech, Belgian, Danish, French, Italian, and U.S. weapons in the National Guard's inventory, and pointed out that Nicaragua was discussing possible arms deals with Italy, Czechoslovakia, and France. Col. Somoza Debayle was even planning visits to Fabrique Nationale in Belgium and the Dansk Industri Syndikat in Copenhagen. All it would take to satisfy the Somozas, the dispatch concluded, was a MAP agreement, a U.S. Army mission, and the freedom to buy arms from the U.S. Army.[47]

"The Nicaraguan Army is very poorly equipped and is nowhere near prepared to resist any armed aggression," the Embassy wrote in August.[48] U.S. intelligence officers considered the Guardia capable of "maintaining internal security and of preventing widespread subversive disorders in the event of emergencies," but unable to prevent "sporadic or isolated instances, particularly in the initial stages of a war." The Caribbean coastal area remained highly vulnerable to "enemy clandestine use." In addition to the weapons just delivered by Western Arms, the Guard could count on no more than about one thousand Mausers (half Czech and the other half Brazilian) and twenty mortars in June 1953. The air force had three bombers, two fighters, one transport, and nineteen trainers, but there were no aircraft repair installations in Nicaragua, no land-air or point-to-point communication networks, and not even any weather forecasting facilities.[49]

Clearly well-informed about the pending shift in military collaboration policy, the Somoza government filed a $6 million request—"if possible, on the basis of a long-term loan, transfer, or sale"—on 30 July for enough arms and equipment to outfit an infantry battalion, plus five transport aircraft, six fighters, a hangar, and aircraft repair equipment. It was favorably received by State, which asked Defense "to take this list into account in developing a hemispheric defense task which Nicaragua might perform under the military assistance program."[50]

The request for an army mission was approved over the summer of 1953 by both State and the army, but the haggling among State, Defense and the White House over grant collaboration with El Salvador, Nicaragua, and Honduras continued until 9 December, when President Eisenhower authorized the opening of grant collaboration negotiations with the three governments. The Defense Department from the start had been inclined to offer grant collaboration to Nicaragua while denying it to El Salvador and Honduras, perceiving in Nicaragua a slight military justification that it was hard pressed to identify in the other two countries. With its argument for grant collaboration with all three countries based on the short-term political impact that it was likely to have on the Arbenz government of Guatemala, State reasoned that if only Nicaragua were to get a MAP agreement, the "psychological impact" on Guatemala would be diminished even as the other three countries would feel threatened by Nicaragua.[51]

Claiming it feared attack from both Costa Rica and Guatemala, Nicaragua agreed instantly to Washington's proposed grant collaboration agreement and its plans for the Guardia and the air force. The contrast with El Salvador's response, during the same period, could not have been more striking. At 5:30 p.m. on 17 April 1954, two U.S. military officers and the U.S. ambassador sat down with President Somoza, his son Anastasio and Sevilla Sacasa. Two hours later the president and the ambassador initialed the draft MAP agreement, which was ceremoniously signed on 23 April.[52] Six planes carrying twenty-three and a half tons of military cargo were immediately scheduled to arrive in Managua on 24 May, the day before a like shipment was due in Tegucigalpa for the just-signed Honduran MAP agreement. The rest of the Nicaraguan equipment was sent by ship on 17 July.[53] Publicly, the State Department attributed its haste in implementing the MAP deal to two recent events: the arrival in Guatemala on 16 May of arms from the Polish-administered port of Stettin aboard the *Alfhem*—arms that might be used "for subversive purposes against the anti-communist Central American governments"—and the "instability" in Central America, which is "an open invitation for the communists and their sympathizers to interfere in those countries."[54] Of course Nicaragua was a potential—and wholly justifiable—target for Guatemala, though scarcely for the reasons publicly claimed by the State Department. The CIA had been training Castillo Armas's invaders at three camps in Nicaragua since February.[55]

Meanwhile, all the equipment needed to set up the MAP battalion was delivered by May 1955 and training had already been underway in the Canal Zone since the previous June. Yet the battalion (with a planned strength of 852 enlisted men and 39 officers) was still far from combat ready. The training of officers and NCOs would take at least until 1959, and field training of recruits could not begin until November, when a twelve-man U.S. mobile training team was scheduled to arrive for six months' duty to undertake thirty-eight to forty-one weeks of basic training. Construction of housing for the battalion would not start until August.[56]

A full year later, however, there was still "no [MAP] battalion as such," the U.S. Army Mission reported, blaming the delay on a "shortage of capable and trusted manpower, political unrest, lack of intent and interest." Moreover, Nicaraguan officers trained in the Canal Zone were being improperly employed once they came home—a common complaint among U.S. military trainers in Central America during the Cold War, who often saw their efforts wasted when their students were assigned to jobs that had nothing to do with their new specialties. The U.S. Army mission itself seemed to be idle, because "there has been no official request for advice, either infantry or artillery, and all attempts by this mission to foster interest in the knowledge available has been in vain." The Mobile Training Team's visit had to be cancelled because the government had failed to recruit soldiers to man the battalion.[57] The Embassy and the U.S. Army Mission chief attributed Nicaragua's sudden indifference to organizing the battalion it had begged for to "reasons that are almost entirely political."[58] The reason, a Pentagon planning unit confidently asserted in September, was simple: the battalion "would be a predominant power in the country capable of controlling the government." The Caribbean Command pointed out that no "organic combat units" greater than company size existed; as a result, the battalion "could be a potential threat to the present government."[59]

The failure of Nicaragua to cooperate in the organization of the MAP battalion was one of many examples of Washington's typical lack of control over military collaboration, even with collaborators thought to be exceptionally submissive to U.S. interests. Somoza knew exactly what the United States wanted to hear, and he said it often and publicly, but always to advance his own interests, which often conflicted with U.S. preferences. The public signing of the MAP agreement and the public delivery of the equipment were events that served both Washington and Managua, at a moment when both governments were collaborating in the overthrow of the Arbenz government. The actual implementation of the MAP, however, was a different story. Even after the resignation of Arbenz on 27 June, Washington continued to press Nicaragua to carry out its obligations to organize the MAP battalion. If the U.S. State Department hadn't immediately grasped the potential threat to Somoza's control of the Guardia that a powerful MAP battalion posed, Somoza clearly had, and he wasn't about to risk his fortune and his life to satisfy U.S. fantasies of military modernization.

But without the MAP unit, it was clear that the forty-two-hundred-member Guardia would remain, in the eyes of the U.S. military establishment, a weak and unreliable collaborator. Control was fully vested in President Somoza, who was the Guard's director-for-life and personally handled the procurement of arms and ammunition. The Guardia's recruits, volunteers who served for three years, averaged a fourth grade education. Most officers had a high-school education, but they "occupy quasi-political positions and are not well trained by American standards." Although in 1949 the Guardia's ability to turn back an invasion was seriously questioned, by the mid-1950s the U.S. Army thought the Guardia could defend

Nicaragua against an invasion by Honduras or Costa Rica. Nevertheless, its training and equipment were geared for protecting the regime from rioters and insurrectionists, not for "modern combat."[60]

Even as it passively blocked the formation of the MAP battalion, the Nicaraguan government was buying enough weapons and equipment to completely remake the other eight battalions and the air force, and even to launch a small navy. In June 1954 Nicaragua asked to buy $32.9 million worth of ground ($24.1 million), sea ($6 million), and air ($2.8 million) weapons and equipment, a huge package that Anastasio Somoza Debayle acknowledged "will take a few years" to implement. He wanted to use it to outfit a second infantry battalion (in addition to the MAP battalion), while adding four bombers, ten F-47 pursuit planes, and two patrol craft escorts to the government's arsenals. The U.S. Army did not consider the request excessive, because the Guardia was underarmed and most of the weapons it had were "old and inadequate." Moreover, the presence of the U.S. Army mission and the resumption of training programs "are raising the military standards of that country," provoking a need for new and better weapons. The Pentagon recommended the sale of the equipment in a planned series of small purchases.[61]

Whereas Nicaragua's purchases of military equipment between 1949 and January 1, 1954 had totaled just $7,125 and consisted entirely of spare parts, over the course of the following twenty-one months it paid for $1.4 million worth of equipment: seven thousand M1 rifles, seven million M1 cartridges, four 105-mm howitzers, two thousand howitzer shells, and three F-47 pursuit planes.[62] Nicaragua received permission from the State Department to buy its first military helicopter in February 1955.[63] In August, State approved the purchase of four tanks equipped with 105-mm howitzers, five thousand ammunition belts, and seven thousand bayonets with scabbards for M1 rifles.[64] In addition to these purchases from U.S. military stocks, the State Department approved $82,000 worth of commercial purchases of rifle and machine gun parts, and four light military aircraft.[65] When Washington was unable to supply F-47s, the State Department gave Managua permission to buy twenty-five Swedish F-51D Mustangs for $600,000, and the U.S. Air Force mission offered to train the Guardia's mechanics in maintaining them.[66]

Even after Arbenz's downfall, President Somoza found plenty of enemies to justify the buying spree. When he told the U.S. Embassy in April 1955 that he needed one thousand rifles right away, he listed his reasons: he didn't trust President Osorio's government in El Salvador, "hostile leftists" could take over in Honduras, Castillo Armas's government might collapse, and Costa Rica's José Figueres was conspiring against him. And inside Nicaragua, the Conservatives opposed his decision to amend the constitution so that he could run for reelection. The U.S. Embassy agreed that the threats were real: "he should receive one thousand rifles soonest."[67]

Even the least sympathetic U.S. officials felt they had little choice but to continue collaborating with the man that Pres. Franklin Roosevelt supposedly called "our son of a bitch," mainly in order to prevent further inroads by European arms competitors. Arguing in favor of approving Nicaragua's request for the seven thousand M1 rifles, Robert Newbegin, the head of Central American Affairs, acknowl-

edged in December 1954 that Nicaragua was "fast reaching a stage where its armaments are all out of proportion to that of most of the other Central American countries." Newbegin even expected Somoza to resell to other governments some of the
weapons he was buying. "However, there appears little that we can do to control the
situation. If we do not go along with the Nicaraguan request, it is probable that the
Nicaraguans will obtain their arms elsewhere."[68]

President Somoza had failed completely to achieve lasting peace with his principal political enemies, Gen. Emiliano Chamorro's Conservative Party and Costa
Rica's Partido Liberación Nacional, the social-democratic movement associated
with José Figueres. In addition, "significant numbers" of Nicaraguans wanted
Somoza to retire from politics.[69] By 1954, the Pact of the Generals was in tatters, in
part owing to doubts that Somoza would adhere to its stipulation that he refrain
from running for reelection in 1956. General Chamorro—now a senator—had himself repudiated the pact by then, having joined Figueres (now president of Costa
Rica), anti-Somoza exiles, and other enemies of the regime in an elaborate plot to
kill Somoza while seizing control of La Loma, the combined presidential palace-
Guardia headquarters in Managua. Figueres had joined the plot shortly after his
inauguration on 8 November 1953, helping the Nicaraguans acquire weapons and
providing trucks and an escort of Costa Rican Guardia Civil officers for them when
they infiltrated Nicaragua from Costa Rica. Somoza received advance knowledge of
the plot, which was thwarted after a highway shootout on 5 April 1954. The inevitable state of siege and the jailing of opposition figures followed. Eleven months
after the uprising, the Supreme Court banished Chamorro and two other Conservative legislators to the Caribbean coast town of Bluefields for eight years.[70]

For Somoza, the timing of the uprising—just twelve days before the scheduled
meeting to "negotiate" the grant collaboration agreement with the United States—
was ideal. He could justifiably claim a three-front "defense of democracy" or at least
a war on communism, one against Guatemala, one against Costa Rica, and another
against the two countries' fifth columns. Figueres's participation also gave Somoza
an excuse to avenge himself against his most notorious non-Nicaraguan enemy. On
11 January 1955 about five hundred mostly Costa Rican exiles who had been training
in Nicaragua carried out their long-expected invasion. Supported by the
Nicaraguan Air Force, the rebel army occupied two border towns. After the United
States rushed four F-51 fighter planes to Costa Rica to aid in its defense against
Nicaragua's U.S.-supplied F-47s, the invasion collapsed, but not before Nicaragua
insisted, unsuccessfully, that the United States provide it with four F-51 to counter-
balance Costa Rica's.[71]

The aborted uprising against Somoza the previous April had not only triggered
the repression of the opposition and support for the Costa Rican exiles, but an even
more audacious act of political revenge against General Chamorro: the passage of a
constitutional amendment by the Nicaraguan Congress on 20 April 1955 allowing
Somoza to seek reelection in 1957. By the time Somoza announced, on 29 November
1955, that he would run in the February 1957 election, he was reportedly "nervous"
about repeated plots on his life and even avoiding interviews with foreign corre-

spondents.[72] But unlike the situation a decade earlier, the U.S. government was now at the dictator's side—above all, as a much more prominent military collaborator, but also in the person of what one historian called the "outlandishly pro-Somoza" behavior of the U.S. ambassador, Thomas E. Whelan.[73]

Somoza's reelection was a certainty, despite what the Embassy called "considerable opposition" to his nomination—even from within the Liberal Party itself. An assassin's bullet stopped him on 29 September 1956. The general's son Luis immediately replaced his father as interim president and as the Liberal Party candidate for president. Although Washington was deeply worried that the assassination might trigger unrest and seemed to be pinning its hopes for stability on the Guardia, it rejected a request by Managua on 17 October to buy what the State Department considered to be a "considerable amount of arms and ammunition," while wondering why the government wasn't organizing the MAP battalion instead of buying more weapons.[74] Immediately after Luis Somoza defeated the Conservative Party's candidate on 3 February 1957, the Embassy assessed the regime's military strength and found it had improved significantly in the last three years, despite the ghostly status of the MAP battalion. The country could "wage all out aggressive warfare by Nicaraguan standards, against a neighboring country, for 30–45 days. Nicaragua can wage reduced scale warfare against a neighboring country indefinitely."[75]

In military matters, Luis initially displayed more independence from Washington than his father. The United States seems to have dissuaded the late dictator from buying sixty Canadian tanks a few months before he was killed. His son Luis quickly made a tank deal with Israel instead, without U.S. consent or even knowledge. From Israel, Nicaragua bought sixty-eight fully armed Staghound armored cars, made in Canada by General Motors for the British Army. The deal included mortars, ammunition, and equipment for a national radio communications network that would have linked some twenty command posts already under construction. "The network and the armored cars will make Nicaraguan forces very mobile," the State Department observed. The Guardia had discovered that the four tanks it bought from Washington for $80,000 were practically useless in Nicaragua, and regretted spending the money. The Staghounds, on the other hand, would be "useful for police action and street fighting as well as field work. . . . There is no doubt that the quantity and type of equipment which Nicaragua has now acquired will create a great deal of apprehension among her Central American neighbors, particularly Honduras and Costa Rica. It is probable that attempts will be made by Nicaragua's neighbors to restore the military balance as soon as possible."[76]

But as Washington had long suspected, the regime was also dabbling in the arms trade, seeking profits that would not necessarily be credited to the national treasury but find their way into private bank accounts.[77] On 20 March 1958, the Nicaraguan government agreed to sell the beleaguered Cuban regime of Fulgencio Batista thirty of the sixty-eight Staghounds for $377,000, the price that Nicaragua had paid to Israel for all of them.[78] The deal was made six days after the State Department decided to block all U.S. arms shipments to Cuba, owing to the Batista government's failure to "create conditions for fair elections" and to the "deteriorating political situation" in

Cuba. A longstanding request by Batista to buy twenty armored cars from the U.S. Army was among the casualties of the U.S. arms embargo.[79]

After the Cuban deal was made, military collaboration with Nicaragua intensified, perhaps because of the ease with which Nicaragua had circumvented objections to its tank purchase. In May, the Embassy recommended approval of Nicaragua's request to buy seven surplus F-51s at $1,090 each mainly to provide spare parts for its air force.[80] And the government had finally begun to set up the MAP battalion; with Anastasio gone, the fear that it might become a competing power source evaporated. Even though the battalion was still not combat ready, it was now "more effective than any other unit of the Nicaraguan Army," according to U.S. military advisers.[81] In October, Nicaragua's request for another major weapons order—mostly automatic rifles, machine guns and grenades—was approved by the Embassy.[82]

But even as the government of "President Luis," as the State Department called him, plied Washington throughout 1958 and 1959 with reports of antigovernment invasion plots and assassination conspiracies emanating variously from Costa Rica, Honduras, and Cuba, the United States sought to avoid associating itself too closely with the regime. The long-running Honduran-Nicaraguan border dispute discouraged any exceptional signs of U.S. friendliness, and the Somoza name had itself become a liability to the United States. In rejecting Luis's persistent requests in 1958 for a formal invitation to visit the United States, the State Department highlighted the fact that everywhere in the hemisphere his name was associated with the continuation of a family dictatorship, despite Luis's announcement that no Somoza would run for president in the 1963 election.[83] Two U.S. police advisers, returning from a twenty-four-hour visit to Managua, reported that "Nicaragua is a semi-feudalistic state with only a tinge of organized law and order. The police are politically repressive and are tools of those in power."[84] Within weeks of the victory of Castro's forces in Cuba, the State Department's top Latin Americanist, Roy R. Rubottom, Jr., emphasized in a confidential letter to the Embassy in Managua the U.S. preference for a non-Somoza government there: "We have been impressed by President Somoza's sincere desire to lead the Nicaraguans to a type of government more democratic than that which existed under his father. If Luis is able to continue his present policy of ample civil liberties, and adheres to his promise of ending the so-called 'Somoza dynasty' when his term is completed on April 30, 1963, I think our interests and those of Latin America as a whole will be served." The situation was further complicated by the rise to power of both Castro and Rómulo Betancourt in Venezuela, notorious enemies of the Somoza regime who, Rubottom thought, may well be preparing guerrilla attacks on Nicaragua.[85]

Two months later, Rubottom had a frank talk in Washington with Gen. Anastasio Somoza Debayle, who inherited command of the Guardia from his father. Nicaragua should "keep itself absolutely clean in its dealings with its neighbors" and should "desist in its efforts to purchase arms in the United States, since we did not want to call undue attention to this subject at this particular time." Cruelly, Rubottom concluded, "the thing of which the Somoza brothers are the most proud, their name, is a serious political liability; they should recognize that public opinion throughout the Americas simply is unable to accept the fact that Nicaragua is being governed with a moderate hand and that the people have civil liberties." Somoza, Rubottom thought, "seemed to accept all this in a friendly way and he even acknowledged the veracity of the points made."[86]

Throughout 1959, Washington exploited opportunities to encourage more tolerance of the opposition to the regime. After the Guard defeated an invasion in June from Costa Rica and Cuba by an exile group that included both Conservative Party activists and leftists, General Somoza became convinced that Nicaragua was "faced with massive threats from both north and south." He seriously considered bombing both Costa Rica and Cuba while unleashing the Honduran exile, Colonel Velásquez, against the Villeda government. President Luis apparently overruled his brother, to the great relief of the U.S. government.[87] Recognizing that attempts to overthrow the Nicaraguan government had the support of the noncommunist opposition, the State Department responded by pressing the Somozas to pact with those factions of the opposition that had so far refrained from engaging in armed insurgency—what the United States called the "responsible" opposition. A pact would make it easier for the government to "thwart efforts of outside-supported groups with doubtful ideologies to make overthrow attempts," while doing "much to discredit any accusation that present Government is dictatorship."[88]

As U.S. distrust of the Cuban government intensified in 1960, association with the Somoza name apparently became less burdensome to Washington. The U.S. Air Force invited General Somoza to tour some of its installations in October 1960. During his visit, the general reported to the U.S. government what was probably its first news that a certain pro-Castro opposition group that would labor in obscurity for another decade "has adopted the flag of the late opposition leader-bandit, Sandino, as its symbol and pays homage to López Pérez, the assassin of his father, as its leader." By then, the Somozas had secretly given Washington their permission to use the airbase at Puerto Cabezas for U.S. air support of the planned Bay of Pigs invasion. In March and early April 1961 the invasion force was moved from Guatemala to Nicaragua. On 14 April the force embarked for Cuba in four merchant ships and two infantry landing crafts. The first air strikes against Cuba were launched from Puerto Cabezas the next day.[89]

In no other Central American country have the domestic and international dimensions of public violence intersected in more complex, even paradoxical, ways than in Nicaragua. The country has often been depicted as little more than the permanent victim of its watery geography and of the imperialist aggressors who sought to exploit it as an interoceanic waterway. But Nicaragua's history yields impressive examples of the ways that Nicaraguans themselves internationalized public violence in their own country, sometimes by inviting foreigners in through the front door, though more often by their conspicuous failure to reduce the limits of public violence.

The outcomes of the policies adopted by the United States have been no less paradoxical. Bent on reducing the limits of public violence in Nicaragua up to the early 1930s, Washington deceived itself with the solution that it worked out with Nicaragua's leaders in the 1920s—the creation of a unified, nonpartisan "constabulary" at the service of the state. Instead, the United States turned out to be the midwife of a peculiar species of state, one improvised by the Guardia's leader and his cronies. Anchored in the authority of the leader's family, the family-controlled Liberal Party, and the family-controlled Guardia until the 1970s, it was a state continually subject to the changing preferences and interests of the Somoza family. If the state's paternity could be traced to the United States, Washington took no pride in the fact and exercised surprisingly little authority over it. The Warren conversation (1945), the withdrawal of diplomatic recognition (1947–48), the five-year interruption in military collaboration (1947–52), and the Rubottom conversation (1959) show not only that the United States throughout this period maintained a reluctant and at times highly critical relationship with the Somozas, but that the United States was often incapable of bending them to its will. Their servile rhetoric aside, the Somozas cooperated with, challenged, or ignored Washington as their own interests dictated, improvising the state on the foundation of the Guardia. Yet despite Washington's obvious distaste for the Somozas and their policies, and despite the fact that Nicaragua displayed more belligerence in its relations with the rest of the Central American governments than any other on the isthmus, Nicaragua received more U.S. military goods and services during the 1950s than any other isthmian government (see figures A-1 to A-6), more even than Guatemala after 1954.

Why did the United States do so much to strengthen the military power of a government that it clearly wished to see replaced? The main reason was the government's dependability; the loyalty of the Somozas to Washington was unquestionable, even if their fitness to rule was doubtful. Nor did any credible political opposition ever pose the slightest threat to Nicaragua's solid anticommunism, which meant that even if one or another liberal or conservative faction might have somehow seized the presidency, its loyalty to the United States could be counted on. The possibility that a powerful Nicaraguan National Guard might therefore be used by someone other than a Somoza in ways that challenged U.S. policy was practically nil. This was not the case in Guatemala, where Arévalo sought a comeback, and even Gen. Ydígoras Fuentes's anticommunism was questioned. Nor was it the case in Honduras, where the Liberal Party was always seen as soft on communism, nor in El Salvador, the most anti-Yankee country in Central America.

Another reason for Washington's generous attitude toward military collaboration was linked to the important role that Somoza played in the U.S. plan to overthrow the Arbenz government of Guatemala. Fully 46 percent of all U.S. military goods and services delivered to Nicaragua in the 1950s were delivered between July 1954 and July 1955, immediately after the anti-Arbenz forces had been trained in Nicaragua and then unleashed from their launch pad in Honduras. U.S. deliveries surged again between July 1959 and June 1960 in response to the Cuba threat. For the Somoza dictatorship, the Cuban revolutionary government was therefore the second deus ex machina of the Cold War, performing the same function that the Guatemalan revolutionary government had in 1950–54.

A third reason for Nicaragua's favored treatment was the same geopolitical logic that, in Washington's eye, set the country apart from all the others in Central America, and which Anastasio Somoza García exploited so cravenly during World War II: its unique suitability for an interoceanic canal route, and therefore a likely target of a foreign adversary.

Finally, the U.S. government had no choice but to accept the fact that in Nicaragua, unlike the other countries of the isthmus, Somoza founded his state on the Guardia, and it was the Guardia (through its leader) that made the state. To allow the Guardia to become undone, to see it wither and factionalize, would have been to invite a return to the 1920s, a scenario whose potentially catastrophic consequences hardly any responsible U.S. leader could doubt. The damage could easily have exceeded whatever potential for harm to U.S. national interests the Arbenz government of Guatemala represented. As the Cold War came to Latin America, the Guardia became the sable cloud that turned out her silver lining. To the United States, its gleam did not dim until 1979, when the *montonera* that claimed both Sandino and Marx as their ideological *caudillos* finally destroyed both the Guardia and the state that the founder, his sons and their collaborators had cobbled together.

14

Costa Rica

An Army Renamed

> The Guardia Civil could become the main nucleus of an Army with a view toward wider objectives than those directed purely at keeping internal public order.
>
> —Fernando Lara, foreign minister of Costa Rica,
> to U.S. ambassador, 11 March 1952

In 1940, Pres. Rafael Angel Calderón Guardia worried that fifth columns of both fascists and communists might undertake operations against his government—or so he told the U.S. minister in San José. On 5 June, with France on the verge of collapse, and perhaps out of a genuine fear that his country would be defenseless were the United States drawn into the war in Europe, Calderón Guardia begged the U.S. envoy for arms and ammunition, and a week later, when pressed for his "actual needs," mentioned four thousand rifles and forty-five submachine guns for the 324-man Army of Costa Rica. Calderón Guardia told the envoy that he expected Washington "to act speedily and effectively in the event the German and Italian elements here make an effort to upset the present Government."[1] The catastrophe in Europe had clearly shaken the confidence of all the Central American governments, including the Costa Rican, in U.S. protection from external aggression:

> In view of the repeated assurances given by Germany, Great Britain and France to the small countries of Europe during the past year as to the maintenance of their sovereignty, all of which were violated with impunity, these people down here have lost faith in treaties, conversations and pledges. They expect and demand something more concrete than words. We are on trial at the present moment in Latin America, and unless we are prepared to make good our assurances by a substantial contribution to the defense of this part of the world in terms of arms and ships, it is not impossible that we may expect as an alternative a successful German "blitzkrieg" in the not too far distant future. . . . [Costa Ricans] expect our material aid as a condition precedent to further cooperation.[2]

In response to Calderón Guardia's request on 11 July for a U.S. military mission to help Costa Rica reorganize its army, Washington agreed, provided that Costa Rica expand the National Police and increase the enlistment terms of both army and police recruits. But Calderón replied that he was studying the matter, possibly hesitating over the cost of the mission, according to the U.S. minister.[3] There the matter rested for nearly a year, until 14 July 1941, when the government finally signed a four-year military mission agreement. After a Lend-Lease agreement was signed on 16 January 1942, Costa Rica authorized the United States to keep a squadron of patrolling warplanes at the airport in La Sabana. By May, the U.S. Military Mission had arrived and was training both officers and enlisted men in the Costa Rican Army.[4]

The president's dread of impending fifth-column attacks must have subsided considerably, for in mid-1941 the U.S. military attaché seemed surprised to discover that "The only apparent mission of the Costa Rican army is that of guarding and cleaning the arms, ammunition and equipment stored in the two barracks located in the capital, San José." Equipped and organized as infantry, the troops had practically no training.[5] In fact, the threat posed to the Calderón Guardia administration by its Costa Rican political opponents overshadowed that of any European fascist fifth columnists. Electoral fraud had increased so dramatically during the 1930s that confidence in Costa Rica's elections was deteriorating markedly when World War II began.[6] In response to the electoral chicanery, as well as to the persistence of other forms of inefficiency and corruption in government, a group of professionals and intellectuals organized themselves in 1940 as the Centro para el Estudio de los Problemas Nacionales (CEPN). The Center's activists, some of whom had already been planning a *golpe de estado*, turned fiercely against Calderón after his Partido Republicano Nacional (PRN) pacted with its most aggressive rival for urban votes, the communist Vanguardia Popular, in 1943.[7] Now, the CEPN and other opponents of the government added communism to the list of failures that could be associated not just with a corrupt and opportunistic administration, but with what many considered to be an irretrievably defective state apparatus.

Nevertheless, the Republicano-communist alliance, calling itself the Bloque de Victoria, easily overcame that opposition with its single slate of candidates in the 1944 elections and gained the presidency for its candidate, Teodoro Picado. The communists won four seats in the legislature, but Picado—seeking to distance himself from communism—declined to offer them a single government ministry. Still, the sudden prominence of the communists in the halls of power polarized politics as never before.[8] Accusations of fraud and other irregularities in the presidential election of 1944 and the legislative elections of 1946 greatly surpassed those of earlier elections, and the incidence of electoral violence—previously limited to rural zones—multiplied considerably in the country's core urban district, the Valle Central.[9]

With two successful presidential campaigns in a row behind it, the PRN once again pacted with the communists' Vanguardia Popular and again nominated Calderón Guardia for president in the election scheduled for 8 February 1948. In response, the antigovernment opposition parties united in February 1947 as the Partido Unión Nacional (PUN). Its candidate, the newspaper publisher Otilio Ulate, publicly declared that he would lead an armed revolt if the government failed to respect the results of the election. Ulate appointed José Figueres, a prominent member of CEPN, to assemble the weapons and organize the revolt—just in case. Figueres had been agitating openly in favor of armed action against the Calderón and Picado governments since 1942, and as the government and opposition parties clashed repeatedly during the 1947 campaign, he traveled to Guatemala to collect arms. Once there, he signed a pact "on behalf of the people of Costa Rica" with opposition leaders from the Dominican Republic and Nicaragua, pledging to liberate their countries from the dictatorships that controlled them, starting with Costa Rica. The "Pact of the Caribbean" gave birth to the fabled international *montonera*, the Caribbean Legion.[10]

After an election marred by missing and destroyed ballots and improper procedures, the national election board declared Ulate the winner, even though the published results were so contradictory that historians still disagree about which party earned the most votes.[11] The fateful decision by the government-controlled legislature to annul the election, thus favoring Calderón, was treated as a declaration of war by the anti-*calderonistas*. Despite a last-minute accord between Calderón and Ulate to recognize an interim president in order to avoid civil war, Figueres, the chief of Ulate's *montonera*, launched his rebellion on 12 March. The tiny Costa Rican Army was irrelevant in the forty-day war, which pitted the police forces and party militias of the government against the militias of the opposition parties, at a cost of two thousand lives.[12] As the fighting intensified, the United States weighed in against the Picado administration and the Calderón-communist alliance. Costa Rica was being compared to Czechoslovakia, where a communist government had just taken office. Washington blocked arms shipments to the Picado government and did nothing to stop the Guatemalan government from assisting Figueres's army, which even benefited from the advice of the U.S. military attaché.[13] The triumphant insurgents under Figueres's leadership established a temporary, eleven-man ruling body that called itself the Junta Fundadora de la Segunda República, which promptly repressed the left and outlawed any form of communist political organization.

On 1 December, newspaper reporters showed up at one of the army garrisons in San José, the Cuartel Bella Vista, where, according to an earlier announcement by the Junta, the minister of public security, Col. Edgar Cardona, would turn over the keys to the garrison so that it could be converted into the National Museum. But Cardona stunned the crowd by announcing the *junta*'s decision to dissolve the army. After Cardona gave the symbolic garrison key to the education minister, Lalo Gámez, the National Museum director, Rómulo Valerio, took a sledgehammer and knocked down part of the garrison's wall. Figueres, the Junta president, then announced that "The Founding Junta of the Second Republic officially declares dissolved the National Army, considering a good police force sufficient for the security of our country." In an interview the next day, Figueres stressed that Colonel Cardona deserved most of the credit for the Junta's decision to dissolve the army because he pushed for it harder than anyone else, insisting that funds being spent on the army were better transferred to education. The colonel's idea was just a reflection of the national character, an editorial writer suggested in praise of the Junta's decision: "We Costa Ricans have a political mystique, a preference, renewed daily, for republican practices. We were born, we were educated, beneath a republican sign, so to say, abjuring completely what may signify the intervention of arms in the decisions of public life or in its maintenance." Two days after the proclamation, *La Prensa Libre* reported, President Figueres had already received "an infinity" of telegrams from overseas congratulating him for the suppression of the army.[14] Costa Rica's most durable modern political myth was born. "Dissolution of Army Causes Sensation in Paris," roared the front page of *La Prensa Libre* on 3 December. On the fifty-second anniversary of the proclamation, a reporter wrote, "Go to any part of the world and even in the most remote little towns they will tell you, 'Ah, Costa Rica, the country without an army!'"[15]

Although no single act of the Junta has been more widely cited and admired than the decision to abolish the army, in fact no evidence of any such decree appears in the records of its deliberations. Only the public statements of Cardona and Figueres on 1 December, preserved in newspaper accounts, attribute the decision to the Junta.[16] Nevertheless, reaction to the decision over the next six months suggested that it enjoyed broad popular support. A nine-man, Junta-appointed committee drafted a new constitution that included the following article: "The army is proscribed as a permanent institution. For the vigilance and conservation of public order, the State will depend on the necessary police forces. Only by continental treaty or for the national defense will military forces be organized."[17]

A constitutional convention, elected on 8 December, began deliberating on 15 January 1949 and retained, with some modifications, the drafting committee's proposal to abolish the army as Article 12 of the new constitution. Attributing the constitutional proscription of the armed forces solely or even principally to the political authority of Figueres or his Junta would therefore be erroneous. Although the convention retained the essential language of the Junta committee's ban on an army, it stunned the Junta by rejecting the committee's draft constitution and opted to base it on that of 1871.[18] This demonstration of political and ideological independence from the Junta was congruent with the convention's makeup. Of its forty-five delegates, 76 percent represented the PUN; only four of the candidates of Figueres's Partido Social Demócrata managed to gain election as delegates. Moreover, the three deputies who proposed Article 12 were all members of Ulate's PUN, and the motion was approved with almost no discussion.[19] What stands out about the constitutional prohibition of the army, therefore, was the strong support it found quite beyond— and perhaps even in spite of—the Junta's or Figueres's backing of the measure.

Whether Article 12 merely acknowledged a decades-old fact of political life in Costa Rica, or represented a boldly original proclamation against violence and war, is a question that still divides historians. Some say it was the evolutionary outcome of a strongly civilian political culture traceable to 1821.[20] If so, it was an evolution whose unfolding was hastened by leaders like those associated with CEPN, convinced since the early 1940s that the time had come to redesign certain elements of the state; in this view, a national army represented a decadent holdover of "an order of things that had to disappear."[21] As for external threats, Costa Ricans could reasonably assume, as they had since the 1920s, that they could go on looking to the United States for unilateral protection against Panama or Nicaragua. In addition, there was now the multilateral commitment of the Rio Treaty, which the Picado administration and most other hemispheric republics had signed on 2 September 1947. By obligating all the signatories to submit "every controversy which may arise between them to methods of peaceful settlement," and to come to the aid of any signatory subject to armed attack, the treaty's required commitment to peaceful resolution of disputes became one of the main arguments for abolishing the army.[22]

There is little doubt that Costa Rica's only serious external threat was (and has remained) Nicaragua, and in this connection the timing of the army's abolition is worth analyzing. Nicaragua's delegation to the Rio Treaty conference was not seated because its government was still not recognized as legitimate, owing to General Somoza's unconstitutional removal of President Arguello. As a result, Nicaragua did not sign the treaty until 15 October 1948, more than a year after almost all the other signatories. Nicaragua ratified it on 1 November. Costa Rica ratified the treaty on 20 November and proclaimed the abolition of its army ten days later. The Rio Treaty officially entered into force two days after that. Figueres had simultaneously managed to convince the Caribbean Legion, whose members had joined him in overthrowing the Picado government, to withdraw from Costa Rica to Guatemala.[23] The timing of the proclamation to abolish the Costa Rican Army might be explained, therefore, by the Junta's conviction that the Nicaraguan threat had dissipated, owing not only to Managua's solemn pledge in the Rio Treaty to seek a peaceful solution in the event of conflict with Costa Rica, but also to the withdrawal from Costa Rica of the Caribbean Legion.

If that was the Junta's logic, it failed. The treaty did not deter the crafty Somoza and on 11 December Costa Rica became the first country to invoke the Rio Treaty. Acting in response to an invasion the previous night by what the Junta called "armed forces proceeding from Nicaragua," Costa Rica called on the Organization of American States for assistance. Somoza, who had supported the Picado government during the March uprising, struck the first blow in a violent rivalry between two utterly disparate regimes (and their respective *caudillos*) that would go on for three decades. By allowing Calderón Guardia to organize and train a small force that accomplished nothing but the brief occupation of a couple of small Costa Rican towns near the border, Somoza succeeded in embarrassing the Junta by drawing attention to its association with the Legion. The ensuing OAS investigation faulted Nicaragua for not preventing Calderón Guardia from using its territory. More important, however, the OAS investigators denounced the Costa Rican Junta's moral and material support for the "so-called Legion of the Caribbean," among whose objectives was the overthrow of "the present regime in Nicaragua."[24] If the Junta had interpreted the Rio Treaty as one more shield behind which it could safely disarm Costa Rica, Somoza may have seen in the treaty's investigative machinery a tool to reveal Costa Rica's complicity with the Legion.

Article 12 of the Constitution of 1949 has not been modified since it became effective on 8 November. But it did not leave Costa Rica entirely without the means to deploy violence against an aggressor. Although its dramatic first sentence "proscribing" an army is all that is usually quoted, the article also authorizes the establishment of a military force under certain conditions, and without any limit on its duration: "The Army as an institution is proscribed. . . . Only by continental treaty or for national defense can military forces be organized."[25] The ambiguity of the constitutional status of an army is reflected also in the fact that the 1941 U.S. Military Mission agreement was regularly renewed, not only in 1945, but in 1950, 1953, 1958, 1962, and 1966. How could the United States send a military mission to a country without a military? Costa Rica begged Washington throughout the 1950s for MAP infantry battalions of the kind that its northern neighbors were getting. In 1955 the Ministerio de Seguridad Pública identified its twin responsibilities as (a) police functions and (b) "functions of the preservation and defense of the country and the national territory (military)." Police functions were carried out mainly by the Guardia Civil, whereas those of the military were fulfilled by an undefined "military organization of the Public Force" under the command of an unidentified "Comandancia en Jefe."[26] Costa Rica, therefore, possessed an army in 1955 during the presidential administration of José Figueres, the man who is probably best known for abolishing it in 1948. What it did not have was a force that anyone dared to call an army.

Although not until the late 1970s did a serious public controversy erupt over the degree to which Costa Rica could be said to have an army, it seems clear that, from the beginning of what Figueres grandly chose to call the "Second Republic," the state maintained a military force, and continuously sought to improve its capacity. Costa Rican police and military forces after 1949 were certainly stronger than the pitiful institution that was called an army before 1949.[27]

The rebuilding of the old army was well under way during the administration of President Ulate (1949–53), who turned to the United States to help the government rearm, largely out of fear that Figueres might launch a revolt to take back the presidency should he lose the presidential election scheduled for 26 July 1953. In 1951, Washington agreed to sell the government $500,000 worth of weapons, just as civil war veterans who were allied with Figueres organized a "veterans association" that looked a lot like a *montonera*.[28] By January 1952 Costa Rica's orders for military equipment at the Defense Department had mounted to $830,000.[29]

By then the Ulate government was begging Washington to be admitted to the small circle of Latin American governments authorized to participate in grant military collaboration under the MAP. When the U.S. government demurred on the grounds that Costa Rica had abolished its army, the foreign minister, Fernando Lara Bustamante, hastened to remind the United States of the loophole in Article 12, which allowed for military forces organized for national defense or under a continent-wide treaty. "The Guardia Civil," Lara told ambassador Philip B. Fleming, "could become the main nucleus of an army with a view toward wider objectives than those directed purely at keeping internal public order." Fleming in turn told the State Department not to take too seriously the propaganda about the country without an army. To the Ulate government, he said, "the Costa Rican Guardia Civil is just as much an army as the so-called armies of any of the other Central American Republics, whose real functions are like those of the Guardia Civil here, principally police duties." Fleming, who agreed with Ulate that the Costa Rican Guardia was not very different from the armies of the rest of the isthmus, recommended a grant military agreement, on the following grounds: Costa Rica's proximity to the Panama Canal, its World War II collaboration, its famously democratic culture, and its value as a food producer, "which might be most helpful in time of emergency."[30]

Ulate's fear that Figueres might launch a revolt if he lost the 1953 election went untested, for Figueres swept to victory with 65 percent of the votes. After taking office on 8 November 1953, Figueres continued to press Washington for a grant military agreement, seizing on news of the impending MAP deal with Nicaragua in April 1954 to renew his demand. After the State Department again rejected the Costa Rican request for grant collaboration later that month, the Figueres government accused Washington of siding with Nicaragua in the ongoing conflict between the two countries.[31] In May, Figueres offered the United States $487,734 for 5,000 rifles, 1,230 machine guns, 70 mortars, 10 rocket launchers, and 500 hand grenades, as well as tear gas, trucks, radios, and other equipment and ammunition. The State Department approved, but secretly asked the U.S. Army to delay fulfillment in order to punish Figueres for the support he had provided to the aborted plot to overthrow Somoza on 4 April, and to induce Costa Rica to vote to condemn the Arbenz government at the upcoming OAS meeting.[32]

Figueres, in turn, demonstrated not only that he could grovel as effectively as his rival Somoza, but that even in the country-without-an-army, the government was eager to use news of increased U.S. military collaboration as a sign of its legitimacy. Summoned to a meeting with Figueres, C. Allan Stewart, the interim U.S. chargé d'affaires in San José, reported on 7 May that "it was plain to see that President Figueres realizes he is in the dog-house with the United States. . . . The President was in a greatly chastened mood." Figueres said he needed the weapons as soon as possible to counter opposition rumors that the Washington was unfriendly to him. He also assured Washington of his loyalty and his opposition to communism and the Arbenz government:

> President Figueres was quite grave and he obviously was fully aware that we were suspicious of his ties with Guatemala, else he would not have been so explicit in his message to be relayed to the Department. He appeared very anxious to have some arms delivered to him as soon as possible. . . . He was very explicit in delivering a message, to be forwarded to the Department, that Costa Rica was through with Guatemala. On the basis of the President's demeanor, the Embassy recommended, . . that a token sale of arms be made and that they be shipped immediately. With this gesture, we will see whether the President has perhaps learned that the United States can also play games.[33]

In the OAS, Figueres fully supported the U.S. position against Guatemala. With Somoza threatening to unleash an exile army headed by ex-presidents Calderón and Picado to invade Costa Rica again, the United States duly released the Costa Rican weapons for immediate delivery, in what the U.S. Embassy said a year later was a straightforward quid pro quo. The news was quickly greeted in Costa Rica as evidence of U.S. support for Figueres.[34] The same month, plans for U.S. combat training of Guardia Civil members were released.[35] At the same time, the U.S. Army took steps to help Costa Rica repel an invasion from Nicaragua if Figueres invoked the Rio Treaty; Nicaragua had placed about fifteen hundred "good troops" at the border towns of Rivas and Peña Blanca but the U.S. Army thought Somoza was bluffing.[36] It guessed wrong. On 11 January 1955 ex-president Picado's son Teodoro led five hundred troops into northern Costa Rica, while rebel planes strafed San José and other cities with support from the Nicaraguan Air Force. The OAS sent an investigating committee and on 14 January condemned Nicaraguan support of the rebel invasion. But it was the emergency delivery to Costa Rica on 17 January of four P-51 fighters by the United States that led to the collapse of the invasion before month's end.[37]

The invasion provoked the greatest surge so far in U.S. military collaboration. Telephone equipment, Browning automatic rifles, .50-cal. machine guns, more than a million rounds of rifle ammunition as well as mortar shells, rockets, hand grenades, and parachutes were on the way by January 20.[38] Costa Rica requested a U.S. Air Force mission, and on 26 January even asked to buy enough equipment and weapons to outfit a reinforced infantry battalion in hopes the government would qualify soon for a grant MAP agreement.[39] Although Washington offered to take the F-51s back after the crisis, Costa Rica decided to buy them for $125,000.[40] San José's seven-man U.S. Army mission, which directed the Guardia's training academy, supervised weapons and basic training, and taught small-unit tactics, was now the second-largest in Central America, after Honduras.[41] To the Pentagon, Costa Rica's 1,791-member Guardia Civil qualified as a "military force" but the country had no naval presence at all and no air force, despite its possession of the four P-51s.[42]

Writing five months after the invasion, Humberto Pacheco Coto, the public security minister, reported that the Guardia was gravely underprepared and underequipped for national defense. Many of the troops slept without mattresses and blankets, and some didn't even have uniforms. Vehicles were in such a deplorable state that they cost more to repair than they were worth. Weapons were so old and in such poor condition that no one, he argued, could oppose a program of rearmament. "No country, no matter how peaceful and democratic it may be, can do without the necessary elements for keeping order and assuring the respect, defense and integrity of the national territory." It was utopian to think that "order can be maintained with a moral code in one hand and the Penal Code in the other."[43]

Despite the fact that more than five hundred Guardia troops had received military training in U.S. military schools in the Canal Zone in recent years, it wasn't the Guardia that the government had sent north to stop the invasion force, but a newly organized Reserva Nacional whose volunteers began training in 1954 in response to the invasion threat. The Reserva did almost all the fighting and accounted for nearly all twenty-nine or so combat deaths. By committing volunteers instead of professional soldiers to the front, the government in part sought to sustain the fiction that the country lacked an army, according to U.S. ambassador Robert Woodward. "The volunteers were sent into combat first, for the military purpose of having trained forces in case of more dire emergency and for the political purpose of having a 'citizens' army' to defend the country."[44]

As a result of the war, the Figueres government confessed to Ambassador Woodward that it had "learned sadly of the inadequacies of its regular defense forces and system" and realized that it had to increase the country's military strength. President Figueres wanted one or two MAP infantry battalions but the U.S. ambassador recommended a MAP engineer battalion "as a possible efficient and relatively non-controversial solution to this problem," bearing in mind Costa Rica's "traditional reluctance to build up armed forces" and the possible opposition to Costa Rican grant collaboration by the Nicaraguan and Venezuelan dictatorships. An engineer battalion could maintain the strategically important Inter-American Highway as well as the country's airstrips, thus fulfilling a hemispheric defense mission. Besides, the ambassador added, "Costa Ricans, because of their high average education and high proportion of Spanish stock, have demonstrated that they make unusually able mechanics.... The Bureau of Public Roads of our Government has found that Costa Ricans make as expert operators of heavy and complicated road-building machinery as do United States citizens."[45]

Woodward and the State Department seemed to agree that Costa Rica did not need a U.S.-trained and equipped infantry battalion. And yet a broad consensus among U.S. policy makers that spanned the Embassy and the highest levels of the Washington security establishment agreed that Figueres wasn't taking communism seriously enough—despite the fact that the Partido Vanguardia Popular (PVP), the communist party, had no more than two hundred members; despite Figueres's constant denunciations of communism; and despite the constitutional prohibition of antidemocratic political parties, which effectively outlawed the PVP. "The government," Woodward wrote in April 1955, "should be urged to maintain closer surveillance over communists and prosecute them more vigorously," and should even amend the constitution to "limit the travel of communists, increase penalties for subversive activities" and exclude communists from labor union leadership. This was just the formula that the United States would be urging on the governments of El Salvador and Guatemala in 1957.[46]

Woodward may have had in mind the arrest two months earlier of Alvaro Montero Vega and Arnaldo Zeledón Seballos, caught in the act of printing El Trabajo, the banned organ of the PVP. Zeledón was identified as a member of the shoemakers' union and of "communist cell '22 of May'"; Montero was a student and the founder of the PVP's youth group. Perhaps what disturbed Woodward was that the pair was released on bail, pending a court appearance, after a public campaign on their behalf. The government's security archives for the 1950s indicate that the Guardia's detective bureau kept close watch on suspected communists, as well as *calderonistas* (who were frequently classified with communists), particularly those active in the labor movement.[47] On 28 August 1954, the Guardia's detective bureau, suspecting a general mobilization of subversives, distributed a confidential message to police officials throughout the country, directing them to discreetly undertake a census in their districts of "individuals known to be *calderonista y comunista*."[48]

But if Woodward is to be believed, the surveillance too rarely resulted in prosecution and punishment. A major study of Costa Rican "internal security" by the U.S. Operations Coordinating Board in August 1956 also criticized Figueres for being soft on communism. "While Figueres took drastic action against communists during the revolution of 1948, the attitude of the government toward their suppression is currently somewhat lackadaisical." The Board was particularly puzzled by Figueres's lack of action in "removing communist influences from the labor movement in the banana zones despite reasonably good opportunities to do so." The Board concluded that the Guardia was incapable of detecting and investigating communist activity, that the government lacked the legal authority "to move against communists" and that most Costa Ricans "do not see communism as a menace and are unsympathetic to the use of force by the authorities." Echoing Woodward's ideas, the Board recommended that the United States "convince" the Figueres government to "limit the international movement of communists," "increase penalties for communist activities," "eliminate communists from union leadership" and "restrict communist propaganda."[49]

Apparently having lost patience with Figueres, the State Department informed Woodward in October that the U.S. government was at that moment taking steps to "undermine the principal center of communist strength in Costa Rica, namely the labor movement in the Pacific banana zone of the country," a task that was being handled "here in Washington."[50] At the same time, Woodward was told to encourage the Figueres administration "to request that the United States undertake an overall survey of Costa Rican internal security capabilities," as a step toward police collaboration. "[I]t is the Department's hope that it will be possible to convince the Government of Costa Rica that the strengthening of the capabilities of its internal security forces is in its own interest rather than in that of the United States" and that the Figueres administration would therefore agree to pay part of the costs of the police program. However, Woodward recommended the postponement of a survey until after the 1958 presidential election, because it would be interpreted as U.S. support for the administration's candidate.[51] In any case, Woodward seemed doubtful that any amount of police collaboration "will prevent their [communists'] activities in this respect as long as the legislation of Costa Rica, a country where there is basic respect for legal guarantees, is relatively unrestrictive against the types of activity in which they engage."[52] It was neither the first nor would it be the last time that a U.S. government official implied that Costa Rica might benefit from a hearty dose of authoritarianism, even while publicly praising the country for its exceptionally democratic record.

The Figueres government's repeated attempts to convince Washington to extend to Costa Rica the grant collaboration status enjoyed by the governments of Guatemala, Honduras, and Nicaragua were rejected by the Pentagon in 1957 on the grounds that "the military potential of Costa Rica is not significant." The Caribbean Command in the Canal Zone pointed out that not only was a battalion unnecessary for defense against an internal threat, but "strong popular aversion to mil [military] forces" among Costa Ricans would probably keep the national legislature from approving grant collaboration.[53] Even the Operations Coordinating Board had acknowledged that "the majority of the people are opposed to anything with a militaristic taint, and efforts to increase armed power would be most controversial."[54] But Figueres pressed on with his plan to strengthen the country's military, ordering Lt. Col. Alvaro Arias Gutiérrez, Director General de Intendencia of the Guardia, to set up in July 1957 "Unidades de Combate de la Guardia Civil."[55] At the same time, President Figueres was fending off charges that his party, Liberación Nacional, was training a party militia with government-owned machine guns. The militia was accused variously of preparing to prevent an antigovernment uprising by the Guardia Civil, and to carry out a coup in the event the party lost the 1958 presidential election.[56]

Meanwhile, Costa Rica continued to boast that, as a state without an army, it was unique in the world. Two months after Arias received his orders to create combat units, the UN General Assembly heard the Costa Rican delegate claim, untruthfully, that his country was "a totally disarmed country" and one whose Constitution "forbids the existence of an army." Costa Rica "has seen the miracle of committing to the business of education, of economic development, and of health, what would otherwise go for weapons and the upkeep of armed bodies."[57]

Thus, even while the Figueres government proclaimed to the world its unique success in achieving the miracle of total disarmament, it was quietly pressing the United States for a military collaboration agreement that would have made it one of the strongest military powers in the isthmus. Yet Washington rejected these overtures, in part because it thought Costa Rican public opinion would have disapproved of a military buildup.

Public opinion also seemed to be turning against Figueres, who was accused of having opened Costa Rica to attack by his obsessive hatred of Somoza and his constant intrigues against other Caribbean dictators. Figueres launched such a vindictive campaign against his domestic opponents that it was said to have contributed to the defeat of his own party, Liberación Nacional, in the presidential election of 2 February 1958.[58] The victor, the PUN's Mario Echandi Jiménez, responded to the antimilitary mood by announcing, three weeks after his election, that he intended to abolish the armed forces and sell the country's weapons to invest in agricultural development and health care. He would enforce the constitutional prohibition of an army, he said.[59]

On his post-election pilgrimage to Washington in March, Echandi acknowledged that even though Costa Rica did not have an army the Guardia was somehow over-armed. He told the State Department that "in keeping with Article 12 of the Costa Rican Constitution he desired to get rid of all excess armaments" because the country neither had an army nor wanted one.[60] Initially true to his word, Echandi tried to get the United States to buy about $200,000 worth of military equipment, including weapons, ammunition, two P-51s fighters and M1 rifles, or at least allow Costa Rica to exchange them for $200,000 worth of cars, trucks, radio equipment, airplanes, and uniforms for the Guardia. The Guardia had only six or seven radio-equipped sedans, down from twenty-five a few years ago, and its largest vehicle was a half-ton pick-up truck. The United States rejected the deal as "not practical."[61]

Meanwhile, the communist threat seemed to grow, and in the summer of 1958 the Embassy again recommended heightened collaboration in the identification and surveillance of communists. Even though Costa Rica's "almost 300 active communists" were "mostly professors, students, and intellectuals" and were "noisy, but not violent," they should be taken seriously. Whiting Willauer, the U.S. ambassador, freshly transferred from Honduras, regretted that Costa Rica's "peculiar position of guaranteeing sanctuary to any political refugee" made it "impossible to take strong action against [them] or those which might enter from the outside."[62] Indeed, the mere arrest, interrogation, and expulsion of two Panamanians suspected of being communists had just become a public scandal after top officials of the Ministerio de Seguridad Pública were accused of abusing and humiliating the suspects before deporting them to Panama.[63]

By deporting the Panamanians, the Echandi administration showed a disposition to consider the "strong action" against suspected communists favored by Washington. The United States also dropped its opposition to grant military collaboration, which began in 1960 when the Guardia began to be trained under the MAP. "The majority of training," the Pentagon reported, "has been conducted in the Canal Zone and has been concentrated on intelligence, maintenance, communication, counterinsurgency, and military police type subjects with naval training for boat crews included." In addition, what the Pentagon called "special grants from other U.S. agencies" of $50,000 in 1960 and $25,000 in 1961 provided vehicles and radios for the Guardia, although formal police collaboration would not start until 1964. In 1962, the last year of the Echandi administration, the Guardia began receiving its first grant military equipment. Washington pledged to "make or continue to make available" to Costa Rica defense articles and services "for internal security purposes and for the defense of the Western Hempisphere."[64] And so the status of grant military collaborator that first Ulate and then Figueres had sought was finally achieved during the administration of the president who pledged the definitive abolition of the army that had supposedly been banned in 1948.

In truth, Costa Rica was not and never has been a nation without an army. Perhaps the real Costa Rican novelty was the army's stable subordination to civilian government, an achievement that no Latin American government except for Mexico has been able to claim, before or since 1949.

15

Conclusions

Until 1940, the limits of public violence were shaped with little or no substantive or sustained interference by groups or interests that could be identified as wholly external to Central America. Although some modest Spanish, German, and Chilean military collaboration aided the upward displacement of the agents of public violence into national armed forces, this too was largely an internal process. The exception was Nicaragua, where the United States created the Guardia Nacional in the late 1920s and early 1930s in order to put an end to the country's chronic public violence. Unavailing in its objective, the U.S. effort in Nicaragua instead spawned a state much like that of its northern neighbors—one that succeeded in concentrating a good deal of public violence in the hands of its own agents, even as they continued to operate within the traditionally permissive limits of that violence.

The process of concentration or upward displacement was scarcely a smooth one. Burdened by the legacy of factionalism and personalism, it was subject to frequent disruption and setbacks. Even under the best of political circumstances, the extreme resource limitations of the Central American states invariably undermined their capacity to reliably concentrate and control public violence. As a result, the isthmian states' armed forces had only become weakly institutionalized by the start of World War II. The war heralded a startling acceleration in the pace and thoroughness of the concentration of the disparate sources of institutional public violence into national armies, air forces, and police forces. What brought it on was the sudden intrusion of the U.S. government as a reliable collaborator, for the first time, in the process of upward displacement. Washington in effect stabilized the process by injecting into it U.S. trainers, academy directors, and advisors—agents of the globalization of public violence. They brought modern tools of warmaking tested in battles around the globe, ranging from the mundane (field rations, combat boots, control, and command systems) to the magnificent (field artillery, warplanes, rockets, high-powered rifles). The fragmentation and incoherence of upward displacement were gradually overcome. The process became less vulnerable to the cyclical quirks of destitution and affluence. Directed almost entirely at the institutional agents of public violence, U.S. collaboration surely dampened, at least temporarily, activity by the counterinstitutional agents of public violence (except where they collaborated with the U.S. government, as in Guatemala in 1954), and probably that of its parainstitutional agents as well.

If the exigencies of the world war led to military collaboration between the United States and the Central American states during the conflict, two strategic reasons accounted for its acceleration after the war. The first rested on Pres. James Monroe's doctrine opposing European territorial acquisitions in the New World. Washington feared that, as the globalization of public violence intensified, the absence of a practical U.S. monopoly on military collaboration would open the door to collaboration with one or more of the armed forces of Europe, converting Guatemala, say, into the quasiprotectorate of a nonhemispheric country. The second reason was the desire to establish closer relations with governments that were typically either dominated by the military or subject to some kind of military veto. U.S. access to such governments, and therefore U.S. influence on them, would be improved by long-term collaborative relationships with their armed forces. The wisdom of this logic was confirmed in Guatemala during the Arbenz administration, when Washington maintained its military mission there in order to preserve relations with the armed forces, which eventually acted on behalf of U.S. interests by betraying Arbenz. By maintaining close ties with the Guatemalan high command, Washington probably saved Guatemala the cost of a direct U.S. military intervention to overthrow the president.

A third, tactical reason for the surge in U.S. military and police collaboration was the power it gave Washington to advance short-term U.S. interests by accelerating or diminishing access to the resources it controlled. For example, in roughly the same period, the United States took such action against two antithetical governments, one famous for its servility to U.S. interests and the other for its disdain of those interests. Washington terminated all military collaboration with Nicaragua from 1947 to 1952 in order to signal its dissatisfaction with General Somoza's refusal to give up power, and sharply diminished its collaboration with the Guatemalan government of President Arbenz. Nicaragua remained cloyingly loyal to Washington throughout. But Arbenz seemed not to notice or care, and so in December 1953, in order to further isolate Guatemala politically (but for no military reason at all) President Eisenhower authorized the Pentagon to open grant collaboration talks with El Salvador, Honduras, and Nicaragua. The result was a surge in Honduran military capacity and a big stride forward in Nicaragua's.[1] Similarly, military collaboration with Guatemala intensified in a very public way after the fall of Arbenz in order to increase the legitimacy of Castillo Armas's putschist regime.

Up to about 1960, U.S. military authorities consistently denied any strictly hemispheric-defense rationale for the kind of collaboration that the Central Americans most desired—outright grants of equipment and training resources. Grant collaboration was supposed to be limited to the kind of equipment and training needed to repel an invasion by a nonhemispheric power such as the Soviet Union. Although the Pentagon rarely opposed Central American requests to buy equipment and services, it strongly resisted grant collaboration on the grounds that no amount of U.S. support would ever qualify the isthmian countries for a role in hemispheric defense. The Pentagon grudgingly approved grant collaboration for the political reasons invariably advanced by the State Department.

If Washington was divided about grant collaboration, all of the Central American governments eagerly sought it for the opportunities it presented for the rapid, low-cost transformation of their military forces. They were just as eager to enter into purchase agreements for equipment and training services that were not available through grants, often submitting purchase requests rejected by Washington as excessive. Democrats were no less vulnerable than dictators to the charms of military collaboration with the United States. Not only was Costa Rican opposition to the Arbenz government purchased by a timely U.S. arms transfer, but Costa Rica even begged for one of the U.S.-organized army battalions that had been bestowed, free of charge, on three of its northern neighbors. Only El Salvador's armed forces, acting out of a singular sense of vanity, hesitated, and soon regretted their failure to seize the grant collaboration agreement that had been proffered in 1954.

In the two decades that followed the start of World War II the military and police forces of the Central American states achieved the greatest gains in capacity in their histories, essentially perfecting the upward displacement of state-sponsored violence into national, centralized agencies. The most spectacular gains were in air power, but exponential improvements in mobility, communications, command efficiency, logistics, firepower, and discipline could be found across the four northern countries. Honduras probably registered the most dramatic changes, followed by Guatemala, Nicaragua, and El Salvador, in that order; even Costa Rica benefited from the continuous presence of a U.S. military mission and U.S. government training and weapons sales. (See figures A-7, A-8, and A-9 in the Appendix.) At the same time, through a combination of both U.S. police and military collaboration, all five states began to create agencies capable of specializing in intelligence gathering, surveillance, and record keeping, effectively institutionalizing the primitive spy networks that personalist dictators had been devising since the late nineteenth century.

The degree to which one may attribute these gains to U.S. collaboration is impossible to measure precisely, because it is likely that—in the era of globalization of public violence—some of them would have occurred in the absence of U.S. collaboration. What Washington was in a unique position to bestow was a rough uniformity—modeled, of course, on U.S. practice—in weaponry, training, and organization, not to mention a fairly consistent ideology to justify collaboration. That ideology was of course anticommunism, seasoned by an underlying commitment to liberal democracy that was never taken too seriously either by Washington or its collaborators. This rough regional consistency in technical and ideological matters was nevertheless strongly shaped, in each country, by distinctive historical experiences in state formation and public violence. In Honduras, the new army retained its pre-collaboration association with the Partido Nacional. In Nicaragua the Guardia Nacional's status as the militia of the Partido Liberal was if anything even more obvious in 1960 than it had been in 1940. The transformative impact of collaboration on the Salvadoran armed forces lagged behind the other countries mainly because of the Salvadoran military's initial fear of U.S. domination. In Guatemala, collaborative activities and transfers of all kinds shot up dramatically after June 1954, but with results that frequently baffled and annoyed U.S. military advisers. There, a current of nationalistic animus within the officer corps toward increasing U.S. military collaboration culminated in a coup attempt in 1960. Nowhere in Central America did U.S. military authorities even seek, let alone achieve, control over the military and police agencies of the region's government. Modernization, understood as a level of efficiency more or less congruent with U.S. standards, was mainly what the Pentagon and the State Department wished to achieve. On the way to that goal, the United States frequently met recalcitrance, resentment, footdragging, indifference, and even (in the case of El Salvador) an attempt to play off a Chilean military mission against the U.S. mission. But except for the Arévalo-Arbenz period in Guatemala, Washington never had reason to doubt the loyalty of the isthmian military authorities to the basic U.S. policy of communist containment. The overall relationship, much less than one of U.S. "control" and yet more than the disinterestedness implied by the term "military assistance," was collaborative. The isthmian authorities were never mere clients of the northern colossus.

The results of collaboration, by 1960, were impressive. The armies, air forces, and police agencies of the region were more lethal, more effective, and therefore more threatening to internal and external opponents. The impact of collaboration was heightened because it coincided with a rapid shift among the states of the region toward a much more intrusive role in their societies, decades after a similar shift took place in the bigger countries of Latin America.

But apart from external collaboration—an instance of the general globalization of public violence—an even more fundamental and decisive choice had already been made by the Central Americans themselves without the collaboration of any foreign power. Institutional public violence, concentrated by 1960 within and practically monopolized by what Washington approvingly called "modern" armed forces, continued to be deployed within the generous limits that had been pegged out in the continual remaking of the improvisational states that followed independence in 1821. U.S. government officials always understood that they were collaborating with forces whose range of action vastly exceeded the limits of U.S. public violence. That understanding often slowed the pace and altered the character of collaboration, but it only stopped it once, in Nicaragua in the late 1940s. U.S. military authorities rarely wavered in their single-minded goal of "modernizing" the military and police forces at the command of the Central American states. Nor is there any evidence that Washington's occasional uneasiness with modernizing them ever inspired it to use its power to force the collaborating governments to take concrete steps to reduce the limits of public violence, at least before the 1960s.

By separating the making of the limits of public violence from the capacity to make public violence, I have tried to show how Central Americans and the U.S. government shared responsibility for what happened. The limits of public violence and the capacity to conduct it have always been among the defining features of the state formation process. The extraordinary breadth of the isthmian limits ensured that the leaps in capacity delivered by U.S. collaboration would, in the absence of any serious effort to shrink those limits, intensify and prolong the destruction to come after 1960: the destruction of innocent people above all—a horror in which Guatemala led the way—but also a destruction of opportunities and practices whose cultivation might have led to a dramatic shrinkage in the limits of public violence, of a kind that Costa Rica achieved.

In exploiting the opportunities provided by the globalization of public violence, the governments of all the Central American countries successfully manipulated two persistent U.S. fears: The threat of enemy infiltration (first fascist, later communist) and the threat of isthmian military collaboration with European governments. The purpose of the manipulation was not to drive the United States away from Central America, but to deepen military collaboration with it. Out of the collaboration of the 1940s and 1950s emerged something new—powerful military and police institutions. Yet they continued to act according to norms of public violence that were already familiar by the mid-nineteenth century. The new military authorities of the 1940s and 1950s still demonized their enemies, killed them readily, and held in the coldest contempt the people in whose name they governed. The United States had collaborated in the making of modern armies, in countries where the state formation process had yet to link itself with a coherent, unifying idea of the state, embodied in a sense of nationhood. Except for Costa Rica, the anomaly that had beset the isthmian countries since independence persisted through the Cold War: armies without nations.

In the history of Central American public violence, 1960 marked a turning point. Agents of para-institutional and counterinstitutional violence, by tapping into newly thriving global circuits of public violence, increasingly challenged the dramatic gains in capacity that the institutional agents of violence had begun to achieve during the 1950s. In response, the United States decisively shifted from a collaboration strategy vaguely geared toward overall force modernization, and influenced by World War II assumptions about the need to defend against an attack emanating from the Eurasian landmass, to one focused tightly on combating the counterinstitutional forces that began to proliferate after the success of the Cuban revolution. Public violence intensified markedly compared to the 1940s and 1950s, taking forms rarely seen on the isthmus: urban terrorism, guerrilla warfare, disappearances, and campaigns of rural mass murder carried out by the armed forces and their para-institutional allies. In the 1980s, the U.S. decision to intervene in

Nicaragua with a counterinstitutional force of exiled and displaced Nicaraguans, and in El Salvador with a program of military collaboration that exceeded anything seen since the Vietnam war, intensified the violence. For Washington, the results were yet another instance of "blowback," consequences that were not merely unintended but positively contrary to the highest goals of U.S foreign policy—peace, prosperity, and democracy. The costs to the people of Central America were practically incalculable, whether reckoned in the tens of thousands of lives lost as the victims of public violence, or in the hundreds of thousands displaced by the violence, or in the innumerable ways that the violence set back economic and social welfare.

The era of the globalization of public violence coincided with a four-decade struggle between two incompatible political systems, communism and democracy. The governments of all five Central American countries joined the democratic side, even though democracy was little more than an aspiration for Guatemala, El Salvador, Honduras, and Nicaragua, places where expressions of public violence had already become singularly engrained and habitual, compared to other Latin American countries, by the late nineteenth century. After World War II, the new conditions of international life produced, in all four countries, armies without nations that resisted democracy almost as fervently as they battled communism. A plausible alternative outcome would have required levels of public virtue—courage, insight, vision, and political dexterity—among leaders in both Washington and the capitals of Central America that few societies have been able to summon even under the most favorable circumstances. In that respect, the history of public violence in Central America is unexceptional. Again and again, as this book has shown, isthmian political leaders identified public violence as the great obstacle to every decent political aspiration, and yet seemed unable to overcome it. The first signs of a radical change in that pattern did not begin to appear until the early 1990s. "Why then?" is the subject of another book. In this one I have addressed a more fundamental question: "Why did it take so long?"

STATISTICAL APPENDIX

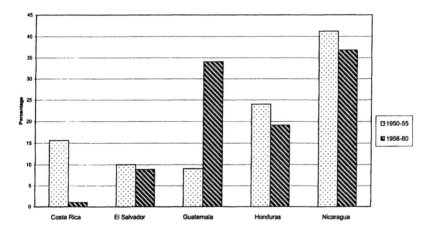

Figure A.1 Shares of Total Deliveries of U.S. Military Goods and Services Compared, 1950–55 and 1956–60, by Country. *Note:* This chart compares the relative distribution among the five countries of total U.S. government military transfers in two periods: 1950–55 and 1956–60. In constant 1990 dollars, the United States delivered $55.3 million in grants and sales over the whole decade. The total of government sales and grants was divided almost perfectly between the two periods, $27.6 million in the first half and $27.8 million in the second. *Source:* Calculations by author, from U.S. Defense Department, "DSAA Fiscal Year Series," 1950–1990, in constant 1990 dollars. Data do not include costs of military missions, which were paid by the host country.

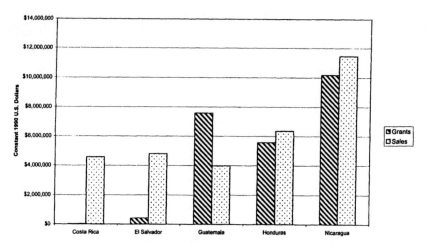

Figure A.2 Value of Deliveries of U.S. Military Goods and Services, Government Sales vs. Grants, 1950–1960, by Country. *Note:* U.S. government grants and sales accounted for virtually all U.S. military transfers of goods and services in this period; a third type, credits, was extended to Guatemala alone ($398,000) in this period. *Source:* Calculations by author, from U.S. Defense Department, "DSAA Fiscal Year Series," 1950–1990, in constant 1990 dollars.

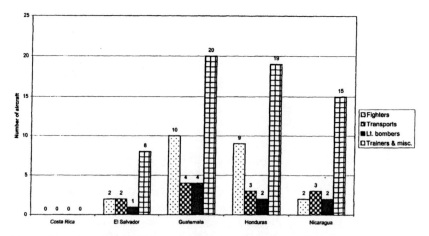

Figure A.3 Operational Military Aircraft, 1954. *Note:* All aircraft were propeller-driven. SOURCE: RTA/FOIA; DDRS (1979/124C),CIA, "National Intelligence Estimate Number 80–54, The Caribbean Republics," 24 Aug. 1954.

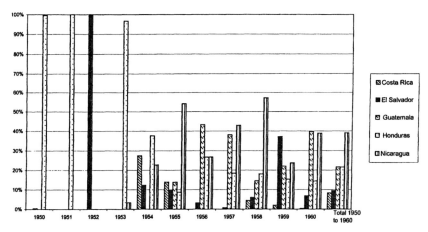

Figure A.4 Annual Shares of Total U.S. Government Military Sales & Grants. *Source:* Calculations by author, from U.S. Defense Department, "DSAA Fiscal Year Series," 1950–1990, in constant 1990 dollars. Data do not include costs of military missions, which were paid by the host country.

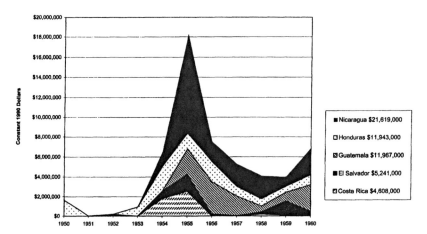

Figure A.5 Total U.S. Government Military Sales and Grants, 1950–1960. *Source:* Calculations by author, from U.S. Defense Department, "DSAA Fiscal Year Series," 1950–90, in constant 1990 dollars. Data do not include costs of military missions, which were paid by the host country.

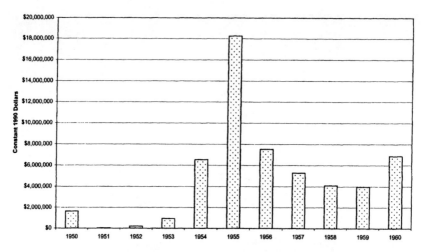

Figure A.6   Annual Totals, U.S. Government Military Sales and Grants. *Source:* Cal-culations by author, from U.S. Defense Department, "DSAA Fiscal Year Series," 1950–1990, in constant 1990 dollars. Data do not include costs of military missions, which were paid by the host country.

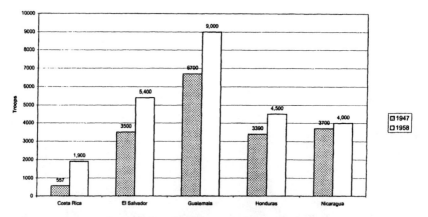

Figure A.7   Ground Force Manpower, 1947–1958. *Notes:* "Ground Troops" included armies and militarized police forces; the only country with naval forces was El Sal-vador, whose naval manpower in 1958 was reported at 162. *Sources:* For 1947, USAMHI/Lib, DA-G2/MSW/Jan 46/Feb 47. "Military Summary of Western Hemi-sphere," War Department, Military Intelligence Division, 23 January 1946. For 1954, DDRS (1979/124C), CIA, "National Intelligence Estimate No. 80–54: The Caribbean Republics," 24 August 1954. For 1958, DDRS (1982/697). White House. "Latin Ameri-can Information," 13 June 1958.

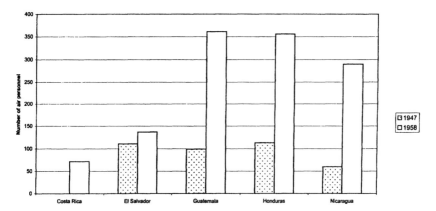

Figure A.8 Air Force Manpower, 1947–58. *Sources:* For 1947, USAMHI/Lib, DA-G2/MSW/Jan 46/Feb 47. "Military Summary of Western Hemisphere," War Department, Military Intelligence Division, 23 January 1946. For 1954, DDRS (1979/124C), CIA, "National Intelligence Estimate No. 80–54: The Caribbean Republics," 24 August 1954. For 1958, DDRS (1982/697). White House. "Latin American Information," 13 June 1958.

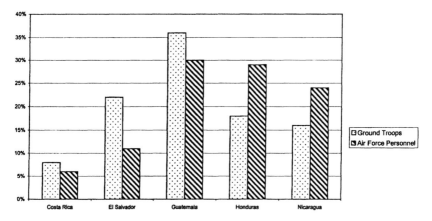

Figure A.9 Relative Shares of Total Ground Troops & Air Force Personnel, 1958. *Notes:* "Ground Troops" included armies and militarized police forces; the only country with naval forces was El Salvador, whose naval manpower in 1958 was reported at 162. *Sources:* For 1947, USAMHI/Lib, DA-G2/MSW/Jan. 46/Feb. 47. "Military Summary of Western Hemisphere," War Department, Military Intelligence Division, 23 January 1946. For 1954, DDRS (1979/124C), CIA, "National Intelligence Estimate No. 80–54: The Caribbean Republics," 24 August 1954. For 1958, DDRS (1982/697). White House. "Latin American Information," 13 June 1958.

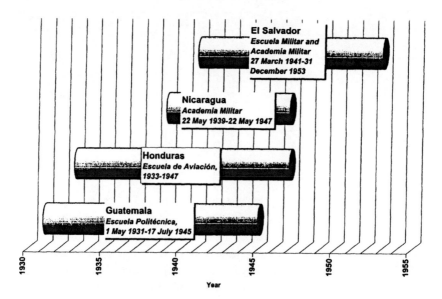

Figure A.10 U.S. Direction of Military Academies

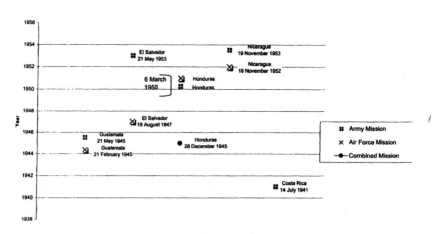

Figure A.11 Founding Dates, U.S. Military Missions. *Sources:* UST. Note: Honduras's combined Army and Aviation Mission agreement expired 28 December 1949, two months before it was replaced with separate army and air force missions.

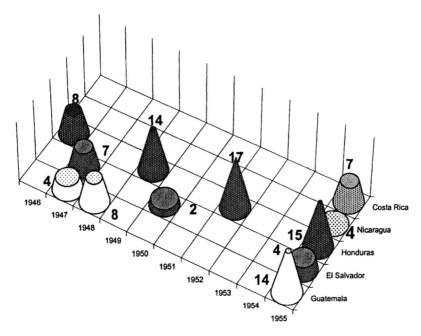

Figure A.12   Changes in U.S. Military Mission Sizes, 1947–55. *Note:* 1946 Honduras includes two aviation specialists. *Sources:* NA, RG218, CCS 092 (8–22–46) (2) Sec. 3, 954–956. Geo. Roderick, assistant secretary of the army, to assistant secretary of defense, 7 February 1955. NA, RG218, CCS 092 (8–22–46) (2) Sec. 3, 954–956. Geo. Roderick, assistant secretary of the army, to assistant secretary of defense, 7 February 1955. AGCA, Min. de Defensa, Legajo 20824. "Organization Chart—U.S. Army Mission to Guatemala—1 November 1948." NA, FOIA, RG 59, 716.56/2–2350. George P. Shaw, U.S. Embassy, San Salvador, to DOS, 23 February 1950. MGES 1947, pp. 21–22. MGH 1945–46, pp. 1–2. MGH 1948–49, pp. 11–13, 67. MGH 1951–52, pp. 24, 44–45.

Table A.1   Guatemalan Police Agencies, 1956

Agency	Manpower	Function
Policía Nacional (more than one-third of force assigned to capital)	3,000	
Guardia de Hacienda (Border Patrol) (directed by army colonel; established in 1955)	663	Stops contraband at borders; investigates illegal immigration, subversion
Departamento de Policía Judicial	184	Gathers intelligence, arrests subversives
Departamento de Seguridad	36	Protects president, gathers intelligence on subversives, arrests subversives
Sección de Defensa Contra Comunismo	30	Investigates communist subversion

Source: NA, RG59, 714.5/6-156, International Cooperation Administration, "Report on the National Police in the Republic of Guatemala," by Fred G. Fimbres, police consultant, 9 April 1956.

Table A.2   Subjects & Hours of
Instruction Taught by U.S. Army Mission
to Officers and NCOs, School of
Application, Honduras, 1951

Subject	Hours
Weapons (bayonet, grenades, bazookas, pistols, carbines, rifles, machine guns and mortars)	292
Physical education	124
Tactics	120
Sports	104
Visual signals and telegraph	93
Soldier training [*escuela del soldado*]	70
Marching	56
Driving and driver training	50
Map reading	50
Military instruction	46
Bivouac	44
Orientation	35
Wire communication	20
Radio	20
Explosive and demolitions	20
Swimming	20
Camouflage	15
Campaign fortifications	15
Mines and obstacles	15
Hygiene and sanitation	15
Personal defense	15
First aid	11
Military justice and military law	10
Administration	10
Chemical warfare	10
Codes and ciphers	10
Transport of sick and wounded	10
Leadership	8
Military courtesy and military ethics	8
Field orders [*órdenes de campo*]	8
Knots and rigging	8
Sentry duties	8
Kitchen management	6
Security	5
Bandaging and splinting	5
Quartermaster operations	4
TOTAL	1,360

Source: NA, RG59, 715.58/7-1851, U.S. Army
Mission Report, Honduras, 9 July 1951.

Table A.3 U.S. Government Military Sales to Honduras, 1952–53

ammunition cartridges	280,000
bayonets	341
binoculars	14
carbines, .30-cal., M1	136
demolition equipment (sets)	10
grenade launchers	48
hand grenades, fragmentation	1,000
machine guns	24
mortar shells	4,300
mortars	10
pistols, automatic, .45-cal.	80
rifle grenades	4,000
rifles	255
rockets	3,000
trucks	67

Source: NA, RG330/21/Honduras, various documents, 1952–53.

NOTES

ABBREVIATIONS

AALCR	République de Costa Rica. Archivo de la Asamblea Legislativa.
AEES	República de El Salvador. Ministerio de Economía, *Anuario estadística*
AGCA	República de Guatemala. Archivo General de Centro América, Guatemala
AGNES	República de El Salvador. Archivo General de la Nacion, San Salvador
AID/Lib	U.S. Agency for International Development, Library, Rosslyn, Va.
AIHN	Archivo del Instituto de Historia de Nicaragua, Universidad Centroamérica, Managua
ANCR	República de Costa Rica. Archivo Nacional, San José
ANH	República de Honduras. Archivo Nacional, Tegucigalpa
ANN	República de Nicaragua. Archivo Nacional, Managua
ARA	Bureau of Inter-American Affairs, U.S. State Department
ASREH	República de Honduras. Archivo de la Secretaría de Relaciones Exteriores, Tegucigalpa
Bevans	*Treaties and other International Agreements of the United States of America 1776–1949*, compiled by Charles I. Bevans. Washington: U.S. Government Printing Office, 1972.
CIA	Central Intelligence Agency
CIEL	República de Honduras. Centro de Informática y Estudios Legislativos, Biblioteca, Congreso Nacional Hondureño (Tegucigalpa)
CONDECA	Consejo de Defensa Centroamericana.
DDRS	Declassified Documents Reference System
FOIA	United States. Released to author via Freedom of Information Act
FRUS	United States. Department of State. *Foreign Relations of the United States*
GPO	Government Printing Office

L	Lejajo
MdeD	Ministerio de Defensa
MGCR	República de Costa Rica. *Memoria* de Guerra
MGES	República de El Salvador. *Memoria* de Guerra
MGG	República de Guatemala. *Memoria* de Guerra
MGH	República de Honduras. *Memoria* de Guerra
MGN	República de Nicaragua.*Memoria* de Guerra.
MGOBH	República de Honduras. *Memoria* de Gobernación
MHH	República de Honduras. *Memoria* de Hacienda
MHI	U.S. Army Military History Institute, Carlisle Barracks, Pa.
MPG	República de Guatemala. *Memoria* de Dirección General de Policía Nacional
MPH	República de Honduras. Mensaje del Presidente.
MRECR	República de Costa Rica. *Memorias* del Ministerio de Relaciones Exteriores y de Culto
MS	Microfiche Supplement
MSEG	República de El Salvador. *Memoria* de Guerra/Defensa
MSP	Mutual Security Program
MSPCR	República de Costa Rica. *Memoria* de Seguridad Pública
NA	United States. National Archives, Washington, D.C.
NAMP	National Archives Microfilm Publications
NYT	*New York Times*
OMA	Office of Military Assistance
OPS	Office of Public Safety
RG	Record Group
SP	Seguridad Pública
USAm	U.S. Ambassador
USEm	U.S. Embassy
USS	*United States Statutes at Large.* Washington, D.C.: Government Printing Office.
UST	Department of State. *United States Treaties and Other International Agreements.* Washington, D.C.: Government Printing Office, 1952.
WNRC	United States. National Archives, Washington National Records Center, Suitland, Md.

INTRODUCTION

1. Raymond Grew, "On the Prospect of Global History," in Bruce Mazlish and Ralph Buultjens, eds., *Conceptualizing Global History* (Boulder, Colo.: Westview Press, 1993), 238.

2. Bruce Mazlish, "An Introduction to Global History," in Mazlish and Ralph Buultjens, eds., *Conceptualizing Global History* (Boulder, Colo.: Westview Press, 1993), 4.

3. Jan Aart Scholte's dictum neatly synthesizes this point of view: "There are no separate local, national and international societies; there is only a world society with local, national and international dimensions." *International Relations of Social Change* (Buckingham, UK: Open University Press, 1993), 27.

4. State formation has been, according to Bruce Buzan, a "massive dialectic" linking both domestic and international forces. Likewise, Anthony Giddens argued that states sought to consolidate power internally to "cope with the vast international political network" of modern state relations. Buzan, *People, States and Fear: An Agenda for International Security Studies in the Post-Cold War Era*, 2d ed. (Boulder, Colo.: Lynne Rienner, 1991), 60–61; Giddens, *A Contemporary Critique of Historical Materialism*, vol. 2, *The Nation-State and Violence* (Berkeley: University of California Press, 1987), 256, 263–64.

5. J. H. Hexter attributed his famous distinction between historians who were "splitters" (those who emphasize distinctions) and "lumpers" (who emphasize connections and similarities) to Donald Kagan in J. H. Hexter, *On Historians* (Cambridge, Mass.: Harvard University Press, 1979), 241–42, though the idea goes back at least to Francis Bacon's parable of the ant, the spider, and the bee: "Those who have handled sciences have been either men of experiment or men of dogmas. The men of experiment are like the ant, they only collect and use; the reasoners resemble spiders, who make cobwebs out of their own substance. But the bee takes a middle course: it gathers its material from the flowers of the garden and of the field, but transforms and digests it by a power of its own. Not unlike this is the true business of philosophy." Francis Bacon, *Novum Organum* (1620), §95. Splitters are likely to remind us of Bacon's spiders; lumpers of his ants. To the inevitable charge of excessive lumpiness in my construction of "public violence," I urge (in hope of being classed with the bees) a careful consideration of the evidence presented in the next fifteen chapters.

CHAPTER 1

1. "Reflections on Violence in the United States," in Hofstadter and Michael Wallace, eds., *American Violence: A Documentary History* (New York: Alfred A. Knopf, 1970), 4.

2. Anthony Giddens, *A Contemporary Critique of Historical Materialism*, vol. 1, *Power Property and the State* (Berkeley: University of California Press, 1981), 177.

3. The "ultimate units of the great society of all mankind are not states (or nations, tribes, empires, classes or parties) but individual human beings, which are permanent and indestructible in a sense in which groupings of them of this or that sort are not." *The Anarchical Society: A Study of Order in World Politics* (New York: Columbia University Press, 1977), 21.

4. By patrimonialism and patrimonial institutions I mean, broadly, sociopolitical practices that depend on a particularistic interpretation of power. Practices that associate power exclusively with a person, rather than an office temporarily occupied by a functionary who exercises that power according to rational-legal or bureaucratic norms, would be an example. The distinction, of course, derives from Max Weber's ideal typology of the forms of "legitimate domination"; see Weber, *Economy and Society: An Outline of Interpretive Sociology*, ed. Guenther Roth and Claus Wittich (Berkeley: University of California Press, 1978), I:231–32. I include, as manifestations of patrimonalism, patron-client relationships and their specifically Latin American variant, *caudillismo*. For a concise theoretical and empirical treatment of patrimonialism as an element of Spanish colonial political culture, see Jorge I. Domínguez, *Insurrection or Loyalty: The Breakdown of the Spanish American Empire* (Cambridge, Mass.: Harvard University Press, 1980), especially 13–15. In Jeremy Adelman's taxonomy of three principal "colonial legacy" narratives, the survival of colonial-era patrimonialism would be a "reconstituted legacy," one in which a break occurs that, although giving rise to certain changes, cannot "demolish old structures"; Adelman, "Introduction: The Problem of Persistence in Latin American History," in Adelman, *Colonial Legacies: The Problem of Persistence in Latin American History* (New York: Routledge, 1999), 10. Guillermo O'Donnell highlighted the persistence of "clientelism, patrimonialism, and corruption" and the personalization of power during the democratic transitions of the 1990s in "Delegative Democracy," *Journal of Democracy* 5 (January 1994) 1:59, 66.

5. Only a hint of that potential for violence is offered in the classic theoretical treatment of *caudillismo* by Eric R. Wolf and Edward C. Hansen. They affirmed that *caudillo* leadership rested heavily on the demonstration of masculinity, which they defined as two closely related attributes: the domination of females and the readiness to deploy violence; see Eric R. Wolf and Edward C. Hansen, "*Caudillo* Politics: A Structural Analysis," *Comparative Studies in Society and History*, vol. 9 (January 1967) 2:174, 177.

6. Historians of the twentieth century increasingly highlight the period's comparative brutality. For the global contours of the great killing, see Eric Hobsbawn, *The Age of Extremes: A History of the World, 1914–1991* (New York: Pantheon, 1994), ch. 1. Omer Bartov brilliantly linked Europe's perfection of "industrial killing" to another of Europe's great gifts, the Enlightenment; see *Murder in Our Midst: The Holocaust, Industrial Killing, and Representation* (New York: Oxford University Press, 1996).

7. Giddens, *Nation-State and Violence*, 4–5. Albrecht and Kaldor put a finer point on Giddens's claim: "Through the twentieth century, the development of the armed forces proceeded alongside the development of the arms industry. Each weapons system was the product of a particular company and the centre of a military unit. The manufacturing capabilities of a company were at one and the same time the performance characteristics of a weapons system and the operational doctrine of a military unit. The relationship between different military units exactly paralleled the structure of industry." Ulrich Albrecht and Mary Kaldor, "Introduction," in Mary Kaldor and Asbjorn Eide, eds., *The World Military Order: The Impact of Military Technology on the Third World* (London: Macmillan, 1979), 11.

8. Buzan, *People, States and Fear*, 59, made the point in just these terms. Charles Tilly's reference to "state-sponsored and state-seeking violence," evidently intended to capture the rough equivalence of these two types of public violence as they are experienced by their victims, implied the existence of the field of state-associated violence that I am proposing here; "State-Incited Violence, 1900–1999," Working Paper No. 177, Center for Studies of Social Change, New School for Social Research (December 1993), 3. Giddens pointed out that armed groups of all kinds "are almost always oriented to the assumption of state power, either by taking over an existing state's territory or by dividing up a territory and establishing a separate state. Such organizations do not and cannot 'opt out' from involvement in state power one way or another as frequently happened" in the pre-modern era; *Nation-State and Violence*, 121.

9. In social theory the concept of field is most closely associated today with Pierre Bourdieu. Rejecting the use of the word "apparatus" to refer to the state, owing to that term's mechanistic implications, Bourdieu specifically identified the state as an example of a "field," a place where "agents and institutions constantly struggle, according to the regularities and the rules constitutive of this space of play." Bourdieu and Loïc J. D. Wacquant, *An Invitation to Reflexive Sociology* (Chicago: University of Chicago, 1992), 102, 110, but see the discussion at 94–114. Also see, in the same volume, Wacquant's interpretation of a field as both a "relational configuration" and "a space of conflict and competition," in "The Structure and Logic of Bourdieu's Sociology," 17. For another reference to the state as an "arena," see Charles Bright and Susan Harding, "Processes of Statemaking and Popular Protest: An Introduction," in Bright and Harding, *Statemaking and Social Movements: Essays in History and Theory* (Ann Arbor: University of Michigan Press, 1984), 2–5.

10. By "violence" I mean physical harm inflicted on people or their property; for a discussion of Latin American politics and violence in these terms, see Torcuato S. DiTella, *Latin American Politics: A Theoretical Framework* (Austin: University of Texas Press, 1990), 76–79.

11. The sharpshooter who picks off total strangers, such as Charles Whitman did on the campus of the University of Texas in 1966, must be considered an agent of public violence, as were the Littleton, Colorado boys who gunned down their classmates in 1999, the anti-technology package-bomber who picked his victims in the 1970s and 1980s, and the bombers of the Oklahoma City Federal Building in 1995. Whether serial killers, who also pick on strangers but whose performance is considerably less public than the above examples, are acting as agents of public or private violence may be debated. Serial killers are in some respects like the death-squad killers; although the latter clearly operate in the public sphere of violence, they may also share the instincts and motivations of a "private" pathological killer. But this is just where the boundary between public and private begins to break down, as all theoretical

boundaries must, though Riane Eisler erred in claiming that the distinction between "private and public violence" is "absurd"; see her "Human Rights and Violence: Integrating the Public and Private Spheres," in Jennifer Turpin and Lester R. Kurtz, eds., *The Web of Violence: From Interpersonal to Global* (Urbana: University of Illinois Press, 1997), 163.

12. Camacho's definition of "public violence" highlights ideology, identifying its agents as acting in the name of forces that are committed to either defending or attacking a particular "social order." See his "Public and Private Dimensions of Urban Violence in Cali," in Charles Bergquist et al., ed., *Violence in Colombia: The Contemporary Crisis in Historical Perspective* (Wilmington, Del.: Scholarly Resources, 1992), 241–60. For a finely argued distinction between collective and private violence, see John Ladd, "The Idea of Collective Violence," in James B. Brady and Newton Garver, eds., *Justice, Law, and Violence* (Philadelphia: Temple University Press, 1991), 22–24.

13. Richard Maxwell Brown, *Strain of Violence: Historical Studies of American Violence and Vigilantism* (Oxford: Oxford University Press, 1975), vii; of course, Brown went on to argue that violence has nevertheless been a "major aspect" of U.S. history. Hofstadter recognized the comparative implications, arguing that while violent episodes were frequent and commonplace in the history of the United States, in a world-historical perspective, they were circumscribed in character and limited in scale, except for the Civil War; "Reflections," 7, 10. Insurrectionary challenges to the U.S. political system have been extremely rare.

14. One important exception, Patricia Alvarenga, *Cultura y ética de la violencia: El Salvador, 1880–1932* (San José, Costa Rica: EDUCA, 1996) will be discussed in chapter 2. On a continental scale, a few recent contributions qualify as partial exceptions. Fernando López-Alves discussed the role of war—particularly what he called "guerrilla war"—in *State Formation and Democracy in Latin America, 1810–1900* (Durham, N.C.: Duke University Press, 2000), attributing differences in the outcomes of state formation in some South American countries in part to the type of wars that the states undertook. The universal tension between coercion and consensus in state making provided the main theme for a collection of essays edited by Riccardo Forte and Guillermo Guajardo, *Consenso y Coacción: Estado e instrumentos de control político y social en México y América Latina (siglos XIX y XX)* (Pedregal de Santa Teresa, Mexico: El Colegio de México, 2000). Miguel Angel Centeno, *Blood and Debt: War and the Nation-State in Latin America* (University Park: Pennsylvania State University, 2002), argued that the scarcity of international wars among Latin American states explains their organizational and ideological weakness, which in turn explains the relatively high level of what the author calls "domestic strife" within their jurisdictions (66). Mere deductive logic rather than historical research seems to have led Centeno to the conclusion that "domestic strife" is just what happens when you don't have a strong state. As a result, what he rather casually dismissed as "domestic strife" led him to understate or to ignore altogether its significance, and may have drawn him into making the incoherent claim that "political violence in Latin America has been relatively muted" (7–8) *and* that "Latin America has experienced much internal or civil conflict" (61). See my discussion in chapter 2 of "war as a way of life" in Central America.

15. For an example drawn from the historiography of El Salvador, see Hector Lindo-Fuentes, *Weak Foundations: The Economy of El Salvador in the Nineteenth Century* (Berkeley: University of California Press, 1990), 4–5, 83, 97–98.

16. Norbert Elias, *The Germans: Power Struggles and the Development of Habitus in the Nineteenth and Twentieth Centuries*, ed. Michael Schröter, trans. by Eric Dunning and Stephen Mennell. (New York: Columbia University Press, 1996), 216.

17. Elias, *The Germans*, 218–20.

18. The formulation is in Buzan, *People, States and Fear*, chapter 2, whose theory seems to underlie the analysis of state weakness and violence by T. David Mason and Dale A. Krane,

"The Political Economy of Death Squads: Toward a Theory of the Impact of State-Sanctioned Terror," *International Studies Quarterly* 33 (1989): 177–78. Buzan's theory also lurks behind Carol Smith's claim that the repressive Guatemalan state of the 1980s, although "stronger" than its predecessors was "weak with respect to ideological (hegemonic) control"; "Conclusion: History and Revolution in Guatemala," in Carol A. Smith, ed., *Guatemalan Indians and the State: 1540 to 1988* (Austin: University of Texas Press, 1990), 282. Evelyne Huber's masterly analysis of the relational, contingent, and highly complex character of state strength should discourage all but the most obstinate reductionists; see her "Assessments of State Strength," in Peter H. Smith, ed., *Latin America in Comparative Perspective: New Approaches to Methods and Analysis* (Boulder, Colo.: Westview Press, 1995), 163–94.

19. Youssef Cohen, Brian R. Brown, and A. F. K. Organski, "The Paradoxical Nature of State Making: The Violent Creation of Order," *American Political Science Review* 75 (December 1981) 4:901–10.

20. It was precisely Centeno's refusal in *Blood and Debt* to lift his gaze beyond the state apparatus, to consider the existence of a field of state power that embraces nonstate agents, and to define the problem not as state but *public* violence, that drew him into the contradictory position noted above, and that undercut his analysis of state formation.

21. The typology of public violence presented here was derived in part from the work of two Colombian social scientists, Carlos Medina Gallego and Mireya Téllez Ardila, *La violencia parainstitucional paramilitar y parapolicial en Colombia* (Bogotá, Colombia: Rodríguez Quito Editores, 1994), 45–46; 39.

22. Between 1966 and 1968 no fewer than twenty-three "grupos paramilitares y irregulares" were operating in Guatemala *against* the guerrilla insurgency led by the Fuerzas Armadas Revolucionarias, but it was hard to distinguish between those that were merely specialized commando groups operating within the armed forces, "which seemed to compete with each other," on the one hand, and "groups organized by parties and forces of the right" that operated more or less independently of the armed forces, on the other hand. It seems likely that the very haziness of their identity, and the ambiguity of their affiliation with the state, further enhanced the climate of terror that they sought to induce. Gabriel Aguilera Peralta and Jorge Romero Imery et al., *Dialéctica del Terror en Guatemala* (San José, Costa Rica: Editorial Universitaria Centroamericana, 1981), 115–16, 125.

23. This situation is comparable to that faced by what Giddens called the premodern or "traditional," state, where "it is almost always the case that significant elements of actual or potential military power exist outside the control of the central state apparatus," in the form of "decentralized military power wielded by local warlords or various sorts of insurrectionary leaders," not to mention robbers and armed tribal groups; *Nation-State and Violence*, 57.

24. This taxonomy draws on, while revising, the model in Michael Mann, *The Sources of Social Power*, vol. 1, *A History of Power from the Beginning to a.d. 1760* (Cambridge: Cambridge University Press, 1986), 2, 6, 30 and vol. 2, *The Rise of Classes and Nation-States, 1760–1914* (Cambridge: Cambridge University Press, 1993), 1–3. The typographical omission of the words "they are economic, ideological and political" in the sentence beginning "Among Marxists" (10, vol. 1) was acknowledged by Mann in e-mail correspondence, 29 April 1998, with the author.

25. Alan Knight showed how class identity sometimes did and did not count in the unfolding of the Mexican Revolution of 1910–20, an exceptionally violent conflict often carelessly oversimplifed in class terms. The variety of coalitions, alliances, and divisions, within and between "classes," was staggering to behold. *The Mexican Revolution* (Cambridge: Cambridge University Press, 1986), vol. 1, 43–44; vol. 2, 263–64, 270. Donna Yashar makes a similar point for the period of radical reform in Costa Rica that began in 1941 and culminated in the 1948 civil war and the founding of the Second Republic; *Demanding Democracy: Reform and*

Reaction in Costa Rica and Guatemala, 1870s–1950s (Stanford, Calif.: Stanford University Press, 1997).

26. Aguilera Peralta and Romero, *Dialéctica*, 114. The authors of this now-classic study of Guatemalan violence were themselves the victims of the state-sponsored violence they documented and analyzed. Romero, a prominent member of the social science faculty of the Universidad de San Carlos, was kidnapped by a Guatemalan army unit on 14 March 1981; his body was found two months later. In February, another researcher, Guillermo Monzón Paz, was killed. The Guatemala City building housing the Centro de Investigación y Documentación Centroamericano, which sponsored the project, was destroyed and a number of other collaborating researchers were killed; *Dialéctica*, 38, 41.

27. David Stoll, *Between Two Armies: In the Ixil Towns of Guatemala* (New York: Columbia University Press, 1993), 278–79.

28. Carlos M. Vilas, "Family Affairs: Class, Lineage and Politics in Contemporary Nicaragua," *Journal of Latin American Studies* 24 (May 1992) 2:309–41; for resistance to the revolution by the poor and lowly, see Charles R. Hale, *Resistance and Contradiction: Miskitu Indians and the Nicaraguan State, 1894–1987* (Stanford, Calif.: Stanford University Press, 1994), chapters 6–8, and Timothy C. Brown, *The Real Contra War: Highlander Peasant Resistance in Nicaragua* (Norman: University of Oklahoma Press, 2001). Jeffrey L. Gould, *To Die in This Way: Nicaraguan Indians and the Myth of Mestizaje, 1880–1965* (Durham, N.C.: Duke University Press, 1998), 283, cited the "massive disaffection of the indigenous peoples" as a source of the counterrevolution.

29. The point was made in Anton Blok's reply to Hobsbawm's social banditry thesis; see "The Peasant and the Brigand: Social Banditry Reconsidered," *Comparative Studies in Society and History* 14 (September 1972) 4:496.

30. For an attempt to reconcile class and personalism, see Peter Flynn, "Class, Clientelism, and Coercion: Some Mechanisms of Internal Dependency and Control," *Journal of Commonwealth and Comparative Politics* 12 (July 1974) 2:133–56.

31. Roberto A. DaMatta, "For an Anthropology of the Brazilian Tradition; or 'A Virtude está no Meio,'" in Hess, *Brazilian Puzzle*, 276–77. For an overview of DaMatta's work, see "Introduction," in David J. Hess and Roberto A. DaMatta, eds., *The Brazilian Puzzle: Culture on the Borderlands of the Western World* (New York: Columbia University Press, 1995), 1–30.

32. Roberto Kant de Lima, "Bureaucratic Rationality in Brazil and in the United States: Criminal Justice Systems in Comparative Perspective," in Hess, *Brazilian Puzzle*, 259, 245.

33. Kant de Lima, "Bureaucratic Rationality," 246. Laura Kalmanowiecki insightfully links police corruption and violence in "Police, People, and Preemption in Argentina," in Martha K. Huggins, ed., *Vigilantism and the State in Modern Latin America* (New York: Praeger, 1991), 47–60.

34. Richard Morse, *New World Soundings: Culture and Ideology in the Americas* (Baltimore, Md.: Johns Hopkins University Press, 1989), 98–106; this argument refines the "cultural" interpretation that Morse had been elaborating since at least the mid-1960s; see, for example, "The Heritage of Latin America" in Louis Hartz, ed., *The Founding of New Societies: Studies in the History of the United States, Latin America, South Africa, Canada, and Australia* (New York: Harcourt, Brace and World, 1964), 123–77, which anticipated (175) Kant de Lima's interpretation of law, cited above, and applied it to all of Latin America. Among the political scientists who have most enthusiastically developed Morse's cultural argument is Howard Wiarda, "Toward a Model of Social Change and Political Development in Latin America: Summary, Implications, Frontiers," in Wiarda, ed., *Politics and Social Change in Latin America: The Distinct Tradition*, 2d ed. (Amherst: University of Massachusetts Press, 1982), 329–59. Also see Glen Caudill Dealy, who traced the *caudillo*'s ability to "to use force with a good conscience" to

a Thomistic "dual morality" and Claudio Véliz, who located Latin America's political culture in a centralist tradition stemming from the Counter-Reformation; Dealy, *The Latin Americans: Spirit and Ethos* (Boulder, Colo.: Westview Press, 1992), 24; Véliz, *The New World of the Gothic Fox: Culture and Economy in English and Spanish America* (Berkeley: University of California Press, 1994), 210.

35. Gabriel A. Almond, "Foreword: The Return to Political Culture," in Larry Diamond, ed., *Political Culture and Democracy in Developing Countries* (Boulder, Colo.: Lynne Rienner, 1993), ix–xi. Political culture as a "historical creation," and its reciprocal relationship with political action, were stressed by Keith Baker, "Introduction," *Inventing the French Revolution: Essays on French Political Culture in the Eighteenth Century* (Cambridge: Cambridge University Press, 1990), 10 . Ruth Lane analyzed the application of the concept since its introduction in 1956 by Almond, favorably assessing its utility for integrating "the sociological and the individual" in "Political Culture: Residual Category or General Theory," *Comparative Political Studies,* 25 (October 1992) 3:362–87. Also see Ann Swidler, "Culture in Action: Symbols and Strategies," *American Sociological Review* 51 (April 1986) 2:284; Harry Eckstein, "A Culturalist Theory of Political Change," *American Political Science Review* 82 (September 1988) 3:789–803; Alicia Hernández Chávez, *La tradición republicana del buen gobierno* (Mexico City: El Colegio de México, 1993), 9; Norbert Lechner, "La democratización," in Lechner, *Cultura política y democratización* (Santiago, Chile: CLASCO, 1987), 253–54 and Lechner, "Presentación," idem., 7–9; Brian Loveman, *The Constitution of Tyranny: Regimes of Exception in Spanish America* (Pittsburgh: University of Pittsburgh Press, 1993), 63.

36. Comisión Especial del Senado sobre las Causas de la Violencia y Alternativas de Pacificación en el Perú, *Violencia y pacificación* (Lima, Peru: División de Impresiones y Publicaciones del Diario de los Debates del Senado, 1989), 34, 124, 39, 43.

37. Enrique Mayer, "Patterns of Violence in the Andes," *Latin American Research Review* 29 (1994) 2:143–44.

38. James B. Greenberg, *Blood Ties: Life and Violence in Rural Mexico* (Tucson: University of Arizona Press, 1989).

39. Mann, *History of Power*, vol. 1, 26.

40. Christopher Clapham, *Third World Politics: An Introduction* (Madison: University of Wisconsin Press, 1985), 48.

41. Octavio Paz, *The Labyrinth of Solitude: Life and Thought in Mexico*, trans. Lysander Kemp (New York: Grove Press, 1961), 122–23.

42. The notion of disguise was highlighted by Medard in his analysis of the African neopatrimonial regime, which "dissimulates the private while simulating the public," privatizing the public and thus making politics a kind of private business. Jean-Francois Medard, "The Underdeveloped State in Tropical Africa: Political Clientelism or neo-patrimonialism?" in Christopher Clapham, ed., *Private Patronage and Public Power: Political Clientelism in the Modern State* (New York: St. Martin's Press, 1982), 181.

43. François-Xavier Guerra, *México: Del Antiguo Régimen a la Revolución*, vol. 1 (Mexico: Fondo de Cultura Económica, 1985), 201–2; also see the analysis of the range of personal ties and the role of "las clientelas," 145–57.

44. Marie-Danielle Demélas-Bohy, "Pactismo y Constitucionalismo," in A. Annino et al., eds., *De los Imperios a las Naciones: Iberoamérica* (Zaragoza, Spain: Ibercaja, 1994), 510; Francois-Xavier Guerra," The Spanish-American Tradition of Representation and its European Roots," in *Journal of Latin American Studies* 26 (February 1994) 1:1–36.

45. F.-X. Guerra and M.-D. Demélas-Bohy, "The Hispanic Revolutions: The Adoption of Modern Forms of Representation in Spain and America, 1808–1820," in Eduardo Posada-Carbó, *Elections before Democracy: The History of Elections in Europe and Latin America* (Houndmills, UK: Macmillan, 1996), 56–57.

46. A pact, or what Hinkelammert called a "concertación," identifies as mere "opponents" those who make the pact, but it also identifies, often specifically, precisely who is the "enemy," in other words, "aquél que se opone al propio sistema social." Franz Hinkelammert, "El concepto de lo político según Carl Schmitt," in Norbert Lechner, comp. *Cultural política y democratización* (Santiago, Chile: CLACSO, 1987), 235–36.

47. Party affiliation became more and more important in determining the identity of local office holders as kinship became less important. The local notable's power increasingly came to depend on his connections in the capital city. There was a blend, therefore, of partisanship and kinship in the structuring of administration opportunities, with the former more important in the later periods, the latter in the early periods and in the more geographically marginal regions. Fernando Uricoechea, *The Patrimonial Foundations of the Brazilian Bureaucratic State* (Berkeley: University of California Press, 1980), 52–57.

48. For studies of political banditry in three very different settings, but which reveal remarkably similar patterns in the way regional power holders sought out and utilized bandit groups, see Michael J. Schroeder, "Horse Thieves to Rebels to Dogs: Political Gang Violence and the State in the Western Segovias, Nicaragua, in the Time of Sandino, 1926–1934," *Journal of Latin American Studies* 28 (May 1996) 2:383–434; Anton Blok, *The Mafia of a Sicilian Village, 1860–1960: A Study of Violent Peasant Entrepreneurs* (New York: Harper Torchbooks, 1974); Roderick Aya, "The Missed Revolution: The Fate of Rural Rebels in Sicily and Southern Spain 1840–1950," *Papers on European and Mediterranean Societies*, 3 (Amsterdam: Anthropologisch-Sociologisch Centrum, 1975), 40–45; and Phil Billingsley, *Bandits in Republican China* (Stanford, Calif.: Stanford University Press, 1988).

49. Graham's study is a brilliant exception to the general lack of attention paid to the role of patronage networks in the history of Latin America; *Patronage and Politics in Nineteenth Century Brazil* (Stanford, Calif.: Stanford University Press, 1990), 78, 122–23, 133, 145. For examples of similar studies that followed his, see Eduardo Posada-Carbó, "Elections and Civil Wars in Nineteenth-Century Colombia: The 1875 Presidential Campaign," *Journal of Latin American Studies* 26 (October 1994) 3:635; Vincent C. Peloso, "Liberals, Electoral Reform, and the Popular Vote in Mid-Nineteenth-Century Peru," in Peloso and Barbara A. Tenenbaum, eds., *Liberals, Politics and Power: State Formation in Nineteenth-Century Latin America* (Athens: University of Georgia Press, 1996), 186–211; Jorge Basadre, *Elecciones y Centralismo en el Perú: Apuntes para un esquema histórico* (Lima, Peru: Centro de Investigaciones de la Universidad del Pacífico, 1980), 29–30; Paula Alonso, "Voting in Buenos Aires, Argentina, Before 1912," in Eduardo Posada-Carbó, *Elections before Democracy: The History of Elections in Europe and Latin America* (Houndmills, UK: Macmillan, 1996), 181–200.

50. David Nugent, *Modernity at the Edge of Empire: State, Individual, and Nation in the Northern Peruvian Andes, 1850–1935* (Stanford, Calif.: Stanford University Press, 1997), 309–13.

51. "Corporatism" refers to the tendency to see society and therefore the polity as a community organized according to "natural" assocations of individuals, as opposed to liberalism's interpretation of society as a mass of individuals with distinctive personal interests and goals. In a classic essay, James M. Malloy joined theories of economic dependency and populist politics to attribute the surge of authoritarian military regimes in the 1960s to a corporatist tradition; see his "Authoritarianism and Corporatism in Latin America: The Modal Pattern," in Malloy, ed., *Authoritarianism and Corporatism in Latin America* (Pittsburgh: University of Pittsburgh Press, 1977), 3–22. Also see, in the same collection, Simon Schwartzmann's "Back to Weber: Corporatism and Patrimonialism in the Seventies," 89–108, which wisely cautioned against a tendency to use these concepts in a way that defined them as essential and unchanging features of a "traditional" Latin American culture.

52. This, he pointed out, is why the "pluralist" or "class" models of politics don't work well in analyzing Latin American politics, and why concepts like "corporatism" and "clien-

telism" are so useful in analyzing the vertical relationships that result; Douglas A. Chalmers, "The Politicized State in Latin America" in Malloy, ed., *Authoritarianism and Corporatism,* 30–35.

53. Hinting at the connection, Giddens observed that patrimonial power in the "traditional" or premodern (i.e., noncapitalist) state "is inherently unstable for the individuals involved, resting as it does upon personal affiliation and kinship relations. Murder, loss of favor, punishment for incompetence or corruption, all these make for a volatile distribution of authority within the higher echelons of the state apparatus and the military"; Giddens, *Nation-State and Violence,* 78.

54. Uricoechea, *Patrimonial Foundations,* 163–64. Uricoechea, however, resorted to the mechanistically deductive claim that the Brazilian tendency to interpret legal redress as vengeance "began to yield, of course, with the gradual development of organic solidarity, which was maturing along with the bourgeois organization of society." He thus seemed to be closing the door to the possibility that patrimonialism may have coexisted with "bourgeois organization," which is the more persuasive claim of DaMatta.

55. Gonzalo Sánchez, G. and Donny Meertens, *Bandoleros, gamonales y campesinos: El caso de la violencia en Colombia* (Bogotá, Colombia: El Ancora Editores, 1983), 48, 52.

56. Chasteen, *Heroes on Horseback: A Life and Times of the Last Gaucho Caudillos* (Albuquerque: University of New Mexico Press, 1995), ch. 13; quote at 141.

57. Posada-Carbó, "Elections and Civil Wars," 645.

58. John D. Kelly, "Diaspora and World War, Blood and Nation in Fiji and Hawaii," *Public Culture* 7 (1995):477, 489.

59. In 1966, just as the trickle of U.S. scholarly output on the Latin American military was about to metamorphose into a cascade, L. N. McAlister complained that too many U.S. scholars regarded the Latin American militaries as "alien and sinister forces existing outside the body social and politic which did not interact with civilian groups and sectors but acted independently through conspiracies organized by greedy and ambitious generals and colonels or by narrow and selfish military cliques." Two decades later, Abraham F. Lowenthal noted approvingly that since McAlister's critique, scholars had "increasingly recognized that the armed forces and civilian politics were often closely intertwined," and that the "armed forces interact continuously with the other elements in Latin American societies." To insist, however, that the militaries have always "interacted" with other "groups" in society is to emphasize in a different way the military's extraneous character, which is what much of the scholarship has done over the last four decades. Scholars of the labor movement have not felt compelled to insist that unions "interact" with the rest of society. L. N. McAlister, "Recent Research and Writings on the Role of the Military in Latin America," *Latin American Research Review* 2 (Fall 1966) 1:6; Lowenthal, "Armies and Politics in Latin America: Introduction to the First Edition," in Lowenthal et al., *Armies and Politics,* 4–5. The premise of the military as a somewhat separated or even alien body can be found in Alfred Stepan, *Rethinking Military Politics: Brazil and the Southern Cone* (Princeton, N.J.: Princeton University Press, 1988); Augusto Varas, "Las relaciones civil-militares en la democracia," in Dirk Kruijt and Edelberto Torres-Rivas, coord., *América Latina: militares y sociedad,* vol. II (San José, Costa Rica: FLACSO, 1991), 153–80 ; J. Samuel Fitch, "Armies and Politics in Latin America: 1975–1985," in Abraham F. Lowenthal and J. Samuel Fitch, eds., *Armies and Politics in Latin America,* rev. ed. (New York: Holmes and Meier, 1986), 26–58; and Jorge Zaverucha, "The Degree of Military Political Autonomy During the Spanish, Argentine and Brazilian Transitions," *Journal of Latin American Studies* 25 (May 1993) 2: 283–300.

60. See Karen L. Remmer's assault on theory making among specialists in the study of democracy and authoritarianism, "New Wine or Old Bottlenecks? The Study of Latin American Democracy," *Comparative Politics* 23 (July 1991) 4:479–95. I do not, however, share her

ardently positivistic recommendations for reviving the corpse. For a critique of that literature, see Holden, "Constructing the Limits," 449–54.

61. Omar G. Encarnación, "Tocqueville's Missionaries: Civil Society Advocacy and the Promotion of Democracy," *World Policy Journal* (Spring 2000):16. Joe Foweraker risked the observation that Latin American civil societies "might themselves suffer from strong authoritarian tendencies"; *Theorizing Social Movements* (London: Pluto Press, 1995), 28.

62. Guillermo O'Donnell, "Democracia en la Argentina micro y macro," in Oscar Oszlak, ed., *Proceso, crisis y transición democrática* (Buenos Aires: Centro Editor de América Latina, 1984), vol. 1, 17, 19, 23. For the popularity of an army general who oversaw the disappearance of 387 Argentines in the province of Tucumán during the Dirty War, see Jonathan Friedland, "Argentine Governor with Notorious Past Is Returned to Office," *Wall Street Journal*, 28 February 1996, 1.

63. See, for example, Decree 17's "Principios de la Revolución," issued by the Junta Revolucionario of Guatemala, composed of two military officers and a civilian, on 27 November 1944, in Francisco Villagrán Kramer, *Biografía política de Guatemala: Los Pactos Políticos de 1944 a 1970* (Guatemala: FLACSO, 1993), 21, especially Principle No. 4.

64. The contrast between the domestic invisibility of public violence and its salience as an export product was similarly suggested by Michael Mann as the difference between a "private, even a secret militarism" that is hidden from public view in the United States in a way that would not have been considered possible or desirable before the Cold War, and the "spectator-sport militarism" that draws U.S. citizens into indirect participants in the foreign applications of U.S. military force, mobilizing the nation as spectators but not fighters. Michael Mann, "The Roots and Contradictions of Modern Militarism," *New Left Review* 162 (March/April 1987):44, 47–48.

65. Robin Luckham, "Of Arms and Culture," *Current Research on Peace and Violence*, 7 (1984) 1:13–16.

66. Juan Forero, "Role of U.S. Companies in Colombia Is Questioned," *New York Times*, 18 May 2001.

67. "The gravest problem in Colombia today is violence; nothing seems capable of resolution without resorting to conflict as a way of living together" ("como forma de convivencia"). Joaquín Estefanía, "Los colombianos hemos utilizado la violencia como relación social," *El País* (Madrid), Edición Internacional, 6 March 1995, 3. Four years later, Pres. Ernesto Zedillo of Mexico condemned the "authoritarianism and . . . vertical power" that Mexico was still attempting to put behind it, as well as political leaders whose "referent, their habits and even their nostalgia is the old authoritarianism of *caudillismo* and the arbitrary subjection of wills"; they "long for the old depository of absolute power who is the arbiter for everybody, who decides for everybody and subjugates everybody." President Ernesto Zedillo, "Clausura de la XVII Reunión Anual de la CONCAMIN," a speech in Veracruz reproduced on the Mexican government web site, available at http://www.presidencia.gob.mx/pages/f_ind_disc.html, 23 March 1999.

68. Nevertheless, research on clientelism "virtually stopped" by the early 1980s; Jonathan Fox, "The Difficult Transition from Clientelism to Citizenship," *World Politics*, 46 (January 1994) 2:154 n. 7.

CHAPTER 2

1. The improvisational state was an example of what Mann called "extensive power [or] the ability to organize large numbers of people over far-flung territories in order to engage in minimally stable cooperation," as opposed to the "intensive power" of a state that can "organize tightly and command a high level of mobilization or commitment from the participants." Mann, *History of Power*, 7.

2. An example of a state that was *not* improvisational, at any time in its history, was that of the United States. On the other hand, Paul Rock's description of England as recently as the early eighteenth century suggests an improvisational quality about the state's search for reliable sources of coercion that is quite familiar to historians of nineteenth-century Latin America. "Law, Order and Power in Late Seventeenth- and Early Eighteenth-century England," in Stanley Cohen and Andrew Scull, eds., *Social Control and the State: Historical and Comparative Essays* (Oxford: Martin Robertson, 1983), 191–221.

3. Hence the irrelevance, in the historical context of Latin American state formation, of the hallowed political science dichotomy "consensus vs. coercion," which supplied the organizing logic behind Forte and Guajardo, eds., *Consenso y Coacción*. Like "strong state-weak state," this is an idea that deserves less reverence from historians.

4. Chalmers, "Politicized State," 23–26.

5. *Montonera* derived from *montón*, whose primary meaning as a disorderly collection of things thrown together, was adopted in the region of the Río de la Plata to refer to the "group of *gauchos* who made war without being instructed in the military art and organization of the European armies," according to Alberto González Arzac, *Caudillos y constituciones* (Buenos Aires: Colección Estrella Federal, 1994), 38–39; the classic study is of course that by the Argentine essayist and politician, Domingo F. Sarmiento, *Facundo: Civilización y Barbarie*, first published in 1845 (Madrid: Ediciones Cátedra, 1990), 49. In rural Honduras, the word *montonera* was commonly in use at least as late as the 1950s to refer to the party militias temporarily organized to contest elections, according to personal informants of the author.

6. States must first monopolize violence before they can nonviolently induce consent to their institutions and laws; Nicos Poulantzas, *State, Power, Socialism*, trans. Patrick Camiller (London: Verso, 1978), 80–82.

7. Norman A. Bailey elaborated inventively on international expressions of *caudillaje* in "The United States as *Caudillo*," *Journal of Inter-American Studies* 5 (July 1963), 313–24. The essential role of the Cold War arms transfers that were to come, as a dimension of international caudillaje, was developed by Christopher C. Shoemaker and John Spanier, *Patron-Client State Relationships: Multilateral Crises in the Nuclear Age* (New York: Praeger, 1984), 14–15.

8. FRUS 1911, Díaz to F. M. Gunther, in Gunther to Department of State, 21 December 1911, 670. Díaz's proposal found its way into the Bryan-Chamorro Treaty of 1914, but the U.S. Senate insisted on its elimination before ratifying the treaty in 1916.

9. FRUS 1920:2, McMillin (Guatemala) to Department of State, 16 March 1920, 726.

10. Norbert Elias tried to show how habitus—"embodied social learning" or "second nature"—can be shaped by the process of state formation; see Elias, *The Germans: Power Struggles and the Development of Habitus in the Nineteenth and Twentieth Centuries*, trans. Eric Dunning and Stephen Mennell (New York: Columbia University Press, 1996), especially "Preface" and "Introduction" by the translators. Later and more famously, Pierre Bourdieu called habitus a "system of dispositions—a present past that tends to perpetuate itself into the future by reactivation in similarly structured practices," and an "embodied history, internalized as a second nature and so forgotten as history . . . the active presence of the whole past of which it is the product," in *The Logic of Practice*, trans. Richard Nice (Cambridge: Polity Press, 1990), 54, 56. Also see Bourdieu's "Men and Machines," in *Advances in Social Theory and Methodology: Toward an Integration of Micro-and Macro-Sociologies* (Boston: Routledge and Kegan Paul, 1981), 304–15, and Morten Schmidt, "Habitus Revisited," *American Behavioral Scientist* 40 (February 1997), 444–54. For the tendency of state makers to become "habituated to violence" see Ted Robert Gurr, "War Revolution, and the Growth of the Coercive State," *Comparative Political Studies* 21 (April 1988) 1:45–65.

11. MPH 1911, 8–11.

12. Eugene Victor Walter, *Terror and Resistance: A Study of Political Violence* (New York: Oxford University Press, 1969), 26, 31.

13. Rodolfo Cerdas, *El desencanto democrático: Crisis de partidos y transición democrática en Centro América y Panamá* (San José, Costa Rica: Red Editorial Iberoamericana Centroamérica, 1993), 21, 23.

14. Mario Monteforte Toledo, *Centro América: Subdesarrollo y dependencia*, vol. 2 (Mexico City: Universidad Nacional Autónoma de Mexico, 1972), 253.

15. Quoted in Gautama Fonseca, "Los Precedentes," in *Cuatro Ensayos sobre la Realidad Política de Honduras* (Tegucigalpa, Honduras: Editorial Universitaria, 1987), 90.

16. Alejandro Serrano Caldera, "En busca de la nación," in *Historia y Violencia en Nicaragua* (Managua: Instituto de Investigaciones y Acción Social "Martin Luther King," de la Universidad Politécnica de Nicaragua y UNESCO, 1997), 14.

17. Edelberto Torres-Rivas, *El tamaño de nuestra democracia* (San Salvador, El Salvador: Istmo Editores, 1992), 38, 41, 29. For further examples see Julio César Pinto S., "Luchas sociales y políticas: en busca de un proyecto estatal viable (1811–1830)," in Edelberto Torres-Rivas and Julio César Pinto S., eds., *Problemas en la formación del estado nacional en centroamérica* (San José, Costa Rica: Instituto Centroamericano de Administración Pública, 1983), 104; Patricia Alvarenga, "Reshaping the Ethics of Power: A History of Violence in Western Rural El Salvador, 1880–1932" (Ph.D. diss., University of Wisconsin, 1994), 153; subsequently published as *Cultura y ética de la violencia: El Salvador, 1880–1932* (San José, Costa Rica: EDUCA, 1996); and Piero Gleijeses, *Politics and Culture in Guatemala* (Ann Arbor, Mich.: Institute for Social Research, 1988), 4–5, for whom violence remains "the taproot of Guatemalan history."

18. Lindo-Fuentes, *Weak Foundations*, 48.

19. This entity encompassed what would become the "traditional" countries of Central America, in the sense that the only other possible contenders, Panama and Belize, should be excluded because they did not achieve national independence until much later than the others, and because their political histories are so different. Panama was a province of Colombia until 1903, when it became a U.S. protectorate, remaining so, arguably, until the Panamanian state acquired full possession of the Panama Canal on 31 December 1999. Belize was a British colony until 1981 and is the only English-speaking state on the isthmus.

20. For the comparison with the United States, see Thomas L. Karnes, *The Failure of Union: Central America, 1824–1975* (Tempe: Center for Latin American Studies, Arizona State University, 1976), 54–55.

21. Lorenzo Montúfar, *Reseña histórica de Centroamérica* (Guatemala City: Tipografia de El Progreso, 1878), vol. 1, 54–55, 340; vol. 2, 32–38, for just three examples; many others could be cited.

22. Declaration by Bonilla in January 1893, quoted in Aro Sanso [Ismael Mejía Deras], *Policarpo Bonilla: Algunos Apuntes Biográficos* (Mexico City: Imprenta Mundial, 1936), 163–64.

23. In this brief comment to a university audience, Cuadra Pasos concisely linked three salient features of patrimonialism—honor, loyalty, and violence. AIHN, "Leyes Varias," Carlos Cuadra Pasos, "Reforma de la Constitución en cuanto a la organización de los Poderes Públicos, Conferencia pronunciada . . . a los alumnos universitarios de la Sociedad Justicia en la Universidad de Granada," January 1932.

24. AIHN/ASD 010. "Discurso pronunciado por . . . Presidente . . . Anastasio Somoza D., durante la conmemoración del 50 aniversario del pacto 'Espino Negro,'" Tipitapa, 4 May 1977.

25. Enrique Sotelo Borgen, "Emiliano Chamorro, el Gobernante," *En Marcha* (Managua; organ of the Partido Conservador Demócrata) 36 (February 1983):8; Clemente Guido, "Ideario de Emiliano," *En Marcha* 36 (February 1983):7.

26. Pinto S., "Luchas sociales," 101.

27. Montúfar, *Reseña*, vol. 1, 365, 368. For more Guatemalan examples, see Ralph Lee Woodward, Jr., "The liberal-Conservative Debate in the Central American Federation, 1823–1840," in Vincent C. Peloso and Barbara A. Tenenbaum, eds., *Liberals, Politics and Power: State Formation in Nineteenth-Century Latin America* (Athens: University of Georgia Press, 1996), 71; Julio César Pinto S., "Los problemas de la transición," in Edelberto Torres-Rivas et al., *Problemas*, 73; and "Proclama del 8 de mayo de 1871, Miguel García Granados a los guatemaltecos," in Comité Pro Festejos de la Revolución de 1871, *Antecedentes Históricos de la Revolución de 1871* (Guatemala City: Editorial "Jose de Pineda Ibarra," 1971), 78–79.

28. MPH 1894, 6; also see Rafael Bardales Bueso, *Historia del Partido Nacional* (San Pedro Sula, Honduras: Central Impresora, 1987), 34, 36.

29. Erik Ching, "Patronage, Politics and Power in El Salvador, 1840–1940" (Greenville, S.C., 1998), 220–21.

30. Salvador Mendieta, *La enfermedad de Centro-América* (Barcelona: Tipografía Maucci, 1934), vol. 1, 270–71.

31. Pinto S., "Luchas sociales," 95, 104, 115.

32. Villagrán Kramer, *Biografía Política*, 61.

33. Serrano Caldera, "En Busca de la Nación," 8.

34. Montúfar, *Reseña*, vol. 1, 313–14.

35. Ivan Molina and Fabrice Lehoucq, *Urnas de lo Inesperado: Fraude Electoral y Lucha Política en Costa Rica (1901–1948)* (San José, Costa Rica: Editorial de la Universidad de Costa Rica), 71. Compare a similar view in that twentieth-century balefire of Latin American thought, José Enrique Rodó's *Ariel* (trans. Margaret Sayers Peden), which was highly suspicious of democracy and taught that the masses were the inert tools of strong leaders (Austin: University of Texas Press, [1900] 1988), 60.

36. Montúfar, *Reseña*, vol. 2, 345–46; 348.

37. Céleo Dávila, "El gobierno fuerte," *Revista Ariel* (Tegucigalpa) 1 (30 March 1925) 2:26; the article was dated 1923; and "Gobierno del sentido común," 1 (15 May 1925) 5:105.

38. For a rare attempt to find systematic evidence of nonviolent, "constructive collaboration" in Central America, see Jordana Dym, "The State, the City and the Priest: Political Participation and Conflict Resolution in Independence-Era Central America," 18 November 1999.

39. Recall the slogan of the federalist government of Gen. Juan Rosas in the Argentina of the 1840s, which may be unequalled in the annals of politically incited hatred: "Mueran los salvajes inmundos unitarios" ("Death to the filthy, savage Unitarians"); Sarmiento, *Facundo*, 195.

40. Carlos Cuadra Pasos, *Explicación de Mi Conducta Política* (Managua, Nicaragua: n.p., 1948), 8.

41. NA, Despatches from United States Consuls in San Salvador, 1868–1906, Microcopy No. T-237, Roll 1, vol. 1, J. Maurice Duke, consul, San Salvador, to James D. Porter, assistant secretary of state, 5 September 1885.

42. Arturo Taracena Arriola, "Liberalismo y poder político en Centroamérica (1870–1929)," in Victor Hugo Acuña Ortega, ed., *Las repúblicas agroexportadoras (1870–1945)*, vol. 4 of *Historia General de Centroamérica* (Madrid: Sociedad Estatal Quinto Cententario y FLACSO, 1993), 189.

43. Mendieta, *Enfermedad*, 231. In a note that Mendieta appended in the 1930s, he wrote that since 1907 there had been free presidential elections in Costa Rica in 1910, 1920, 1924 and 1928; in Nicaragua in 1924, 1928 and 1932 "por intervención yanqui"; in Honduras in 1928 and 1932; in El Salvador in 1931; and in Guatemala in 1920 and 1931.

44. CIEL, "Antecedentes de Decretos del Congreso Nacional," "Dictamen," 4 May 1934.

45. CIEL, "Libro de Actas de la Asamblea Nacional Constituyente de la Federación de Centroamérica," 138, speech by Miguel F. Alvarado, 20 August 1921.

46. Molina and Lehoucq, *Urnas*, 115. The "politics-is-hell" argument was not invented to deny women the vote; the proponents of women's suffrage resorted to identical reasoning, as follows: Not only had women already shown themselves to be worthy combatants in the political wars, and thus deserved the right to vote, but extending the vote to women would likely make politics less violent because of women's gentle nature. See the speeches by Policarpo Bonilla and Juan E. Paredes in CIEL, "Libro de Actas," 127 ff and 133 ff.

47. Graciela Bográn, "¿Debe o no concederse el sufragio a la mujer hondureña?" *Alma Latina* 2 (Noviembre 1933) 31:5.

48. Interview with Manuel Mora Valderde, "Anexo 4," Oscar Alguilar Bulgarelli, *Costa Rica y Sus Hechos Políticos de 1948* (San José, Costa Rica: Editorial Costa Rica, 1993), 531–32.

49. "Entregar el Poder Anunció Figueres," *La Nación* (San José, Costa Rica), 8 February 1958, 12. The introduction of the secret ballot may have helped reduce electoral violence; it was not adopted in El Salvador, for example, until 1950.

50. "Liberals switched sides with a facility explainable only on the basis of crass calculations of personal advantage," according to Gudmundson; "Society and Politics in Central America, 1821–1871," in Gudmundson and Hector Lindo-Fuentes, *Central America, 1821–1871: Liberalism Before liberal Reform* (Tuscaloosa: University of Alabama Press, 1995), 90–93. The relative insignificance of ideology was also stressed by Mario Argüeta, *Tiburcio Carías: Anatomía de Una Epoca, 1923–1948* (Tegucigalpa, Honduras: Editorial Guaymuras, 1989), 85–97; William S. Stokes, *Honduras: An Area Study in Government* (Madison: University of Wisconsin Press, 1950), ch. 9; and Molina and Lehoucq, *Urnas*, 143–44. Contemporary observers also made the point; see Mendieta, *La enfermedad*, vol. 1, 186–90 and Gustavo A. Castañeda S., *El General Domingo Vásquez y Su Tiempo* (Tegucigalpa, Honduras: Imprenta Calderón, 1934), 33.

51. Arturo J. Cruz, Jr., *Nicaragua's Conservative Republic, 1858–93* (Basingstoke, UK: Palgrave, 2002), 63n43; 8. For a similar evaluation of the tertulias, see E. Bradford Burns, *Patriarch and Folk: The Emergence of Nicaragua, 1798–1858* (Cambridge, Mass.: Harvard University Press, 1991), 47.

52. Ricardo Alduvin, "Policarpo Bonilla," in Sanso, *Policarpo Bonilla*, xi.

53. Ibid., xi

54. Castañeda, *El General*, 33.

55. The Liberal Party of Honduras was not noticeably strengthened even after President Bonilla's five years in office (1894–99) but "divided" and "had no organization whatsoever." Sanso, *Policarpo Bonilla*, 335–38.

56. Most of the words are uniquely Nicaraguan and refer, loosely, to the kind of people an English speaker might refer to as "riff-raff," or worse. Enrique Guzmán, *Escritos Históricos y Políticos*, vol. 1, *1867–1879* (San José, Costa Rica: Libro Libre, 1986), 199, quoted in Cruz, *Nicaragua's Conservative Republic*, 61.

57. The quote is from Chasteen, *Heroes on Horseback*, 141.

58. Because of the corporate-clientelistic environment, Foweraker suggested, Latin American social movements do not necessarily lead to demands for political rights but instead to the extension of special privileges or social rights for a particular social movement, creating "not political citizens but political dependents or clients." *Theorizing Social Movements*, 92–93.

59. ANH, Fondo Policarpo Bonilla, Vespaciano Garín, "(Hospital) Tegucigalpa," to Policarpo Bonilla, 14 November 1894.

60. See, for example, ANH, Fondo Policarpo Bonilla, Raimundo Rodriguez to Gen. Manuel Bonilla, 16 October 1894; Concepción Toro to Policarpo Bonilla, 23 October 1894.

61. AIHN. Fondo Sacasa. José A. Gámez (Rivas) to President Sacasa, 10 January 1890 and 3 December 1890.

62. ANN, Fondo Presidencial, Guardia Nacional/Comandantes Departamentales, Año 1933–68, Midence to José María Zelaya, private secretary of the president, 8 November 1968.

63. ANN], Fondo Presidencial/Guardia Nacional/Comandantes Departamentales/Año 1933–1968, "Comandante Departamental." Somoza transmitted the complaint to the comandante of Matagalpa Department and assured the letter writers that it would be investigated.

64. Robert M. Carmack, "State and Community in Nineteenth-Century Guatemala: The Mosmostenango Case," in Carol A. Smith, ed., *Guatemalan Indians and the State: 1540 to 1988* (Austin: University of Texas Press, 1990), 135.

65. La República 1 (20 July 1871) 4:1, cited in Wayne M. Clegern, *Origins of liberal Dictatorship in Central America: Guatemala, 1865–1873.* (Niwot: University Press of Colorado, 1994), 125.

66. David McCreery, *Rural Guatemala 1760–1940* (Stanford, Calif.: Stanford University Press, 1994), 180–81. McCreery noted that the new liberal regime succeeded for the first time in clearly distinguishing the militia from the army. The army, posted in the major cities and on the borders, defended Guatemala against foreign invasions; the militia, scattered in 173 detachments throughout the country, controlled the rural inhabitants, the vast majority of whom identified themselves as Indians, a fact that logically excluded them from membership in the militia itself, because they were now not trusted to police their own people. They were, however, forcibly recruited into the outward-looking army. Also see Edelberto Torres-Rivas, "Evolución Histórico del Sector Público en Centroamérica y Panamá," in Torres-Rivas et al., *Problemas*, 23.

67. Nicolás Mariscal, "Militares y reformismo en El Salvador," *Estudios Centroamericanos* 351/352 (January–February 1978):12.

68. Ching, "Patronage," 195–96.

69. I borrowed the phrase "upward displacement" from Perry Anderson, who applied it to the process by which power was transferred from feudal lords to the absolutist state in *Lineages of the Absolutist State* (London: Verso, 1979), 19.

70. Charles Tilly, *Coercion, Capital and European States, a.d. 990–1990* (Cambridge, Mass.: Basil Blackwell, 1990), 68–69, and his *Big Structures, Large Processes, Huge Comparisons* (New York: Russell Sage Foundation Press, 1984), 9–10.

71. S. N. Eisenstadt and L. Roniger, *Patrons, Clients and Friends: Interpersonal Relations and the Structure of Trust in Society* (Cambridge: Cambridge University Press, 1984), 49.

72. See John Lynch's important interpretation of the origins and development of *caudillismo* generally in Latin America; the result was a view of government less as a source of policy than a source of patronage, with promises to "people as clients with expectations, not citizens with rights." *Caudillos in Spanish America 1800–1850* (New York: Oxford University Press, 1992), 433–37, 4–5, 406.

73. Ching, "Patronage," ch. 4, especially 130–31.

74. The classic expositions of this model are Eric Wolf, "Aspects of Group Relations in a Complex Society: Mexico," *American Anthropologist* 58 (1956):1065–78 and John Duncan Powell, "Peasant Society and Clientelist Politics," *American Political Science Review* 64 (June 1970) 2:411–25. For a subsequent refinement, see Eisenstadt et al., *Patrons*, 231–44.

75. Mendieta, *Enfermedad*, vol. 1, 249, 220–21.

76. Ibid., 215; in a note he appended in the 1930s, Mendieta said that while the two posts were still combined in Guatemala, they were now separate in Honduras and El Salvador. The Nicaraguan jefe político had been effectively replaced by the departmental Guardia Nacional commander, while in Costa Rica "the departmental governor takes command of military forces as needed because there is no permanent army."

77. Until at least 1922, when the central government sought to end the practice, Guatemalan garrison commanders kept whatever funds they could extract from men in their districts seeking legal exemption from military service; NAMP, Roll 11, "Correspondence and

Record Cards. . . ." U.S. Military Attaché, "Buying Exemption from Military Service," 28 July 1922. For evidence that garrison commanders in Honduras operated like feudal barons until the 1940s, see Argüeta, *Tiburcio Carías*, 109–10.

78. Pastor, *Historia*, 210–11.

79. Rodolfo Pastor, *Historia de Centroamérica* (Guatemala City: Editorial Piedra Santa, 1990), 210–12; James Dunkerley, *Power in the Isthmus: A Political History of Modern Central America* (London: Verso, 1988), 58, 65; Victor Bulmer-Thomas, *The Political Economy of Central America Since 1920* (Cambridge: Cambridge University Press, 1987), 43–46, 48–49, 84–85; Taracena, "Liberalismo y poder político," 225–49.

80. Bulmer-Thomas, *Political Economy*, 84–85; also see Dunkerley, *Power in the Isthmus*, 94, 58, 65.

81. Bulmer-Thomas, *Political Economy*, 65–67, attributed the difference to the isthmian dictatorships' decision to protect the supremacy of the export-led growth model (abandoned elsewhere in Latin America) and to roll back the modest social reforms of the 1920s. They probably had no choice, given the scarcity of capital relative to other Latin America countries.

82. This paragraph draws on Edelberto Torres Rivas, "Central America Since 1930: An Overview," in Leslie Bethell, ed., *Latin American Since 1930: Mexico, Central America and the Caribbean*, vol. 7 of *The Cambridge History of Latin America* (Cambridge: Cambridge University Press, 1990), 173–80; also see Dunkerley, *Power in the Isthmus*, 117.

83. Summaries of the open political meddling and manipulation by Washington, as well as its military intervention in the cases of Honduras and Nicaragua, can be found Thomas M. Leonard, *Central America and the United States: The Search for Stability* (Athens: University of Georgia Press, 1991), chs. 4–5 and J. Lloyd Mecham, *A Survey of United States-Latin American Relations* (Boston: Houghton Mifflin, 1965), ch. 12.

84. NAMP No. M1488, 9, especially rolls 11 and 12, "Correspondence and Record Cards of the Military Intelligence Division Related to General, Political, Economic, and Military Conditions in Central America, 1918–1941."

85. NAMP, "Correspondence and Record Cards. . . . ," Roll 2, Maj. M. Churchill, Military Intelligence Division, War Department, Washington, to U.S. military attaché, Panama City, 20 October 1921.

86. Bulmer Thomas, *Political Economy*, 46.

87. Dana Munro, *Intervention and Dollar Diplomacy in the Caribbean* (Princeton, N.J.: Princeton University Press, 1964), 215. Some twenty-six hundred U.S. Marines landed in Nicaragua in August 1912 to protect the newly elected Pres. Adolfo Díaz from an insurgent general incensed by Díaz's proposal for a U.S. protectorate over the country; Buell, "The United States," 173.

88. FRUS 1911, Elliott Northcott, U.S. minister in Managua, to Department of State, 25 February 1911, 655; on 27 March, Northcott reported that Estrada's hold on power was owing entirely to the U.S. Marines, 656.

89. Its resolution against the proposal was reprinted in full in FRUS 1912:578–80; for references to popular opposition to the plan, and the "violently anti-American" nature of some of the opposition, see Munro, *Intervention*, 218, 220, 222, 226.

90. Raymond Leslie Buell, "The United States and Central American Stability," *Foreign Policy Reports* 7 (8 July 1931) 9:176–77.

91. Buell, "The United States," 181–84.

92. Leonard, *Central America*, 59–60, 72–73; Taracena, "Liberalismo," 222–24, notes that the 1907 treaties failed to include mechanisms to regulate "U.S. interventionism in both the internal and inter-state affairs of the area."

93. Thomas L. Karnes, *The Failure of Union: Central America, 1824–1960* (Chapel Hill: University of North Carolina Press, 1961), 223.

94. Conference on Central American Affairs, Washington, December 4, 1922–February 7, 1923 (Washington, D.C.: Government Printing Office, 1923), 339–43.

95. Thomas M. Leonard, "U.S. Policy and Arms Limitation in Central America: The Washington Conference of 1923," Occasional Papers Series, No. 10 (Los Angeles: Center for the Study of Armament and Disarmament, California State University, 1982), 38; also see NAMP, "Correspondence and Record Cards....," Roll 12, for correspondence, 1925–26, from and to Lt. Col. Jean H. A. Day, U.S. Army Resereve, who had been tentatively hired by the Honduran government to direct its proposed constabulary.

96. In the 1920s and 1930s, U.S. direct investments in Nicaragua were the lowest in the isthmus but it had the longest and most dramatic record of U.S. intervention. Guatemala had the highest level of U.S. investment, followed by Honduras. See Raul Migone et al., *Inter-American Statistical Yearbook 1942* (New York: Macmillan, 1942), 799.

97. Costa Rica remained somewhat exceptional even in this, however, and the civil war of 1948, which was fought almost entirely among political-party militias, highlighted the weakness and marginal character of its extremely small army.

98. For Costa Rica, see Mercedes Muñoz Guillen, *El Estado y la Abolición del Ejército 1914–1949* (San José, Costa Rica: Editorial Porvenir,1990), 104; for Guatemala, Villagrán Kramer, *Biografía Política*, 192. For *la mancha brava*, I am grateful to Marvin Barahona for information supplied; see David Calderón, *Orígen de la Mancha Brava* (San Salvador, El Salvador: n.p., 1970), 11ff.

99. Buzan, *People, States and Fear*, ch. 2. Buzan's notion of state is considerably broader than that used throughout this book, but his theory interlocks nicely with Clapham's proposition that the fragility (not the "capacity") of the Third World state derives from the "disjunction between the state and any shared set of social values," where "neo-patrimonialism" replaces national identity; Clapham, *Third World State*, ch. 3.

100. Samuel L. Baily, "Introduction," in Baily, ed. *Nationalism in Latin America* (New York: Alfred A. Knopf, 1971), 6–7. A spurt of scholarship in the 1990s adducing evidence for "peasant nationalism" in the nineteenth century supports my argument, for it tended to emphasize the local, particularistic, heterogeneous, and evanescent nature of what these scholars insisted on calling "nationalism." See Florencia E. Mallon, *Peasant and Nation: The Making of Postcolonial Mexico and Peru* (Berkeley: University of California Press, 1995) and Peter Guardino, "Identity and Nationalism in Mexico: Guerrero, 1780–1840," *Journal of Historical Sociology* 7 (September 1994) 3:314–42. By contrast, Tocqueville wrote in the early 1830s, "Every citizen of the United States transfers, so to speak, his attachment to his little republic into the common share of American patriotism," identifying (rather than separating) local and national interests; Alexis de Tocqueville, *Democracy in America* (New York: Vintage Books, [1835] 1990), 1:164.

101. See the essays in the revealingly entitled *Nicaragua en Busca de Su Indentidad*, ed. Frances Kinloch Tijerino (Managua, Nicaragua: Instituto de Historia de Nicaragua, Universidad Centroamericana, 1995), which uniformly emphasize the fragmentation of identities and the need to create a common idea of citizenship for political democracy and economic development to take root, especially Serrano Caldera, "En Busca de la Nación." Marvin Barahona's *Evolución Histórica de la Identidad Nacional* (Tegucigalpa, Honduras: Editorial Guaymuras, 1991), 16, highlighted the "deformation" of a highly uneven and frustrated process of nation-building.

102. Isthmian nationalism, often rooted in "resentment, fear, frustration, and a sense of inferiority, was frequently angry and violent." Ralph Lee Woodward, Jr., *Central America: A Nation Divided*, 3d ed. (New York: Oxford University Press, 1999), 211.

103. Tocqueville, *Democracy in America*, 1:242.

104. Villagrán Kramer, *Biografía Política*, 224; for his insightful analysis of anticommunism as the newly imposed ideology of the state, and its utter lack of constructive intent, see 204–20.

105. Luis Carrión Cruz, interview, "Luis Carrión," in *Historia y Violencia*, 351. Serrano, "En Busca," 21, likewise observed that the Sandinista revolution was no more than another example of the making of the "nación intermitente" that is Nicaragua.

106. Such demands encompassed labor rights, the creation of social security funds, the extension of public education and health services, among others; see Torres-Rivas, "Evolución histórica," 33.

CHAPTER 3

1. Ralph Lee Woodward, Jr., *Rafael Carrera and the Emergence of the Republic of Guatemala, 1821–1871* (Athens: University of Georgia Press, 1993), 60–66.

2. Ibid., 241, 251.

3. Ibid., 253; under Carrera, the army became "the most powerful institution in Guatemalan society," Woodward concluded (464).

4. For scattered evidence see ibid., 241, 251, 281. Woodward concluded (463) that "Beginning with Carrera, the army became a place where young Indian men could escape their villages or urban slums and make a transition to Ladino life under the leadership of Ladino officers who could now aspire to high political office and economic opportunity." The army's prestige was also probably enhanced by its important role in the National War against William Walker of Nicaragua in 1856–57, and its subsequent domination of Honduras and El Salvador (464).

5. Comisión Nacional de Festejos del Centenario de la Escuela Politécnica, *Historial de la Escuela Politécnica* (Guatemala City: Editorial del Ejército, 1973), 12.

6. Passing references to such events, but no summarization of them, can be found here and there in Woodward, *Rafael Carrera*, chs. 11, 12, 14, though the author concluded that the very revolt that Carrera led in 1837 "continued a pattern of guerrilla warfare . . . that would continue intermittently to the present. Much of Carrera's efforts as caudillo were spent in quelling these recurring uprisings." (462)

7. Block quote in Pedro Zamora Castellanos, *Vida Militar de Centro América*, vol. 2 (Guatemala City: Tipografía Nacional, 1924), 428; other details, 409–32; Woodward, *Rafael Carrera*, ch. 16.

8. Montúfar, *Reseña Histórica*, vol. 1, 208

9. Hector Pérez Brignoli, *Breve Historia de Centroamérica* (Madrid: Alianza Editorial, 1985), 77.

10. Clegern, *Origins of Liberal Dictatorship*, 141.

11. Taracena, "Liberalismo y poder," 181.

12. "Decreto de Unión Centroamericana del General Justo Rufino Barrios," in Comité Pro Festejos de la Revolución de 1871, *Antecedentes Históricos de la Revolución de 1871* (Guatemala City: Editorial "Jose de Pineda Ibarra," 1971), 137.

13. Zamora Castellanos, *Vida Militar*, vol. 2, 449, 451; also see Thomas L. Karnes, *The Failure of Union: Central America, 1824–1960* (Chapel Hill: University of North Carolina Press, 1961), 158–63.

14. Such is the standard interpretation; see, for example, Fernando González Davison, *El Régimen liberal en Guatemala (1871–1944)* (San Carlos, Guatemala: Editorial Universitaria, Universidad de San Carlos, 1990), 11, 13.

15. Taracena, "Liberalismo y poder," 181.

16. Zamora Castellanos, *Vida Militar*, vol. 2, 433–40; "remincheros" was a contraction fashioned from "Remington de shere," a self-mocking reference to the primitive arms they carried—machetes and clubs—made of a species of evergreen oak; Zamora equated "shere" with "encina," wood from the holm oak tree (433).

17. Zamora Castellanos, *Vida Militar*, vol. 2, 441–47

18. Taracena, "Liberalismo y poder político," 184–185, 212–14; Dana Munro, *The Five Republics of Central America: Their Political and Economic Development and Their Relations with the United States* (New York: Oxford University Press, 1918), 53–54; Paul J. Dosal, *Doing Business with Dictators: A Political History of United Fruit in Guatemala, 1899–1944* (Wilmington, Del.: Scholarly Resources, 1993), 37–38, 71.

19. For a summary of rebellions that the army under Estrada successfully defeated until the collapse of the dictatorship in 1920, see Zamora Castellanos, *Vida Militar*, vol. 2, 510–21; 537–39.

20. Ibid., 537–539; FRUS 1920:2, McMillan (Guatemala City) to Department of State, 22 March 1920, 732. For the death estimate, see Taracena, "Liberalismo y poder político," 232. For an interpretation that stresses the depth and power of the popular opposition to Estrada, see Wade Kit, "The Fall of Guatemalan Dictator, Manuel Estrada Cabrera: U.S. Pressure or National Opposition?" *Canadian Journal of Latin American and Caribbean Studies* 15 (1990) 29:105–28.

21. NAMP, "Correspondence and Record Cards . . . ," Roll 11, U.S. Military Attaché, "Reorganization of Guatemalan Army by General Ubico," 24 December 1921; "Army of Guatemala," 30 June 1922.

22. Grieb, *Guatemalan Caudillo*, 32, 42.

23. MGG 1931, 51–54.

24. MPG 1932, 3, 13–17.

25. MPG 1934, 14–16.

26. MPG 1936, 9.

27. Ibid.

28. MGG 1940, 14–16; MGG 1941, 8.

29. MGG 1942, 6.

30. Leonard, *U.S. Policy*, 34.

31. The following U.S. Army officers, with the dates their appointments became effective, ran the Politécnica during Ubico's dictatorship: Considine (1 May 1931), Lt. Col. John F. Davis (11 February 1935), Maj. Victor W. Wales (30 April 1937), Lt. Col. Edward L. N. Glass (26 April 1939), and Lt. Col. William H. Hennig (1943). When Hennig's contract expired in 1945, he was replaced by Guatemalan Lt. Col. Roberto Barrios Peña. MGG 1931, 8; MGG 1935, 77; MGG 1937, 13; MGG 1939, 19; MGG 1943, 23; MGG 1945, 26.

32. A French army lieutenant, Henry Massot, continued as the chief instructor of the air force from 1934 to 1943; MGG 1931, 6, 9; MGG 1934, 100; MGG 1943, 30.

CHAPTER 4

1. According to Montúfar, *Reseña*, vol. 2, 166, the name was bestowed by the notoriously cruel Pedro de Alvarado, in gratitude to God for his conquest of the Indians in the region they called Cuscutlán on 6 August 1524, the Feast of the Transfiguration of Christ, also known as the feast of the "Santísmo Salvador" ("most holy savior"). Also see Lilly de Jongh Osborne, *Four Keys to El Salvador* (New York: Funk and Wagnalls, 1956), 20, 25.

2. Alvarenga, "Reshaping," 103–105; 112, 114, 116–17, 118, 121, 130–32, 153.

3. Ching, "Patronage," 131–32, 136, 137, 150.

4. Ibid., 142.

5. Ibid., 149–50.

6. Ibid., 168, 171–72.

7. Alvarenga, "Reshaping," 153 and ch. 4, 267.

8. Ibid., 268, 274, 276, 278–79, 282–83, 286. Ching, "Patronage," 229–38, challenged Alvarenga's interpretation of the Liga as a populistic mass organization, emphasizing its party-militia character as an elite tool of the ruling PND when its relations with the military were deteriorating. If he is right, the Liga was thus formed by one group of institutional agents of public violence (the civilian governments of 1918–23) in part to protect itself from another group of institutional agents (the military). By the early 1960s, the armed forces everywhere in Central America had become utterly intolerant of competitors in the field of institutional violence; see chapter 13 for the Honduran military's violent response to a nascent national police force in 1963.

9. Lindo-Fuentes, *Weak Foundations*, 62.

10. Aldo Lauria-Santiago, *An Agrarian Republic: Commercial Agriculture and the Politics of Peasant Communities in El Salvador, 1823–1914* (Pittsburgh: University of Pittsburgh Press, 1999), ch. 5. Some historians, such as Alvarenga, use militia to refer exclusively to the state's official reserve military force.

11. Lauria-Santiago, *Agrarian Republic*, 114.

12. NAMP, No. T-237, *Despatches from United States Consuls in San Salvador, 1868–1906*, Roll 1, vol. 1, J. Maurice Duke, U.S. consul, San Salvador, to James D. Porter, assistant secretary of state, 13 June 1885. In this case, the Indians were allied with the leader of the rebellion, Gen. Francisco Menéndez, whose forces did indeed enter San Salvador in victory as Porter had anticipated on 22 June. According to Taracena, Menéndez, a militant liberal and a coffee grower, had organized the revolt with the support of the Guatemalan government; he represented the interests of western coffee growers opposed to the high taxes on coffee imposed by the previous government headed by Rafael Zaldívar; Taracena, "Liberalismo y poder político," 189.

13. Lauria-Santiago attributed the end of the disorder to the professionalization of the army, the civilian elite's success in containing political conflicts among themselves, the end of a land privatization campaign, and the fragmentation of the Indian communities; *Agrarian Republic*, 127; for a similar interpretation, see Taracena, "Liberalismo y poder político," 190.

14. Three of the five Chilean officers stayed in El Salvador after the expiration of the four-year mission agreement. Two lieutenants, Armando Llanos Calderón and Julio Salinas Alarcón, became Salvadoran citizens and were promoted to senior positions in the Salvadoran army. Lt. Carlos Ibáñez del Campo married into the powerful Quiroz family, saw combat in a border dispute with Honduras, and directed the Salvadoran military academy. Ibáñez returned to Chile in 1909 to lead "a new generation of Chilean military officers who despised parliamentary practices, politicians, and, above all else, politics." Ibáñez joined two military rebellions in Chile before he was elected president in 1927, governing as a dictator until a general strike forced him to resign in 1931, but winning reelection in 1952. A second Chilean military mission advised the Salvadorans from 1950 until 1964—the only non-U.S. military mission in Central America after 1940. Brian Loveman, *Chile: The Legacy of Hispanic Capitalism*, 3d ed. (New York: Oxford University Press, 2001), 162; Ejército de Chile, Misiones Militares del, Ejército de Chile, available at http://www.ejercito.cl/internacional/misiones.htm, 15 May 2001. Also see William F. Sater and Holger H. Herwig, *The Grand Illusion: The Prussianization of the Chilean Army* (Lincoln: University of Nebraska Press, 1999), 84–89, for the impact of the Prussianization in Chile up to 1903.

15. NAMP, "Correspondence and Record Cards. . . . ," Roll 12, "Military Information, El Salvador," 29 January 1919.

16. Munro, *Five Republics*, 108–109. Munro's assessment followed several months of travel in Central America, not later than 1917, and presumably not much earlier than about 1914, to gather information for his doctoral thesis at the University of Pennsylvania.

17. NAMP, Roll 12, "Correspondence and Record Cards...." "Pay, rations, etc. of Army of Salvador," 10 December 1921.

18. Ibid., "Recent revolt of troops in San Salvador," 3 June 1922.

19. Ibid., "El Salvador—Inspection of Units of Army," 17 October 1923; "El Salvador, Estimate of the Military Situation," 7 April 1924. The author of the last report observed that the end of the depression and rising prosperity decisively undercut the strength of the political opposition and helped restore stability.

20. The military education reorganization was characteristic of the presidency of Pío Romero Bosque (1927–31), whose reformism was interpreted as a threat to the traditional privileges of the rich, not least in Romero's insistence that the elections over which he presided in January 1931 be open to all candidates regardless of party; Robert Varney Elam, "Appeal to Arms: The Army and Politics in El Salvador, 1931–1964," Ph.D. diss., University of New Mexico, 1968, 14–19.

21. U.S. Army Col. Ramón A. Nadal wrote that description of pre-1940 school life while he was director of the school in 1952. He told the U.S. Embassy he would quit if he had to restore the old punishment system that President Osorio favored; a Salvadoran officer succeeded Nadal as director in 1953. NA, RG59, 716.58/12–1152, Andrew E. Donavan II, chargé d'affaires, U.S. Embassy, El Salvador, to Department of State, 11 December 1952.

22. As late as 1924 the Guard was still led by a Spanish military mission. NA, Roll 12, National Archives Microform Publications, "Correspondence and Record Cards...." "Military Information, El Salvador," 29 January 1919; "El Salvador—Military and Semi-Military Organizations," 13 March 1924.

23. Elam, "Appeal to Arms," 9–10; Alvarenga, "Reshaping," 176–79.

24. NA. Roll 12, National Archives Microform Publications, "Correspondence and Record Cards...." "Military Information, El Salvador," 29 January 1919.

25. Elam, "Appeal to Arms," 10 and Juan Mario Castellanos, *El Salvador 1930–1960: Antecedentes Históricos de la Guerra Civil* (San Salvador, El Salvador: Consejo Nacional para la Cultura y el Arte, 2001), 115–16. The entire Policía Nacional—created in the 1880s—"receives constant military training," a U.S. military observer reported in 1933; NA, Roll 12, National Archives Microform Publications, "Correspondence and Record Cards. . . ." Alex A. Cohen, Office of U.S. Military Attaché, "El Salvador (Combat), Composition and Strength, National Police Forces," 9 June 1933; MPG 1936, 9.

26. Mariano Castro Morán, *Función Política del Ejército Salvadoreño en el Presente Siglo* (San Salvador, El Salvador: UCA Editores, 1989), 57–59; the fatalities reported on p. 58 are the conservative estimate of Thomas P. Anderson, the author of the standard account of the massacre, *Matanza*, 2d ed. (Willimantic, Conn.: Curbstone Press, 1992). Ching, "Patronage," 374–75, 401, convincingly challenged the longstanding assumption that the communist party organized the revolt, tentatively attributing it instead to Indian *cofradías*. For the long-term impact, see Jeffrey M. Paige, *Coffee and Power: Revolution and the Rise of Democracy in Central America* (Cambridge, Mass.: Harvard University Press, 1997), 103–104.

27. NAMP, Roll 12, "Correspondence and Record Cards. . . ." Lt. Col. J. B. Pate, Panama, U.S. military attaché, "El Salvador—Combat, Army; Subject: Militarized Societies,." 20 July 1937.

28. Alvarenga, "Reshaping," 365–78; Philip J. Williams and Knut Walter, *Militarization and Demilitarization in El Salvador's Transition to Democracy* (Pittsburgh: University of Pittsburgh Press, 1997), 29. The organization of the Legión and the Guardias Cívicas were the Salvadoran manifestations—typically local and dispersed, with populistic and even nationalistic

features—of the much more intrusive, state-directed militarization of institutions, such as the teachers' colleges that Guatemala's Ubico government was simultaneously implementing.

29. NA, FOIA, "Supplement: Outlook for El Salvador's New Administration," DIA Intelligence Bulletin, 28 July 1967. Also see República de El Salvador, Casa Presidencial, *Mensajes y Discursos del Señor presidente de la república Coronel Arturo Armando Molina* 5 (July–December 1974) (San Salvador, El Salvador: Publicaciones del Departamento de Relaciones Públicas, Casa Presidencial), "Al asumir el mando supremo de la Organización Democrática Nacionalista (ORDEN)," 25–29. Williams and Walter, *Militarizarion*, 62, argued that the state's reliance on rural paramilitary units since the 1920s had by the 1950s become an unalterable feature of rural politics, with the units functioning "as the permanent political party of the armed forces,..."

30. Lindo-Fuentes, *Weak Foundations*, 2.

31. Thomas D. Schoonover, *The United States in Central America, 1860–1911: Episodes of Social Imperialism and Imperial Rivalry in the World System* (Durham, N.C.: Duke University Press, 1991), 159.

32. Karnes, *Failure of Union*, 200–202. The decade of dollar diplomacy and Wilsonian intervention led, Munro reported, to "a rather marked distrust and dislike of the United States among certain classes" of Salvdorans; Munro, *Five Republics*, 117.

33. NAMP, Roll 2, "Correspondence and Record Cards...." Douglas Macduff, military attaché to Central America, San Salvador, to Military Intelligence Division, General Staff, Washington, 21 December 1918. For references to Guirola's status as a member of the "economic oligarchy," see Lauria-Santiago, *Agrarian Republic*, 138, 226; for municipal-election casualty estimates, see Ching, "Patronage," 214–15.

34. NA, Roll 12, National Archives Microform Publications, "Correspondence and Record Cards...." "Military Information, El Salvador," 29 January 1919.

35. Patricia Parkman, *Nonviolent Insurrection in El Salvador: The Fall of Maximiliano Hernández Martínez* (Tucson: University of Arizona Press, 1988), 10–11; Richard Alan White, *The Morass: United States Intervention in Central America* (New York: Harper and Row, 1984), 165.

36. Elam, "Appeal to Arms," 20–21.

37. By contrast, Guatemalan Pres. Jorge Ubico, who owed his election in 1931 to Washington's insistence that Guatemala adhere to the 1923 treaty, repeatedly urged the United States to act more forcefully against Hernández-Martinez than Washington thought prudent. Ubico's position derived not from any lofty devotion to the principle of constitutional legitimacy; he merely wanted to weaken a traditional rival. Grieb, *Guatemalan Caudillo*, 5, 72–73, 86–92; Edward O. Guerrant, *Roosevelt's Good Neighbor Policy* (Albuquerque: University of New Mexico Press, 1950), 30–31; also see Philip F. Dur, "U.S. Diplomacy and the Salvadorean Revolution of 1931," *Journal of Latin American Studies* 30 (February 1998) 1:95–119.

38. Leonard, *U.S. Policy*, 36.

39. NAMP, Roll 11, "Correspondence and Record Cards...." Lt. Col. J. B. Pate, Military Attaché, "El Salvador—Aviation—Foreign Purchases," 29 November 1938. Pate reported that the Hernández-Martínez government had lied when it announced that it was exchanging coffee for the planes; that was just a "cloak" to ease the shock over the government's readiness to deal with the fascist government of Italy. He also noted that the purchase was arranged by the "head of the local fascist organization," who was married to a daughter of a Salvadoran congressional deputy.

40. República de El Salvador, Ejército de El Salvador, Escuela Militar, *Prospecto de Admisión* (La Ceiba, Cuscatlán, 1958[?]); Elam, "Appeal to Arms," 48–49; NAMP, Roll 11, "Correspondence and Record Cards...," Alex A. Cohen, military attaché office, Costa Rica, "El Salvador—Aviation—Military," 5 December 1938 and 13 December 1938; Lt. Col. J. B. Pate, military attaché, "El Salvador—Aviation—Military," 16 February 1939.

CHAPTER 5

1. From 1827–1900 there were 213 "acciones de guerra civil," an average of 2.9 per year, and 159 in the first thirty-three years of the twentieth century, which at 4.8 a year represents a 66 percent increase over the previous period; Mario Posas and Rafael Del Cid, *La construcción del sector público y del estado nacional de Honduras, 1876–1979* (San José, Costa Rica: Editorial Universitaria Centroamericana, 1981), 51.

2. Stokes, *Honduras,* 181.

3. Charles A. Brand, "The Background of Capitalistic Development: Honduras to 1913." Ph.D. diss., University of Pittsburgh, 1972, 124, 241 n. 407. From 1894 until 1933 all but one of the presidents identified themselves politically as Liberal Party adherents, ideological descendants of the party's modern founder, Policarpo Bonilla, who although not a military man took power in 1894 after the militias associated with his faction of the Liberal Party defeated those of the incumbent, Gen. Domingo Vásquez, in a civil war. The only president who was not a Bonilla liberal in this period was Miguel Paz Baraona (1925–29); Alduvin, "Policarpo Bonilla," xii.

4. *Recopilación de las constituciones de Honduras (1825–1965)* (Tegucigalpa, Honduras: Universidad Nacional Autónoma de Honduras, 1977.)

5. *El Redactor Oficial de Honduras* (Comayagua) 60 (30 June 1843), 300.

6. *Recopilación de las constituciones de Honduras.*

7. The conservative candidate for president in 1852 yielded to the liberal candidate, Trinidad Cabañas, less out of respect for the constitution than because he recognized that "Cabañas commanded the army and thereby held the real power in the state." Woodward, *Rafael Carrera,* 242.

8. *Recopilación de las constituciones de Honduras.*

9. República de Honduras, *Mensaje del presidente de Honduras, contestación del congreso* (Tegucigalpa, Honduras: Tipografía Nacional, 1879), 26–27.

10. Ramón Rosa, "Memoria de Instrucción Pública (1879)," in *Oro de Honduras: Antología de Ramón Rosa,* 2d ed. (Tegucigalpa, Honduras: Editorial Universitaria, 1993), 140.

11. *Recopilación de las constituciones de Honduras.*

12. MGH 1889, 7–8

13. Jesús Evelio Inestroza M., *Genesis y evolución de las escuelas militares del ejército 1831–1937,* vol. 1 (Tegucigalpa, Honduras: Litografía López, 1990), 20–30, 38.

14. *Recopilación de las constituciones de Honduras.*

15. MPH 1894, 15, 17.

16. Ibid., 7–8, 10, 11.

17. MPH 1895–96, 7–8, 14.

18. MGH 1897 [bound with MPH 1895–96], Máximo B. Rosales, comandante de armas of Choluteca, to Ministerio de Guerra, 22 October 1896, 372.

19. MGH 1898–99 [bound with MPH 1898–99], 341, 339.

20. MGOBH 1909–10, v–vi.

21. MPH 1911, 8–11.

22. P. Romero, Coronel del Ejército, "Algunas consideraciones sobre nuestro Ejército," *Boletín del Ejército* 1 (15 October 1913) 2:35–38.

23. M. Bertrand Anduray, "El Ejército y sus protectores," *Boletín del Ejército* 1 (15 September 1913) 1:19–21

24. NAMP, Roll 12, "Correspondence and Record Cards . . . ," "Specific Military Information, Honduras," 18 January 1919.

25. MGH 1922–23, 77–80; NAMP, Roll 12, "Correspondence and Record Cards . . . ," "Changes in military commanders in Honduras," 6 November 1922.

26. MGH 1922–23, 12

27. NAMP, Roll 12, "Correspondence and Record Cards . . . ," "Honduras," 12 November 1921. The attache made similar observations in a report, "Summary of Military Situation in Central America," of 26 October 1922.

28. MGH 1922–23, 7–8, 9, 10–11.

29. MGH 1923–24, 16–17. In the midst of the war, the United States sent two hundred Marines to occupy the capital and called all sides to a peace conference that resulted in a treaty signed 28 April. Under the treaty, one of Carías's officers, Vicente Tosta, took power but was obligated to hold another election in thirty days. In August, Tosta's war minister rebelled but was finally defeated in October, just two months before an election returned a compromise civilian candidate, Miguel Paz Baraona, as president (1925–29).

30. NAMP, Roll 12, "Correspondence and Record Cards . . . ," Maj. Fred T. Cruse, "Honduras—Combat Information," 1 April 1928.

31. NAMP, Roll 12, "Correspondence and Record Cards . . . ," Maj. Fred T. Cruse, "Honduras—Combat Information," 1 April 1928.

32. Argüeta, *Tiburcio Carías*, 109–110.

33. Argüeta, *Tiburcio Carías*, 76–81

34. MGH 1935–36, 7.

35. MGH 1936–37, 6.

36. Posas and Del Cid, *La Construcción*, 68–71.

37. MGH 1934–35, 3–4.

38. "Breve semblanza de la Organización y Evolución de la Fuerza Aérea Nacional," *Boletín Militar* (Tegucigalpa) May–June 1952, 1–3.

39. MGH 1935–36, 13.

40. Argüeta, *Tiburcio Carías*, 114–15; MGH 1935–36, 13. For the liberal revolt and its suppression, see Argüeta, *Tiburcio Carías*, 298.

41. NAMP, Roll 12, "Correspondence and Record Cards . . . ," Col. J. B. Pate, "Honduras: The School of Aviation," 29 July 1940.

42. NAMP, Roll 12, "Correspondence and Record Cards . . . ," Lt. Col. J. B. Pate, "Honduras—Combat—Army," 21 November 1938.

CHAPTER 6

1. Burns, *Patriarch and Folk*, ably summarized and convincingly documented the scope and frequency of the violence, 13–50; quote by official, 50.

2. Cruz, *Nicaragua's Conservative Republic*, 46.

3. For a refutation of the economistic interpretations of nineteenth-century Nicaraguan politics, see Cruz, *Nicaragua's Conservative Republic*, especially 8–12, as well as Burns, *Patriarch and Folk*, 20–28, 33–34. For the relevance in early Latin America of the proliferation of mutually antagonistic "regional kindreds," see Wolf and Hansen, "Caudillo Politics," 171–72; the decisive significance of a "strong patriarchal family structure" in early Nicaragua was argued by Burns, 2, 71–72.

4. Knut Walter, *The Regime of Anastasio Somoza, 1936–1956* (Chapel Hill: University of North Carolina Press, 1993), 5–7.

5. Cruz, *Nicaragua's Conservative Republic*, 38–44; Burns, *Patriarch and Folk*, 194, 197.

6. "Documento No. 60, El Pacto Providencial," in Antonio Esgueva Gómez, ed., *Las Constituciones Políticas y sus Reformas en la Historia de Nicaragua* (Managua, Nicaragua: Editorial El Parlamento, 1994), 329.

7. Cruz, *Nicaragua's Conservative Republic*, 47–52; Walter, *Regime*, 7, and Burns, *Patriarach and Folk*, 220, also attributed the long peace to the devastation of the war.

8. Pablo Levy, *Notas geográficas y económicas sobre la república de Nicaragua* (Paris: Librería Española de E. Denné Schmitz, 1873), 332–33.

9. Cruz, *Nicaragua's Conservative Republic,* 102, 105.

10. Ibid., 54–55.

11. Levy, *Notas,* 328; 340–43.

12. Ibid., 343.

13. Cruz, *Nicaragua's Conservative Republic,* 54–55, 113. See chapter 3 above for Barrios's ill-fated campaign to unify the isthmus under his command.

14. Ibid., 57–63.

15. Ibid., 56, 61, 75, 93–94, 97, 107–109.

16. Ibid., 18, 122–32.

17. Ibid., 153–55.

18. *El gobierno liberal de Nicaragua: Documentos 1893–1908,* vol. 1 (Managua, Nicaragua: Tip. y Encuadernación Internacional, 1909), 30.

19. ANH, Fondo Policarpo Bonilla, Pres. José Santos Zelaya (Managua), to Pres. Policarpo Bonilla (Tegucigalpa), 1 August 1894.

20. AIHN, *Leyes Varias,* "Ley Reglamentaria de Jefes Políticos," 11 October 1894.

21. Somoza García's formal occupation of the presidency (1 January 1937–31 December 1946, and 21 May 1950–29 September 1956), exceeded that of Zelaya (15 September 1893–16 December 1909) by just thirty-one days (5,968 days for Somoza, and 5,937 for Zelaya).

22. MGN 04–05, 259–60.

23. Orient Bolívar Juárez, *Causas de la Creación, Supresión y Restablecimineto del Departamento de Estelí a Fines del Siglo XIX* (Managua, Nicaragua: Centro de Investigaciones Históricas de Nicaragua "Adolfo Altamirano C.," 1995), 33–46.

24. Zamora Castellanos, *Vida Militar,* vol. II, 528–31.

25. The Marines were subsequently court-martialed and punished; see NAMP, Roll 2, "Correspondence and Record Cards . . . ," "Summary of Intelligence, Managua, Nicaragua, from Feb. 1–Feb. 28, 1921," 28 February 1921.

26. Dana G. Munro, *The United States and the Caribbean Area* (Boston: World Peace Foundation, 1934), 241–46. For the names of the parties, see *Current History* 21 (October 1924) 1:105.

27. Munro, *The United States,* 247–48; Richard V. Salisbury, *Anti-Imperialism and International Competition in Central America 1920–1929* (Wilmington, Del.: Scholarly Resources, 1989), 67–82; Neill Macaulay, *The Sandino Affair* (Durham, N.C.: Duke University Press, 1985), 28–30.

28. Macaulay, *Sandino Affairs,* 62–66, 75, 83–84, 96.

29. Ibid., 130, 135, 239. Macaulay reports that the five thousand included some army personnel dispatched to Nicaragua to supervise the election of 1928 but most were Marines.

30. FRUS 1923:2, "Memorandum by the Secretary of State of a Conversation with the Nicaraguan Minister (Chamorro)," 28 September 1923, 606–607; "The Secretary of State to the Chargé in Nicaragua (Thurston)," 8 October 1923, 607–12; "The Minister in Nicaragua (Ramer) to the Secretary of State," 14 December 1923, 613–14.

31. FRUS 1925:2, "Plan for the Establishment of a Constabulary in Nicaragua," 624–27; "The Chargé in Nicaragua (Thurston) to the Secretary of State," 15 May 1925, 628–30; idem., 20 May 1925, 630–32; "The Secretary of State to the Chargé in Nicaragua (Thurston)," 27 May 1925, 632–33; NAMP, Roll 12, "Correspondence and Record Cards. . . ." "Nicaragua—Establishment of Constabulary Service," 13 March 1925; "Nicaragua—Establishment of Constabulary," 8 April 1925; C. B. Carter, chief, National Guard of Nicaragua, Managua, to Charles C. Eberhardt, U.S. minister, Managua, 1 October 1925.

32. FRUS 1925:2, "The Secretary of State to the Chargé in Nicaragua (Thurston), 16 June 1925, 633–34; Leonard, *U.S. Policy*, 30–32; NAMP, Roll 12, "Correspondence and Record Cards. . . .," A. W. Bloor, military attaché, Managua, to G-2, War Department, 23 May 1927.

33. NAMP, Roll 12, "Correspondence and Record Cards. . . .," "Guardia Nacional de Nicaragua, General Order No. 1, 21 May 1927."

34. Marine Corps commandant Maj. Gen. Ben H. Fuller, in testmony to a U.S. congressional committee in 1931, called the Guardsmen "those Indians," and added: "Also, it takes a good while to make a good soldier out of anybody, and it takes much longer to make one out of a Nicaraguan." NAMP, Roll 12, "Correspondence and Record Cards. . . .," Maj. Fred T. Cruse, military attaché, "Nicaragua—Combat," 3 June 1929. During the intervention, 136 Marines died in what Macaulay called "an impossible task"—to "win a war that had no military solution"; Macaulay, *Sandino Affair*, 135, 151, 161, 173, 184, 239, 241.

35. NAMP, Roll 12, "Correspondence and Record Cards. . . .," Maj. A. R. Harris, military attaché, "Nicaragua (Combat)," 18 November 1932. Italics in original.

36. According to Walter, *The Regime*, 212, Somoza by the late 1940s had engineered a "fusion" of his two main institutional tools—the Liberal Party and the Guardia.

37. AIHN, *Leyes Varias*, Carlos Cuadra Pasos, "Reforma de la Constitución en cuanto a la organización de los Poderes Públicos, Conferencia pronunciada . . . a los alumnos universitarios de la Sociedad Justicia en la Universidad de Granada," January 1932.

38. ANN. Fondo Presidencial/Guardia Nacional/Comandantes Departamentales, 1933–68.

39. NAMP, Roll 12, "Correspondence and Record Cards. . . .," reports by Alex A. Cohen undated and 5 September 1935, and Maj. A. R. Harris undated and 1 March 1935.

40. Walter, *Regime*, 57–58, 97. For the best analysis of the early years of the Guard's existence, see Richard Millett, *Guardians of the Dynasty: A History of the U.S. Created Guardia Nacional de Nicaragua and the Somoza Family* (Maryknoll, N.Y.: Orbis Books), 1977.

41. Walter, *Regime*, 81–82.

42. MGN 1937, 127–28.

43. Paul Coe Clark, Jr., *The United States and Somoza, 1933–1956* (Westport, Conn.: Praeger, 1992), 39, 51, 56.

44. "Wonderful Turnout," *Time* 33 (May 15, 1939) 20:15. © 1939 Time Inc. Reprinted by permission.

45. Felix Belair, Jr., "Washington Pomp Welcomes Somoza," *New York Times*, 6 May 1939, 1, 3.

46. U.S. Congress, *Congressional Record*, 8 May 1939, 5206–7 (Senate) and 5254–55 (House).

47. FRUS 1939:5, Somoza to Roosevelt, 22 May 1939, 727; MGN 1937, 211–12.

48. FRUS 1939:5, "Editorial note," 747; MGN 1939, 7.

49. 10 Bevans 408, 415.

CHAPTER 7

1. Montúfar, *Reseña*, vol. 1, 121–22.

2. José Luis Vega Carballo, *Orden y progreso: La formación del estado nacional en Costa Rica* (San José, Costa Rica: Instituto Centroamericano de Administración Pública, 1981), 36.

3. Vega Carballo, *Orden y progreso*, 62, 71, 44. For an account of the Guerra de la Liga, also see Montúfar, *Reseña*, vol. 2, 211–36.

4. Vega Carballo, *Orden y progreso*, 77–78.

5. Ibid., 97.

6. This interpretation is of course subject to the caveat that the political historiography of nineteenth century Costa Rica is still in its infancy. At this moment, little can be found to directly gainsay it, beyond Urcuyo's judgement that "Violence was a constant in the country's political life during much of the nineteenth century," and even this does not challenge the essential point of Costa Rica's *relative* tranquility; Constantino Urcuyo, "Civil-Military Relations in Costa Rica: Militarization or Adaptation to New Circumstances?" in Louis W. Goodman, Johanna S. R. Mendelson, and Juan Rial, eds., *The Military and Democracy: The Future of Civil-Military Relations in Latin America* (Lexington, Mass.: Lexington Books, 1990), 239–40.

7. Vega Carballo, *Orden y progreso*, 127–31, 134–35.

8. Ibid., in numerous passages, for example, 202–7.

9. Ibid., 161–62.

10. Ibid., 241.

11. Ibid., 245–49. But the military's relationship to the coffee oligarchy has not been clarified; Edwin Solís and Carlos González, *El ejército en Costa Rica: Poder Político, Poder Militar 1821–1890* (San José, Costa Rica: Ediciones Guayacán, 1992), 41–42, 48, 54, argue that the army was just a pawn of the coffee barons during this period.

12. Vega Carballo, *Orden y progreso*, 270, 322.

13. Solís and González, *El ejército*, 71.

14. Pérez Brignoli, *Breve Historia Contemporanea*, 99.

15. MGCR 1880, 2, 4; in 1883, the forces on active service totaled 454 not counting the four military bands; MGCR 1883, 1.

16. Solís and González, *El ejército*, 42–45

17. MGCR 1885, 1–25.

18. Vega Carballo, *Orden y progreso*, 303–4.

19. James L. Busey, "The Presidents of Costa Rica," *The Americas* 18 (July 1961) 1:56–58.

20. Fernando Zamora Castellanos, *Militarismo y Estado Constitucional en Costa Rica* (San José, Costa Rica: Investigaciones Jurídicas, 1997), 85–95.

21. Vega Carballo, *Orden y progreso*, 127–28, 158, 161.

22. Tellingly, the minister's report of the size of the three classes of army service— Operaciones (men eighteen to forty years old), Reserva (men forty-one to fifty), and the Guardia Nacional (men fifty-one to sixty)—was based, not on an army roster but on estimates derived from the last national census, in 1892. The age ranges had been expanded slightly from 1883 to draw in more men, yielding an estimate of 49,200 men who were theoretically available for military service. A military registration campaign was underway that would permit the government to construct a roster and identify those who had received garrison training, the minister said. MGCR 1900, vii–ix.

23. Muñoz Guillen, *El estado*, 111.

24. Pérez Brignoli, *Historia Contemporanea*, 105; Buell, "The United States," 181–83; FRUS 1918, Johnson to Department of State, 244.

25. Zamora Castellanos, *Militarismo y Estado*, 96; for a corroborating view, see Taracena, "Liberalismo y poder político," 221.

26. That the *idea* of a real national army nevertheless remained intact even when it didn't exist in reality is suggested by the officers' roster for 1930, which listed the names of an astonishing total of 4,013 army officers, ranging from 2,106 *subtenientes* to 5 generals; MSPCR 1929, 149–87. For the U.S. attaché d'affaire's estimates, see NAMP, Roll 11, "Correspondence and Record Cards . . . ," "Costa Rica, Service Report," 19 March 1921; "Combat Factor, Costa Rica," 3 May 1922; Maj. Fred T. Cruse, "Costa Rica, Combat," 13 August 1929.

27. Muñoz Guillén, *El estado*, 111.

28. NAMP, Roll 11, "Correspondence and Record Cards . . . ," Maj. A. R. Harris, "G-2 Report, Costa Rica (Combat)," 4 December 1933.

29. José Luis Vega Carballo, *Poder político y democracia en Costa Rica* (San José, Costa Rica: Editorial Porvenir, 1982), 98, 99. For a remarkable analysis of electoral fraud, including the use of force against voters, based on government records, see Molina and Lehoucq, *Urnas*, especially 44–48, 86, 109; for the strength of personalism, see *Urnas*, 139, 144.

30. Muñoz Guillén, *El Estado*, 31, 33, 130, 132.

31. Fabrice Edouard Lehoucq, "The Institutional Foundations of Democratic Cooperation in Costa Rica," *Journal of Latin American Studies* 28 (May 1996) 2:335, 338.

32. Molina and Lehoucq, *Urnas*, 109–12; for a detailed description of the interference by the police and army in the 1932 election, see Muñoz Guillén, *El Estado*, 130–32.

33. NAMP, Roll 11, "Correspondence and Record Cards . . . ," Alex A. Cohen, "G-2 Report, Costa Rica (Combat)," 6 February 1934.

CHAPTER 8

1. For authoritarianism, see Juan J. Linz, "Totalitarian and Authoritarian Regimes," in *Handbook of Political Science: Macropolitical Theory*, eds. F. I. Greenstein and N. W. Polsby (Reading, Mass.: Addison-Wesley, 1975), 175–373; Enrique Baloyra-Herp, "Reactionary Despotism in Central America," *Journal of Latin American Studies* 15 (November 1983) 2:295–319; for the last two categories see Alain Rouquie, *The Military and the State in Latin America*, trans. Paul E. Sigmund (Berkeley: University of California Press, 1987), chs. 5 and 6.

2. Dosal expertly summarized the exploitation of public violence by U.S.-owned banana companies in Honduras and Guatemala in *Doing Business with Dictators*, especially 80–81, 152–53. For the best treatment of Honduras, see Marvin Barahona, *La Hegemonía de los Estados Unidos en Honduras (1907–1932)* (Tegucigalpa, Honduras: Centro de Documentación de Honduras, 1989). Lester D. Langley and Thomas Schoonover chronicled the pre-1930 activities of U.S. fruit and mineral exporters, as well as U.S. mercenary soldiers, in *The Banana Men: American Mercenaries and Entrepreneurs in Central America, 1880–1930* (Lexington: University Press of Kentucky, 1995); also see Darío Euraque, *Reinterpreting the Banana Republic: Region and State in Honduras, 1870–1972* (Chapel Hill: University of North Carolina Press, 1996), especially 43–44, 48.

3. My approach to globalization and my understanding of both its historical sources and the role of military power in that process were strongly influenced by Anthony Giddens, *The Consequences of Modernity* (Oxford: Polity Press, 1990), chs. 1–2.

4. Although Krause argued that a "genuinely global arms transfer and production system" emerged in the fifteenth and sixteenth centuries, it was, he added, nevertheless a "system" largely devoid of active state control: "Arms are widely traded, but this represents more a triumph of primitive capitalism and the prestige and power of modern technology than a triumph of conscious state policies." Production and even technological innovation were limited by mercantilism and the instinct for autarky. Keith Krause, *Arms and the State: Patterns of Military Production and Trade* (Cambridge: Cambridge University Press, 1992), 36, 53. Of course, the local impact of imported European arms and military methods could be considerable, as David B. Ralston argued in the cases of Russia, the Ottoman Empire, Egypt, China, and Japan at different moments between 1600 and 1914, in *Importing the European Army: The Introduction of European Military Techniques and Institutions into the Extra-European World, 1600–1914* (Chicago: University of Chicago Press, 1990), ix, 2–3, ch. 7.

5. Krause, *Arms and the State*, 58.

6. Ibid., 72–79.

7. For fascinating signs of both the genesis of Cold War globalization in the age of second-wave imperialism, and the extraordinary mutations to which that hereditary material was subjected, compare *Small Wars: Their Principles and Practice*, written in the late 1890s by

Royal Army Maj. Charles E. Callwell, and the twelve essays produced a century later in *Small Wars*, William J. Olson, ed., vol. 541 (September 1995) of the *Annals of the American Academy of Political and Social Science*.

8. John Stanley and Maurice Pearton, *The International Trade in Arms*. (London: Chatto and Windus, 1972), 5–7; for a historical discussion, see Asjorn Eide and Mary Kaldor, "Conclusion," *The World Military Order: The Impact of Military Technology on the Third World*, eds. Mary Kaldor and Asbjorn Eide (London: Macmillan, 1979), 265–66.

9. Albrecht and Kaldor, "Introduction," 4; David Mussington, *Arms Unbound: The Globalization of Defense Production* (Washington, D.C.: Brassey's, 1994), 79–80.

10. Ronald Steel, *Pax Americana* (New York: Viking Press, 1967), 10.

11. Containment was position defense, the deployment of most of one's defensive forces "in selected tactical localities where the decisive battle is to be fought. Principal reliance is placed on the ability of the forces in the defended localities to maintain their positions and to control the terrain between them." Wolfram F. Hanrieder and Larry V. Buel, *Words and Arms: A Dictionary of Security and Defense Terms* (Boulder, Colo.: Westview Press, 1979), 96. Also, "Warfare in which the defensive is confined chiefly to fixed positions, for keeping the enemy out of strategic areas"; Frank Gaynor, ed., *The New Military and Naval Dictionary* (New York: Greenwood Press, 1951), 197.

12. Leon Martel, *Lend-Lease, Loans, and the Coming of the Cold War: A Study of the Implementation of Foreign Policy* (Boulder, Colo.: Westview Press, 1979), 4–5.

13. For Draper, see United States, President, The President's Committee to Study the United States Military Assistance Program, "Composite Report," 17 August 1959, vol. I, 4. Attempts to quantify the global arms trade are notoriously risky. This estimate by Council on Foreign Relations researcher Andrew J. Pierre in his *The Global Politics of Arms Sales* (Princeton, N.J.: Princeton University Press, 1982), 45, bore the imprimatur of the Council (a conservative channel for elite opinion) as "a responsible treatment of a significant international topic."

14. Richard F. Grimmett, "An Overview of United States Military Assistance Programs," Congressional Research Service, based on statement before Foreign Operations Subcommittee of the House Committee on Appropriations, March 9, 1988, in U.S. Congress, House, *Background Materials on Foreign Assistance*, Report of the Task Force on Foreign Assistance to the Committee on Foreign Affairs, February 1989, 101st Cong., 1st Sess. (Washington, D.C.: Government Printing Office, 1989), 279.

15. *USS* 63:1, Sec. 411, 401:720–721, 716 (1949).

16. *USS* 63:1, Sec. 408(e):720 (1949).

17. *USS* 65, Sec. 511:381 (1951). For the hemispheric restriction, see Sec. 401:377.

18. Mark L. Morgan and Mark A. Berhow, *Rings of Supersonic Steel: Air Defenses of the United States Army 1950–1979, an Introductory History and Site Guide* (San Pedro, Calif.: Fort MacArthur Museum, 1996), 8–9, 29. My thanks to Christopher Bright for pointing this out to me, and supplying the source.

19. *USS* 69, Sec. 2(c):284 (1955). For a historical survey of credit sales, see U.S. Congress, Senate, Committee on Banking, Housing and Urban Affairs, *Financing of Foreign Military Sales. Hearing*. 95th Cong., 2d Sess., January 30, 1978 (Washington, D.C.: Government Printing Office, 1978), 22–29.

20. *USS* 68:1, Sec. 131(a):838 (1954) and *USS* 68:1, Sec. 131:838 (1955).

21. For historical overviews and interpretations of these programs, see Larry Q. Nowels, "An Overview of the Economic Support Fund," Congressional Research Service, in U.S., Congress, House, *Background Materials on Foreign Assistance; Report of the Task Force on Foreign Assistance to the Committee on Foreign Affairs, February 1989*. 101st Cong., 1st Sess. (Y4.F76/

1:F76/71) (Washington, D.C.: Government Printing Office, 1989), 260–68; and Paul L. Ferrari, Raul L. Madrid and Jeff Knopf, *U.S. Arms Exports: Policies and Contractors* (Cambridge, Mass.: Ballinger, 1988), 66.

22. U.S. Congress, House, *International Security Assistance Act of 1976; Report of the Committee on International Relations*, 94th Cong., 2d Sess., House Report No. 94–848, 24 February 1976, 30–31.

23. Philip J. Farley, Stephen S. Kaplan, and William H. Lewis, *Arms Across the Sea* (Washington, D.C.: Brookings Institution Press, 1978), 34.

24. Murray Stedman, *Exporting Arms: The Federal Arms Exports Administration, 1935–1945*. (New York: Kings Crown Press, 1947), 1–3; Joseph P. Smaldone, "U.S. Commercial Arms Exports: Policy, Process, and Patterns," in David J. Louscher and Michael D. Salomone, eds., *Marketing Security Assistance: New Perspectives on Arms Sales* (Lexington, Mass.: Lexington Books, 1987), 187–88.

25. Calculations by author, based on tabular data supplied to author via FOIA by the U.S. Department of Defense, Defense Security Assistance Agency, "DSAA Fiscal Year Series," 1950–90.

26. DDRS (1987/1081), White House, memorandum by Col. E. G. Lansdale, Office of Special Operations, Department of Defense [no destination], 27 April 1959.

27. NA, WNRC, RG286, AID/OPS: Director's Numerical Files, Box 3, "General Reports and Statistics," "Internal Security Programs," 20 March 1961.

28. DDRS (R/962B), Institute for Defense Analysis, "Studies for the President's Committee to Study the U.S. Military Assistance Program (Final Report)," 3 March 1959, 10–31 to 10–35. NA, WNRC, RG286, AID/OPS: Director's Numerical File. Box 2. IPS-1, General Policy, "Report," 14 December 1956. Police training was considered a " technical cooperation activity" under the authority of Section 302 of the Mutual Security Act of 1954. "The act in delineating permissible technical cooperation activities includes 'training in public administration.' Public Safety is one phase of public administration." In addition, support for civil police forces after 1956 was justified "under Defense Support, Development Assistance, and Special Assistance authority." See DDRS (1987/1080), White House, Edwin H. Arnold, DD/S, to J. H. Smith Jr., D/ICA, 12 November 1958.

29. DDRS (1987/1080), White House, Edwin H. Arnold, DD/S, to J. H. Smith, Jr., D/ICA, 12 November 1958.

30. NA, WNRC, RG286, AID/OPS, Director's Numerical Files, Box 3, "General Reports and Statistics," "Internal Security Programs," 20 March 1961.

31. Created by President Eisenhower in 1953 and chaired by the under secretary of state, the OCB was made up of the deputy secretary of defense, the directors of the Central Intelligence Agency and the Foreign Operations Administration, and a representative of the President. It was to "provide for the integrated implementation of national security policies by the several agencies concerned," reporting to the Natonal Security Council. FRUS 1952–54:2:1:455.

32. DDRS (1987/2274), White House, Operations Coordinating Board, "Operational and Coordinating Arrangements for the NSC Action No. 1290-d Program," 19 September 1956.

33. NA, WNRC, RG286, AID/OPS, Director's Numerical Files, Box 3, "General Reports and Statistics," "Internal Security Programs," 20 March 1961. One source claims the CIA affiliation was terminated briefly in 1961 but resumed with the appointment of Byron Engle as head of the newly formed Office of Public Safety in 1962; Charles Maechling, Jr., "Camelot, Robert Kennedy, and Counter-Insurgency—A Memoir," *Virginia Quarterly Review* 75 (Summer 1999) 3:450. Engle's precise connection with the CIA has yet to be clearly established, though more than one source—including Robert Amory, Jr., quoted below—point to an affiliation with the agency, which may even have been his primary employer; see Maechling, 450.

34. John F. Kennedy Library, Boston, "Second Oral History Interview with Robert Amory Jr., February 17, 1966, Washington, D.C.," by Joseph E. O'Connor for the John F. Kennedy Library, 99–103.

35. Collaboration with state terrorism in the supply of training and material resources, and the supervision that inevitably accompanied it, continued in Guatemala even after the Cold War, according to the U.S. government's Intelligence Oversight Board. The human rights records of the Guatemalan " security services . . . were generally known to have been reprehensible by all who were familiar with Guatemala," yet the U.S. Central Intelligence Agency provided those services with between $1 million and $3.5 million a year between 1989 and 1995, the Board reported on 28 June 1996. U.S. Intelligence Oversight Board, "Report on the Guatemala Review."

36. Nor would it be prudent to assume any ideological consistency in the collaborative relationships developed by counterinstitutional agents of Central American public violence. In 1949, the Costa Rican insurgency led by José Figueres was thoroughly anticommunist, whereas that of the Nicaraguan Frente Sandinista de la Liberación Nacional in the 1970s drew on Panamanian and Venezuelan sources as well as Cuban communist ones, and that of the anti-Sandinista "contras" in the 1980s relied first on Argentine and later on U.S. collaboration.

CHAPTER 9

Part of chapter 9 appeared under the title "Securing Central America Against Communism: The United States and the Modernization of Surveillance in the Cold War," *Journal of Interamerican Studies and World Affairs* 41 (1) (Spring 1999), 1–30.

1. As late as 1954, according to the chief U.S. military advisor in Honduras, "this country manufactures nothing and every item necessary to equip the [U.S.-created infantry] unit, including but not limited to uniforms, personal equipment, housekeeping equipment, tentage, building hardware, and transportation must be imported." NA, RG59, 715.5-MSP/6–854, Col. M. C. Shattuck, acting chief MAAG, Tegucigalpa, to Department of the Army, 8 June 1954.

2. The War Department's policy statement on collaboration with Latin American governments, as approved by Roosevelt, was reproduced in Stetson Conn and Byron Fairchild, *The Framework of Hemisphere Defense* (Washington, D.C.: Office of the Chief of Military History, Department of the Army, 1960), 213.

3. FRUS 1940:5, John M. Cabot (U.S. chargé d'affaires, Guatemala) to Department of State, 3 July 1940, 113; Cabot thought Pate was exaggerating the speed and thoroughness with which Germany could take over the governments of the isthmus, but agreed that a German threat existed (114).

4. Hanson W. Baldwin, *United We Stand! Defense of the Western Hemisphere* (New York: Whittlesey House, 1941), 89.

5. Central American defense budgets broken out by major spending categories could not be found except for El Salvador, where spending on "materiales, artículos, repuestos" and "equipo" for 1959–64 ranged from a low of 9 percent to a high of 14 percent. See República de El Salvador, Ministerio de Economía, Dirección General, de Estadística y Censos, *Anuario Estadístico* for years 1955 through 1986 (San Salvador: Imprenta Nacional, 1955–86).

6. AGCA, MdeD, L 20455, Embassy of Guatemala in Washington to U.S. Secretary of State James F. Byrnes, 17 September 1946.

7. U.S. Congress, "Thirty-Ninth Report to Congress on Lend-Lease Operations: Message from the President of the United States . . . for the year ending December 31, 1957," 85th Cong., 2d Sess., House Document No. 449 (Washington, D.C.: Government Printing Office, 1958), Appendix I (b).

8. Mission agreements can be found in Bevans and UST. When collaborator governments accepted grant military aid under the MAP, mission members administered the grant material and training; while doing so, they were responsible not to the government but to the chief of the U.S. diplomatic mission.

9. Walter, *Regime*, 134; Posas and Del Cid, *La construcción*, 73–74; Dunkerley, *Power in the Isthmus*, 122–24.

10. FRUS 1944:7, Secretary of State Edward R. Stettinius, Jr., to U.S. representatives in the five Central American republics, 2 February 1944, 1391–92.

11. For the U.S.-influenced "Thermidoran reaction" *against* the popular mobilizations immediately *following* World War II all across Latin America, see Leslie Bethell and Ian Roxborough, "Latin America between the Second World War and the Cold War: Some Reflections on the 1945–8 Conjuncture," in *Journal of Latin American Studies* 20 (1988):167–89.

12. A copy of the pact was sent to the Department of State by the U.S. chargé d'affaires in Managua, who said it was given to him by General Somoza on 21 March 1948, nearly a year after it was signed. Somoza, according to the chargé d'affaires, cited the pact as one of the reasons for "his proposed intervention in Costa Rica against 'the communist menace.'" NA, RG59, 818.00/4–248, Enclosure with memorandum, Maurice M. Bernbaum, chargé d'affaires ad interim, Managua, to Department of State, 2 April 1948.

13. Bulmer-Thomas, *Political Economy*, especially chs. 6–7.

14. Dunkerley, *Power in the Isthmus*, 87.

15. MRECR 1951–52, "Carta de San Salvador," 61–64.

16. MRECR 1952–53, "Organización de Estados Centroamericanos," 13–14; MRECR 1952–53, 188–190. Raúl Osegueda, ministro de relaciones exteriores de Guatemala, to Fernando Lara Bustamante, ministro de relaciones exteriores de Costa Rica, 4 April 1953; MRECR, 1954–55, x; MRECR 1955–56, 10, 59–60. For Operation Fortune, the Berle recommendation and the initiation of Operation Success, see Gleijeses, *Shattered Hope*, 228–31, 239–41, 243, and Herbert Matthews, *A World in Revolution: A Newspaperman's Memoir* (New York: Charles Scribner's Sons, 1971), 262–63.

17. Briefing prepared at Conference on CONDECA at Headquarters, USSOUTHCOM July 1967, 1, cited in Laun C. Smith, Jr., "Central American Defense Council: Some Problems and Achievements," *Air University Review* XX (March–April 1969) 3:69.

18. See, for example, FRUS 1955–57:7, "Memorandum from Richard B. Moon of the Office of Middle American Affairs to the Director of the Office (Wieland)," July 9, 1957, 235–37.

19. NA, RG59, 716.5-MSP/4–953, John Foster Dulles, secretary of state, to Charles E. Wilson, secretary of defense, April 9, 1953. Also see FRUS 1952–54:4, "Memorandum on Substance of Discussions at a Dept. of State-JCS Meeting," 22 May 1953, 151–52.

20. NA, RG59, 717.5-MSP/6–2453, F. C. Nash, assistant secretary of defense, to secretary of state, 18 June 1953; FRUS 1952–54:4, "Memorandum on Substance of Discussions at a Dept. of State-JCS Meeting," 22 May 1953, 151–53.

21. NA, RG59, 717.5-MSP/7–2353, Woodward to the Secretary, 16 July 1953; 717.5-MSP/6–2453, Burrows to Mann, 24 June 1953; F. C. Nash, assistant secretary of defense, to secretary of state, 18 June 1953; 717.5-MSP/7–2353, H. Freeman Matthews, deputy undersecretary of state, to Charles E. Wilson, secretary of defense, 23 July 1953; 717.5-MSP/11–1753, secretary of defense to secretary of state, 17 November 1953; 717.5-MSP/12–1453, President Eisenhower to director, Foreign Operations Administration, 9 December 1953, 717.5-MSP/5–1154, Frederick C. Nolting, Jr., special assistant to the president, National Security Affairs, to Maj. Gen. George C. Stewart, director, Office of Military Assistance, Department of Defense, 11 May 1954; 717.5-MSP/5–2154, Commander, Caribbean Command, to secretary of state, 21 May 1954; 717.5-MSP/5–2154, Dulles to U.S. Embassy, Nicaragua, 21 May 1954.

22. NA, RG218, CCS 092 (8–22–46) Sec. 106, 1954–56, Box 12, Brig. Gen. Edwin H. J. Carns, secretary, Joint Chiefs of Staff, to chairman, Inter-American Defense Board, 17 February 1954.

23. UST 5.1.843 (Honduras) and UST 5.1.453 (Nicaragua).

24. DDRS (1979/124C), Central Intelligence Agency, "National Intelligence Estimate Number 80–54. The Caribbean Republics," August 1954, 8–9.

25. NA, FOIA, RG59, 720.5/5–2256, Dulles to various diplomatic posts in the Americas, 22 May 1956.

26. NA, RG218, 092 (8–22–46) (2) B.O. Part 15-A, N. F. Twining, chairman, Joint Chiefs of Staff, to secretary of defense, 14 November 1957.

27. DDRS (1983/156), Department of Defense, "Report by the Joint Strategic Plans Commitee to the Joint Chiefs of Staff on Military Assistance Program: Honduras, Nicaragua and Guatemala," 30 January 1958; USAMHI/Lib. OO/DD-ISA/MAPG/1958. "Military Assistance Programming Guidance," Department of Defense, International Security Affairs, 1958.

28. DDRS (1979/124C), Central Intelligence Agency, "National Intelligence Estimate Number 80–54, the Caribbean Republics." August 1954, 8–9.

29. NA, FOIA, RG 59, 1954–55, 716.521/6–154 [Salazar]; 714.521/1–1255 CS/W [St. Croix]; 715.521/8–354 [Stephansky]; 716.521/5–553 CS/W [Honduran]; 716.521/6–2855 [Gamero].

30. NA, RG59. 718.5/6–2656 FOIA, U.S. Embassy, Costa Rica, Costa Rica, to Department of State, 26 June 1956.

31. NA, RG59, 1957, 714.551/8–1357, Thomas C. Mann, U.S. Embassy, El Salvador to Department of State, 13 August 1957.

32. FRUS 1958–60:5MS, Guatemala, "Summary of Discussions in Guatemala during Milton Eisenhower's Visit, July 30–August 1, 1958," 1081–83.

33. NA, WNRC, RG286, AID/OPS, Director's Numerical File, Box 4, IPS 2–3, Program Surveys, "Department of Defense Internal Security Program," enclosure to Department of State instruction to all Latin American diplomatic posts, 7 November 1960.

34. NA, FOIA, RG59. 713.5/8–761. Williams, San Salvador, to Department of State, 7 August 1961.

35. Manuel Rojas Bolaños, "La Política," in Héctor Pérez Brignoli, ed., *De la posguerra a la crisis (1945–1979)*, vol. 5 of *Historia general de centroamérica*, Edelberto Torres-Rivas, coordinator (Madrid: Sociedad Estatal Quinto Cententario y FLACSO, 1993), 118–19.

36. Rojas Bolaños, "La Política," 134; Rafael Obregón Loria, *Hechos Militares y Políticos de Nuestra Historia Patria* (Alajuela, Costa Rica: Museo Histórico Cultural Juan Santamaría, 1981), 355.

37. DDRS (1988/2072), Department of State, Christian A. Herter, secretary of state, to President Eisenhower, 16 November 1960.

38. It was front-page news in Central America; see United Press International, "Eisenhower Ordena Protección a Nicaragua y Guatemala," *La Nación* (San José), 18 November 1960, 1, 16; *Department of State Bulletin*, 12 December 1960, 888, and 19 December 1960, 924.

39. FRUS 1952–54:4, "National Intelligence Estimate, NIE-80–54, The Caribbean Republics," 24 August 1954, 380, 396.

40. FRUS 1955–57:6, "National Intelligence Estimate. Political Stability in Central America and the Caribbean Through 1958." 23 April 1957, 642.

CHAPTER 10

Epigraph source: NA, RG59, 714.5 MSP/8–1158 H BS, L. D. Mallory, U.S. ambassador, Guatemala, to Department of State, 11 August 1958.

1. FRUS 1940:5, U.S. Ambassador Fay Allen Des Portes to Department of State, 4 June 1940, 112.

2. FRUS 1940:5, various correspondence, 114–22. Ubico also wanted the United States to force Great Britain to cede British Honduras to Guatemala, according to Grieb, *Guatemalan Caudillo*, 260; the military mission agreement is at 8 Bevans 568, 577.

3. Conn and Fairchild, *Framework*, 254, 347–48; Stetson Conn, Rose C. Engelman and Byron Fairchild, *Guarding the United States and Its Outposts* (Washington, D.C.: Office of the Chief of Military History, Department of the Army, 1964), 343; MGG 1941, 23; AGCA, MdeD, L 20498; U.S. House, Report No. 950, 78th Cong., 1st Sess., 13 December 1943 (Washington, D.C.: Government Printing Office, 1944), 3.

4. For the agreements and related correspondence, see FRUS 1942:6, 433–51.

5. MGG 1942, 29–30

6. MGG 1943, 68–69; 28.

7. Ibid., 4

8. For Ubico's downfall, the U.S. reaction, and the transition to constitutional rule, see Gleijeses, *Shattered Hope*, 23–26.

9. Juan José Arévalo, *El Presidente Electo al Pueblo de la República* (Guatemala City: Tipografía Nacional, February 1945), 8–9.

10. AGCA, MdeD, Lejago 20821, "Acta de la sesión de inauguración de las conversaciones bilaterales de estado mayor entre representantes de los Estados Unidos de América y de Guatemala," "Discurso del Teniente General Brett." and related "Reseñas" of subsequent meetings, 9–14 May 1945.

11. AGCA, MdeD, L 20821, "Respuestas a las Preguntas de la Misión Militar Norteamericana," 15 May 1945; FRUS 1945:9, Kyle, U.S. ambassador, to Department of State, 28 August 1945, 1083; for corroboration of Arévalo's subordination to the will of the Army, see USAMHI/Lib, Intelligence Division, General Staff, U.S. Army, "Intelligence Research Project: Characteristics and Capabilities of Latin American Armies," 17 June 1949.

12. AGCA, MdeD, L 20821, "Agreement Between the Government of the Republic of Guatemala and the Government of the U.S.A.," 21 May 1945.

13. MGG 1945, 3–4, 22–24; for the prereform system of organization, see MGG 1931, 52–54.

14. MGG 1945, 10. Another seventeen went to Mexico for advanced study.

15. Ibid., 9–10.

16. According to Gleijeses, *Shattered Hope*, 53, the president-elect met privately twice with Arana and "had little choice but to agree" to Arana's demand.

17. AGCA, MdeD, L 20821, "Reseña de la Reunión de Clausura de las Conferencias Bilaterales de Estado Mayor, entre Representantes de los Estados Unidos de America y de Guatemala."

18. AGCA, MdeD, L 20456, Col. Oscar Morales López, agregado militar y aéreo, Embassy of Guatemala in Washington, to Jacobo Arbenz, minister of defense, 12 March 1947.

19. Gleijeses, *Shattered Hope*, 59–60; 67–69, 72.

20. Gleijeses, *Shattered Hope*, 82.

21. NA, RG330/21/Guatemala, various documents; RG59, 714.56/12–1550, memorandum of conversation, Mann and Antonio Goubaud Carrera, ambassador of Guatemala in the United States, and Colonel Giron, chief of the Guatemalan Air Force, 15 December 1950.

22. AGCA, MdeD, L 20821, Col. Clyde E. Steele, chief of U.S. Military Ground Mission, Guatemala, to minister of defense, 19 January 1946.

23. AGCA, MdeD, L 20821, Col. Clyde E. Steele, chief of U.S. Military Ground Mission, Guatemala, to minister of defense, 29 October 1946.

24. AGCA, MdeD, L 20822, Col. Clyde E. Steele, chief of U.S. Military Ground Mission, Guatemala, to Ray Tasco Davis, dirctor, Consejo de Servicio de Escuelas Americanas, Washington DC, 15 January 1947; L 20823, Lt. Col. Stephen D. McElroy, chief of U.S. Military Air Mission, Guatemala, to Ministry of Defense, 4 March 1948.

25. MGG 1945, 9–10; AGCA; Ministry of Defense, L 20822, Lt. Col. Stephen D. McElroy, chief of U.S. Military Air Mission, Guatemala, to Ministry of Defense, 12 September 1947; L 21171, "Memoria de labores del ramo de la defensa nacional. Año 1947," L 20824, Col. W. W. O'Connor, chief of U.S. Army Mission to Guatemala, to Ministry of Defense, 22 November 1948; Ls 20821–27, U.S. Military Missions in Guatemala; L 20826, "Guatemalan Officers Who Have Attended Courses at U.S. Army Service Schools Since 1941, in U.S. and Panama," February 1949; L 20826, Col. W. W. O'Connor, chief of U.S. Army Mission in Guatemala, to minister of defense, 30 March 1949.

26. AGCA, MdeD, L 21167, Col. W. W. O'Connor, chief, U.S. Military Mission in Guatemala, to minister of national defense, 15 December 1947.

27. AGCA, MdeD, L 20822, Lt. Col. Stephen D. McElroy, chief of U.S. Military Air Mission, Guatemala, to Ministry of Defense, 30 July 1947.

28. AGCA, MdeD, L 20826, untitled document, 30 March 1949.

29. Peurifoy to Secretary of State John Foster Dulles, 19 November 1953, cited in Gleijeses, *Shattered Hope*, 255–56.

30. NA, RG469, Latin American Geographical File, Guatemala, General, 1954, U.S. Embassy, Paris to Department of State, 24 June 1954; RG 59, 714.5-MSP/10–2554, Holland to secretary of state, 25 October 1954.

31. This analysis is consistent with the account of the army's behavior reported by Gleijeses, *Shattered Hope*. Gleijeses emphasized the failure of the army to defend the Arbenz government as the proximate cause of its downfall, but offered no interpretation of the army's role in the persistence of the Guatemalan revolution of 1944–54, except to observe, at p. 50, that Arbenz pampered it in order to preserve its loyalty. Arbenz's government was, if not pro-communist, at least "riddled with communists" according to Gleijeses, 318; also see 196–205, 246–47, 304–305, 308, 333, 339, 341–42; Tim Weiner, "CIA in 1950's Drew Up List of Guatemalan Leaders to Be Assassinated," *New York Times*, 28 May 1997, 5.

32. For the best chronology of events, see Gleijeses, *Shattered Hope*, ch. 14.

33. The planes only cost $5,400 apiece ($16,200 altogether) but spare parts, ground handling equipment and special tools cost $83,337; see NA, RG330/21/Guatemala, case summary sheet; Peurifoy to secretary of state, 24 July 1954; Frederick E. Nolting, Jr., special assistant to secretary for mutual security affairs, to H. Struve Hensel, assistant secretary of defense, ISA, [date illegible]; Col. S. F. Langley, Air Force, to director, Office of Military Assistance, OSD, 14 September 1954; RG330/21A/Guatemala, letters between Puerifoy and Carlos Salazar, Guatemalan foreign minister, 27 July 1954; WNRC, RG469, Latin American Geographical File/Guatemala/General/1954, Hoover, Department of State, to U.S. Embassy, Guatemala, 22 October 1954.

34. Villagrán Kramer, *Biografía Política*, 251–63; but Ebel, in *Misunderstood Caudillo*, 43, reported that eight of the sixty-six delegates were unaligned with the *junta*.

35. NA, RG59, 714.5622/10–1354, Thomas C. Mann, counselor of the U.S. Embassy, Guatemala, to secretary of state, 13 October 1954.

36. NA, RG59, 714.5-MSP/10–2054, U.S. Embassy, Guatemala to John Foster Dulles, secretary of state, 16 October 1954.

37. NA, RG59, 714.56/10–2754, John Foster Dulles, secretary of state, to Charles E. Wilson, secretary of defense, 27 October 1954.

38. NA, RG218, CCS092 (8–22–46) 1954–56, Sec. 123, "Report by the Joint Stategic Plans Committee to the Joint Chiefs of Staff on Military Assistance for Guatemala," 3 December 1954.

39. NA, RG59, 714.5622/11.554, Thomas C. Mann, counsellor of the U.S. Embassy, Guatemala, to Department of State, 5 November 1954.

40. NA, RG59, 714.5622/12–2854, U.S. Embassy, Guatemala to Dulles, 28 December 1954; 714.5-MSP/12–154, Nolting to Wilson, 1 December 1954; 714.5-MSP/11–2954, Nolting to Stassen, 29 November 1954; 714.5-MSP/11–1654, Memorandum of Conversation, "Military Assistance to Guatemala," 16 November 1954; 714.56/12–854, Dulles to U.S. Embassy, Guatemala, 8 December 1954; 714.5622/11.554, Mann, U.S. Embassy, Guatemala, to Department of State, 5 November 1954; RG330/2A/Guatemala, Armour, U.S. Embassy, Guatemala, to Dulles, 4 November 1954; RG330/21/Guatemala, Armour, U.S. Embassy, Guatemala, to Dulles, 16 November 1954; Frederick E. Nolting, Jr., special assistant to secretary for mutual security affairs, to Col. James K. Wilson, acting director, Office of Military Assistance, Department of Defense, 18 November 1954; "Estimated Costs, Case No. OMA/Guatemala 6," 22 November 1954; Nolting to Wilson, 3 December 1954; "Guatemala 6," 30 August 1955; FRUS 1952–54:4, "Editorial Note," 1217; Dulles to Wilson 27 October 1954, 1234–1236; Dulles to Stassen, 26 November 1954, 1237.

41. NA, RG59, 714.5-MSP/3–155, George O. Spencer, Bureau of Inter-American Affairs, Department of State, to Mr. Sparks, Bureau of Inter-American Affairs, 1 March 1955; 714.5-MSP/3–255 CS/W, Spencer to Jamison, 2 March 1955; 714.5-MSP/4–1955, U.S. Embassy, Guatemala to Department of State, 19 April 1955; 714.5-MSP/3–1655, U.S. Embassy, Guatemala to secretary of state, 16 March 1955.

42. FRUS 1955–57:7, "Letter from the Deputy Under Secretary of State for Political Affairs (Murphy) to the Director of the Foreign Operations Administration (Stassen)," 4 March 1955, 68–69.

43. NA, 714.5-MSP/3–1655, U.S. Embassy, Guatemala to secretary of state, 16 March 1955.

44. NA, RG55, 720.5 MSP/4–155, Robert Murphy, deputy undersecretary of state, to H. Struve Hensel, assistant secretary of international security, Department of Defense, 1 April 1955.

45. FRUS 1955–57:6, Davis (Department of Defense) to secretary of state, 20 April 1955, 223–24.

46. NA, RG59, FW714.5-MSP/5–555, Eisenhower to director, Foreign Operations Adminsitration, 2 May 1955. The authorization invoked not only Sec. 105 (b) (4) of the Mutual Security Act of 1954, which specified that military assistance to Latin America may only be provided for hemispheric defense, but Sec. 105 (a), which allowed military assistance "to any nation whose increased ability to defend itself the President shall have determined to be important to the security of the United States. . . ." See USS 68, 1, 834–835 (1954). The implementation of the MAP agreement had to await the approval of Guatemala's National Constituent Assembly on 27 October, and the signature of Castillo Armas the next day; NA, RG59,714.5-MSP/11–855, U.S. Embassy, Guatemala, to Department of State, 8 November 1955.

47. NA, RG59,n714.5-MSP/5–355 CS/W, Mr. Holland, ARA, to Secretary of State Dulles, 3 May 1955.

48. NA, FOIA, RG59,714.5/5–855, U.S. Ambassador Armour, Guatemala City, to Department of State, 9 May 1955.

49. Both countries agreed to publish the full text (except for a secret annex), but after much haggling the United States denied Guatemala's request that the text of the agreement refer to military "cooperación" instead of "asistencia." NA, RG59,714.5-MSP/6–1155, U.S. Embassy, Guatemala, to secretary of state, 11 June 1955; 714.5-MSP/6–1455, U.S. Embassy, Guatemala, to secretary of state, 14 June 1955; 611.147/6–1455, Henry F. Holland, ARA, to Mr. Phleger, 14 June 1955; 714.5-MSP/6–1755, U.S. Embassy, Guatemala, to secretary of state, 17 June 1955; 714.5-MSP/6–2055, U.S. Embassy, Guatemala, to secrtary of state, 20 June 1955.

50. FRUS 1955–57:7, "National Intelligence Estimate. Probable Developments in Guatemala," 26 July 1955, 94.

51. NA, RG59,714.56/8–255, U.S. Embassy, Guatemala, to Department of State, 2 August 1955; 714.56/8–255, Frederick E. Nolting, Jr., special assistant to secretary for mutual security affairs, to Department of Defense, 15 August 1955; 714.5 MSP/8–1655, Memorandum of Conversation, "Purchase of Military Equipment," 16 August 1955; 714.5-MSP/8–1755, Mr. Neal, MID, to Mr. Lyon, ARA, 17 August 1955; 714.56/8–1955, Nolting to Department of Defense, 19 August 1955.

52. NA, RG59,714.5-MSP/8–3055. Sparks, U.S. Embassy, Guatemala, to secretary of state, 30 August 1955. NA, RG330/21A/Guatemala, "Reimbursable Military Assistance," 30 September 1955.

53. NA, RG273. Operations Coordinating Board (OCB), "Report to the National Security Council Pursuant to NSC Action 1290-d," 23 November 1955.

54. AID/Lib, "Mutual Security Program, Vol. IV, Program Estimates Fiscal Year 1957: Latin America Non-Regional"; U.S. Congress, House, 84th Cong., 1st Sess., "Report of the Special Study Mission to Central America on International Organizations and Movements," House Report No. 1155 (Washington, D.C.: Government Printing Office, 1955), 16.

55. NA, FOIA, RG59, 714.5/12–1856 HBS, William B. Connett, Jr., second secretary of the U.S. Embassy, Guatemala, to Department of State, 18 December 1956.

56. Villagrán Kramer, Biografía Política, 290–92.

57. NA, RG59, 714.5-MSP/11–1457, Dulles to U.S. Embassy, Guatemala, 15 November 1957.

58. Villagrán Kramer, Biografía Política, 314.

59. For the pact, see Villagrán Kramer, Biografía Política, 317–24; for Ydígoras's politics and the reapertura política that his election represented, see 316, 337.

60. DDRS(R/495G), Dulles, Department of State, to U.S. Embassy, Guatemala, 25 October 1957. Years later, Ydígoras told a U.S. journalist that the U.S. government had given his opponent, Col. Juan Luis Cruz Salazar, $97,000 in campaign funds and that he himself had been offered $500,000 to drop out of the race; see Georgie Ann Geyer, "Twists and Turns of Our Guatemala Policy," Chicago Daily News, 24 December 1966, 3.

61. FRUS 1958–60:5MS, Guatemala, Stewart, director of Office of Central American and Panamanian Affairs, to Rubottom, assistant secretary of state for inter-American affairs, 12 June 1959, 1115–18. Washington's doubts about Ydígoras were well grounded. In 1953, he not only rejected as humiliating the terms offered by the U.S. government in return for his participation in an anti-Arbenz insurgency, but his politics were solidly centrist (if anticommunist) rather than reactionary; Roland H. Ebel, Misunderstood Caudillo: Miguel Ydígoras Fuentes and the Failure of Democracy in Guatemala (Lanham, Md.: University Press of America, 1998), 37, 21, 82–85.

62. USAMHI/Lib, OO/DD-ISA/MAP/PR/Mar'59, "Department of Defense Progress Report, Military Assistance Program," 16 March 1959; OO/MAAG/G95/NS/1959, "U.S. Military Assistance Advisory Group, Guatemala. Narrative Statement, Guatemala, 1958–," 30 June 1959.

63. NA, RG59, 714.58/4–2359, Kennedy M. Crockett, first secretary, U.S. Embassy, Guatemala, to Department of State, 23 April 1959.

64. USAMHI/Lib.,OO/MAAG/G95/NS/1959, "U.S. Military Assistance Advisory Group, Guatemala. Narrative Statement, Guatemala, 1958–," 30 June 1959; NA, WNRC, RG286/Op Div/LA Br/Guatemala, Col. Berry, U.S. Army attaché, Guatemala, to Corrigan, U.S. Embassy, Guatemala, 16 March 1960.

65. NA, RG59, 714.58/12–3159, Jesús Rubén González Siguí, minister of national defense, Guatemala, to U.S. Embassy, Guatemala, 10 December 1959; U.S. Embassy, Guatemala, to Department of State, 31 December 1959.

66. FRUS 1958–60:5MS, Guatemala, Stewart, director of Office of Central American and Panamanian Affairs, to Rubottom, assistant secretary of state for inter-American affairs, 12 June 1959, 1115–20.

67. FRUS 1958–60:5MS, Guatemala, Mallory, U.S. ambassador to Guatemala, to Department of State, 11 November 1959, 1138, 1141. Arévalo would eventually bring down Ydígoras's government; three days after Arévalo returned to Guatemala on 27 March 1963, an army revolt threw Ydígoras out of office, and Arévalo in turn fled the country for good.

68. NA, FOIA, RG59, 714.56300/10–1760 HBS, Muccio, U.S. Embassy, Guatemala, to Department of State, 17 October 1960; 714.563/1–2561, Muccio, U.S. Embassy, Guatemala, to Department of State, 25 January 1961; 714.563/1–2061 CAA, Muccio, U.S. Embassy, Guatemala, to Department of State, 20 January 1961. Alejos was the Ydígoras administration's official in charge of "technical assistance" from the U.S. government, and as such handled the U.S. police collaboration program, which was already associated with the CIA. For Alejos's position in the government, see NA, WNRC, RG286, OPS/Oper/LA Guatemala 1955–61, Box 60, 1955–58, David Laughlin, PSD, Guatemala, to Roberto Alejos, Personero del Gobierno para los Asuntos de Cooperacion Tecnica, 9 May 1958; Guatemala 1955–63, "Guatemala Reports," "Public Safety Program, USOM, Guatemala," November 1958; *Operation Zapata: The "Ultrasensitive" Report and Testimony of the Board of Inquiry on the Bay of Pigs* (Frederick, Md.: University Publications of America, 1981), 10, 117, 170. For the B-52 sale, see NA, FOIA, RG59, 714.5622/1–2560, Corrigan, U.S. Embassy, Guatemala, to State Dept., 25 January 1960; RG59, 714.5622/2–2060, Livingston T. Merchant, Department of State, to John N. Irwin II, Department of Defense, 6 April 60; 714.5622/4–760, Memorandum of Conversation, Edwin E. Vallon, deputy director, CMA, to Department of State, 7 April 1960; FRUS 1958–60:5MS, Guatemala, Rubottom, assistant secretary of state for inter-American affairs, to Merchant, undersecretary of state for political affairs, 4 April 1960, 1149–52 (see "Editorial Note" for 27 April approval).

69. NA, FOIA, RG59, 714.5-MSP/5–1060, "Memorandum of Conversation," C. Allan Stewart, Office of Central American and Panamian Affairs, Department of State, 10 May 1960; WNRC/FOIA, RG286/Op Div/LA Br/Guatemala, Muccio, U.S. Embassy, Guatemala, to secretary of state, July 24–25, 1960; RG59, 714.5-MSP/11–1360, Muccio, Guatemala City, to Department of State, 13 November 1960; 714.5-MSP/12–860. Muccio to Department of State, 8 December 1960.

70. FRUS 1958–60:6, "Memorandum of a Meeting with the President," 29 November 1960, 1128.

71. Lawrence A. Yates, "The United States and Rural Insurgency in Guatemala, 1960–1970: An Inter-American 'Success Story'?" in Ralph Lee Woodward, Jr., *Central America: Historical Perspectives on the Contemporary Crises* (New York: Greenwood Press, 1988), 49–51.

72. Villagrán Kramer, *Biografía Política*, 354–59.

73. The anti-U.S. nationalism within the armed forces that had contributed to the November 1960 uprising—and thus to the guerrilla insurgency—would be reborn in 1978, when the chiefs of the Guatemalan armed forces, who had taken charge of the country's government, joined the chiefs of the military governments of El Salvador, Argentina, and Brazil in rejecting any further military collaboration with the United States that required them to submit to reviews of their "human rights" records.

74. NA, FOIA, RG59,714.58/3–2155 CSBM, Jameson to Holland, "Assignment of Intelligence Advisers to U.S. Army Missions in Latin America," 21 March 1955; FOIA, RG59, 714.58/3–2455 CS/E, George O. Spencer, acting officer in charge, Inter-American Military Assistance Affairs, Department of State, to Col. William F. Kaufman, chief, Latin American Branch, O3, Department of the Army, 24 March 1955.

75. FRUS 1955–57:7, "Telegram from the Ambassador in Guatemala (Armour) to the Dept. of State," 8 May 1955, 77.

76. NA, RG59. 714.5-MSP/6–756. U.S. Embassy, Guatemala, to Department of State, June 7, 1955.

77. By 1960, U.S. Army training in counterintelligence had advanced sufficiently for the Guatemalan government to advise Washington that it needn't replace the mission's current intelligence adviser, Lt. Col. Harold M. Frindell, once his toured ended. "The School of Counterintelligence can now begin to develop upon its own, with the help of its graduates," the defense minister reported, implying that the U.S. had established the School and trained its staff. Seven months later, however, the government reversed itself and asked that the Lieutenant Colonel Frindell's position be renewed when his tour ended on 31 October 1961; see NA, RG59, 714.58/12–3159, Jesús Rubén González Siguí, minister of national defense, Guatemala, to U.S. Embassy, Guatemala, 10 December 1959; also see NA, FOIA, RG59, 714.58/7–2660, Robert Foster Corrigan, counselor, U.S. Embassy, Guatemala, to Department of State, 26 July 1960.

78. NA, FOIA, RG59, 714.5/6–456, U.S. Embassy, Guatemala, to Department of State, 4 June 1956.

79. NA, RG273, Operations Coordinating Board, "Report to the National Security Council Pursuant to NSC Action 1290-d," 23 November 1955.

80. NA, RG59, 714.5-MSP/6–756, U.S. Embassy, Guatemala, to Department of State, 7 June 1956.

81. NA, WNRC, RG 286, AID/OPS: Operations Division, LA Branch, Guatemala, Box 60, file unit: Guatemala—General, Department of State-ICA to U.S. Embassy, Guatemala, 1 December 1955; WNRC, RG 469, Office of Latin American Operations, 1952–58, Guatemala—General—1955, Box. 34, Edward J. Martin, director, U.S. Operations Mission in Guatemala, to U.S. Ambassardor, 29 November 1955.

82. NA, RG59, 714.5/6–156, International Cooperation Administration, "Report on the National Police in the Republic of Guatemala," by Fred G. Fimbres, police consultant, 9 April 1956.

83. NA, WNRC, RG286, AID/OPS, Director's Numerical File, Box 2, IPS-1, General Policy. "Report," 14 December 1956; for budget, see RG59, 714.5-MSP/6–756, U.S. Embassy, Guatemala, to Department of State, 7 June 1956.

84. See, for example, NA, WNRC, RG286, OPS/Oper/LA Guatemala 1955–61 Box 60, 1955–58, ICA, Guatemala, to ICA (Washington), 14 November 1956, which noted the division of police funding between MAP and the ICA. Also see NA, WNRC, RG286. OPS/Oper/LA Guatemala 1955–61 Box 60, 1955–58. ICA, Program Approval, 15 April 1957, for the use of Defense Support Funds.

85. NA, WNRC, RG286. OPS/Oper/LA Guatemala 1955–61 Box 60, 1955–58, USOM, Guatemala, to ICA (Washington), 27 February 1957.

86. NA, WNRC, RG286. OPS/Oper/LA Guatemala 1955–61, Box 60, 1955–58, "Guatemala," 17 April 1957.

87. NA, WNRC, RG286, OPS/Oper/LA, Guatemala 1955–61, Box 60, 1955–58, Dave Laughlin, USOM,Guatemala, to Byron Engle, chief, Civil Police Administration, ICA, 9 May 1957.

88. NA, WNRC, RG286, OPS/Oper/LA Guatemala 1955–61, Box 60, 1955–58, Rubottom, Department of State, to Atwood, 3 June 1957.

89. NA, WNRC, RG286. OPS/Oper/LA Guatemala 1955–61 Box 60, 1955–58, USOM, Guatemala, to ICA (Washington), 27 February 1957.

90. NA, WNRC, RG286, OPS/Oper/LA Guatemala 1955–61, Box 60, 1955–58, PSD, Guatemala, to ICA (Washington), 7 March 1958.

91. NA, WNRC, RG286, OPS/Oper/LA. Guatemala 1955–61, Box 60, 1955–58, "Guatemala Public Safety Program Summary," November 1958; OPS/Oper/LA Guatemala 1955–63, Guatemala Reports, "Public Safety Program, USOM, Guatemala," November 1958.

92. NA, WNRC, RG286. OPS/Op Div/LA, Guatemala 1955–61, Box 60, Programs 1959–61, David Laughlin, chief public safety adviser, USOM, Guatemala, to Theo E. Hall, chief, Public Safety Division, 10 April 1959; OPS/Oper/LA Guatemala 1955–63, Guatemala Reports, "Public Safety Program, USOM, Guatemala," November 1958.

93. NA, WNRC, RG286, OPS/Oper/LA Guatemala 1955–63, Guatemala Reports, "Public Safety Program, USOM, Guatemala," November 1958.

94. NA, WNRC, RG286, OPS/Oper/LA Guatemala 1955–63, Guatemala Reports, "Public Safety Program, USOM, Guatemala," November 1958; OPS/Op Div/LA, Guatemala 1961–63, Box 62, IPS 2, "Report—Public Safety Division, USOM/Guatemala," July 1961.

95. NA, WNRC, RG286, OPS/Oper/LA Guatemala 1955–63, Guatemala Reports, "Public Safety Program, USOM, Guatemala," November 1958.

96. NA, WNRC, RG286, OPS/Oper/LA, Guatemala 1955–61, Box 60, 1955–58, Theo E. Hall, chief, Public Safety Division, ICA, to Gen. J. M. Swing, commissioner, Immigration and Naturalization Service, 18 November 1957.

97. NA, WNRC, RG286, OPS/Oper/LA Guatemala 1955–61, Box 60, 1955–58, Howard R. Keough to Theo Hall, chief, Public Safety Division, February 4, 1958; OPS/Oper/LA Guatemala 1955–61, Box 60, 1955–58, Howard R. Keough to Theodore E. Hall, chief, Civil Police Administration Division, ICA, 30 September 1957, and to Herbert O. Hardin, 3 December 1957.

98. NA, WNRC, RG286, OPS/Oper/LA Guatemala 1955–63, Guatemala Reports, "Public Safety Program, USOM, Guatemala," November 1958.

99. NA, WNRC, RG286, OPS/Op Div/LA, Guatemala 1955–61, Box 60, Programs 1959–61, "Evaluation of Guatemala Program," 16 March 1959.

100. NA, WNRC, RG286, OPS/Oper/LA. Guatemala 1955–61, Box 60, 1955–58, "Guatemala Public Safety Program Summary," November 1958.

101. NA, WNRC, RG286, OPS/Oper/LA Guatemala 1955–63, Guatemala Reports, "Completion of Tour Report," David L. Laughlin, chief public safety advisor, Guatemala City, 27 April 1960.

102. NA, WNRC, RG286, Op div/LA br/Guatemala, FOIA, USOM, Guatemala, to ICA, 25 August 1960.

103. NA, FOIA, Dept. of State, 714.5-MSP/5.2261. R. F. Corrigan, U.S. Embassy, Guatemala, to Department of State, 23 May 1961.

104. Larry Rohter, "A War So Long, Its Origin Is Dim to the Guatemalans," *New York Times*, 20 September 1996, 16; the death toll estimate was by Commission for Historical Clarification, *Guatemala: Memory of Silence* (1999), available at http://hrdata.aaas.org/ceh/report/english/ [26 July 2002].

105. "Remarks in a Roundtable Discussion on Peace Efforts in Guatemala City March 10, 1999," in U.S., President, *Weekly Compilation of Presidential Documents* 35 (15 March 1999) 10:395.

CHAPTER 11

The epigraph source—a letter from Thomas C. Mann dated 16 May 1957—is located in NA, RG59, 716.56/5–1657, U.S. Ambassador Mann to Department of State.

1. Patricia Parkman, *Nonviolent Insurrection in El Salvador: The Fall of Maximiliano Hernández-Martínez* (Tucson: University of Arizona Press, 1988), 24–27.

2. MGES 1941, 29; also see MGES 1942 and 1944.

3. See chapter 9.

4. NA, RG59, 716.58/12–1152, Andrew E. Donavan II, chargé d'affaires, U.S. Embassy, El Salvador, to Department of State, 11 December 1952.

5. Parkman, *Nonviolent*, 21.

6. FRUS 1943:6, various, 308–12.

7. Parkman, *Nonviolent*, 33–37.

8. Castro Morán, *Función política*, 159–86.

9. Ibid., 187–206

10. The officer corps of both armies, of course, were divided politically between those favoring civilian rule and those favoring a continuation of dictatorship. Why the Guatemalan officers, as a group, *stepped aside* for the likely election of a popular civilian (Juan José Arévalo) while the Salvadorans, as a group, *blocked* the likely electoral victory of a popular civilian (Arturo Romero), at precisely the same moment, is a problem that merits more attention than it has received in the historiography. The explanation may hinge on nothing more complicated than the timing itself, as the historiography tends to imply; in other words, it was just because of the success of the Guatemalan antidictatorship movement, and its heady impact on the Salvadoran enemies of dictatorship, that the Salvadoran army reacted against the democratic threat when it did. Williams and Walter, *Militarization*, imply as much (33), but a more satisfactory explanation must await a closer comparison of the two politico-military contexts.

11. Parkman, *Nonviolent*, 102.

12. FRUS 1945:9, 1062–65.

13. MGES 1947, 21–22.

14. MGES 1949, 21–22.

15. NA, FOIA, RG 59, 716.56/2–2350, George P. Shaw, U.S. Embassy, El Salvador, to Department of State, 23 February 1950.

16. Ibid.

17. *Hispanic World Report* 2 (June 1949) 6:10, and 2 (August 1949) 8:12.

18. *Hispanic World Report* 2 (September 1949) 9:11; for the Partido Nacional Pro-Patria, see Williams and Walter, *Militarization*, 28–29.

19. Roberto Turcios, *Autoritarismo y modernización: El Salvador 1950–1960* (San Salvador, El Salvador: Ediciones Tendencias, 1993), 29–32, 52–54, 66–68, 70, 71.

20. Turcios, *Autoritarismo*, 73–82.

21. The complete text of the law, Decree No. 876, was attached to NA, FOIA, RG59, 716.5/8–1456, U.S. Embassy, El Salvador, to Department of State, 14 August 1956.

22. Williams and Walter, *Militarization*, 45–46; 47.

23. USAMHI/Lib., Intelligence Division, General Staff, U.S. Army, "Intelligence Research Project: Characteristics and Capabilities of Latin American Armies," 17 June 1949.

24. The government's list, drawn up with the help of the U.S. military attaché, included another C-47, trucks, mortars, machine guns, bazookas, two howitzer batteries, hand grenades and grenade launchers, mines, and more than 2 million rounds of machine gun ammunition, as well as motorcycles, radios, and stoves. NA, FOIA, RG 59, 716.56/2–2350, George P. Shaw, U.S. Embassy, El Salvador, to Department of State, 23 February 1950; 716.56/2–2550, George P. Shaw, U.S. Embassy, El Salvador, to Department of State, 25 February 1950. For the rise in coffee prices and rearmament, see Turcios, *Autoritarismo*, 33–34.

25. NA, RG330/18/El Salvador, Maj. Gen. L. L. Lemnitzer, U.S. Army, director, Office of Military Assistance, to Maj. Gen. R. E. Duff, U.S. Army, deputy assistant chief of staff, 19 July 1950; 716.58/11–950, U.S. Ambassador Shaw to Maj. Alberto Escamilla, Salvadoran undersecretary of defense, 17 October 1950; RG330/21/El Salvador, "Assistance Request No.: El Salvador-I," 6 September 1950.

26. NA, RG59, 716.58/5–2951, U.S. Ambassador Shaw to Department of State, 29 May 1951; 716.58/11–950, Shaw to Department of State, 9 November 1950.

27. NA, RG59, 716.58/10–2050, Shaw to Department of State, 20 October 1950; 716.58/12–1150, Shaw to Department of State, 11 December 1950.

28. NA, RG 59, 716.58/12–1150, Shaw to Department of State, 11 December 1950; UST 3.4.4799; 5.1.416.

29. UST 4.2.1579; 5.3.2870. The agreement merely obligated El Salvador to refrain from hiring military advisers from third countries *unless* Washington was unable to furnish the advisers requested. Even that limitation was considerably softened in the 1954 Army mission agreement; UST 5.3.2882, Article 23. By contrast, the Nicaraguan agreement, which was typical, required Managua to seek U.S. approval before contracting with third-country military advisers; UST 4.2.2244, Article 25.

30. NA, RG59, 716.56/2–2453, "Memorandum of Conversation, Purchase of Arms by Government of El Salvador"; 24 February 1953; RG330/21A/El Sal, Edward A. Jamison, deputy director, Office of Regional American Affairs, Department of State, to Col. Paul A. Gavan, chief, Liasion Division, OMA, Pentagon, 25 February 1953; RG59, 716.56/2–2553, Leddy to Mann, 25 February 1953; 716.56/2–2753, Leddy to Mann, 27 February 1953; 716.56/2–2753, Mann to the undersecretary, 27 February 1953; FW 716.56/2–2753, Cabot to the undersecretary, 6 March 1953; RG330/21A/El Sal, Col. Sam C. Russell, G-4 for Foreign Military Aid, Pentagon, to Gen. George C. Stewart, director, OMA, 10 March 1953; RG59, 716.56/4–2453, "Memorandum," San Salvador, 24 April 1953, and "Armament and Equipment"; RG330/21/El Sal, "Case Summary Sheet, Case No. OMA El Salvador 6," and accompanying documents; RG59, 716.56/10–153 CS/W, Sayre to Fisher, 1 October 1953.

31. NA, RG59, 716.56/10–153 CS/W, U.S. Embassy, El Salvador, to Department of State, 1 October 1953.

32. NA, RG59, 716.56/4–2453, "Memorandum," 24 April 1953.

33. NA, RG59, 716.5-MSP/5–3154, "Memorandum of Conversation, " U.S. Ambassador Michael J. McDermott, El Salvador, 31 May 1954.

34. NA, RG59, 715.5 MSP/6–2454, U.S. Ambassador McDermott to Department of State, 24 June 1954.

35. NA, RG59, 716.5-MSP/1–755, Dulles to U.S. Embassy, El Salvador, 7 and 21 January 1955.

36. MGES 1952–53, 55.

37. Juan Forch Petit, *Organización de Defensa Nacional y Organización Militar* (San Salvador: Ministerio de Defensa Nacional, 1955); also see, by another Chilean mission member, Julio Campo Sepúlveda, *Estrategia: Los Problemas de la Defensa Nacional y la Preparación del Estratega Contemporaneo* (San Salvador, El Salvador: Ministerio de Defensa, 1955).

38. NA, RG59, 716.5 MSP/4–2955, Frederick E. Nolting, Jr., special assistant to secretary for mutual security affairs, to director, Office of Military Assistance, Department of Defense, 29 April 1955; RG330/21/El Sal, "Case Summary Sheet, Case No. OMAP/El Salvador 12," and related documents.

39. NA, RG59, 716.58/12–1355, U.S. Ambassador Mann to secretary to state, 13 December 1955. As assistant secretary of state for inter-American affairs in 1964, Mann shaped what became known as the Mann Doctrine—a turn away from Kennedy-era interest in democracy and social reform, toward more tolerance for military rule, and renewed stress on protecting U.S. investments.

40. Turcios, *Autoritarismo*, ch. 3

41. NA, RG59, 716.5 MSP/4–557, Alton W. Hemba, first secretary, U.S. Embassy, El Salvador, to Department of State, 5 April 1957.

42. Turcios, *Autoritarismo*, ch. 4.

43. NA, RG59, 716.5 MSP/4–557, Alton W. Hemba, first secretary, U.S. Embassy, El Salvador, to Department of State, 5 April 1957; Dulles to U.S. Embassy, El Salvador, 18 April 1957.

44. Although El Salvador's share of total isthmian ground troops exceeded that of Honduras and Nicaragua, its share of Air Force personnel and equipment was far behind that of all the other countries except Costa Rica; see Appendix, figures A-7, A-8, and A-9.

45. NA, RG59, 716.56/5–1657, U.S. Ambassador Mann to secretary to state, 16 May 1957.

46. NA, RG59, 716.56/6–755, U.S. Embassy, El Salvador, to Department of State, 7 June 1955.

47. NA, FOIA, RG59, 716.5/8–2456, Hemba, U.S. Embassy, El Salvador, to Department of State, 24 August 1956.

48. NA, RG286, OPS/Oper/LA, El Salvador, 1956–63, Box 55, Programs 1956–59, Dulles to U.S. Embassy, El Salvador, 10 June 1957.

49. NA, RG59, 716.58/3–2658, U.S. Ambassador Kalijarvi to Department of State, 26 March 1958.

50. NA, RG59, 716.5-MSP/4–159, "Memorandum of Conversation: Salvadoran Interest in a Mutual Assistance Agreement," 1 April 1959; 716.5-MSP/4–359, Herbert B. Leggett, CAP, to Rubottom, 3 April 1959; 716.5-MSP/5–1959, Edwin E. Vallon, chargé d'affaires ad interim, U.S. Embassy, El Salvador, to Department of State, 9 May 1959.

51. NA, RG59, 716.5-MSP/11–2059, U.S. Ambassador Kalijarvi to Department of State, 20 November 1959; RG84, FOIA, Box 55, Dillon, acting Secretary of State, to U.S. Embassy, El Salvador, 18 May 1960.

52. NA, WNRC, RG286, OPS/Oper/LA El Sal 1956–63, Box 55, Programs 1956–59, "Public Safety Program in El Salvador," 4 December 1959.

53. NA, FOIA, RG84, Box 55, U.S. Embassy, El Salvador, to Department of State, 26 July 1960.

54. NA, FOIA, RG84, Box 55, John F. McDermott, PSD, El Salvador, to the record, 25 August 1960.

55. NA, RG59, FW716–5-MSP/5–1160, Col. Robert A. Matter, chief, U.S. Army Mission, "Joint Military Assistance Plan for El Salvador (FY62–66)," 28 April 1960.

56. NA, FOIA, RG84, Box 55, U.S. Embassy, El Salvador, to Department of State, 26 July 1960.

57. NA, FOIA, RG84, Box 55, U.S. Ambassador Kalijarvi to Department of State, 20 October 1960.

58. Williams and Walter, *Militarization*, 57–59.

59. NA, FOIA, RG84, Box 55, U.S. Ambassador Kalijarvi to secretary of state, 26 October 1960; DDRS 1989/1445, Secretary of State Herter to president, 10 November 1960; FRUS 1958–60:5MS, El Salvador, Christian A. Herter to President Eisenhower, 26 November 1960, 1048; DDRS, 1985/166, Department of State to U.S. Embassy, El Salvador, 1 December 1960; DDRS, 1985/566, White House, "Memorandum of Conference with the President," 1 December 1960.

60. NA, RG59, 716.5811/4–1461. James A. McNamara, third secretary, U.S. Embassy, El Salvador, to State, 14 April 1961.

61. FRUS 1961–63:12, Acting Secretary of State Chester Bowles to President Kennedy, 29 September 1961, n. 1, 190.

CHAPTER 12

1. ASREH, Albert H. Cousins, Jr., chargé d'affaires ad interim, U.S. Embassy, Honduras, to Dr. Salvador Aguirre, Honduran minister for foreign affairs, 25 July 1940.

2. ASREH, Cousins to Aguirre, 29 July 1940.

3. MGH 1941–42, 3–11

4. ASREH, John D. Erwin, chief of the U.S. legation in Honduras, to Dr. Salvador Aguirre, minister for foreign affairs, 6 December 1940; R. D. Gatewood, U.S. chargé d'affaires ad interim, and Cousins to Aguirre, 11 October 1941 and 22 October 1941; Erwin to Aguirre, 15 December 1941; Erwin to Aguirre, 7 February and 9 February, 1942; Erwin to Aguirre, 26

December 1941 and 24 February 1942; "Strictly Confidential," jointly signed by Summer Welles, acting secretary of state, and Julián R. Cáceres, Honduran ambassador to the United States, 28 February 1942; Cáceres to Aguirre, 25 February 1942; MGH 1941–42, 3–11.

5. ASREH, "Memorandum," John D. Erwin, chief, U.S. Legation, Honduras, 20 March 1942.

6. ASREH, "Memorandum," Erwin, 22 June 1942. By 1945, a quarter of the Highway's 3,334 miles was still consisted of trails or dry-weather roadway; Bulmer-Thomas, *Political Economy*, 350n7.

7. ASREH, "Memorandum," Erwin, U.S. ambassador, Honduras, 22 March 1945.

8. Posas and Del Cid, *La construcción*, 73–74.

9. Alejandro Salomon Sagastume F., *Carías: El caudillo de Zambrano, 1933–1948* (Tegucigalpa, Honduras: Graficentro Editores, 1988), 100, 116. Carías not only outlived the isthmus' other three dictators of that period, he was the only one to die in his own *tierra*. Ubico died at sixty-seven in Baptist Hospital, New Orleans, on 14 June 1946. The other two died violently. Somoza, sixty-one, was shot on 21 September 1956 and died on 29 September in Gorgas Hospital in the Canal Zone. Hernández-Martínez, eighty-four, was stabbed to death by his chauffeur on 15 May 1966 in the dining room of his home in Jamastrán, Honduras. See "Gen. Ubico, Ex-Head of Guatemala, Dies," *New York Times*, 16 June 1946, 40; for Somoza, see FRUS 1955–57:7, "Editorial Note," 211, 218; for Hernández-Martínez, see Leonidas Arturo Durán Altamirano, *Trayectoria: Vida, Proyección y Muerte de Dos Salvadoreños Notables Que el Destino Puso Frente a Frente* (San Salvador, El Salvador: n.p., 1987), 96–97.

10. Argüeta, *Tiburcio Carías*, 104–107, 109–110; for an entertaining example, see Matías Funes, *Los deliberantes: El poder militar en Honduras* (Tegucigalpa, Honduras: Editorial Guaymuras, 1995), 140–41.

11. Argüeta, *Tiburcio Carías*, 123.

12. Dunkerley, *Power in the Isthmus*, 122; Posas and Del Cid, *La Constructión*, 86–87.

13. MGH 1946–47, 1–2, 10.

14. When Gálvez died in 1972, practically the entire high command of the armed forces attended the funeral; by contrast, military officers had been hard to find at Carías's funeral in 1969. Funes, *Los deliberantes*, 155.

15. MGH 1945–46, 1–2.

16. MGH 1946–47, Anexo A.

17. MGH 1946–47, 3–5, and Anexo A; MGH 1945–46

18. MGH 1945–46, 2–4.

19. MGH 1948–49, 11–13, 67.

20. USAMHI/Lib., Intelligence Division, General Staff, U.S. Army, "Intelligence Research Project: Characteristics and Capabilities of Latin American Armies," 17 June 1949; FRUS 1951:2, "Policy Statement Prepared by the Department of State [on Honduras]," 6 February 1951, 1466–67.

21. The five-thousand-man army already had 2,083 Springfield rifles (first produced for the U.S. Army in 1903) and "a considerable number of foreign rifles, some of which are serviceable." NA, RG330/21/Honduras, various documents, 1950; RG59, 715.5-MAP/4–1150 CS/W, John C. Dreier, Department of State, to Thomas Mann, Department of State, 11 April 1950; 715.MAP/3–2450 CS/W, Memorandum of Conversation, "Honduran Request for Arms," 24 March 1950; 715.5614/10–1350, Herbert S. Bursley, U.S. ambassador, Honduras, to Department of State, 13 October 1950.

22. NA, RG59, 715.58/7–1851, U.S. Army Mission Report, Honduras, 9 July 1951; MGH 1950–51, 6, 15, 126–28; MGH 1949–50, 5–6, 60. For new mission agreements, see UST 1.212 and 1.199.

23. NA, RG59, 715.58/7–2451, "Annual Report of USAF Mission to Honduras," 18 July 1951.

24. MGH 1951–52, 24, 44–45.

25. NA, RG59, 715.56/6–2453, John D. Irwin, U.S. Embassy, Honduras, to Department of State, 24 June 1953.

26. NA, RG330, 21A/Honduras, "Resume of Military Assistance to Honduras," 18 June 1954; RG330/21/Honduras, various documents, 1952–53.

27. Nick Cullather, *Secret History: The CIA's Classified Account of Its Operations in Guatemala, 1952–1954* (Stanford, Calif.: Stanford University Press, 1999), 29–30.

28. Cullather, *Secret History*, 48–49.

29. Stephen Schlesinger and Stephen Kinzer, *Bitter Fruit: The Story of the American Coup in Guatemala*, expanded ed. (Cambridge, Mass.: Harvard University Press, 1999), 126–29.

30. For the strike, see Euraque, *Reinterpreting*, 94–95, and James A. Morris, *Honduras: Caudillo Politics and Military Rulers* (Boulder, Colo.: Westview Press, 1984), 10–11; for United Fruit, see Schlesinger and Stephen Kinzer, *Bitter Fruit*, 88–93, 126.

31. "General Strike in Honduras," *Department of State Bulletin* 30 (24 May 1954):778–801.

32. FRUS 1952–54:4, Dulles to President Eisenhower, 11 May 1954, 1303–4.

33. NA, RG 218, 1954–56, CCS 381 Western Hemisphere (3–22–48), Sec. 20, "Plan for Military Support of Inter-American Treaty of Reciprocal Assistance," 4 June 1954; RG 218, 1954–56, 381 (6–15–49), Sec. 3, COMCARIB to Joint Chiefs of Staff, 9 June 1954.

34. Gleijeses, *Shattered Hope*, 301; NA, RG59, 715.56/5–2754, Frederick E. Nolting, Jr., special assistant to the secretary for mutual security affairs, to U.S. Rep. Frances P. Bolton, 27 May 1954. Nolting also linked the general strike and the *Alfhem* to the attempted assassination of President Somoza in April—all signs of an instability that was "an open invitation for the communists and their sympathizers to interfere in those countries."

35. NA, RG59, 715.5MSP/5–2554, U.S. Embassy, Honduras to Department of State, 25 May 1954.

36. Ramón E. Cruz, *La lucha política de 1954 y la ruptura del orden constitucional* (Tegucigalpa, Honduras: Editorial Universitaria, 1982), 17.

37. NA, RG59, 715.5-MSP/6–854, Whiting Willauer, U.S. ambassador, Honduras, to Department of State, 8 June 1954.

38. U.S. Congress, Senate, Committee on the Judiciary, "Communist Threat to the United States Through the Caribbean," *Hearings*, part 13, 27 July 1961 (Washington, D.C.: Government Printing Office, 1962), 865–66. After Arbenz resigned, CIA Director Allen Dulles sent Willauer a telegram crediting him with ensuring the success of the plot to overthrow Arbenz. "I am very proud of that telegram."

39. NA, FOIA, RG59, 715.5 MSP/6–2854, Col. M. C. Shattuck, acting chief, MAAG, Tegucigalpa, to commanding general, U.S. Army Caribbean, Ft. Amador, CZ, 28 June 1954 (attached to U.S. Ambassador Whiting Willauer, Honduras, to Department of State, 28 June 1954).

40. NA, RG59, 715.5 MSP/6–1357, Whiting Willauer, U.S. ambassador, Tegucigalpa, to Department of State, 13 June 1957.

41. NA, FOIA, RG59, 715.5 MSP/6–2854, Col. M. C. Shattuck, acting chief, MAAG, Tegucigalpa, to commanding general, U.S. Army Caribbean, Ft. Amador, CZ, 28 June 1954 (attached to U.S. Ambassador Whiting Willauer, Honduras, to Department of State, 28 June 1954).

42. NA, RG59, 715.5 MSP/6–1154, Lt. Col. Charles E. Bailey, USAF mission chief, to Gen. Leonidas Pineda, minister of war, 8 June 1954; Whiting Willauer, U.S. ambassador, Honduras, to Department of State, 11 June 1954; FOIA, RG59, 715.5 MSP/6–2854, Col. M. C. Shattuck, acting chief, MAAG, Tegucigalpa, to commanding general, U.S. Army Caribbean, Ft. Amador, CZ, 28 June 1954 (attached to U.S. Ambassador Whiting Willauer, Honduras, to Department of State, 28 June 1954).

43. NA, FOIA, RG59, 715.5 MSP/6–2854, Col. M. C. Shattuck, acting chief, MAAG, Tegucigalpa, to commanding general, U.S. Army Caribbean, Ft. Amador, CZ, 28 June 1954 (attached to U.S. Ambassador Whiting Willauer, Honduras, to Department of State, 28 June 1954).

44. NA, RG 218, 1954–56. 381 (6–15–49), Sec. 3, Joint Chiefs of Staff to CINCARIB, 12 July 1954.

45. FRUS 1952–54:4, "The Assistant Secretary of State for Inter-American Affairs (Holland) to the Ambassador in Honduras (Willauer)," 16 July 1954, 1310.

46. FRUS 1952–54:4, Murphy to Hensel, 10 August 1954, 1311–12; Hensel to Murphy, 30 October 1954, 1315–16; NA, RG218, CCS092 (8–22–46) Sec. 119, 1954–56, "Report by the Joint Strategic Plans Committee to the Joint Chiefs of Staff on C-47 Aircraft for Honduras," 16 September 1954.

47. NA, RG 218, CCS 092 (8–22–46) (2) 1954–1956, B. P. Pt. #1, "Military Aspects of Mutual Security Programs as of 31 December 1954."

48. Cruz, *La Lucha Política*, 16–18, 21.

49. FRUS 1952–54:4, U.S. Ambassador Willauer to Department of State, 24 September 1954, 1313–15.

50. FRUS 1952–54:4, Newbegin to Holland, 12 November 1954, 1316–17; FRUS 1952–54:4, Memorandum for the files, 19 November 1954, 1319–20.

51. FRUS 1952–54:4, Willauer to Department of State, 6 December 1954, 1322–23; Stefania Natalini de Castro, María de los Angeles Mendoza Saborio and Joaquín Pagán Solórzano, *Significado Histórico del Gobierno del Dr. Ramón Villeda Morales* (Tegucigalpa, Honduras: Editorial Universitaria, 1985), 45.

52. NA, RG59, 715.5-MSP/6–854, Col. M.C. Shattuck, acting chief, MAAG, Tegucigalpa, to Department of the Army, 8 June 1954.

53. NA, RG218, CCS092(8–22–46) (2) Sec. 4, "Report by the Joint Strategic Plans Committee to the Joint Chiefs of Staff on the MDA Programming Guidance for FY 1957," 4 March 1955.

54. NA, RG218, 092 (8–22–46) (2) 1954–56 B.P. Pt. 2, Maj. Gordon A. Schraeder, acting chief, MAAG, Honduras, to secretary of defense, 27 May 1955.

55. NA, RG 218, 092 (8–22–46) (2) 1954–1956, Sec. 11, F.H. Higgins, assistant secretary of the army, to assistant secretary of defense (ISA), 15 June 1955.

56. NA, FOIA, RG 59. 715.5622/6–1655, Wymberley DeR. Coerr, chargé d'affaires, ad interim, U.S. Embassy, Honduras, to Department of State, 16 June 1955; for the age of the fleet, see NA. RG218, CCS092 (8–22–46) (2) 1954–56 Sec. 22, "Honduras MDAP Statement," 31 December 1955.

57. NA, RG59, 715.5622/6–1655, Frederick E. Nolting, Jr., special assistant to the secretary for mutual security affairs, to director, Office of Military Assistance, International Security Affairs, Department of Defense, no date; 715.5622/12–255, Whiting Willauer, U.S. ambassador, Honduras, to Department of State, 2 December 1955. For the 1954 fighter inventory, see DDRS (1979/124C), CIA, "National Intelligence Estimate Number 80–54, The Caribbean Republics," 24 August 1954.

58. NA, RG218, CCS092 (8–22–46) (2) 1954–56 Sec. 22, "Honduras MDAP Statement," 31 December 1955.

59. Ibid.

60. Ibid.

61. NA, RG59, 715.5-MSP/7–2356, U.S. Embassy, Honduras, to Department of State, 23 July 1956.

62. Natalini et al., *Significado*, 46–47; Rojas Bolaños, "La Política," 110; *Facts on File* 16 (August 1–7, 1956) 823:259; Willauer attributed the defeat of the revolt to the MAP battalion; see NA, FOIA, RG59,715.5-MSP/3–1957, Willauer to Department of State, 19 March 1957.

63. NA, RG59, 715.56/8–956, U.S. Embassy, Honduras, to Department of State, 9 August 1956; 715.5-MSP/8–2356, Honduran Embassy to Department of State, 23 August 1956; 715.56/9–456, "Memorandum of Conversation: Honduran Arms Purchase," 4 September 1956; 715.56/9–2156, U.S. Embassy, Honduras, Department of State, 22 September 1956; 715.56/9–2556, Dulles to U.S. Embassy, Honduras, 25 September 1956; 715.56/9–2556, U.S. Embassy, Honduras, to Department of State, 26 September 1956; 715.56/10–2456, U.S. Embassy, Honduras, to Department of State, 24 October 1956.

64. Natalini et al., *Significado*, 48; *Facts on File* 16 (October 3–9, 1956), 832, 334.

65. USAMHI/Lib., 0/MAAG/H7/NS/Je59, U.S. Military Assistance Advisory Group, Tegucigalpa, Honduras, "Narrative Statement," 29 July 1959.

66. Funes, *Los Deliberantes*, 186–90.

67. NA, RG59, 715.56/7–1757, U.S. Embassy, Honduras, to Department of State, 17 July 1957; 715.56/7–2657, Department of State to U.S. Embassy, Honduras, 26 July 1957; 715.56/ 8–557, Robert G. Barnes, special assistant to under secretary for mutual security affairs, to Department of Defense, 5 August 1957; 715.56/8–757, U.S. Embassy, Honduras, to Department of State, 7 August 1957.

68. Ramón Oquelí, "Gobiernos Hondureños Durante el Presente Siglo," *Economía Política* 9 (II época) 1974–75, 13, quoted in Leticia Salomón, *Militarismo y Reformismo en Honduras* (Tegucigalpa, Honduras: Editorial Guaymuras, 1982), 33–34.

69. NA, RG59, 715.5/10–3059, U.S. Embassy, Honduras, to Department of State, 30 October 1959.

70. For references to a written pact between the Liberal Party and the armed forces, whose material existence all sources agreed has yet to be proven, see Natalini et al., *Significado*, 50–51; Rojas Bolaños, "La Política," 128; Posas and Del Cid, *La Construcción*, 114–15; Funes, *Los Deliberantes*, 194–98. For the timing of events, see two *New York Times*'s reports, "Honduras Names Head" (16 November 1957, 10) and "Honduras to Give Autonomy to Army" (28 November 1957, 71). In "Some Hondurans Fear Army Role," *New York Times* (1 December 1958, 22) reported that the Assembly's final approval of the constitutional provisions favoring military autonomy was explained "by informed observers [in Tegucigalpa] as stemming from an agreement between Liberal Party leaders and the armed forces to insure the military's acceptance of a Liberal Party victory." It became known as the Pacto del Agua Azul for the place, near Yojoa Lake, where it was supposedly signed, according to Funes, *Los Deliberantes*, 198.

71. The armed forces' letter to Villeda of 8 December 1958 was printed in *El Día* (Tegucigalpa) 25 May 1968 under the headline "Villeda No Contestó Nota del Consejo de la Defensa," 1. This is also cited by Natalini et al., *Significado*, for the terms of the Pacto de Agua Azul, as if it were the Pact, but in fact the letter contains no more than a passing reference to the signing of an agreement on 14 November 1957.

72. According to Fonseca, the governing *junta* itself (by then reduced to two men, Gálvez and Caracciolo) had no knowledge of the deal, which obligated the liberals to (1) insert verbatim into the constitution a chapter governing the armed forces that had been drafted by the defense ministry's lawyer, Ricardo Zúñiga Augustinus; (2) appoint an armed forces chief from among three candidates proposed by the to-be-created Consejo Superior de la Defensa Nacional, with the understanding that López Arellano would be picked; and (3) "luchar contra el comunismo." In return, the military would accept Villeda's appointment as president by the constitutional convention and "struggle against communism." Fonseca, "Los precedentes," 115–16.

73. The 1965 and 1982 constitutions omitted the extraordinary second sentence of Article 319, allowing the armed forces chief to appeal to the Congress in the event he disagreed with the president. See *Recopilación de las Constituciones de Honduras*, "Constitución de la República de 1957," Title XIII, 530–31, and "Constitución de la República de 1965," Title XII,

609–10. For the abolition of constitutional autonomy (by elimination of the post of chief of the armed forces and the Consejo Superior de las Fuerzas Armadas, the military's governing body), see "Suprimida Jefatura de Fuerzas Armadas, *La Prensa* (San Pedro Sula), 26 January 1999, and "Presidente Flores: Con Este Acto 'Honduras le Habla al Mundo de su Madurez Política,'" *La Prensa* 28 January 1999.

74. NA, WNRC, RG469, Latin American Geographical File/Honduras/Budget, FY57/Box 50, ICA, "Non-Military Country Program, Honduras," for FY59, 21 October 1957 and "Comments by the American Ambassador," 19–20.

75. NA, RG59, 715.55/12–2757, Lawrence S. Eagleburger, third secretary of U.S. Embassy, Honduras, to Department of State, 27 December 1957.

76. NA, RG59, 715.5 MSP/12–1456, J. L. Hummel, director, USOM, Honduras, to Willauer, 31 October 1956.

77. NA, RG59, 715.5 MSP/6–1357, Willauer to Department of State, 13 June 1957.

78. NA, RG59, 715.5-MSP/8–158 HBS, Robert Newbegin, U.S. Embassy, Honduras, to Douglas Dillon, undersecretary for economic affairs, Department of State, 1 August 1958; NA, RG59, 715.5-MSP/11–558, Memorandum of Conversation, "Engineering Construction Unit Project in Honduras," 5 November 1958.

79. Art. 327, Constitution of 1957; Salomón, *Militarismo y Reformismo*, 36–37.

80. The letter was reprinted in *El Día* (Tegucigalpa) 25 May 1968 under the headline "Villeda No Contestó Nota del Consejo de la Defensa," 1.

81. NA, RG59, 715.551/12–158, Stewart (OAP) to Snow (ARA), 1 December 1958.

82. NA, RG59, 715.5-MSP/2–6 59, Robert Newbegin, U.S. Embassy, Honduras, to Department of State, 6 February 1959; USAMHI/Lib. OO/DD-ISA/MAP/PR/Mar'59. "Department of Defense Progress Report, Military Assistance Program," 16 March 1959; RG59, 715.5-MSP/9–1659, Christian Herter, secretary to state, to U.S. Embassy, Honduras, 15 September 1959.

83. USAMHI/Lib., o/MAAG/H7/NS/Je59, U.S. Military Assistance Advisory Group, Tegucigalpa, Honduras, "Narrative Statement," 29 July 1959.

84. NA, RG59, 715.58/9–1059, Robert Newbegin, U.S. ambassador, Honduras, Department of State, 10 September 1959.

85. NA, RG59, 715.56/4–1558 CS/G, Robert G. Barnes, special assistant for mutual security coordination, to Department of Defense, 1 May 1958.

86. USAMHI/Lib., o/MAAG/H7/NS/Je59, U.S. Military Assistance Advisory Group, Tegucigalpa, Honduras, "Narrative Statement," 29 July 1959.

87. The uprisings were reported in some detail by the *New York Times* on 10 February (1), 11 February (13), 12 February (11), 15 February (4), 16 February (8), 19 February (10), 31 March (3), 13 May (5).

88. Funes, *Los Deliberantes*, 220–22; "Army and Party Feud in Honduras," *New York Times*, 12 July 1959, 20; a search of the *Herald* failed to turn up the article.

89. Lt. Col. Velásquez surrendered on condition that he receive safe conduct to the Costa Rican embassy. Funes, *Los Deliberantes*, 228; Longino Becerra, *Evolución Histórica de Honduras* (Tegucigalpa, Honduras: Baktun Editorial, 1989), 172.

90. Paul P. Kennedy, "Snipers Retard Honduran Peace," *New York Times*, 16 July 1959, 3.

91. Posas and Del Cid, *La Construcción*, 127; Natalini et al., *Significado*, 124; Funes, *Los Deliberantes*, 228–29.

92. Becerra, *Evolución Histórica*, 172.

93. NA, RG59, 715.5/10–3059, U.S. Embassy, Honduras, to Department of State, 30 October 1959.

94. NA, FOIA, RG59, 715.561/2–1060 HBS, Robert Newbegin, U.S. ambassador, Tegucigalpa, to Department of State, 10 February 1960.

95. NA, FOIA, RG59,715.561/2–2360, Herbert O. Hardin, chief, Latin American Branch Public Safety Division, ICA/W, to U.S. Ambassador Newbegin, 17 February 1960.

96. NA, WNRC, RG286, OPS/Oper/LA, Guatemala 1955–63, "Guatemala Reports." David L. Laughlin, public safety advisor, to ICA (Washington), 31 March 1960.

97. NA, FOIA, RG59, 715.561/2–2660, Newbegin to Department of State, 26 February 1960.

98. NA, FOIA, RG59, Newbegin to Department of State, 27 July 1960; Newbegin to Department of State, 26 February 1960; 715.561/2–2660, Department of State to U.S. Embassy, Honduras, 5 March 1960; 715.561/7–2260, Newbegin to Department of State, 22 and 23 July 1960.

99. NA, RG286, OPS/Technical Services Division/Geographic Files/1961–70/Honduras, OPS/Tegucigalpa to AID/Washington, "Cumulative Report of Commodities Received during FY-61, 62 and 63," 11 July 1963.

100. NA, FOIA, RG59, 715.5-MSP/9–960, Albert B. Franklin, chargé d'affaires ad interim, U.S. Embassy, Honduras, to Department of State, 9 September 1960.

101. FRUS 1958–60:5MS, Honduras, Merchant, acting secretary of state, to U.S. Embassy, Honduras, 2 September 1960, 1223.

102. Cuba "acknowledged with pride" its atttempt to overthrow Somoza, according to Jorge I. Domínguez, *To Make a World Safe for Revolution: Cuba's Foreign Policy* (Cambridge, Mass.: Harvard University Press, 1989), 26, 118.

103. Paul P. Kennedy, "Hondurans' Chief Says Revolt Ebbs," *New York Times*, 11 February 1959, 13; Paul P. Kennedy, "Nicaragua Fears Leftist Attacks," *New York Times*, 15 February 1959, 4.

104. Robert D. Crassweller reported that Trujillo financed Velásquez and that Somoza provided a training camp for his men in Nicaragua. *Trujillo: The Life and Times of a Caribbean Dictator* (New York: Macmillan, 1966), 340–41.

105. NA, FOIA, RG59, 717.00/1–860 EMW, Robert Newbegin, Memorandum of Conversation, Tegucigalpa, 6 January 1960; and 717.00/1–360 CAA, Whelan (Managua) to Department of State, 3 January 1960; 717.00/1–360, Dillon to Newbegin, 4 January 1960; Whelan (Managua) to Department of State, 5 January 1960.

106. NA, FOIA, RG59, 715.5-MSP/10–1400 HBS, Albert B. Franklin, chargé d'affaires ad interim, U.S. Embassy, Honduras, to Department of State, 14 October 1960.

107. Fonseca, "Los Precedentes," 119, 128.

108. NA, RG59, 715.5 MSP/6–1357, Willauer to Department of State, 13 June 1957.

109. To say that the U.S. government *made* the Honduran armed forces in 1954–56 might not be an exaggeration. Honduras's highest military authorities have publicly said as much. See, for example, Lt. Col. José Oscar Flores, director de Historia Militar, Armed Forces of Honduras, "Reseña Histórica de la Rama Ejército en Honduras," *Proyecciones Militares* (Organ of the Armed Forces of Honduras) (January 1984):13–15, 20–21. In 1992, at a public exhibit ("Expomil-21," 17 October 1992) sponsored by the armed forces at a Tegucigalpa parade grounds, a poster commemorating the establishment of the First Infantry Battalion declared: "With the creation of the First Infantry Battalion the growth and evolution of the national army was initiated, and for that reason it can be said of the battalion, in all justice, that it was the genesis of the modern national army and cradle of the Honduran infantry." The poster went on to identify U.S. Army Col. Thomas M. McGrail, the head of the U.S. Army mission in 1954, as the founder and first commander of the battalion. Another display credited six U.S. Army soldiers as the "pioneers" whose supervision of the Toncontín construction crews in the late 1940s led to the creation in 1959 of the First Engineers Battalion.

NOTES TO PAGES 196–200

CHAPTER 13

1. FRUS 1940:5, Meredith Nicholson (U.S. minister in Nicaragua) to Department of State, 6 June 1940, 146–47.

2. See chapter 9 for a comparative analysis of Lend-Lease support.

3. Conn and Fairchild, *Framework*, 254, 264

4. FRUS 1939:5, Roosevelt to Somoza, 22 May 1939, 728; FRUS 1942:6, Welles to Roosevelt, 3 April 1942, 571; General Eisenhower to Welles, 2 April 1942, 570; also see editorial notes in FRUS 1939:5, 747 and FRUS 1942:6, 575–76; for martial law, see Walter, *The Regime*, 112. For the vulnerability of Rama to guerrilla action, see Macaulay, *Sandino Affair*, 207–8. The project turned out to be a colossal boondoggle, costing four times the original estimate of $4 million and unfinished until the late 1960s; see Clark, *The United States*, 91.

5. FRUS 1945:9, Finley, U.S. Embassy, Nicaragua, to Department of State, 26 February 1945, 1197.

6. Ibid.

7. AIHN/ASG 136, Gen. LeRoy Bartlett, Jr., GN [Guardia Nacional], director of the Academia Militar, and colonel in the U.S. Military Mission, to President Somoza, 25 May 1945; for martial law and the antisubversive statute, see Walter, *The Regime*, 112.

8. AIHN/ASG070, "Speech of General Somoza."

9. AIHN/ASG070, "Minutes of the Initial Plenary Conference of the Bi-Lateral Staff Conversations Between the United States and the Republic of Nicaragua."

10. FRUS 1945:9, A. M. Warren, Department of State, to U.S. Ambassador Fletcher Warren, 13 July 1945, 1201.

11. FRUS 1945:9, U.S. Ambassador Fletcher Warren to A. M. Warren, Department of State, 18 July 1945, 1202–04; A. M. Warren, Department of State, to U.S. Ambassador Fletcher Warren, 20 August 1945, 1205–8; for evidence of efforts to block transfers, see correspondence, 1208–13.

12. For "dictator" comment, see FRUS 1945:9, U.S. Ambassador Fletcher Warren to Department of State, 29 November 1945, 1226; also see related correspondence, 1213–30, and Walter, *Regime*, 146–49; Walter's claim (144) that Somoza's final decision against running for reelection "was determined in good measure" by the opposition of the United States seems well supported by the diplomatic correspondence he cites, though Walter does not explicitly weigh the influence of internal political opposition to Somoza on his decision not to run.

13. FRUS 1947:8, various correspondence, 9 May–27 May 1947, 848–58.

14. FRUS 1947:8, correspondence, 28 May–10 June 1947, 858–60.

15. FRUS 1947:8, Department of State to U.S. Embassy, Nicaragua, 26 May 1947, 854, and Bernbaum to Department of State, 26 May 1947, 854–56; FRUS 1947–52MS, "Secretary's Memoranda of Conversations," memorandum of conversation, "Nicaraguan Political Situation," 5 June 1947.

16. FRUS 1947:8, Bernbaum to Department of State, 1 July 1947, 862–63.

17. FRUS 1947:8, Bernbaum to Department of State, 7 August 1947, 865.

18. Walter, *Regime*, 165; FRUS 1947:8, Norman Armour memorandum of conversation, 24 August 1947, 871–72.

19. FRUS 1947:8, Bernbaum to Department of State, 19 August 1947, 866. For a bitterly critical legal analysis of this familiar maneuver, see Fonseca, "Los Precedentes," 95–106, dealing with the Honduran constitutional convention's appointment of Ramón Villeda Morales in 1957.

20. Walter, *The Regime*, 167, 213.

21. "Mexico Suggested as New Canal Site," *New York Times*, 25 December 1947, 14.

22. "Nicaraguan Backs Canal," *New York Times*, 27 December 1947, 27; "Nicaragua Discusses Canal Plan," *New York Times*, 29 December 1947, 9.

23. "26 Seized in Managua Raid," *New York Times*, 20 January 1948, 10; "Managua Holds 14 More as Reds," *New York Times*, 23 January 1948, 12.

24. "Nicaraguan Charges Plot," *New York Times*, 29 January 1948, 20. On 17 December 1947 Arévalo had indeed presided over the signing of the Pacto del Caribe, an alliance of revolutionary exiles from Costa Rica, Nicaragua, and the Dominican Republic bent on overthrowing the dictatorships that governed their countries; Gleijesis, *Shattered Hope*, 110; Charles D. Ameringer, *Don Pepe: A Political Biography of José Figueres of Costa Rica* (Albuquerque: University of New Mexico Press, 1978), 40, 76ff.

25. The pact was reproduced in Carlos Cuadra Pasos, *El Pensamiento Político del Doctor Carlos Cuadra Pasos* (Granada, Spain: Editorial La Prensa, June 1950); also see Cuadra Pasos, *Explicación*, and Walter, *Regime*, 172–73. Cuadra Pasos's faction favored the election of party leaders, and opposed the militarism and authoritarianism that it associated with the party's leader, General Chamorro, according to Cuadra; *Hispanic American Report* 4 (June 1951) 6:15.

26. FRUS 1948:9, Bernbaum to Department of State, 12 February 1948 and 3 March 1948, 101–105; 102n2.

27. FRUS 1948:9, Secretary of State Marshall to the acting secretary of state, Bogotá, 31 March 1948, 24; Bernbaum to Department of State, 3 March 1948, 104; Marshall to U.S. diplomats in Latin America, 30 April 1948, 108n2.

28. The pact was reproduced in Esgueva Gómez, *Las Constituciones Políticas*, 903–12.

29. Walter, *The Regime*, 175–77, 275n37; 197. Somoza proved to be "very respectful" of Conservative business and property interests (198).

30. Walter, *The Regime*, 178–79.

31. Carlos Cuadra Pasos, *Mensaje a los Conservadores de Nicaragua* (Managua, Nicaragua: Fondo del Grupo Conservador Tradicionalista, 1950), 3, 8–9.

32. C. H. Calhoun, "Nicaragua to Seek New Foreign Loan," *New York Times*, 23 May 1950, 24. The voting procedures, the *Times* editorialized, proved that Nicaragua was just what many Nicaraguans called it—"hacienda de Somoza"; "Hacienda de Somoza," *New York Times*, 28 May 1950, Sec. 4, 2.

33. "Nicaraguan Admits Obtaining Arms Here; Somoza Says Contraband Nullfies Ban," *New York Times*, 14 January 1949, 16.

34. FRUS 1947–52MS, "Secretary's Memoranda of Conversation," and State Department memorandum, "Unusual Publicity in Bogotá Concerning Nicaraguan 'Invasion' of Costa Rica," 19 April 1948. On 11 December, Costa Rica invoked the Río Treaty in response to an armed invasion from Nicaragua; Nicaragua denied the accusation, but denounced Costa Rica for fostering anti-Nicaraguan conspiracies. "Costa Rica and Nicaragua 1948–1949," in Pan American Union, *Inter-American Treaty of Reciprocal Assistance Applications*, vol. 1, *1948–1959* (Washington, D.C.: Pan American Union, 1964), 27–29.

35. Clark, *The United States*, 182.

36. USAMHI/Lib., Intelligence Division, General Staff, U.S. Army, "Intelligence Research Project: Characteristics and Capabilities of Latin American Armies," 17 June 1949.

37. NA, RG59, 717.5-MAP/5–951, Duncan A. D. Mackay, Office of Regional American Affairs, to Ernest V. Siracusa, Central American Affairs, "Military Policy with Regard to Nicaragua," 9 May 1951.

38. NA, RG59, 717.58/5–1651, Maxwell D. Taylor, assistant chief of staff, U.S. Army, to Department of State, 16 May 1951; FRUS 1951:2, "Memorandum by the Acting Secretary of State to the Executive Secretary of the National Security Council (Lay)," 13 September 1951, 1021–22.

39. The lunch story was told to *New York Times* correspondent Herbert L. Matthews by Edward G. Miller, Jr., assistant secretary of state for inter-American affairs; Matthews, *A World*, 262–63. Also see Gleijeses's *(Shattered Hope*, 228–30) account of "Operation Fortune," which is based mainly on Matthews's report but contains corroborating details.

40. UST 3.4.5027, 4.2.2238.

41. FRUS 1952–54:4, "The Ambassador in Nicaragua (Whelan) to the Dept. of State," 6 March 1953, 1375–6. Somoza's servility to the United States even caught the attention of a *New York Times* editorial writer. "In the United Nations, the Organization of American States and other international bodies, Nicaraguan delegates support United States policies so quickly and so enthusiastically that they have given a new meaning to the phrase, 'me too.'" "Unchanging Nicaragua," *New York Times*, 9 May 1950, 28.

42. NA, FOIA, RG59,717.5-MSP/3–953, U.S. Embassy, Nicaragua, to Department of State, 9 March 1953.

43. NA, FOIA, RG 59, 717.5 MSP/3–1153, U.S. Embassy, Nicaragua, to Department of State, 11 March 1953.

44. NA, RG59, 717.5/5–553, "Proposal for a Military Agreement between the U.S. and Nicaragua," 5 May 1953.

45. NA, FOIA, RG59, 717.56/5–2153, U.S. Embassy, Nicaragua, to Department of State, 21 May 1953.

46. NA, RG 218,1954–56, 381 Western Hemisphere (3–22–48), Sec. 23, "Memorandum by the Chief of Staff, U.S. Army, for the Joint Chiefs of Staff on Sale of Military Equipment to Latin American Countries," 9 November 1954.

47. NA, FOIA, RG59,717.56/6–2453 LWC, Rolland Welch, first secretary of the U.S. Embassy, Nicaragua, to Department of State, 24 June 1953.

48. NA, RG59,717.5-MSP/8–1153, Rolland Welch, first secretary of U.S. Embassy, Nicaragua, to Department of State, 11 August 1953.

49. USAMHI/Lib., Intelligence Division, General Staff, U.S. Army, "Intelligence Research Project: Characteristics and Capabilities of Latin American Armies," 17 June 1949; NA, RG59, 717.56/6–2453, Rolland Welch, first secretary, U.S. Embassy, Nicaragua, to Department of State, 24 June 1953; 710.5/3–1751, Junta Interamericana de Defensa, Estado Mayor, "Cuestionario," 18 January 1951.

50. NA, RG330/17/Nicaragua, Guillermo Sevilla-Sacasa, Nicaraguan ambassador to the United States, to John Foster Dulles, U.S. secretary of state, 20 July 1953; RG330/21A/Nicaragua, Department of Defense, Office of Military Assistance, to John Foster Dulles, 13 August 1953; RG330/21A/Nicaragua, Logisitics Division, Reimbursable Aid Branch, "Subject: Nicaragua," 30 December 1953.

51. NA, RG59, 717.5-MSP/7–2353, Burrows to Mann, 24 June 1953.

52. NA, RG59, 717.5-MSP/4–1754, U.S. Embassy, Nicaragua, to secretary of state, 17 April 1954.

53. NA, RG59, 717.5-MSP/5–1154, Frederick C. Nolting, Jr., special assistant to the president, National Security Affairs, to Maj. Gen. George C. Stewart, director, Office of Military Assistance, Department of Defense, 11 May 1954; 717.5622/1–1755, Ohmans, MID, to Newbegin, MID, 17 January 1955.

54. NA, RG59, 715.56/5–2754, Frederick E. Nolting, Jr., special assisant to the secretary for mutual security affairs, to U.S. Rep. Frances P. Bolton, 27 May 1954.

55. Gleijesis, *Shattered Hope*, 292.

56. NA, RG59, 717.5-MSP/5–2455, Col. James W. Pumpelly, chief, MAAG, Nicaragua, "General Considerations," 24 May 1955.

57. NA, RG59, 717.53/6–156, U.S. Army Mission, Nicaragua, Report to Ambassador, 1 June 1956.

58. NA, RG59, 717.5-MSP/7–2656, U.S. Embassy to Department of State, 26 July 1956,

59. NA, RG 218, 092 (8–22–46) (2) B.P. Pt. 11, 1954–56, "Report by the Joint Strategic Plans Committee to the Joint Chiefs of Staff on Status of Military Assistance Programs on 30 June 1956," 8 September 1956; RG218, 1954–56. 381 Western Hemisphere (3–22–48) Sec. 30, Headquarters Caribbean Command, Canal Zone, "Study of MDAP Force Base Units for Latin America." Somoza may even have feared that the MAP battalion commander would bypass Somoza completely in the acqusition of weapons and might seek U.S. favor "at the expense of family sovereignty," according to Michael D. Gambone, *Eisenhower, Somoza, and the Cold War in Nicaragua, 1953–1961* (Westport, Conn.: Praeger, 1997), 94–95.

60. NA, RG218, 1954–56, 381 Western Hemisphere (3–22–48) Sec. 30. Headquarters Caribbean Command, Canal Zone, "Study of MDAP Force Base Units for Latin America."

61. NA, RG330/21/Nicaragua, Sec. 408(e), sales cases No. 1, 2, and 3, 1954; Frederick Nolting, Jr., special assistant to the secretary for mutual security affairs, Department of State, to Maj. Gen. George C. Stewart, Office of Military Assistance, Department of Defense, 25 June 1954; Guillermo Sevilla Sacasa, ambassador of Nicaragua, to John Foster Dulles, 17 July 1954; Nolting to Stewart, 2 September 1954; A. Somoza D., jefe del estado mayor, Nicaragua, to Thomas E. Whelan, U.S. ambassador, Nicaragua, 14 June 1954; Nolting to Stewart, 17 August 1954; Col. S. M. Langley, Department of Air Force, to director, Office of Military Assistance, Department of Defense, 25 October 1954; Capt. H. T. Deutermann, Department of the Navy, to Stewart, 10 September 1954; Gen. Sam C. Russell, Foreign Aid Division, Department of the Army, to Office of Military Assistance, Department of Defense, 24 November 1954.

62. NA, RG330/21A/Nicaragua, Logisitics Division, Reimbursable Aid Branch, "Subject: Nicaragua," 30 December 1953; RG330/21A/Nicaragua. "Reimbursable Military Assistance, Sales of Military Equipment and Materials, Government of Nicaragua, as of 30 September 1955; NA, RG59. 717.5 MSP/1–3155, Ohmans to Holland, 1 February 1955.

63. NA, RG330/21/Nicaragua, Frederick C. Nolting, Jr., special assistant to secretary for mutual security affairs, Department of State, to Office of Military Assistance, Department of Defense, 11 February 1955.

64. NA, RG59, 717.5-MSP/7–2755, Sevilla-Sacasa to Dulles, 27 July 1955; Nolting to Department of Defense/ISA, 26 August 1955,

65. NA, RG59, 717.5622/1–1755, Ohmans, MID, to Newbegin, MID, 17 January 1955.

66. FRUS 1955–57:7, "Memorandum from John L. Ohmans of the Office of Middle American Affairs to the Director of the Office (Newbegin)," 17 January 1955, 195–6; RG59, 717.5622/10–2554, Carlos J. Warner, first secretary, U.S. Embassy, Nicaragua, to Department of State, 25 October 1954; RG 59, 717.5 MSP/1–2155, Dulles to U.S. Embassy in Managua, 21 January 1955; 717.5-MSP/1–2455, Dulles to U.S. Embassy, 26 January 1955.

67. NA, RG59, 717.5614/4–2555, Whelan, U.S. Embassy, Nicaragua, to secretary of state, 25 April 1955.

68. NA, RG59, 717.56/12–1554, Newbegin to Holland, 15 December 1954.

69. Walter, *The Regime*, 206; for an acute analysis of the anti-Somoza opposition, see 216–33.

70. Ibid., 230–33; "3 Nicaraguans Banished," *New York Times*, 15 February 1955, 2; Ameringer, *Don Pepe*, 119–20.

71. Ameringer, *Don Pepe*, 121–23; also see the Organization of American States's investigative report, which concluded that Costa Rica had been the victim of "foreign intervention" but delicately declined to identify the guilty government; "Costa Rica and Nicaragua 1955," in Pan American Union, *Inter-American Treaty*, 196. Nicaragua's demand for the F-51s was seriously considered but rejected; see NA, RG 59, 717.5 MSP/1–2155, Dulles to U.S. Embassy in Managua, 21 January 1955; 717.5-MSP/1–2455, Dulles to U.S. Embassy, 26 January 1955.

72. Paul P. Kennedy, "Nicaragua Found in Nervous State," *New York Times*, 11 August 1955, 4; "Somoza to Run in 1956 for 4th 6-Year Term," *New York Times*, 30 November 1955, 13.

73. Clark, *The United States*, 190. The former North Dakota potato farmer presented his credentials on 3 November 1951, just as U.S.-Nicaraguan relations were beginning to glow again, and stayed until 22 March 1961, making Whelan's the longest tenure of any U.S. mission chief in Managua.

74. FRUS 1955–57:7, "Letter from the Director of the Office of Middle American Affairs (Neal) to the Ambassador in Nicaragua (Whelan)," 30 October 1956, 232–33; NA, RG59, 717.56/10–1756, U.S. Embassy, Nicaragua, to John Foster Dulles, 17 October 1956.

75. NA, RG59,717.51/5–1057, U.S. Embassy, Nicaragua, to Department of State, 10 May 1957.

76. NA, FOIA, RG59, 717.56/5–3157 CS/DLS, "Memorandum of Conversation: Nicaragua-Israel Deal for Purchase of Staghound Armored Vehicles," by Park F. Wollam, Nicaraguan desk officer, Department of State, 31 May 1957; FRUS 1955–57:7, Moon to Wieland, 9 July 1957, 235–37.

77. For these suspicions, and for the pre-assassination tank deal proposed by Anastasio, see NA, RG59,717.5622/6–2656, Barnes to Department of Defense/ISA, 11 July 1956; RG59,717.561/5–256, Hoover, acting, Department, to U.S. Embassy, Nicaragua, 4 May 1956; 717.561/5–756, Park F. Wollam, Department of State, to Thomas E. Whelan, U.S. ambassador, Nicaragua, 7 May 1956; Whelan to secretary of state, 10 May 1956. After the assassination, the regime became more active in the purchase and resale of arms worldwide; see Gambone, *Eisenhower, Somoza*, 196–201.

78. NA, RG59, 717.56/4–153, U.S. Embassy, Nicaragua, to Department of State, 1 April 1958.

79. FRUS 1958–60:6, U.S. Embassy, Cuba, to Department of State, 11 January 1958, 7; Department of State to U.S. Embassy, Cuba, 14 March 1958, 60.

80. NA, RG59, 717.5622/5.658, Whelan, U.S. Embassy, Nicaragua, to secretary of state, 7 May 1958.

81. AID/Lib.,"Mutual Security Program, Fiscal Year 1959 Estimates, Latin America."

82. NA, RG59, FW717.56/9–857, Nicaraguan Embassy, Washington, D.C., to Department of State, 8 September 1958; 717.5614/10–258, Whelan, U.S. Embassy, Nicaragua, to secretary of state, 2 October 1958.

83. For the invasion and rebel plots, see various documents in FRUS 1958–60:5MS, "Nicaragua." For the "dictatorship" concern, see FRUS 1958–60:5MS, "Nicaragua," Roy R. Rubottom, Jr., assistant secretary of state for inter-American affairs, to U.S. Ambassador Thomas Whelan, Managua, 7 April 1958, and C. Allan Stewart, Office of Middle American Affairs, to Rubottom, 26 November 1958.

84. NA, RG286, OPS/LA/Nica/IPS-1, Herbert O. Hardin and John C. Neely to "the files," 12 September 1958.

85. FRUS 1958–60:5MS, "Nicaragua," Rubottom to Whelan, U.S. Embassy, Nicaragua, 31 January 1959.

86. FRUS 1958–60:5MS, "Nicaragua," Memorandum of conversation, Rubottom, 4 April 1959.

87. FRUS 1958–60:5MS, "Nicaragua," U.S. Embassy, Nicaragua, to Department of State, 19 June 1959; Rojas Bolaños, "La Política," 132.

88. FRUS 1958–60:5MS, "Nicaragua," Department of State to U.S. Embassy, Nicaragua, 7 July 1959 (HU-15).

89. *Operation Zapata*, 69–70, 80; Albert C. Persons, *Bay of Pigs: A Firsthand Account . . .* (Jefferson, N.C.: McFarland, 1990), 62, 77. For Somoza's U.S. visit, see FRUS 1958–60:5MS, "Nicaragua," Memorandum of Conversation, 21 October 1960.

CHAPTER 14

1. FRUS 1940:5, William H. Hornibrook, U.S. Embassy, Costa Rica, San José, to Department of State, 5 June and 11 June, 1940, 83–84, 85–86; for the size of the army see NAMP, Roll 11, "Correspondence and Record Cards....," Col. J. B. Pate, "Personnel Strength, Active Army," 30 July 1940, and "Actual Composition of Costa Rican Army," 3 July 1941.

2. FRUS 1940:5, Hornibrook to Department of State, 24 June 1940, 87–88.

3. Ibid., 11 July, 4 September, 17 September, 1940, 88–93.

4. Pres. Rafael A. Calderón, speech to Congreso Constitucional, 1 May 1942, in Carlos Meléndez Chaverri, ed., *Mensajes Presidenciales 1940–1958* (San José, Costa Rica: Imprenta Nacional, 1990), 54.

5. NAMP, Roll 11, "Correspondence and Record Cards....," Col. J. B. Pate, "Actual Composition of Costa Rican Army," 3 July 1941.

6. Molina and Lehoucq, *Urnas*, ch. 11, attributed the deterioration to a sharpening of interparty competition brought on by electoral law changes in the 1920s, which among other things bestowed excessive authority on the president to settle election controversies.

7. Molina and Lehoucq, *Urnas*, 137, 150, 151, 156.

8. Ibid., 161.

9. Ibid., 172–77.

10. Ameringer, *Don Pepe*, ch. 2.

11. See the analysis in Molina and Lehoucq, *Urnas*, 185–89, which concluded that Ulate probably did not win, although his victory has been widely assumed in the historiography.

12. For the Calderón-Ulate accord, see Molina and Lehoucq, *Urnas*, 184. For a chronicle of the violence that emphasized the Figueres-led opposition movement's early resort to terrorism and violence, see John Patrick Bell, *Crisis in Costa Rica: The 1948 Revolution* (Austin: University of Texas Press, 1971), ch. 5. For the communist "brigadas de choque" see Muñoz Guillén, *El estado*, 143.

13. Longley, *Sparrow*, 63–64, 69–83.

14. From *La Prensa Libre* (San José) of 1 December 1948: "Exto. del Discurso del Presidente de la Junta de Gobierno," 7; "Texto del Discurso del Ministro de Seguridad Pública," 3; "Disuelto el Ejército Nacional," 1, 3. Of 2 December: "Al Coronel Cardona se Debe la Medida que Supreme el Ejército Regular de Costa Rica," 1, 5; "Temas del Momento: Sin Ejército," 2; Of 3 December: "En Paris Causa Sensación la Disolución del Ejército," 1, 4.

15. Lilly Edgerton, "Un sello muy tico," *Al Día* (San José), 1 December 2000, 17.

16. See ANCR, Junta Fundadora de la Segunda Republica, bks 2 and 3, for records of both the minutes and the decrees of the Junta; no decree abolishing the army was recorded, nor could archivists locate a record of such a decision. That the decision was made spontaneously by Figueres himself is suggested by Zamora Castellanos, *Militarismo*, 104, but the newspaper reports cited above consistently quote Figueres and Cardona as attributing the decision to the Junta.

17. Quoted in Zamora Castellanos, *Militarismo y Estado*, 105.

18. Alguilar Bulgarelli, *Costa Rica y Sus Hechos Políticos* 462; Oscar Castro Vega, *Fin de la Segunda República: Figueres y la Constituyente del 49* (San José, Costa Rica: Imprenta LIL, 1996), 64, 245–46.

19. Zamora Castellanos, *Militarismo y estado*, 106. For the bitter political rivalry between Ulate's PUN and Figueres in 1948, see Ameringer, *Don Pepe*, 88–89, 93.

20. Oscar Alguilar Bulgarelli, *La Constitución de 1949: Antecedentes y Proyecciones* (San José, Costa Rica: Editorial Costa Rica, 1991), 105.

21. Zamora Castellanos, *Militarismo y estado*, 100.

22. Of course, it also became an argument for *not* abolishing the army, because the treaty also required its signatories to use their armies to aid other threatened signatores; Zamora Castellanos, *Militarismo y estado*, 137–38.

23. The Legion was known to be organizing an assault on the Nicaraguan government and its presence would obviously complicate a diplomatic solution in the event of Nicaraguan aggression; Ameringer, *Don Pepe*, 80.

24. Both countries signed, at the urging of the OAS, a Pact of Amity on 21 February 1949. See "Costa Rica and Nicaragua 1948–1949," in Pan American Union, *Inter-American Treaty*, 35; Ameringer, *Don Pepe*, 80–83.

25. *Constitución Política de la República de Costa Rica* (San José, Costa Rica: Editec Editores, 2000), 13.

26. MSPCR 1953–54, 5–6.

27. Urcuyo, "Civil-Military," 241.

28. NA, RG59, 716.5/5–2251, Department of State, Memorandum of Conversation, "Military Equipment for Costa Rica," 22 May 1951; RG 59, 718.5/6–2151, Memorandum, 21 June 1951; 718.5/6–1351. Oreamuno to Acheson, 13 June 1951; 718.5-MAP/7–2651, Miller to Bendetsen, 26 July 1951. For the "paramilitary characteristics" of the 1948 veterans, see Ameringer, *Don Pepe*, 100.

29. NA, FOIA, RG59,718.56/1–2952, Memorandum of Conversation by Albert F. Nufer, director, MID, 29 January 1952.

30. NA, FOIA, RG59, 718.5 MSP/3–1352, Philip B. Fleming, U.S. Embassy, Costa Rica, to Department of State, 13 March 1952; attached letter, Lara to Fleming, 11 March 1952.

31. NA, RG59, 717.5-MSP/4–1754, "Costa Rican Reaction to United States-Nicaragua Military Aid Pact," 17 April 1954; FRUS 1952–54:4, memorandum of conversation, Ohmans, 27 April 1954, 843.

32. NA, RG 59, 718.5-MSP/5–454. Costa Rican Embassy to Department of State, 4 May 1954; 718.5-MSP/5–454, Department of State to Costa Rican Embassy, 11 May 1954; 718.5-MSP/5–2654, General Stewart to Department of State, 26 May 1954; 718.5-MSP/4–2054. U.S. Embassy, Costa Rica, to Department of State, 5 April 1954; 718.56/5–2654, memorandum, 26 May 1954; 718.56/6–954. Ohmans to Burrows, 9 June 1954; 718.5-MSP/7–154, Dulles to U.S. Embassy in Nicaragua, 1 July 1954; 718.56/10–154, U.S. Embassy, Costa Rica, to Department of State, 1 October 1954; 718.5-MSP/11–1654, Costa Rican Embassy to Department of State, 16 November 1954.

33. NA, FOIA, RG59,718.561/5–754, C. Allan Stewart, chargé d'affaires ad interim, to Department of State, 7 May 1954.

34. FRUS 1952–54:4, " Ohmans to Hill, 7 July 1954, 845–46; secretary of state to U.S. Embassy, Guatemala, 9 July 1954, 851; FRUS 1955–57:7, Woodward to Department of State, 26 April 1955, 4.

35. ANCR, SP, 84/1381, Maj. Enrique Martén, jefe de planes y operaciones, to director general de detectives, 5 July 1954.

36. NA, RG 218, 1954–56, 381 Western Hemisphere, Sec. 22, U.S. Army chief of staff to CINCARIB, 30 July 1954; CINCARIB to CSUSA, 1 August, 1954.

37. "Costa Rica and Nicaragua 1955," in Pan American Union, *Inter-American Treaty*, 181; Ameringer, *Don Pepe*, 121–23, and ch. 13 above.

38. NA, RG59, 718.5614/1–1955, Woodward, U.S. Embassy, Costa Rica, 19 January 1955; 718.56/1–2055, Holland to Jamison, 20 January 1955; 718.5614/1–2155, Dulles to U.S. Embassy, Costa Rica, 21 January 1955; 718.5614/1–2055, Frederick E. Nolting, Jr., Department of State, special assistant to secretary for mutual security, to director, Office of Military Assistance, Department of Defense, 10 February 1955.

39. NA, RG59, 718.56/1–2055, Holland to Jamison, 20 January 1955; 718.56/1–2655, Robert F. Woodward, U.S. Embassy, Costa Rica, to Department of State, 26 January 1955.

40. NA, RG59, 718.5622/1–1555, Woodward to secretary of state, 16 January 1955; 718.5622/1–1655, Memorandum of Conversation, "Planes for Costa Rica," 16 January 1955; 718.5622/1–1755, State Department memorandum, 17 January 1955; 718.5622/1–1855, Dulles to U.S. Embassy, Costa Rica, 18 January 1955; 718.5 MSP/1–2555, Frederick F. Nolting, Jr., Department of State, special assistant for mutual security affairs, to Office of Military Assistance, Department of Defense, 25 January 1955.

41. NA, RG218, CCS 092 (8–22–46) (2) Sec. 3, 954–56, George Roderick, assistant secretary of the Army, to assistant secretary of defense, 7 February 1955; FRUS 1955–57:7, "Paper presented by the Operations Coordinating Board. Analysis of Internal Security Situation in Costa Rica and Recommended Action," 15 August 1956, 23.

42. NA, RG218, 1954–56, 381 Western Hemisphere (3–22–48) Sec. 27, Joint Chiefs of Staff, "U.S. Military Policy for Latin America," 16 November 1955; RG59, 718.5-MSP/4–1255, Robert F. Woodward, U.S. ambassador, Costa Rica, to Department of State, 12 April 1955.

43. MSPCR 1953–54, 7–8.

44. For Guardia training, MSPCR 1953–54, 11; for organization of the Reserva in 1954–55, ANCR, SP, 43/474, Col. Alvaro Arias Guitiérrez, director general, Reserva de la Fuerza Pública, to Benjamín Piza, minister of public security, 21 November 1985; RG59, 718.5-MSP/4–1255, Woodward to Department of State, 12 April 1955.

45. NA, RG59, 718.5-MSP/4–1255, Woodward to Department of State, 12 April 1955.

46. FRUS 1955–57:7, Woodward to Department of State, 26 April 1955, 9; for similar U.S. pressures on Guatemala and El Salvador in 1957, see chapters 10 and 11.

47. ANCR, SP, 101/1923, Maj. Raul Cambronero, subdirector general de detectives, to Humberto Pacheco Coto, secretario general de la presidencia, 17 February 1955; Cambronero to Pacheco, 23 February 1955. See this file and others in "Seguridad Pública" for various records of investigations of suspected communists—particularly those active in the banana strike of 1955—and *calderonistas*, who were typically referred to as if they were practically identical categories of political subversives.

48. ANCR, SP, 90/1544, Circular letter, from Lt. Col. Guillermo Salazar R., director general de detectives, 28 August 1954.

49. FRUS 1955–57:7, "Paper presented by the Operations Coordinating Board. Analysis of Internal Security Situation in Costa Rica and Recommended Action," 15 August 1956, 23, 30.

50. FRUS 1955–57:7, Rubottom to Woodward, 17 October 1956, 31.

51. NA, RG59, 718.5/11–2856, Hoover, acting (Department of State) to U.S. Embassy, Costa Rica, 28 November 1956; 718.5/12–1156, Woodward to Department of State, 11 December 1956.

52. NA. RG59, 718.5/12–1156, Woodward to Department of State, 11 December 1956.

53. NA, RG 218, 1957, 381 Western Hemisphere (3–22–48) Sec. 34, "Note by the Secretaries to the Holders of JCS 1976/204," 27 May 1957; RG 218,1957, CCS 381 Western Hemisphere (3–22–48), Sec. 33, messages between U.S. Army staff in Washington and CINCARIB in Canal Zone, February 1957.

54. FRUS 1955–57:7, "Paper presented by the Operations Coordinating Board. Analysis of Internal Security Situation in Costa Rica and Recommended Action," 15 August 1956, 29.

55. MSPCR 1957–58, 59

56. AALCR. See Ramiro Brenes Gutiérrez et al., for the Partido Unión Cívico Revolucionario, to the Asamblea Legislativa, 27 March 1957, accompanying Decreto No. A15#2094, "Comisión Investigadora de Tráfico de Armas," 3 April 1957.

57. The speaker was Alberto Cañas; see MRECR 1957–58, 70–71, and UN General Assembly, *Official Records*, 31 October 1957, 102.

58. Ameringer, *Don Pepe*, 125–28.

59. "President-Elect Pledges Disarming of Costa Rica," *New York Times*, 26 February 1958, 2; "Costa Rica," *Hispanic American Report* 11 (1958) 2:82 and 11 (1958) 3:141–42.

60. FRUS 1958–60:5MS, "Costa Rica," "Briefing Paper for Visit of Costa Rican President-Elect Echandi," n.d., 837; "Memorandum of Conversation: Costa Rica 1958," 27 March 1958, 845.

61. NA, RG59, 718.56/8–2558, Manuel G. Escalante, ambassador of Costa Rica to the United States, to John Foster Dulles, secretary of state, August 25, 1958; 718.5-MSP/7–359, Col. Maurice C. Holden, chief, U.S. Army Mission, Costa Rica, to Commander, Caribbean Command, 26 May 1959.

62. NA, RG286, OPS/LA/Costa Rica/IPS 1, Herbert O. Hardin and John C. Neely to The Files, 25 September 1958, including memorandum of conversation of 19 September 1958.

63. AALCR. Correspondence and testimony filed with Decreto No. A15E2196, Comisión para Investigar las Denuncias Hechas Contra el Servicio de Inteligencia, 1 July 1958.

64. USAMHI/Lib., DD/ISA/MAP/C8/Jy'63, Department of Defense, Office of Military Assistance, Military Assistance Plan, Costa Rica, 15 July 1963; UST 13.2.2094.

CHAPTER 15

1. Of course, the same tactical and strategic reasoning underlay all U.S.-Latin American military collaboration in this period, with the difference that, in the larger countries of the region, a third strategic reason could be argued: to avoid the need for the United States, in the event of another world war, to again carry nearly all the burden of hemispheric defense.

WORKS CITED

MANUSCRIPT SOURCES

AALCR   Républica de Costa Rica. Archivo de la Asamblea Legislativa.

AGCA   República de Guatemala. Archivo General de Centro América, Guatemala.

AGNES   República de El Salvador. Archivo General de la Nación, San Salvador.

AID/Lib   U.S. Agency for International Development, Library, Rosslyn, Va.

AIHN   Archivo del Instituto de Historia de Nicaragua, Universidad Centroamérica, Managua.

ANCR   República de Costa Rica. Archivo Nacional, San José.

ANH   República de Honduras. Archivo Nacional, Tegucigalpa.

ANN   República de Nicaragua. Archivo Nacional, Managua.

ASREH   República de Honduras. Archivo de la Secretaría de Relaciones Exteriores, Tegucigalpa.

CIEL   República de Honduras. Centro de Informática y Estudios Legislativos, Biblioteca, Congreso Nacional Hondureño (Tegucigalpa)

DDRS   Declassified Documents Reference System.

MHI   U.S. Army Military History Institute, Carlisle Barracks, Pa.

NA   United States. National Archives, Washington, D.C.

NAMP   National Archives Microfilm Publications.

WNRC   United States. National Archives, Washington National Records Center, Suitland, Md.

PUBLISHED SOURCES

Adelman, Jeremy. "Introduction: The Problem of Persistence in Latin American History." In *Colonial Legacies: The Problem of Persistence in Latin American History*, ed. Jeremy Adelman. New York: Routledge, 1999.

Aguilera Peralta, Gabriel, and Jorge Romero Imery et al. *Dialéctica del Terror en Guatemala*. San José, Costa Rica: Editorial Universitaria Centroamericana, 1981.

Albrecht, Ulrich, and Mary Kaldor. "Introduction." In *The World Military Order: The Impact of Military Technology on the Third World*, ed. Mary Kaldor and Asbjorn Eide. London: Macmillan, 1979.

Alduvin, Ricardo. "Policarpo Bonilla." In *Policarpo Bonilla: Algunos Apuntes Biográficos* by Aro Sanso [Ismael Mejía Deras]. Mexico City: Imprenta Mundial, 1936.

Alguilar Bulgarelli, Oscar. *Costa Rica y Sus Hechos Políticos de 1948*. San José, Costa Rica: Editorial Costa Rica, 1993.

———. *La Constitución de 1949: Antecedentes y Proyecciones*. San José, Costa Rica: Editorial Costa Rica, 1991.

Almond, Gabriel A. "Foreword: The Return to Political Culture." In *Political Culture and Democracy in Developing Countries*, ed. Larry Diamond Boulder. Boulder, Colo.: Lynne Rienner, 1993.

Alonso, Paula. "Voting in Buenos Aires, Argentina, before 1912." In *Elections before Democracy: The History of Elections in Europe and Latin America*, ed. Eduardo Posada-Carbó. Houndmills, UK: Macmillan, 1996.

Alvarenga, Patricia. "Reshaping the Ethics of Power: A History of Violence in Western Rural El Salvador, 1880–1932." Ph.D. diss., University of Wisconsin, 1994.

Alvarenga, Patricia. *Cultura y ética de la violencia : El Salvador, 1880–1932*. San José, Costa Rica: EDUCA, 1996.

American Political Science Association. "Home Page of the Conflict Processes Section of the APSA." Available at http://wizard.ucr.edu/cps/cps.html. 2000.

Ameringer, Charles D. *Don Pepe: A Political Biography of José Figueres of Costa Rica*. Albuquerque: University of New Mexico Press, 1978.

Anderson, Perry. *Lineages of the Absolutist State*. London: Verso, 1979.

Anderson, Thomas P. *Matanza*, 2d ed. Willimantic, Conn.: Curbstone Press, 1992.

Arévalo, Juan José. *El Presidente Electo al Pueblo de la República*. Guatemala City: Tipografía Nacional, February 1945.

Argüeta, Mario. *Tiburcio Carías: Anatomía de Una Epoca, 1923–1948*. Tegucigalpa, Honduras: Editorial Guaymuras, 1989.

Aya, Roderick. "The Missed Revolution: The Fate of Rural Rebels in Sicily and Southern Spain 1840–1950." *Papers on European and Mediterranean Societies* 3. Amsterdam: Anthropologisch-Sociologisch Centrum, 1975.

Bailey, Norman A. "The United States as *Caudillo*." *Journal of Inter-American Studies* 5 (July 1963): 313–24.

Baily, Samuel L. "Introduction." In *Nationalism in Latin America*, ed. Samuel L. Baily. New York: Alfred A. Knopf, 1971.

Baker, Keith. "Introduction." In *Inventing the French Revolution: Essays on French Political Culture in the Eighteenth Century*. Cambridge: Cambridge University Press, 1990.

Baldwin, Hanson W. *United We Stand! Defense of the Western Hemisphere*. New York: Whittlesey House, 1941.

Baloyra-Herp, Enrique. "Reactionary Despotism in Central America." *Journal of Latin American Studies* 15, no. 2 (November 1983): 295–319.

Barahona, Marvin. *Evolución Histórica de la Identidad Nacional.* Tegucigalpa, Honduras: Editorial Guaymuras, 1991.

———. *La Hegemonía de los Estados Unidos en Honduras, 1907–1932.* Tegucigalpa, Honduras: Centro de Documentación de Honduras, 1989.

Bardales Bueso, Rafael. *Historia del Partido Nacional.* San Pedro Sula, Honduras: Central Impresora, 1987.

Barraclough, Geoffrey. *History in a Changing World.* Oxford: Basil Blackwell, 1957.

———. *Main Trends in History.* New York: Holmes and Meier, 1979.

Bartov, Omer. *Murder in Our Midst: The Holocaust, Industrial Killing, and Representation.* New York: Oxford University Press, 1996.

Basadre, Jorge. *Elecciones y centralismo en el Perú: Apuntes para un esquema histórico.* Lima, Peru: Centro de Investigaciones de la Universidad del Pacífico, 1980.

Becerra, Longino. *Evolución histórica de Honduras.* Tegucigalpa, Honduras: Baktun Editorial, 1989.

Bell, John Patrick. *Crisis in Costa Rica: The 1948 Revolution.* Austin: University of Texas Press, 1971.

Bethell, Leslie, and Ian Roxborough. "Latin America between the Second World War and the Cold War: Some Reflections on the 1945–48 Conjuncture." *Journal of Latin American Studies* 20 (1988): 167–89.

Bevans, Charles I., ed. *Treaties and Other International Agreements of the United States of America, 1776–1949.* Washington, D.C.: Government Printing Office, 1972.

Billingsley, Phil. *Bandits in Republican China.* Stanford, Calif.: Stanford University Press, 1988.

Blok, Anton. "The Peasant and the Brigand: Social Banditry Reconsidered." *Comparative Studies in Society and History* 14, no. 4 (September 1972): 494–503.

———. *The Mafia of a Sicilian Village, 1860–1960: A Study of Violent Peasant Entrepreneurs.* New York: Harper Torchbooks, 1974.

Bourdieu, Pierre, and Loïc J. D. Wacquant. *An Invitation to Reflexive Sociology.* Chicago: University of Chicago, 1992.

———. "Men and Machines." In *Advances in Social Theory and Methodology: Toward an Integration of Micro- and Macro-Sociologies,* ed. K. Knorr-Cetina and A. V. Cicourel. Boston: Routledge and Kegan Paul, 1981.

———. *The Logic of Practice,* trans. Richard Nice. Cambridge: Polity Press, 1990.

Brand, Charles A. "The Background of Capitalistic Development: Honduras to 1913." Ph.D. diss., University of Pittsburgh, 1972.

Bright, Charles, and Susan Harding. "Processes of Statemaking and Popular Protest: An Introduction." In *Statemaking and Social Movements: Essays in History and Theory,* ed. Charles Bright and Susan Harding. Ann Arbor: University of Michigan Press, 1984.

Brown, Richard Maxwell. *Strain of Violence: Historical Studies of American Violence and Vigilantism.* Oxford: Oxford University Press, 1975.

Brown, Timothy C. *The Real Contra War: Highlander Peasant Resistance in Nicaragua.* Norman: University of Oklahoma Press, 2001.

Bull, Hedley. *The Anarchical Society: A Study of Order in World Politics.* New York: Columbia University Press, 1977.

Bulmer-Thomas, Victor. *The Political Economy of Central America Since 1920.* Cambridge: Cambridge University Press, 1987.

Burns, E. Bradford. *Patriarch and Folk: The Emergence of Nicaragua, 1798–1858.* Cambridge, Mass.: Harvard University Press, 1991.

Busey, James L. "The Presidents of Costa Rica." *The Americas* 18, no. 1 (July 1961): 55–70.

Buzan, Barry. *People, States and Fear: An Agenda for International Security Studies in the Post-Cold War Era*, 2d ed. Boulder, Colo.: Lynne Rienner, 1991.

Calderón, David. *Orígen de la Mancha Brava*. San Salvador, El Salvador: n.p., 1970.

Callwell, Charles E. *Small Wars: Their Principles and Practice*. London: H.M.S.O., 1906.

Camacho, Alvaro. "Public and Private Dimensions of Urban Violence in Cali." In *Violence in Colombia: The Contemporary Crisis in Historical Perspective*, ed. Charles Bergquist et al. Wilmington, Del.: Scholarly Resources, 1992.

Campo Sepúlveda, Julio. *Estrategia: Los Problemas de la Defensa Nacional y la Preparación del Estratega Contemporaneo*. San Salvador, El Salvador: Ministerio de Defensa, 1955.

Carmack, Robert M. "State and Community in Nineteenth-Century Guatemala: The Mosmostenango Case." In *Guatemalan Indians and the State: 1540 to 1988*, ed. Carol A. Smith. Austin: University of Texas Press, 1990.

Castañeda S., Gustavo A. *El General Domingo Vásquez y Su Tiempo*. Tegucigalpa, Honduras: Imprenta Calderón, 1934.

Castellanos, Juan Mario. *El Salvador, 1930–1960: Antecedentes Históricos de la Guerra Civil*. San Salvador, El Salvador: Consejo Nacional para la Cultura y el Arte, 2001.

Castro Morán, Mariano. *Función política del ejército salvadoreño en el presente siglo*. San Salvador, El Salvador: UCA Editores, 1989.

Castro Vega, Oscar. *Fin de la Segunda República: Figueres y la Constituyente del 49*. San José, Costa Rica: Imprenta LIL, 1996.

Centeno, Miguel Angel. *Blood and Debt: War and the Nation-State in Latin America*. University Park: Pennsylvania State University Press, 2002.

Cerdas, Rodolfo. *El desencanto democrático: Crisis de partidos y transición democrática en Centro América y Panamá*. San José, Costa Rica: Ediciones Sanabria, 1993.

César Pinto S., Julio. "Luchas Sociales y Políticas: En Busca de un Proyecto Estatal Viable 1811–1830." In *Problemas en la formación del estado nacional en centroamérica*, ed. Edelberto Torres-Rivas and Julio César Pinto S. San José, Costa Rica: Instituto Centroamericano de Administración Pública, 1983.

Chalmers, Douglas A. "The Politicized State in Latin America." In *Authoritarianism and Corporatism*, ed. James M. Malloy. Pittsburgh, Pa.: University of Pittsburgh Press, 1977.

Chasteen, John Charles. *Heroes on Horseback: A Life and Times of the Last Gaucho Caudillos*. Albuquerque: University of New Mexico Press, 1995.

Chile. Ejército de Chile. *Misiones Militares del Ejército de Chile*. Available at http://www.ejercito.cl/internacional/misiones.htm. Last accessed 15 May 2001.

Ching, Erik. "Patronage, Politics and Power in El Salvador, 1840–1940." Photocopy. Department of History, Furman University, Greenville, S.C.

Clapham, Christopher. *Third World Politics: An Introduction*. Madison: University of Wisconsin Press, 1985.

Clark, Paul Coe, Jr. *The United States and Somoza, 1933–1956*. Westport, Conn.: Praeger, 1992.

Clegern, Wayne M. *Origins of Liberal Dictatorship in Central America: Guatemala, 1865–1873*. Niwot: University Press of Colorado, 1994.

Cohen, Youssef, Brian R. Brown, and A. F. K. Organski. "The Paradoxical Nature of State Making: The Violent Creation of Order." *American Political Science Review* 75, no. 4 (December 1981): 901–10.

Comisión Nacional de Festejos del Centenario de la Escuela Politécnica. *Historial de la Escuela Politécnica*. Guatemala City: Editorial del Ejército, 1973.

Commission for Historical Clarification. *Guatemala: Memory of Silence*. 1999. Available at http://hrdata.aaas.org/ceh/report/english. Last accessed 26 July 2002.

Comité Pro Festejos de la Revolución de 1871. *Antecedentes Históricos de la Revolución de 1871*. Guatemala City: Editorial "Jose de Pineda Ibarra" 1971.

Conference on Central American Affairs, Washington, December 4, 1922–February 7, 1923. Washington, D.C.: Government Printing Office, 1923.

Conn, Stetson, and Byron Fairchild. *The Framework of Hemisphere Defense.* Washington, D.C.: Office of the Chief of Military History, Department of the Army, 1960.

Conn, Stetson, Rose C. Engelman, and Byron Fairchild. *Guarding the United States and Its Outposts.* Washington, D.C.: Office of the Chief of Military History, Department of the Army, 1964.

Constitución Política de la República de Costa Rica. San José, Costa Rica: Editec Editores, 2000.

Costa Rica. *Informe dirigido al Excmo. Señor Presidente . . . por el Secretario de Estado en los Despachos de Guerra y Marina, . .* San José, Costa Rica: Imprenta Nacional, 1880.

———. *Memoria presentada al Congreso Constitucional por el Secretario de Estado en las Carteras de Guerra, Marina y Policia.* San José, Costa Rica: Imprenta Nacional, 1883.

———. *Memoria presentada por el honorable señor Don Santiago de la Guardia, secretario de estado en los despachos de Guerra y Marina . . . el 6 de julio de 1885.* San José, Costa Rica: Imprenta Nacional, n.d.

———. *Memoria de Guerra y Marina presentada al Congreso Constitucional de 1900. . . .* San José, Costa Rica: Tipografía Nacional, 1900.

———. *Memoria de la Secretaría de Seguridad Pública correspondiente al año de 1929. . . .* San José, Costa Rica: Imprenta Nacional, 1930.

———. *Memoria del Ministerio de Relaciones Exteriores y de Culto. . . . 1951–1952.* San José, Costa Rica: Imprenta Nacional, 1952.

———. *Memoria del Ministerio de Relaciones Exteriores y de Culto. . . . 1952–1953.* San José, Costa Rica: Imprenta Nacional, 1953.

———. *Memoria del Ministerio de Seguridad Pública . . . 1953–1954.* San José, Costa Rica: Imprenta Nacional, 1955.

———. *Memoria del Ministerio de Relaciones Exteriores y de Culto. . . . 1954–1955.* San José, Costa Rica: Imprenta Nacional, 1955.

———. *Memoria del Ministerio de Relaciones Exteriores y de Culto. . . . 1955–1956.* San José, Costa Rica: Imprenta Nacional, 1956.

———. *Memoria del Ministerio de Seguridad Pública . . . 1957–1958.* San José, Costa Rica: Imprenta Nacional, 1959.

Crassweller, Robert D. *Trujillo: The Life and Times of a Caribbean Dictator.* New York: Macmillan, 1966.

Cruz, Arturo J., Jr. *Nicaragua's Conservative Republic, 1858–93.* Basingstoke, UK: Palgrave, 2002.

Cruz, Ramón E. *La Lucha Política de 1954 y la Ruptura del Orden Constitucional.* Tegucigalpa, Honduras: Editorial Universitaria, 1982.

Cuadra Pasos, Carlos. *El Pensamiento Político del Doctor Carlos Cuadra Pasos.* Granada, Nicaragua: Editorial La Prensa, June 1950.

———. *Explicación de Mi Conducta Política.* Managua, Nicaragua: n.p., 1948.

———. *Mensaje a los Conservadores de Nicaragua.* Managua, Nicaragua: Fondo del Grupo Conservador Tradicionalista, 1950.

Cullather, Nick. *Secret History: The CIA's Classified Account of Its Operations in Guatemala, 1952–1954.* Stanford, Calif.: Stanford University Press, 1999.

DaMatta, Roberto A. "For an Anthropology of the Brazilian Tradition; or 'A Virtude está no Meio.'" In *Brazilian Puzzle,* ed. David J. Hess and Robert A. DaMatta. New York: Columbia University Press, 1995.

De Jongh Osborne, Lilly. *Four Keys to El Salvador.* New York: Funk and Wagnalls, 1956.

Dealy, Glenn. *The Latin Americans: Spirit and Ethos.* Boulder, Colo.: Westview Press, 1992.

Demélas-Bohy, Marie-Danielle. "Pactismo y Constitucionalismo." In *De los Imperios a las Naciones: Iberoamérica*, ed. A. Annino et al. Zaragoza, Spain: Ibercaja, 1994.

DiTella, Torcuato S. *Latin American Politics: A Theoretical Framework*. Austin: University of Texas Press, 1990.

Domínguez, Jorge I. *Insurrection or Loyalty: The Breakdown of the Spanish American Empire.* Cambridge, Mass.: Harvard University Press, 1980.

———. *To Make a World Safe for Revolution: Cuba's Foreign Policy*. Cambridge, Mass.: Harvard University Press, 1989.

Dosal, Paul J. *Doing Business with Dictators: A Political History of United Fruit in Guatemala, 1899–1944*. Wilmington, Del.: Scholarly Resources, 1993.

Dunkerley, James. *Power in the Isthmus: A Political History of Modern Central America*. London: Verso, 1988.

Dur, Philip F. "U.S. Diplomacy and the Salvadorean Revolution of 1931." *Journal of Latin American Studies* 30, no. 1 (February 1998): 95–119.

Durán Altamirano, Leonidas Arturo. *Trayectoria: Vida, Proyección y Muerte de Dos Salvadoreños Notables Que el Destino Puso Frente a Frente*. San Salvador, El Salvador: n.p., 1987.

Dym, Jordana. "The State, the City and the Priest: Political Participation and Conflict Resolution in Independence-Era Central America." Unpublished manuscript, 18 November 1999.

Ebel, Roland H. *Misunderstood Caudillo: Miguel Ydígoras Fuentes and the Failure of Democracy in Guatemala*. Lanham, Md.: University Press of America, 1998.

Eckstein, Harry. "A Culturalist Theory of Political Change." *American Political Science Review* 82, no. 3 (September 1988) : 789–803.

Eide, Asjorn, and Mary Kaldor. "Conclusion." In *The World Military Order: The Impact of Military Technology on the Third World*, ed. Mary Kaldor and Asjorn Eide. London: Macmillan, 1979.

Eisenstadt, S. N., and L. Roniger. *Patrons, Clients and Friends: Interpersonal Relations and the Structure of Trust in Society*. Cambridge: Cambridge University Press, 1984.

Eisler, Riane. "Human Rights and Violence: Integrating the Public and Private Spheres." *The Web of Violence: From Interpersonal to Global*, ed. Jennifer Turpin and Lester R. Kurtz. Urbana: University of Illinois Press, 1997.

El Gobierno Liberal de Nicaragua: Documentos 1893–1908, vol. 1. Managua, Nicaragua: Tipografía y Encuadernación Internacional, 1909.

El Salvador. Ministerio de Guerra. *Memoria de la gestión desarollada en los ramos de guerra, marina y aviación . . . 1941*. San Salvador, El Salvador: publisher unknown, n.d.

———. Ministerio de Defensa. *Memoria del Ministerio de Defensa . . . 1947 . . . por el General Mauro Espinola Castro*. San Salvador, El Salvador, Imprenta Nacional, 1949.

———. Ministerio de Defensa. *Memoria de las labores realizadas por el Ministerio de Defensa . . . entre el 14 de septiembre de 1952 y el 13 de septiembre de 1953, . . . por el Señor Ministro de Defensa, Teniente Coronel Oscar A. Bolaños*. San Salvador, El Salvador: publisher unknown, n.d.

———. Ministerio de Economía. Dirección General de Estadística y Censos. *Anuario Estadístico*. San Salvador, El Salvador: Imprenta Nacional, 1955–86.

———. Ejército de El Salvador. Escuela Militar. *Prospecto de Admisión*. La Ceiba, Honduras: Cuscatlán, 1958 [?].

———. Casa Presidencial. *Mensajes y Discursos del Señor presidente de la república Coronel Arturo Armando Molina*, vol. 5, July–December 1974. San Salvador, El Salvador: Publicaciones del Departamento de Relaciones Públicas, Casa Presidencial, 1974.

Elam, Robert Varney. "Appeal to Arms: The Army and Politics in El Salvador, 1931–1964." Ph.D. diss., University of New Mexico, 1968.

Elias, Norbert. *The Germans: Power Struggles and the Development of Habitus in the Nineteenth and Twentieth Centuries*, ed. Michael Schröter, trans. Eric Dunning and Stephen Mennell. New York: Columbia University Press, 1996.

Elman, Colin, and Miriam Fendius Elman. "Introduction: Negotiating International History and Politics." In *Bridges and Boundaries: Historians, Political Scientists, and the Study of International Relations*, ed. Colin Elman and Miriam Fendius Elman. Cambridge, Mass.: MIT Press, 2001.

Encarnación, Omar G. "Tocqueville's Missionaries: Civil Society Advocacy and the Promotion of Democracy." *World Policy Journal* (Spring 2000): 9–18.

Esgueva Gómez, Antonio. *Las Constituciones Políticas y sus Reformas en la Historia de Nicaragua*. Managua, Nicaragua: Editorial El Parlamento, 1994.

Euraque, Darío A. *Reinterpreting the Banana Republic: Region and State in Honduras, 1870–1972*. Chapel Hill: University of North Carolina Press, 1996.

Farley, Philip J., Stephen S. Kaplan, and William H. Lewis. *Arms Across the Sea*. Washington, D.C.: Brookings Institution Press, 1978.

Ferrari, Paul L., Raul L. Madrid, and Jeff Knopf. *U.S. Arms Exports: Policies and Contractors*. Cambridge, Mass.: Ballinger, 1988.

Fitch, J. Samuel Fitch. "Armies and Politics in Latin America: 1975–1985." In *Armies and Politics in Latin America*, rev. ed., ed. Abraham F. Lowenthal and J. Samuel Fitch. New York: Holmes and Meier, 1986.

Flynn, Peter. "Class, Clientelism, and Coercion: Some Mechanisms of Internal Dependency and Control." *Journal of Commonwealth and Comparative Politics* 12, no. 2 (July 1974): 133–56.

Fonseca, Gautama. "Los Precedentes." In *Cuatro Ensayos sobre la Realidad Política de Honduras*, ed. Gautama Fonseca. Tegucigalpa, Honduras: Editorial Universitaria, 1987.

Forch Petit, Juan. *Organización de Defensa Nacional y Organización Militar*. San Salvador, El Salvador: Ministerio de Defensa Nacional, 1955.

Forte, Riccardo, and Guillermo Guajardo, eds. *Consenso y Coacción: Estado e Instrumentos de Control Político y Social en México y América Latina (Siglos XIX y XX)*. Mexico City: El Colegio de México, 2000.

Foweraker, Joe. *Theorizing Social Movements*. London: Pluto Press, 1995.

Fox, Jonathan. "The Difficult Transition from Clientelism to Citizenship." *World Politics* 46, no. 2 (January 1994) : 151–84.

Funes, Matías. *Los Deliberantes: El Poder Militar en Honduras*. Tegucigalpa, Honduras: Editorial Guaymuras, 1995.

Gambone, Michael D. *Eisenhower, Somoza, and the Cold War in Nicaragua 1953–1961*. Westport, Conn.: Praeger, 1997.

Gates, John M. "Indians and Insurrectos: The U.S. Army's Experience with Insurgency." *Parameters: Journal of the U.S. Army War College* 13 (March 1983) 1:59–68.

Giddens, Anthony. *The Consequences of Modernity*. Oxford: Polity Press, 1990.

———. *The Nation-State and Violence*, vol. 2 of *A Contemporary Critique of Historical Materialism*. Berkeley: University of California Press, 1987.

———. *Power, Property and the State*, vol. 1 of *A Contemporary Critique of Historical Materialism*. Berkeley: University of California Press, 1981.

Gleijeses, Piero. *Politics and Culture in Guatemala*. Ann Arbor: Center for Political Studies, Institute for Social Research, University of Michigan, 1988.

———. *Shattered Hope: The Guatemalan Revolution and the United States, 1944–1954*. Princeton, N.J.: Princeton University Press, 1991.

González Arzac, Alberto. *Caudillos y constituciones*. Buenos Aires, Argentina: Colección Estrella Federal, 1994.

González Davison, Fernando. *El Régimen Liberal en Guatemala, 1871–1944.* Guatemala: Editorial Universitaria, Universidad de San Carlos, 1990.

Gould, Jeffrey L. *To Die in This Way: Nicaraguan Indians and the Myth of Mestizaje, 1880–1965.* Durham, N.C.: Duke University Press, 1998.

Graham, Richard. *Patronage and Politics in Nineteenth Century Brazil.* Stanford, Calif.: Stanford University Press, 1990.

Greenberg, James B. *Blood Ties: Life and Violence in Rural Mexico.* Tucson: University of Arizona Press, 1989.

Grew, Raymond. "On the Prospect of Global History." In *Conceptualizing Global History,* ed. Bruce Mazlish and Ralph Buultjens. Boulder, Colo.: Westview Press, 1993.

Grieb, Kenneth. *Guatemalan Caudillo, the Regime of Jorge Ubico: Guatemala, 1931–1944.* Athens: Ohio University Press, 1979.

Grimmett, Richard F. "An Overview of United States Military Assistance Programs." Statement, 9 March 1988. In U.S., House, Foreign Operations Subcommittee of the House Committee on Appropriations, *Background Materials on Foreign Assistance,* Report of the Task Force on Foreign Assistance to the Committee on Foreign Affairs. 101st Cong., 1st Sess., February 1989.

Guardino, Peter. "Identity and Nationalism in Mexico: Guerrero, 1780–1840." *Journal of Historical Sociology* 7, no. 3 (September 1994): 314–42.

Guatemala. Dirección General de Policía Nacional. *Memoria de los trabajos de la dirección general de la policía nacional correspondiente al año de 1932.* Guatemala City: Tipografia Nacional, 1933.

———. Dirección General de Policía Nacional. *Memoria de los trabajos realizados por la dirección general de la policía nacional, durante el año de 1934.* Guatemala City: Tipografia Nacional, 1935.

———. Dirección General de Policía Nacional. *Memoria de los trabajos realizados por la dirección general de la policía nacional, durante el año de 1936.* Guatemala City: Tipografia Nacional, 1937.

———. Ministerio de Guerra. *Memoria de las labores del ejecutivo en el ramo de Guerra durante el año administrativo de 1931, presentada a la asamblea legislativa en sus sesiones ordinarias de 1932.* Guatemala City: Tipografia Nacional, 1932.

———. Ministerio de Guerra. *Memoria de las labores del ejecutivo en el ramo de Guerra durante el año administrativo de 1934, presentada a la asamblea legislativa en sus sesiones ordinarias de 1935.* Guatemala City: Tipografia Nacional, 1935.

———. Ministerio de Guerra. *Memoria de las labores del ejecutivo en el ramo de Guerra durante el año administrativo de 1937, presentada a la asamblea legislativa en sus sesiones ordinarias de 1938.* Guatemala City: Tipografia Nacional, 1938.

———. Ministerio de Guerra. *Memoria de las labores del ejecutivo en el ramo de Guerra durante el año administrativo de 1940, presentada a la asamblea legislativa en sus sesiones ordinarias de 1941.* Guatemala City: Tipografia Nacional, 1941.

———. Ministerio de Guerra. *Memoria de las labores del ejecutivo en el ramo de Guerra durante el año administrativo de 1941, presentada a la asamblea legislativa en sus sesiones ordinarias de 1942.* Guatemala City: Tipografia Nacional, 1942.

———. Ministerio de Guerra. *Memoria de las labores del ejecutivo en el ramo de Guerra durante el año administrativo de 1942, presentada a la asamblea legislativa en sus sesiones ordinarias de 1943.* Guatemala City: Tipografia Nacional, 1943.

———. Ministerio de Guerra. *Memoria de las labores del ejecutivo en el ramo de Guerra durante el año administrativo de 1943, presentada a la asamblea legislativa en sus sesiones ordinarias de 1944.* Guatemala City: Tipografia Nacional, 1944.

————. Ministerio de Guerra. *Memoria de las labores del organismo ejecutivo en el ramo de la defensa nacional durante el año administrativo de 1945, presentada a la asamblea legislativa en sus sesiones ordinarias de 1946.* Guatemala City: 1946.

Gudmundson, Lowell. "Society and Politics in Central America, 1821–1871." In *Central America, 1821–1871: Liberalism Before Liberal Reform*, ed. Lowell Gudmundson and Hector Lindo-Fuentes. Tuscaloosa: University of Alabama Press, 1995.

Guerra, François-Xavier. *México: Del Antiguo Régimen a la Revolución*, vol. 1. Mexico City: Fondo de Cultura Económica, 1985.

————. "The Spanish-American Tradition of Representation and Its European Roots." *Journal of Latin American Studies* 26, no. 1 (February 1994) : 1–36.

Guerra, François-Xavier, and M.-D. Demélas-Bohy. "The Hispanic Revolutions: The Adoption of Modern Forms of Representation in Spain and America, 1808–1820." In *Elections before Democracy: The History of Elections in Europe and Latin America*, ed. Eduardo Posada-Carbó. Houndmills, UK: Macmillan, 1996.

Guerrant, Edward O. *Roosevelt's Good Neighbor Policy.* Albuquerque: University of New Mexico Press, 1950.

Guidos, Rafael. *El ascenso del militarismo en El Salvador.* San Salvador, El Salvador, 1988.

Gurr, Ted Robert. "War, Revolution, and the Growth of the Coercive State." *Comparative Political Studies* 21, no. 1 (April 1988): 45–65.

Hale, Charles R. *Resistance and Contradiction: Miskitu Indians and the Nicaraguan State, 1894–1987.* Stanford, Calif.: Stanford University Press, 1994.

Hanrieder, Wolfram F., and Larry V. Buel. *Words and Arms: A Dictionary of Security and Defense Terms.* Boulder, Colo.: Westview Press, 1979.

Hernández Chávez, Alicia. *La tradición republicana del buen gobierno.* Mexico City: El Colegio de Mexico, 1993.

Hersh, Seymour. *Cover-Up.* New York: Random House, 1972.

Hess, David J., and Roberto A. DaMatta. "Introduction." In *The Brazilian Puzzle: Culture on the Borderlands of the Western World*, ed. David J. Hess and Robert A. DaMatta. New York: Columbia University Press, 1995.

Hexter, J. H. *On Historians.* Cambridge, Mass.: Harvard University Press, 1979.

Higham, John. *History.* Englewood Cliffs, N.J.: Prentice-Hall, 1965.

Hinkelammert, Franz. "El concepto de lo político según Carl Schmitt." In *Cultural política y democratización*, ed. Norbert Lechner. Santiago, Chile: CLACSO, 1987.

Hobsbawm, Eric. *The Age of Extremes: A History of the World, 1914–1991.* New York: Pantheon Books, 1994.

Hofstadter, Richard. "Reflections on Violence in the United States." In *American Violence: A Documentary History*, ed. Richard Hofstadter and Michael Wallace. New York: Alfred A. Knopf, 1970.

Holden, Robert H. "Constructing the Limits of State Violence in Central America: Towards a New Research Agenda." *Journal of Latin American Studies* 28, no. 2 (May 1996): 438–46.

————. "Securing Central America Against Communism: The United States and the Modernization of Surveillance in the Cold War." *Journal of Interamerican Studies and World Affairs* 41 (1) (Spring 1999), 1–30.

Honduras. *Mensaje del presidente de Honduras, contestación del congreso.* Tegucigalpa, Honduras: Tipografia Nacional, 1879.

————. Ministerio de Instrucción Pública. *Memoria de Instrucción Pública 1879.* In *Oro de Honduras: Antología de Ramón Rosa*, vol. 2. Tegucigalpa, Honduras: Editorial Universitaria, [1948] 1993.

————. *Informe del Secretario de Estado en el despacho de la Guerra presentado al Congreso Nacional del año de 1889.* Tegucigalpa, Honduras: Tipografia del Gobierno, 1889.

————. *Mensaje del Presidente de la República de Honduras y Anexos presentados a la Asamblea Nacional Constituyente de 1894.* Tegucigalpa, Honduras: Tipografia Nacional, 1896.

————. *Mensaje del señor Presidente del Estado de Honduras, Doctor Don Policarpo Bonilla, sobre los actos de su administración, en el año económico de 1895 a 1896, presentado al Congreso Nacional Legislativo.* [Title page missing].

————. *Memoria que el Secretario de Estado en el Despacho de la Guerra presentada al Congreso Nacional en sus sesiones ordinarias de 1897.* In Honduras. *Mensaje del señor Presidente del Estado de Honduras, Doctor Don Policarpo Bonilla, sobre los actos de su administración, en el año económico de 1895 a 1896, presentado al Congreso Nacional Legislativo.* [Title page missing.]

————. *Memoria presentada al Soberano Congreso Nacional por el Secretario . . . de la Guerra, 1898–1899."* In Honduras. *Mensaje del Presidente de la República, Contestación del Congreso y Memorias de los Secretarios de Estado, referentes a los actos del poder ejecutivo durante el año económico de 1898 a 1899.* Tegucigalpa, Honduras: Tipografía Nacional, 1900.

————. *Mensaje del Presidente de la República, Contestación del Congreso y Memorias de los Secretarios de Estado, referentes a los actos del poder ejecutivo durante el año economico de 1898 a 1899.* Tegucigalpa, Honduras: Tipografía Nacional, 1900.

————. *Memoria presentada por el secretario de estado en los despachos de Gobernación, Justicia y Obras Públicas Dr. Don Marcos Carías A. al Congreso Nacional 1909–1910.* Tegucigalpa, Honduras: Tipografia Nacional, 1910.

————. *Mensaje dirigido al Soberano Congreso Nacional en sus sesiones ordinarias de 1911 por el Dr. Don Miguel R. Davila, Presidente de la República de Honduras.* Tegucigalpa, Honduras: Tipografia Nacional, 1911.

————. *Memoria del secretario de estado en el despacho de Guerra y Marina Dr. Y Gral. Dionisio Gutiérrez dirigida al Congreso Nacional 1922–1923.* Tegucigalpa, Honduras: Tipografia Nacional, 1924.

————. *Memoria del secretario de estado en el despacho de Guerra y Marina Gen. Don Andres Leiva presentada al Congreso Nacional 1923–1924.* Tegucigalpa, Honduras: Tipografia Nacional, 1925.

————. *Memoria Guerra, Marina y Aviación presentada al Congreso Nacional por el secretario del ramo Dr. Juan Manuel Gálvez 1933–1934.* Tegucigalpa, Honduras: Talleres Tipografia Nacionales, 1937.

————. *Memoria Guerra, Marina y Aviación presentada al Congreso Nacional por el secretario del ramo Dr. Juan Manuel Gálvez 1934–1935.* Tegucigalpa, Honduras: Talleres Tipografia Nacionales, 1935.

————. *Memoria Guerra, Marina y Aviación presentada al Congreso Nacional por el secretario del ramo Dr. Juan Manuel Gálvez 1935–1936.* Tegucigalpa, Honduras: Talleres Tipografia Nacionales, 1936.

————. *Memoria presentada al soberano Congreso Nacional por el señor secretario de estado en los despachos de Guerra, Marina y Aviación Dr. Juan Manuel Gálvez 1945–1946.* N.p., n.d.

————. *Memoria presentada al soberano Congreso Nacional por el señor secretario de estado en los despachos de Guerra, Marina y Aviación 1946–1947.* N.p., n.d.

————. *Informe del sub-secretario encargado del los despachos de Guerra, Marina y Aviación Gral. Leonidas Pineda M. presentado al Congreso Nacional año económico de 1948 a 1949.* Tegucigalpa, Honduras: Imprenta Coello, n.d.

————. *Informe del sub-secretario encargado del los despachos de Guerra, Marina y Aviación Gral. Leonidas Pineda M. presentado al Congreso Nacional año económico de 1951 a 1952.* Tegucigalpa, Honduras: Imprenta Honduras, n.d.

Huber, Evelyne. "Assessments of State Strength." In *Latin America in Comparative Perspective: New Approaches to Methods and Analysis*, ed. Peter H. Smith. Boulder, Colo.: Westview Press, 1995.

Huggins, Martha K. *Political Policing: The United States and Latin America*. Durham, N.C.: Duke University Press, 1998.

Hughes, H. Stuart. *Consciousness and Society: The Reorientation of European Social Thought, 1890–1930*. New York: Vintage Books, 1961.

Ikegami, Eiko. *The Taming of the Samurai: Honorific Individualism and the Making of Modern Japan*. Cambridge, Mass.: Harvard University Press, 1995.

Inestroza M., Jesús Evelio. *Genesis y evolución de las Escuelas Militares del Ejército 1831–1937*, vol. 1. Tegucigalpa, Honduras: Litografía López, 1990.

Juárez, Orient Bolívar. *Causas de la Creación, Supresión y Restablecimineto del Departamento de Estelí a Fines del Siglo XIX*. Managua, Nicaragua: Centro de Investigaciones Históricas de Nicaragua "Adolfo Altamirano C.," 1995.

Kaldor, Mary. *New and Old Wars: Organized Violence in a Global Era*. Stanford, Calif.: Stanford University Press, 1999.

Kalmanowiecki, Laura. "Police, People, and Preemption in Argentina." In *Vigilantism and the State in Modern Latin America*, ed. Martha K. Huggins. New York: Praeger, 1991.

Kant de Lima, Roberto. "Bureaucratic Rationality in Brazil and in the United States: Criminal Justice Systems in Comparative Perspective." In *Brazilian Puzzle: Culture on the Borderlands of the Western World*, ed. David J. Hess and Roberta A. DaMatta. New York: Columbia University Press, 1995.

Karnes, Thomas L. *The Failure of Union: Central America, 1824–1975*. Tempe: Center for Latin American Studies, Arizona State University, 1976.

———. *The Failure of Union: Central America, 1824–1960*. Chapel Hill: University of North Carolina Press, 1961.

Kelly, John D. "Diaspora and World War, Blood and Nation in Fiji and Hawaii." *Public Culture* 7, no. 3 (1995) : 475–97.

Kinloch Tijerino, Frances, ed. *Nicaragua en Busca de Su Indentidad*. Managua, Nicaragua: Instituto de Historia de Nicaragua, Universidad Centroamericana, 1995.

Kit, Wade. "The Fall of Guatemalan Dictator, Manuel Estrada Cabrera: U.S. Pressure or National Opposition?" *Canadian Journal of Latin American and Caribbean Studies* 15, no. 29 (1990) : 105–28.

Knight, Alan. *The Mexican Revolution: The Sources of Social Power*. Cambridge: Cambridge University Press, 1986.

Krause, Keith. *Arms and the State: Patterns of Military Production and Trade*. Cambridge: Cambridge University Press, 1992.

Ladd, John. "The Idea of Collective Violence." In *Justice, Law, and Violence*, ed. James B. Brady and Newton Garver. Philadelphia: Temple University Press, 1991.

LaFeber, Walter. *Inevitable Revolutions: The United States in Central America*. New York: Norton, 1993.

Lane, Ruth. "Political Culture: Residual Category or General Theory?" *Comparative Political Studies* 25, no. 3 (October 1992): 362–87.

Langley, Lester D., and Thomas Schoonover. *The Banana Men: American Mercenaries and Entrepreneurs in Central America, 1880–1930*. Lexington: University Press of Kentucky, 1995.

Lauria-Santiago, Aldo. *An Agrarian Republic: Commercial Agriculture and the Politics of Peasant Communities in El Salvador, 1823–1914*. Pittsburgh, Pa.: University of Pittsburgh Press, 1999.

Lebow, Richard Ned. "Social Science, History, and the Cold War: Pushing the Conceptual Envelope." In *Reviewing the Cold War: Approaches, Interpretations, Theory*, ed. Odd Arne Westad. London: Frank Cass, 2000.

Lechner, Norbert. "La democratización." In *Cultura política y democratización*, ed. Norbert Lechner. Santiago, Chile: CLACSO, 1987.

———. "Presentación." In *Cultura política y democratización*, ed. Norbert Lechner. Santiago, Chile: CLACSO, 1987.

Lehoucq, Fabrice Edouard. "The Institutional Foundations of Democratic Cooperation in Costa Rica." *Journal of Latin American Studies* 28, no. 2 (May 1996): 335, 338.

Leonard, Thomas M. *Central America and the United States: The Search for Stability*. Athens: University of Georgia Press, 1991.

———. *U.S. Policy and Arms Limitation in Central America: The Washington Conference of 1923*. Occasional Papers Series, No. 10. Los Angeles: Center for the Study of Armament and Disarmament, California State University, 1982.

Levy, Pablo. *Notas geográficas y económicas sobre la república de Nicaragua*. Paris: Librería Española de E. Denné Schmitz, 1873.

Lindo-Fuentes, Hector. *Weak Foundations: The Economy of El Salvador in the Nineteenth Century*. Berkeley: University of California Press, 1990.

Linz, Juan J. "Totalitarian and Authoritarian Regimes." In *Handbook of Political Science: Macropolitical Theory*, ed. F. I. Greenstein and N. W. Polsby. Reading, Mass.: Addison-Wesley, 1975.

Longley, Kyle. *The Sparrow and the Hawk: Costa Rica and the United States During the Rise of José Figueres*. Tuscaloosa: University of Alabama Press, 1997.

López-Alves, Fernando. *State Formation and Democracy in Latin America, 1810–1900*. Durham, N.C.: Duke University Press, 2000.

Loveman, Brian. *Chile: The Legacy of Hispanic Capitalism*, 3d ed. New York: Oxford University Press, 2001.

———. *The Constitution of Tyranny: Regimes of Exception in Spanish America*. Pittsburgh, Pa.: University of Pittsburgh Press, 1993.

Lowenthal, Abraham F. "Armies and Politics in Latin America: Introduction to the First Edition." In *Armies and Politics in Latin America*, rev. ed., ed. Abraham F. Lowenthal and J. Samuel Fitch. New York: Holmes and Meier, 1986.

Luckham, Robin. "Of Arms and Culture." *Current Research on Peace and Violence* 7, no. 1 (1984): 1–64.

Lynch, John. *Caudillos in Spanish America, 1800–1850*. New York: Oxford University Press, 1992.

Macaulay, Neill. *The Sandino Affair*. Durham, N.C.: Duke University Press, 1985.

Maechling, Charles, Jr. "Camelot, Robert Kennedy, and Counter-Insurgency—A Memoir." *Virginia Quarterly Review* 75, no. 3 (Summer 1999): 438–58.

Mallon, Florencia E. *Peasant and Nation: The Making of Postcolonial Mexico and Peru*. Berkeley: University of California Press, 1995.

Malloy, James M. "Authoritarianism and Corporatism in Latin America: The Modal Pattern." In *Authoritarianism and Corporatism in Latin America*, ed. James M. Malloy. Pittsburgh, Pa.: University of Pittsburgh Press, 1977.

Mann, Michael. "The Roots and Contradictions of Modern Militarism." *New Left Review* 162 (March/April 1987): 35–50.

———. *The Sources of Social Power*. Vol. 1. *A History of Power from the Beginning to a.d. 1760*. Cambridge: Cambridge University Press, 1986.

———. *The Sources of Social Power*. Vol. 2. *The Rise of Classes and Nation-States, 1760–1914*. Cambridge: Cambridge University Press, 1993.

Mariscal, Nicolás. "Militares y reformismo en El Salvador." *Estudios Centroamericanos* 351/352 (January–February 1978): 12.

Martel, Leon. *Lend-Lease, Loans, and the Coming of the Cold War: A Study of the Implementation of Foreign Policy.* Boulder, Colo.: Westview Press, 1979.

Mason, T. David, and Dale A. Krane. "The Political Economy of Death Squads: Toward a Theory of the Impact of State-Sanctioned Terror." *International Studies Quarterly* 33 (1989): 177–78.

Matthews, Herbert. *A World in Revolution: A Newspaperman's Memoir.* New York: Charles Scribner's Sons, 1971.

Mayer, Enrique. "Patterns of Violence in the Andes." *Latin American Research Review* 29, no. 2 (1994): 141–71.

Mazlish, Bruce. "An Introduction to Global History." In *Conceptualizing Global History*, ed. Bruce Mazlish and Ralph Buultjens. Boulder, Colo.: Westview Press, 1993.

McAlister, L. N. "Recent Research and Writings on the Role of the Military in Latin America." *Latin American Research Review* 2, no. 1 (Fall 1966): 5–36.

McCreery, David. *Rural Guatemala, 1760–1940.* Stanford, Calif.: Stanford University Press, 1994.

Mecham, J. Lloyd. *A Survey of United States–Latin American Relations.* Boston: Houghton Mifflin, 1965.

Medard, Jean-Francois. "The Underdeveloped State in Tropical Africa: Political Clientelism or Neo-Patrimonialism?" In *Private Patronage and Public Power: Political Clientelism in the Modern State*, ed. Christopher Clapham. New York: St. Martin's Press, 1982.

Medina Gallego, Carlos, and Mireya Téllez Ardila. *La violencia parainstitucional paramilitar y parapolicial en Colombia.* Bogotá, Colombia: Rodríguez Quito Editores, 1994.

Meléndez Chaverri, Carlos, ed. *Mensajes Presidenciales, 1940–1958.* San José, Costa Rica: Imprenta Nacional, 1990.

Mendieta, Salvador. *La Enfermedad de Centro-América*, vol. 1. Barcelona: Tipografia Maucci, 1934.

Mexico. Office of the President. "Clausura de la XVII Reunión Anual de la CONCAMIN." Available: http://www.presidencia.gob.mx/pages/f_ind_disc.htm. Last accessed 23 March 1999.

Migdal, Joel S. "The State in Society: An Approach to Struggles for Domination." In *State Power and Social Forces: Domination and Transformation in the Third World*, ed. Joel S. Migdal, Atul Kohli, and Vivienne Shue. Cambridge: Cambridge University Press, 1994.

Mignone, Raul et al. *Inter-American Statistical Yearbook 1942.* New York: Macmillan, 1942.

Millett, Richard. *Guardians of the Dynasty: A History of the U.S. Created Guardia Nacional de Nicaragua and the Somoza Family.* Maryknoll, N.Y.: Orbis Books, 1977.

Molina, Ivan, and Fabrice Lehoucq. *Urnas de lo Inesperado: Fraude Electoral y Lucha Política en Costa Rica, 1901–1948.* San José: Editorial de la Universidad de Costa Rica, 1999.

Monteforte Toledo, Mario. *Centro América: Subdesarrollo y dependencia.* Mexico City: Universidad Nacional Autónoma de México, 1972.

Montúfar, Lorenzo. *Reseña histórica de Centroamérica.* Guatemala City: Tipografia de El Progreso, 1878.

Morgan, Mark L., and Mark A. Berhow. *Rings of Supersonic Steel: Air Defenses of the United States Army, 1950–1979, an Introductory History and Site Guide.* San Pedro, Calif.: Fort MacArthur Museum Association, 1996.

Morris, James A. *Honduras: Caudillo Politics and Military Rulers.* Boulder, Colo.: Westview Press, 1984.

Morse, Richard. "The Heritage of Latin America." In *The Founding of New Societies: Studies in the History of the United States, Latin America, South Africa, Canada, and Australia*, ed. Louis Hartz. New York: Harcourt, Brace and World, 1964.

Morse, Richard. *New World Soundings: Culture and Ideology in the Americas.* Baltimore: Johns Hopkins University Press, 1989.

Muñoz Guillen, Mercedes. *El estado y la abolición del ejército, 1914–1949.* San José, Costa Rica: Editorial Porvenir, 1990.

Munro, Dana. *The United States and the Caribbean Area.* Boston: World Peace Foundation, 1934.

———. *Intervention and Dollar Diplomacy in the Caribbean.* Princeton, N.J.: Princeton University Press, 1964.

———. *The Five Republics of Central America: Their Political and Economic Development and Their Relations with the United States.* New York: Oxford University Press, 1918.

Mussington, David. *Arms Unbound: The Globalization of Defense Production.* Washington, D.C.: Brassey's, 1994.

Natalini de Castro, Stefania, María de los Angeles Mendoza Saborio, and Joaquín Pagán Solórzano. *Significado Histórico del Gobierno del Dr. Ramón Villeda Morales.* Tegucigalpa, Honduras: Editorial Universitaria, 1985.

Nicaragua. *Memoria de los actos del poder ejecutivo en los departamentos de la Guerra y Marina durante el período del 1 de julio de 1904 al 30 de septiembre de 1905, presentada a la Asamblea Nacional Legislativa, por el Secretario del Ramo, Ing. Don Camilo Castellón.* Managua, Nicaragua: Imprenta Nacional, 1906.

———. *Memoria de la Secretaria de Guerra Marina y Aviación* [Gen. J. Rigoberto Reyes]. Managua, Nicaragua: Talleres Nacionales, 1937.

———. *Memoria de la Secretaria de Guerra, Marina y Aviación* [Gen. J. Rigoberto Reyes]. Managua, Nicaragua: Talleres Nacionales, 1939.

Nowels, Larry Q. "An Overview of the Economic Support Fund." Congressional Research Service. In U.S., Congress, House, *Background Materials on Foreign Assistance; Report of the Task Force on Foreign Assistance to the Committee on Foreign Affairs, February 1989.* 101st Cong., 1st Sess. (Y4.F76/1:F76/71). Washington, D.C.: Government Printing Office, 1989.

Nugent, David. *Modernity at the Edge of Empire: State, Individual, and Nation in the Northern Peruvian Andes, 1850–1935.* Stanford, Calif.: Stanford University Press, 1997.

O'Donnell, Guillermo. "Delegative Democracy." *Journal of Democracy* 5 (January 1994) 1:55–69.

———. "Democracia en la Argentina micro y macro." In *Proceso, Crisis y Transición Democrática,* vol. 1, ed. Oscar Oszlak. Buenos Aires, Argentina: Centro Editor de América Latina, 1984.

Obregón Loria, Rafael. *Hechos Militares y Políticos de Nuestra Historia Patria.* Alajuela, Costa Rica: Museo Histórico Cultural Juan Santamaría, 1981.

Olson, William J., ed. *Small Wars.* In *Annals of the American Academy of Political and Social Science* 541 (September 1995).

Operation Zapata: The "Ultrasensitive" Report and Testimony of the Board of Inquiry on the Bay of Pigs. Frederick, Md.: University Publications of America, 1981.

Paige, Jeffrey M. *Coffee and Power: Revolution and the Rise of Democracy in Central America.* Cambridge, Mass.: Harvard University Press, 1997.

Pan American Union. *Inter-American Treaty of Reciprocal Assistance Applications,* vol. 1, 1948–1959. Washington, D.C.: Pan American Union, 1964.

Parkman, Patricia. *Nonviolent Insurrection in El Salvador: The Fall of Maximiliano Hernández-Martínez.* Tucson: University of Arizona Press, 1988.

Pastor, Rodolfo. *Historia de Centroamérica.* Guatemala City: Editorial Piedra Santa, 1990.

Paz, Octavio. *The Labyrinth of Solitude: Life and Thought in Mexico,* trans. Lysander Kemp. New York: Grove Press, 1961.

Peloso, Vincent C. "Liberals, Electoral Reform, and the Popular Vote in Mid-Nineteenth-Century Peru." In *Liberals, Politics and Power: State Formation in Nineteenth-Century Latin America*, ed. Vincent C. Peloso and Barbara A. Tenenbaum. Athens: University of Georgia, 1996.

Pérez Brignoli, Hector. *Breve Historia de Centroamérica*. Mexico City: Alianza Editorial, 1985.

Persons, Albert C. *Bay of Pigs: A Firsthand Account*. Jefferson, N.C.: McFarland, 1990.

Peru. Senado. Comisión Especial del Senado sobre las Causas de la Violencia y Alternativas de Pacificación en el Perú. *Violencia y pacificación*. Lima, Peru: División de Impresiones y Publicaciones del Diario de los Debates del Senado, 1988.

Pierre, Andrew J. *The Global Politics of Arms Sales*. Princeton, N.J.: Princeton University Press, 1982.

Pinto S., Julio César. "Los problemas de la transición." In *Problemas en la formación del estado nacional en centroamérica*, ed. Edelberto Torres-Rivas and Julio César Pinto S. San José, Costa Rica: Instituto Centroamericano de Administración Pública, 1983.

Posada-Carbó, Eduardo. "Elections and Civil Wars in Nineteenth-Century Colombia: The 1875 Presidential Campaign." *Journal of Latin American Studies* 26, no. 3 (October 1994): 621–49.

Posas, Mario, and Rafael Del Cid. *La Construcción del Sector Público y del Estado Nacional de Honduras, 1876–1979*. San José, Costa Rica: Editorial Universitaria Centroamericana, 1981.

Poulantzas, Nicos. *State, Power, Socialism*. Trans. Patrick Camiller. London: Verso, 1978.

Powell, John Duncan. "Peasant Society and Clientelist Politics." *American Political Science Review* 64, no. 2 (June 1970): 411–25.

Rabe, Stephen G. *The Most Dangerous Area in the World: John F. Kennedy Confronts Communist Revolution in Latin America*. Chapel Hill: University of North Carolina Press, 1999.

Ralston, David B. *Importing the European Army: The Introduction of European Military Techniques and Institutions into the Extra-European World, 1600–1914*. Chicago: University of Chicago Press, 1990.

Recopilación de las constituciones de Honduras, 1825–1965. Tegucigalpa, Honduras: Universidad Nacional Autónoma de Honduras, 1977.

Remmer, Karen L. "New Wine or Old Bottlenecks? The Study of Latin American Democracy." *Comparative Politics* 23, no. 4 (July 1991): 479–95.

Rock, Paul. "Law, Order and Power in Late Seventeenth- and Early Eighteenth-Century England." In *Social Control and the State: Historical and Comparative Essays*, ed. Stanley Cohen and Andrew Scull. Oxford: Martin Robertson, 1983.

Rodó, José Enrique. *Ariel*. Trans. Margaret Sayers Peden. Austin: University of Texas Press, [1900] 1988.

Rojas Bolaños, Manuel. "La Política." In *Historia general de centroamérica*, ed. Edelberto Torres-Rivas, vol. 5, *De la posguerra a la crisis 1945–1979*, ed. Héctor Pérez Brignoli. Madrid, Spain: Sociedad Estatal Quinto Cententario y FLACSO, 1993.

Rouquie, Alain. *The Military and the State in Latin America*, trans. Paul E. Sigmund. Berkeley: University of California Press, 1987.

Sagastume F., Alejandro Salomon. *Carías: El Caudillo de Zambrano, 1933–1948*. Tegucigalpa, Honduras: Graficentro Editores, 1988.

Salisbury, Richard V. *Anti-Imperialism and International Competition in Central America, 1920–1929*. Wilmington, Del.: Scholarly Resources, 1989.

Salomón, Leticia. *Militarismo y Reformismo en Honduras*. Tegucigalpa, Honduras: Editorial Guaymuras, 1982.

Sánchez G., Gonzalo Meertens, and Donny Meertens. *Bandoleros, Gamonales y Campesinos: El caso de la violencia en Colombia*. Bogotá, Colombia: El Ancora Editores, 1983.

Sanso, Aro. [Ismael Mejía Deras]. *Policarpo Bonilla: Algunos Apuntes Biográficos.* Mexico City: Imprenta Mundial, 1936.

Sarmiento, Domingo F. *Facundo: Civilización y Barbarie.* Madrid, Spain: Ediciones Cátedra, [1845] 1990.

Sater, William F., and Holger H. Herwig. *The Grand Illusion: The Prussianization of the Chilean Army.* Lincoln: University of Nebraska Press, 1999.

Schlesinger, Stephen, and Stephen Kinzer. *Bitter Fruit: The Story of the American Coup in Guatemala,* expanded ed. Cambridge, Mass.: Harvard University Press, 1999.

Schmidt, Morten. "Habitus Revisited." *American Behavioral Scientist* 40 (February 1997): 444–54.

Scholte, Jan Aart. *International Relations of Social Change* Buckingham, UK: Open University Press, 1993.

Schoonover, Thomas D. *The United States in Central America, 1860–1911: Episodes of Social Imperialism and Imperial Rivalry in the World System.* Durham, N.C.: Duke University Press, 1991.

Schroeder, Michael J. "Horse Thieves to Rebels to Dogs: Political Gang Violence and the State in the Western Segovias, Nicaragua, in the Time of Sandino, 1926–1934." *Journal of Latin American Studies* 28, no. 2 (May 1996): 383–434.

Schultz, Jr., Richard H. et al., eds. *Guerrilla Warfare and Counterinsurgency: U.S.-Soviet Policy in the Third World.* Lexington, Mass.: Lexington Books, 1989.

Schwartzmann, Simon. "Back to Weber: Corporatism and Patrimonialism in the Seventies." In *Authoritarianism and Corporatism,* ed. James M. Malloy. Pittsburgh, Pa.: University of Pittsburgh Press, 1977.

Serrano Caldera, Alejandro. "En Busca de la Nación." In *Historia y violencia en Nicaragua,* 3–26. Managua, Nicaragua: Instituto de Investigaciones y Acción Social "Martin Luther King" de la Universidad Politécnica de Nicaragua y UNESCO, 1997.

Shoemaker, Christopher C., and John Spanier. *Patron-Client State Relationships: Multilateral Crises in the Nuclear Age.* New York: Praeger, 1984.

Smaldone, Joseph P. "U.S. Commercial Arms Exports: Policy, Process, and Patterns." In *Marketing Security Assistance: New Perspectives on Arms Sales,* ed. David J. Louscher and Michael D. Salomone. Lexington, Mass.: Lexington Books, 1987.

Smith Jr., Laun C. "Central American Defense Council: Some Problems and Achievements." *Air University Review* 20 (March–April 1969): 67–75.

Smith, Carol. "Conclusion: History and Revolution in Guatemala." In *Guatemalan Indians and the State: 1540 to 1988,* ed. Carol A. Smith. Austin: University of Texas Press, 1990.

Solís, Edwin, and Carlos González. *El ejército en Costa Rica: Poder Político, Poder Militar, 1821–1890.* San José, Costa Rica: Ediciones Guayacán, 1992.

Stanley, John, and Maurice Pearton. *The International Trade in Arms.* London: Chatto and Windus, 1972.

Stedman, Murray. *Exporting Arms: The Federal Arms Exports Administration, 1935–1945.* New York: Kings Crown Press, 1947.

Steel, Ronald. *Pax Americana.* New York: Viking, 1967.

Stepan, Alfred. *Rethinking Military Politics: Brazil and the Southern Cone.* Princeton, N.J.: Princeton University Press, 1988.

Stokes, William S. *Honduras: An Area Study in Government.* Madison: University of Wisconsin Press, 1950.

Stoll, David. *Between Two Armies: In the Ixil Towns of Guatemala.* New York: Columbia University Press, 1993.

Swidler, Ann. "Culture in Action: Symbols and Strategies." *American Sociological Review* 51, no. 2 (April 1986): 273–86.

Taracena Arriola, Arturo. "Liberalismo y poder político en Centroamérica, 1870–1929." In *Historia General de Centroamérica*, vol. 4, *Las repúblicas agroexportadoras, 1870–1945*, ed. Victor Hugo Acuña Ortega. Madrid, Spain: Sociedad Estatal Quinto Cententario y FLACSO, 1993.

Tilly, Charles. *Big Structures, Large Processes, Huge Comparisons.* New York: Russell Sage Foundation Press, 1984.

———. *Coercion, Capital and European States, AD 990–1990.* Cambridge, Mass.: Basil Blackwell, 1990.

———. "State-Incited Violence, 1900–1999." Working Paper No. 177. New York: Center for Studies of Social Change, New School for Social Research, December 1993.

Tocqueville, Alexis de. *Democracy in America.* New York: Vintage Books, [1835] 1990.

Torres-Rivas, Edelberto. "Central America Since 1930: An Overview." In *Latin American Since 1930: Mexico, Central America and the Caribbean*, vol. 7 of *The Cambridge History of Latin America.* Cambridge: Cambridge University Press, 1990.

———. "Evolución Histórico del Sector Público en Centroamérica y Panamá." In *Problemas en la formación del estado nacional en centroamérica*, ed. Edelberto Torres-Rivas and Julio César Pinto S. San José, Costa Rica: Instituto Centroamericano de Administración Pública, 1983.

———. *El tamaño de nuestra democracia.* San Salvador, El Salvador: Istmo Editores, 1992.

Turcios, Froylán. "Los Estados Unidos No Tienen Ningún Derecho Para Mezclarse en Nuestros Asuntos Internos." *Boletín de la Defensa Nacional* 1 (21 March 1924), reprinted in *Boletín de la Defensa Nacional.* Tegucigalpa, Honduras: Editorial Guaymuras, 1980.

Turcuyo, Roberto. *Autoritarismo y modernización: El Salvador 1950–1960.* San Salvador, El Salvador: Ediciones Tendencias, 1993.

United States. Congress. Appendix I-b. In "Thirty-Ninth Report to Congress on Lend-Lease Operations: Message from the President of the United States . . . for the year ending December 31, 1957." 85th Cong., 2d Sess., House Document No. 449.

———. Congress. House. *International Security Assistance Act of 1976; Report of the Committee on International Relations.* 94th Cong., 2d Sess., House Report No. 94–848, 24 Feb. 1976.

———. "Report of the Special Study Mission to Central America on International Organizations and Movements." 84th Cong., 1st Sess., House Report No. 1155. Washington, D.C.: Government Printing Office, 1955.

———. Congress. Senate. Committee on Banking, Housing and Urban Affairs. *Financing of Foreign Military Sales: Hearing.* 95th Cong., 2d Sess., 30 January 1978.

———. Congress. Senate. Committee on the Judiciary. "Communist Threat to the United States Through the Caribbean." *Hearings*, pt. 13, 27 July 1961.

———. Department of State. *Foreign Relations of the United States.* Washington, D.C.: Government Printing Office, 1912–58.

———. Department of State. *United States Treaties and Other International Agreements.* Washington, D.C.: Government Printing Office, 1952.

———. Intelligence Oversight Board. "Report on the Guatemala Review." 28 June 1996.

———. *United States Statutes at Large.* Washington, D.C.: Government Printing Office.

———. President. "Remarks in a Roundtable Discussion on Peace Efforts in Guatemala City March 10, 1999." *Weekly Compilation of Presidential Documents* 35, no. 10 (15 March 1999): 395–98.

Urcuyo, Constantino. "Civil-Military Relations in Costa Rica: Militarization or Adaptation to New Circumstances?" In *The Military and Democracy: The Future of Civil-Military Relations in Latin America*, ed. Louis W. Goodman, Johanna S. R. Mendelson, and Juan Rial. Lexington, Mass.: Lexington Books, 1990.

Uricoechea, Fernando. *The Patrimonial Foundations of the Brazilian Bureaucratic State.* Berkeley: University of California Press, 1980.

Varas, Augusto. "Las relaciones civil-militares en la democracia." In *América Latina: militares y sociedad,* vol. 1, ed. Dirk Kruijt and Edelberto Torres-Rivas. San José, Costa Rica: FLACSO, 1991.

Vega Carballo, José Luis. *Orden y progreso: La formación del estado nacional en Costa Rica.* San José, Costa Rica: Instituto Centroamericano de Administración Pública, 1981.

———. *Poder político y Democracia en Costa Rica.* San José, Costa Rica: Editorial Porvenir, 1982.

Véliz, Claudio. *The New World of the Gothic Fox: Culture and Economy in English and Spanish America.* Berkeley: University of California Press, 1994.

Vilas, Carlos M. "Family Affairs: Class, Lineage and Politics in Contemporary Nicaragua." *Journal of Latin American Studies* 24, no. 2 (May 1992): 309–41.

Villagrán Kramer, Francisco. *Biografía política de Guatemala: Los Pactos Políticos de 1944 a 1970.* Guatemala City: FLACSO, 1993.

Wacquant, J. D. "Toward a Social Praxeology: The Structure and Logic of Bourdieu's Sociology." In *An Invitation to Reflexive Sociology,* ed. Pierre Bourdieu and J. D. Wacquant. Chicago: University of Chicago Press, 1992.

Walter, Eugene Victor. *Terror and Resistance: A Study of Political Violence.* New York: Oxford University Press, 1969.

Walter, Knut. *The Regime of Anastasio Somoza, 1936–1956.* Chapel Hill: University of North Carolina Press, 1993.

Weathers, Bynum E. "Factors Affecting the Emergence of Low-Intensity Conflict in Latin America." In *Low-Intensity Conflict in the Third World,* ed. Stephen Blank et al. Maxwell Air Force Base, Ala.: Air University Press, 1988.

Weber, Max. *Economy and Society: An Outline of Interpretive Sociology,* vol. 1, ed. Guenther Roth and Claus Wittich. Berkeley: University of California Press, 1978.

White, Richard Alan. *The Morass: United States Intervention in Central America.* New York: Harper and Row, 1984.

Whitehead, Laurence. "Explaining Washington's Central American Policies." *Journal of Latin American Studies* 15 (1983): 321–63.

Wiarda, Howard. "Toward a Model of Social Change and Political Development in Latin America: Summary, Implications, Frontiers." In *Politics and Social Change in Latin America: The Distinct Tradition,* ed. Howard Wiarda. Amherst: University of Massachusetts Press, 1982.

Williams, Philip J., and Knut Walter. *Militarization and Demilitarization in El Salvador's Transition to Democracy.* Pittsburgh, Pa.: University of Pittsburgh Press, 1997.

Wolf, Eric. "Aspects of Group Relations in a Complex Society: Mexico." *American Anthropologist* 58 (1956): 1065–78.

Wolf, Eric, and Edward C. Hansen. "*Caudillo* Politics: A Structural Analysis." *Comparative Studies in Society and History* 9, no. 2 (January 1967): 168–79.

Woodward, Ralph Lee, Jr. *Central America: A Nation Divided,* 3d ed. New York: Oxford University Press, 1999.

———. "The Liberal-Conservative Debate in the Central American Federation, 1823–1840." In *Liberals, Politics, and Power: State Formation in Nineteenth-Century Latin America,* ed. Vincent C. Peloso and Barbara A. Tenenbaum. Athens: University of Georgia Press, 1996.

———. *Rafael Carrera and the Emergence of the Republic of Guatemala, 1821–1871.* Athens: University of Georgia Press, 1993.

Yashar, Donna. *Demanding Democracy: Reform and Reaction in Costa Rica and Guatemala, 1870s–1950s.* Stanford, Calif.: Stanford University Press, 1997.

Yates, Lawrence A. "The United States and Rural Insurgency in Guatemala, 1960–1970: An Inter-American 'Success Story'?" In *Central America: Historical Perspectives on the Contemporary Crises*, ed. Ralph Lee Woodward, Jr. New York: Greenwood Press, 1988.

Zamora Castellanos, Fernando. *Militarismo y Estado Constitucional en Costa Rica*. San José, Costa Rica: Investigaciones Jurídicas, 1997.

Zamora Castellanos, Pedro. *Vida Militar de Centro América*, vol. 2. Guatemala City: Tipografia Nacional, 1924.

Zaverucha, Jorge. "The Degree of Military Political Autonomy During the Spanish, Argentine and Brazilian Transitions." *Journal of Latin American Studies* 25, no. 2 (May 1993): 283–300.

INDEX

Ft. Benning (Ga.), 135, 159, 178
Ft. Leavenworth (Kans.), 135, 137
Ft. Sill (Okla.), 135
fuero, 70–72

Gálvez, Juan Manuel, 78, 176–79
  death of, 287 n.9
  and election of 1954, 182–83
  and Honduran army, 78, 176, 195
  resignation as president, 183
  and U.S. military collaboration, 177, 181
Gálvez Barnes, Roberto, 187, 290 n.72
García Granados, Miguel, 38, 52–53
gender, 12, 16
General Treaty of Peace and Amity (1923),
  66
Germany
  and Central America, 120, 274 n.3
  and Costa Rica, 214
  and El Salvador, 64, 65, 66, 159, 168
  and globalization of public violence, 112
  and Guatemala, 56, 134, 135
  and Honduras, 74, 178
Giddens, Anthony, 9, 10, 244, n.4, 248 n.23,
  271 n.3
Gleijeses, Piero, 139, 278 n.31
global history, 3
globalization, 3–4, 271 n.3
government, changes of, 68, 109
Graham, Richard, 20
Great Britain, 277 n.2
Greco, John F., 200
Greece, 114
Greenberg, James B., 18
Greene, Corston A., 186
Guardia, Tomás, 99, 100–101, 107–8
Guatemala, 16, 31, 50–57, 134–58, 255 n.17
  armies of, 38
  caudillismo in, 57
  communism in, 56, 129, 138–39, 151
  and Costa Rica, 100, 216
  and Cuba, 132
  death squads, 47
  defense budget of 1941, 120
  democracy in, 232
  and El Salvador, 60, 164
  Fuerzas Armadas Revolucionarias, 248
    n.22
  and Germany, 56
  Guardia Cívica, 56
  and Honduras, 26, 53, 70, 71, 100
  institutional public violence, 11

  and isthmian intelligence collaboration,
    131
  Kingdom of, 28–29, 97
  La Aurora (airfield), 135
  Lend-Lease agreement, 120–21
  and liberalism, 38
  mob violence, 46
  national army, 41, 56, 63, 66, 95, 107–8,
    127–28, 134, 145, 148, 150, 258 n.66
  nation and national identity, 149
  and the Organization of Central Ameri-
    can States, 126
  police, 56, 154, 156; table, 240
  Remincheros revolt, 53, 262 n.16
  Revolution of 1871, 38
  and Rio Treaty, 141
  state, 110
  state formation, 68
  state terrorism, 231, 274 n.35
  and subaltern collaboration in violence, 63
  U.S. bases in World War II, 120, 135
  and U.S. hostility to Pres. Arbenz, 168
  U.S. intelligence collaboration, 150, 282
    n.77
  U.S. intervention in 1954, 165, 181
  U.S. military attaché, 43
  U.S. military collaboration, 56, 128, 134,
    136, 140, 142–43, 145, 151, 158, 229, 230
  U.S. military mission, 57, 134, 137
  U.S. police collaboration, 117, 150–58,
    152–54, 156
  and U.S. relations, 27
Guayape Valley (Honduras), 189, 197
Guerra Nacional, 82, 84, 124, 261 n.4
Guerra, F.-X., 19
guerrillas
  in Central America, 26
  and counterinsurgency warfare, 116, 129,
    166, 271 n.7
  and Cuba, 194
  in Guatemala, 16, 149, 158, 248 n.22, 261
    n.6
  in Nicaragua, 83, 210
  and Panama Canal, 127
  and public violence, 4, 10, 13–14, 23, 111,
    113, 231
  and state formation, 247 n.14
Guirola, Rafael, 64
Gulf of Fonseca, 64, 174–75, 196

habitus, 5, 28, 33, 38
hacendados, 25, 40, 176

Printed in the United States
80303LV00003B/40